The Long Road to Unity

Preaching in Paris

MARC BOEGNER

The Long Road to Unity

MEMORIES AND ANTICIPATIONS

Translated from the French by
RENÉ HAGUE

With an Introduction by
DR W. A. VISSER 'T HOOFT

COLLINS
ST JAMES'S PLACE, LONDON
1970

179719

This book was first published
by Éditions Albin Michel, Paris, in 1968 under the title
L'Exigence Œcuménique

ISBN 0 00 215460 9

© Éditions Albin Michel, 1968

© in the English translation

William Collins Sons & Co. Ltd., London, 1970

Printed in Great Britain by
Collins Clear-Type Press, London and Glasgow

Contents

PART TWO

The Maturity of the Ecumenical Movement
1939 – 1959

PART THREE

The Extension of the Ecumenical Movement
1959 – 1967

Contents

Illustrations

7. Meeting of the Central Committee of the World Council of Churches, Toronto, 1950. 1. Dr Franklin Clark Fry (U.S.A.). 2. Bishop G. Bromley Oxnam (U.S.A.). 3. Rt. Rev. George K. A. Bell, Bishop of Chichester (England). 4. Rt. Rev. Eivind Berggrav (Norway). 5. Dr Marc Boegner (France). 6. Dr Henry Smith Leiper (U.S.A.). 7. Sir Kenneth Grubb (England). 8. Dr A. Koechlin (Switzerland). 9. Dr W. A. Visser 't Hooft (Holland). 10. Dr Nils Ehrenström (Sweden). 11. Dr Martin Niemöller (Germany). 12. Dr O. Frederick Nolde (U.S.A.). 13 Rev. Oliver S. Tomkins (England). (Photo: Agence Diffusion Presse)

8. At the Evanston Assembly, 1954. From left to right: Rt Rev. Eivind Berggrav (Norway), Rt Rev. Athenagoras, Archbishop of Thyteira, Dr Marc Boegner, Dr Fisher, Archbishop of Canterbury, Bishop G. Bromley Oxnam (U.S.A.). (Photo: John Dominis, Courtesy LIFE Magazine, © Time Inc.)

9. Marc Boegner giving an address on the occasion of his reception at the Académie Française, 1963.

10. With Cardinal Tisserant in the latter's library, Rome, 1964.

11. With Cardinal Bea, World Council of Churches, Geneva, 1965. (Photo: John Taylor, World Council of Churches)

Between pages 368 and 369

12. Listening to a lecture given by Dr Martin Luther King, Paris, 1965. (Photo: Jean Pottier)

13. Marc Boegner in his Paris study. (Photo: Philippe Pouliopoulos)

14. With Father Blondel in the courtyard of the Convent of St Anne, Jerusalem, 1964.

15. With Father De Vaux, looking at the Dead Sea Scrolls, Rockefeller Museum, Jerusalem, 1964.

16. With Abbot Starky (right), visiting the ruins of Qumran where the Dead Sea Scrolls were found, 1964.

17. By the River Jordan, at the traditional place of Christ's baptism.

Introduction

WITH apologies to Ecclesiastes it must be said today that of making many books on the ecumenical movement there is no end. But there is one type of ecumenical literature of which we have only very few examples. That is the telling of the story of the emergence and growth of the movement in terms of personal experience and human contacts by men who have been deeply involved in ecumenical life. Most of the early pioneers who could have told that story died without having had the opportunity to write their memoirs. The biographies written about them tell us part of the human story, but cannot give us that intimate picture and that 'feel' of the real history which we need in order to understand the full significance of this new development in the life of the Churches. So we are in danger of thinking of the ecumenical movement in terms of conferences and resolutions rather than in terms of persons.

That is why I urged Pastor Marc Boegner to write down his reminiscences. He is one of the very few remaining leaders of the early days; he could count all the early pioneers among his friends. He has played a decisive role in the creation of the World Council of Churches. As chairman of the administrative committee of the World Council, during the ten stormy years from 1938 to 1948, when the Council was still in process of formation, he has played a decisive role in maintaining its cohesion and its integrity. Then in the period between the first Assembly in 1948 and the second Assembly in 1954 he was one of the presidents of the Council. And ever since he has continued to give time and energy to the further development of the ecumenical movement. He has especially become deeply involved in the dialogue between the Roman Catholic Church and the Protestant Churches which has accompanied and followed the Second Vatican Council.

So he has all the objective qualifications to tell us what really happened in those years when the whole movement for unity was still in its infancy and when it took courage and imagination to urge the Churches to open their windows and when there was the joy of discovery of the treasure of common conviction which Christians of all Churches had received together. But this account would still not meet our need if its author were not a man with a special gift for human contacts. Now Pastor Boegner is known among all his friends and acquaintances as one who has that gift in an exceptional measure. He thinks in terms of people. He takes a personal interest in each of them. He does not forget them. And so the story as he tells it becomes in the first place a story of men of different nations and Churches getting to know each other, entering into real friendship with each other and so laying the indispensable personal foundation for the structures which they create together.

This book is also important in that it shows that the ecumenical movement was never an introverted, inward-looking movement, concerned only with church affairs. Pastor Boegner played an important role in the national life of his country. Some of the finest pages of the book are those about the struggle to save the Jews in France from extermination. That a pastor of the Reformed Church would ever become a member of the famous Académie française seemed quite out of the question. But Pastor Boegner's election to that august body was the natural result of all that he had done for the nation during and after the war.

I hope that many people, particularly younger people, who suspect that the ecumenical movement is a rather dull affair which concerns only ecclesiastical administrators, will read this book and discover that it is above all a laboratory where new human relations are established.

W. A. VISSER 'T HOOFT

Foreword

In writing this short foreword I have had two things in mind.

In the first place I must anticipate a misunderstanding that might be entertained by some of my readers. Anyone who on opening this book is expecting to find an 'autobiography' or 'memoirs' will certainly be disappointed. Over sixty years ago, the challenge of ecumenism made itself heard in my mind with a force that has reverberated throughout my whole life. What I wish to do here is to show how it has given my life a fundamental orientation, introducing it into the modern ecumenical movement and associating it not only with the movement's development and activity, but also with its theological thinking, from the Edinburgh World Conference of 1910 to the Vatican Council of 1962–65.

In what follows, therefore, there will be nothing about my childhood and youth, nor about the intimate family circle to which I owe so much. My pastoral ministry in the valley of the Drôme and later in Paris will remain in the background, emerging only in so far as it has been bound up with my ecumenical life. No more than a glimpse will be given of my church or priestly life or of my ministry as a Lenten preacher. As for the fundamental affirmations of my Christian faith, my devotion to the Reformed Church of France and the great doctrines of the Reformation, these may be found echoed in the thirty-one published series of my Lenten sermons.

Secondly, I wish to express my gratitude to a number of friends without whose help this book would not now be appearing.

Had I not been urged to do so, with the most affectionate insistence, by Visser 't Hooft, Madeleine Barot, Pastor Bourguet, Frère Roger Schutz and Jacques Beaumont, I am sure that I would never have had the courage to undertake this task and to relive sixty years of my life in a light which mercilessly brings out its shortcomings and vacillations.

Mme Lucie Joseph, my dearly valued collaborator for so many years, typed my manuscript with tireless patience; and so eased the task of M. André Sabatier, long the literary editor of Éditions Albin Michel, from whom I have received most valuable suggestions and advice. To both I offer my affectionate gratitude.

Finally, what words can I find that can adequately express my thanks to my daughter Denyse Berthoud? She has been by my side during the detailed planning, the writing, and the revisions of the book whose title I owe to her. Without the peaceful seclusion, far from the din of Paris, which she made possible for me, I would never have begun nor finished what I am now offering to my readers. Such solicitude in a daughter calls for the warmest and most tender return from a father. She will hear, I hope, the thanks that spring from my heart.

Vulaines-sur-Seine, July 1966.
Paris, December 1967.

PART ONE

The Youth of the Ecumenical Movement
1905-1939

CHAPTER I

Introduction to the Ecumenical Life
1898-1906

I. Consequences of a conversion. The rise of ecumenism: Fallot, Oberlin and Christophe Dieterlen. II. Entry into pastoral ministry 1905. An imperative summons.

I

WHEN I allow myself to look back on what I cannot but call my ecumenical life, with its own particular dimension, I can hear, through constant calls to repentance, a voice which tirelessly reminds me that, for all that I have thought and lived in the service of Christian unity, I am in the first place indebted to a number of servants of Jesus Christ for whom the divisions which separate the Churches have always been an agonizing scandal.

I was not yet eighteen years of age when the first symptoms of myopia obliged me to abandon my preparation for the Naval College; shortly afterwards, having obtained my baccalaureate in philosophy, I started as a law student, with the idea that this would lead me either to the bar or to competing for an important position in Government service. It was then that, immediately after a spiritual revolution that was completely to reshape my life, Pastor Fallot, my mother's elder brother, agreed to receive me in his household for a prolonged stay.

What, in fact, was happening to me was a conversion. To lead me to it, or rather to pave the way to it in me, God made use of a Christian of a rare breadth of mind, my cousin Blanche Fallot. She was my uncle's elder daughter – 'my daughter of light', he liked to call her – and a few very simple words she spoke shook my whole being, which at that time was eaten up by pride and far removed from any Christian life; those words impelled me along a road which, a few days earlier, I would certainly never have imagined myself following:[1] a road of humiliation, of

1. Perhaps, without realizing it, I had been led in this direction by the

repentance, of the beginnings of death to self, but also of emancipation, of salvation, of joy in gratitude and adoration. It was then that I first came to appreciate the rich store of love, of forgiveness, and of power to atone contained in the word 'grace'.

It will not be difficult to understand how, standing on the threshold of a life which I envisaged as radically different from that which until then I was proposing to live, I felt the urgent need for as close as possible a contact with the uncle whose true greatness I had hardly suspected in the years gone by.

After a long illness, which prevented him from taking up his ministry in Paris again and still more from continuing with his constant lecture tours all over France, Fallot settled down in 1893, in the valley of the Drôme, on the outskirts of the little town of Crest, where a large parish of the Reformed Church seemed to offer a field of activity for his wife and daughters. From November 1898 until July 1900 I lived at Les Auberts a life of study, of recollection, of apprenticeship to the Christian life and to the life of the Church community, which has left me with wonderful memories.

Fallot may truly be called the father of social Christianity in French Protestantism; he had ruined his health in organizing and conducting, parallel with his pastoral ministry, campaigns against pornography and for the emancipation of 'female slave-labour'. As pastor, since 1876, of the free Church in Paris known as the 'Chapelle du Nord',[2] he had begun by attracting a wide audience; but those who had come to listen to him had gradually deserted him when his preaching had seemed to them dangerously social: the muttered accusation of 'socialist' was only too popular. When, with a number of friends, he founded the 'Protestant Association for the Study of Social Questions', he had gathered around him, in addition to Charles Gide, Emmanuel de Boyve, Louis Comte and Élie Neel, some young pastors who regarded themselves as his disciples: Wilfred Monod, Élie Gounelle, and Henry Babut; these were later to be the pioneers of the ecumenical

Dreyfus affair. I was an ardent supporter of Dreyfus's innocence and the trial of Zola, which I had been able to attend, had forced me to look beyond the horizon of my own life.

2. 17 Rue des Petits-Hôtels; the 'Chapelle du Nord' is now combined with the 'Chapelle Milton'.

movement in our Reformed Churches. With his health broken by years of incessant fighting, he was now obliged to sever his connection with causes whose ardent and frequently vehement defender he had often been. Nevertheless, since 1895, he had been able to undertake again a limited ministry in a small Reformed parish, in the Diois, at Sainte-Croix. At the very time when he was receiving me into his home, he had just agreed to become pastor at the nearest church to Crest, Aouste-sur-Sye.

It is now sixty-nine years since I arrived for the first time at this country house, Les Auberts: and how many things I discovered there, which had a profound influence on my life and thought!

My first discovery was Fallot himself: not that I can linger now to give you a picture of him in his home, surrounded by the most devoted care, following a strict diet, often thwarted by terrible attacks of migraine, and already suffering from the kidney disease from which some years later he was to die. I must go straight to what was essential, and that was the pastor, the preacher, the servant of the human soul. From the very beginning I had the revelation of what I can only call a 'unifier'. His parishioners were for the most part small farmers, or, in Aouste, workers in a paper mill or silk factory; and, come what may, he was determined to make them a brotherly community, a living Church, a family of true disciples of Christ. Among the pastors of the Diois, orthodox and liberal, enslaved to an ecclesiasticism which was empty of any spiritual substance and understanding of the apostolic vocation of every true Church, it was his ambition to pave the way to a mutual approach, to be followed later by co-operation and even communion in the cause of the great missionary work of French Protestantism. The first sermon I heard him preach, some days after my arrival, was on 'the harvest of righteousness' which 'is sown in peace' (James 3:18); and it gripped me, not only by the forcefulness of his words, but by the fundamental conviction that only the persevering and joyful practice of love, permeated by humility and respect, can overcome the perpetual temptations to separation and conflict, and build up a Church of Jesus Christ.

I found myself in the presence of a giant of the spiritual life, and at the same time in that of a pastor passionately devoted to the service of his most humble parishioners – rough and un-

educated, sometimes, and with no knowledge of the most
elementary realities of faith, in whom, nevertheless, he could
distinguish the soul, with its sin, its misery, its ugliness, and yet
its thirst also, its often unconscious expectation, and its possible
attainment of beauty, of glory, of life in God and for God. To
hear him pray in public worship was to feel a thrill of contact
with the invisible.

In his youth Fallot had responded to the influence of three men
of an unusual breadth of spirituality: Pastor Jean-Frédéric
Oberlin, his own maternal grandfather Daniel Le Grand, and a
manufacturer from the valley of the Bruche, Christophe Dieterlen,
whose nephew by marriage he was one day to become. By living
in contact with Fallot, by gradually discovering the roots of his
life and his thought, I learnt to know these Christian men and I
became, if I may be allowed to make that claim, one of their
spiritual heirs. In my later ecumenical work I have never forgotten
the enthusiasm I received from them, and not only from Fallot,
for the service of Christian unity.

Oberlin, pastor in the time of the Revolution and the Empire
of a small canton in the Vosges called Le Ban-de-la-Roche, was
both a mystic, enamoured of everything that impinged on the
invisible world, and at the same time a socially-minded Christian
devoted to the well-being of the poverty-stricken families who
were so dear to him as their pastor. In him contemplation was
always the inspiration and nourishment of action. In order to
release his parishioners from their isolation he had a bridge over
the Bruche built for them, the Charité bridge, which gave them
access to the Schirmeck and Strasbourg road; and in order to
rescue them from their poverty he conceived the plan of starting
a home industry which would supplement the meagre income
from farming their fields and from their goats, which at that
time was the only source of money for the people of Le Ban-de-la-
Roche. He accordingly looked around for some Christian to
support him in carrying out this plan. Jean-Luc Le Grand and his
son Daniel, who had a cotton tape factory near Altkirch, were
won over to his views and fell under the spell of his faith; they
answered his appeal, and taking with them some of their best
workers they moved to Le Ban-de-la-Roche where they set up

looms in every house and so started the manufacture of tape, soon to be well known under the name of 'Le Grand Frères'.

There was another characteristic of Oberlin, which I must mention, since Fallot was to remark on it long afterwards. He liked to describe himself as an *evangelical Catholic*, thereby revealing in his profession of faith an attitude far removed from any Protestant sectarianism and open, by contrast, to contacts and closer relationships that were never less than personal. In this attitude there was more than a hint of the coming of ecumenism in the next century.

Fouday is one of the five communes of which Oberlin was pastor. It was there that Daniel Le Grand went to live, with his wife, his son and his daughters, in a cottage to be replaced after the war of 1870-71 by a very large house which, since he died in 1856, he never saw. In managing his business he came up against the scandal of female and child labour in heavy industry, in particular in the coal mines of France and England. Once his mind was convinced he tried to find out what remedies were possible: only one seemed to him effective, the introduction of international legislation which, by agreement of the great powers, would control the labour of women and children in the mines and in what were then called manufactories.

Women and children were victims of a murderous exploitation. The wretched wage doled out to them in exchange for long hours of work was regarded as perfectly reasonable by those who paid it, but it was the cause of innumerable diseases and deaths. The Churches, faced with a situation that should have forced them to vehement protest, maintained a silence that was violently denounced by Karl Marx. To the nascent proletariat (which was not yet known by that name) they appeared as accomplices of their exploiters, and from that time the gap between Church and worker, which was to reach the dimensions we know today, was continually to grow wider.

It was then that two men rose up in the name of the Gospel and gave voice to the condemnation of Christian consciences: Daniel Le Grand in France, and Lord Shaftesbury in England. Le Grand, however, was not satisfied with protest. Once he had formed an idea of where the remedy lay, he embarked on a crusade aimed at heads of state, governments and parliaments,

in an endeavour to persuade them to start discussions with a view
to producing the international legislation without which he could
see no effective solution. To the service of this cause he devoted,
with long years of his life, the full force of his mind, his heart,
his Christian faith and his unceasing prayer. He was fated to die
before he could see his efforts bear fruit. But when the Congress
met in Berlin which was to introduce international legislation to
control the labour of women and children in industry, Bismarck,
the then Chancellor of the German Empire, recalled the memory
of Daniel Le Grand, the pioneer of the agreement that was being
sought, and paid him the tribute that was due to him. Later again,
in the period between the two world wars, in the entrance hall
of the International Labour Office, Professor Henri Monnier,
the youngest of Daniel Le Grand's grandsons, and I, the youngest
of his great-grandsons, were present at the erection of a tablet
to commemorate this noble protagonist of an international law
of justice and humanity.

Daniel Le Grand's numerous writings, appeals and reports
appeared under the name of 'Un industriel des Vosges'. It was
the same with his religious publications. I remember a leaflet
whose title was: 'What is Christianity? Answer: Jesus Christ'.
Going beyond all dogmatism and denominationalism, he went
straight to the blessed Person by whom and for whom he lived,
and whose service he had at heart in succouring the victims of
social injustice.

There was a nice delicacy in his thoughtfulness, always inspired
by his desire to help Christians in the fulfilment of their vocation.
After Princess Helena of Mecklenburg, a Lutheran, had married
the Duke of Orléans, eldest son of King Louis-Philippe, Le
Grand thought that the young princess royal would no doubt
have difficulty in finding religious books to sustain her evangelical
faith. For some years in succession, he had sent to her, completely
anonymously, a collection of the best works of Christian literature.
One day, the bill, made out to Daniel Le Grand, was found by
chance among the books sent to the Duchess of Orléans. She
was anxious to know so loyal and so tactful a donor, and there
followed an ever-closer relationship and correspondence, which
was to continue until well after the revolution of 1848. In July
1842 the princess royal was taking a cure at Plombières, and

decided to go to Le Ban-de-la-Roche and give herself the pleasure of visiting Daniel Le Grand. She was just stepping into the carriage and starting on the Fouday road when a messenger, hurrying from Paris, brought her the tragic news of the accident which had occurred the day before and had cost the Duke of Orléans his life.

Tommy Fallot, the eldest of Daniel Le Grand's grandsons, was twelve when his grandfather died. He had been very close to him before going to Lausanne for his secondary schooling. He never forgot the stories Le Grand used to tell him as they walked in the woods of Le Ban-de-la-Roche. One can well imagine what precious seeds were sown by the grandfather – grown old in his work for the cause of justice and in faithful service to Christ – in the mind of the small boy walking by his side, who was one day to be possessed by the same passion for justice, the same respect for women and children – because he too was to be possessed by Christ.

The influence on Fallot of Pastor Oberlin and of his grand-father, was deep and lasting; nevertheless, it cannot be compared with the powerful and permanent effect that Christophe Dieterlen, even after his death, constantly produced in one who always called him 'my master'.

In my life of Fallot[3] I tried to bring out the spiritual greatness of this Christian layman: a man of independent mind who was never properly understood by the majority of those close to him, but the scale of whose spirituality had been apparent to Fallot while he was still very young.

Long before Fallot's 'conversion', which burst upon him in 1865, when he was finishing a textile-engineering course in Elberfeld – feeling the impulse, as he said himself, to 'kick down the barriers that hemmed him in' – he felt the magnetic force of this strange Christian, whose horror of all sectarian narrowness cut him off from the Lutheran Church which recognized the Concordat of 1801 and often even made it impossible for him to assist at its Sunday services, but who every Sunday evening would expound, in a non-religious hall and for the benefit of a few Protestants in Rothau, a passage from the Bible from which his life of meditation and intercession drew its roots.

3. *La Vie et la pensée de T. Fallot*, 2 vols., Paris, 1914 and 1926.

A man uncommonly given to prayer, he once wrote, 'As a general rule, the Our Father is enough for me'; and he was the author of a little treatise on prayer, published anonymously,[4] which has sustained many Christians who have grown tired of the endless repetitions of so many liturgical prayers, and has guided them in their intercessions.

In that little book, and in others such as *La Religion de la Bible* and *La Religion pure et sans tache*, one can already see the *irenicism* of Christophe Dieterlen – the word *ecumenism* had not yet come in – his concern never to allow himself to be imprisoned within the boundaries of one particular Church. His Christianity knew no frontiers; it was truly biblical, but without being in any way enslaved to the doctrine of 'literal inspiration', and it was dominated by expectation of the kingdom of God. He was intimately connected with Christoph Blumhardt (the father), whom he had helped financially in acquiring his house in Bad-Boll, which gradually became the centre of an intense religious life of which irenicism in profession of faith was always a fundamental element.

I cannot characterize Christophe Dieterlen's ecumenism better than by quoting some words written at the foot of a letter to his friend Louis Fallot (father of Tommy) in which he declines to join a committee for the evangelization of the Vosges: 'A Protestant who would willingly be a Protestant if the Protestants were not so protestant'. Although without the precise definition of the necessary terms, he was already instinctively making the distinction between evangelism and proselytism which has been the inspiration of so much thought and so many resolutions (often, moreover, contested) at ecumenical gatherings in recent years.

Fallot gradually became more and more intimate with this great, lone, character. None of Christophe Dieterlen's ten sons knew or understood him so profoundly as did Fallot. It is difficult to say whether it was to Dieterlen that the younger man owed his pastoral vocation, which, immediately after the war of 1870-71 when he had already joined his father as an engineer and had already married, revolutionized his whole life. There can be no doubt that it was from him that he received the sense of the summons of the absolute which always harassed 'the master' and so often caused the disciple to suffer acutely. Dieterlen,

4. Later re-published by *La Cause*, with the author's name.

however, was too indifferent, not to say hostile, to ecclesiastical institutions to confine himself merely to following with tender interest and prayer the spiritual crisis which converted the young manufacturer of Fouday into a theological student in the faculty of Strasbourg.

We know for a fact, however, that until his last days Fallot attributed to Christophe Dieterlen the fundamental inspiration of his *spiritual* ministry. When he was engaged in the social battle, he sometimes felt that he was no longer following the road Dieterlen had marked out for him; but when, after his long and painful illness from 1889 to 1892, he felt himself called by that very ordeal once again to devote himself exclusively to the service of souls, to the preaching of the good deed, to the biblical revival, and to the building up of churches which would be real brotherhoods, then he had the joy of living, with an intensity that was full of gratitude, in communion with the master who had given him what he valued above all things, an understanding of the invisible world. The moving pages entitled *On the Threshold (Sur le Seuil)* which he wrote in the purifying furnace of a cruel trial, contain a final testimony.[5]

Such was the spiritual heritage I received from my family circle at Le Ban-de-la-Roche. Through his mother, who was the elder daughter of Daniel Le Grand, Fallot had lived since his childhood in the sphere of Oberlin's influence. In 1871, his second sister had married a nephew of Christophe Dieterlen, Paul Boegner, and it was in their home that I was born. Through many channels, redolent of irenicism and of love of the universal Church, glimpses of ecumenism had made their way to me. And I need hardly add that while still very young the reading of Gratry's *Sources* and his *Henri Perreyve* had taught me to love children of light, as St Paul calls them, brought up in the Catholic faith and steeped in evangelical teaching of the Gospel. I was none the less shaken to the very core by the shock I received when I was still a very young pastor: and it is of this that I must now speak.

5. *Sur le Seuil*, a little book published by Fischbacher in 1902. See also *La Vie et la pensée de T. Fallot*, Vol. 2, the final chapter.

The death of Fallot, which occurred on 3 September 1904 before he had completed his sixtieth year, left me with two duties which, although they were not contradictory, were to cause me to live on two different planes.

If I was to meet the wish which he had himself expressed in moving conversations we had had some weeks before his death, and which coincided with my own dearest ambition, I had to be able to take up as soon as possible the duty of pastoral ministry in the parish of Aouste. Moreover, I received a pressing invitation to do so from the Council of elders, in the month after the death of its pastor. I had, therefore, to finish my theological studies and, giving up any plans for staying abroad, receive ordination as a pastor and take up residence among the five hundred-odd Protestants included at that time in the parish.

On the other hand, I had the task of looking through the manuscripts Fallot had left and selecting those which it would be opportune to publish: in the first place there was his *Le Livre de l'Action bonne*, to which he attached particular importance. I was thus obliged to make an inventory of all his papers: notebooks, texts of lectures and sermons, drafts of studies, letters from numerous correspondents or written by Fallot and later returned to him.

It is with this second task alone that I am now concerned.

As I got on with the work, which was made difficult by the lack of order in the papers, I felt the emotion of living again, in all their depth, the 'epochs' of a life and the movements of a thought whose extreme diversity within a fundamental unity I later tried to bring out. But what a shock I received when I took up a packet of letters and found in it those of which I am now going to reproduce some short extracts.

These letters were from Fallot, some to the philosopher Ernest Naville in Geneva, with whom Fallot had a bond of friendship and respect, and the others to the Abbé Birot, at that time Vicar-General to Mgr Mignot, Archbishop of Albi. I do not know the circumstances in which they were returned to the writer; and on the other hand I have never been able to find those written by the addressees before or after receiving Fallot's letters. All my searches and enquiries have been fruitless.

An earlier study of Naville's on the unity of the Christian world had led Fallot to think seriously about the relationship between Catholicism and Protestantism; and to Naville he confided that he had helped him 'to have done once and for all with Protestant prejudice in all its forms' and 'to have a better understanding of the pedagogic value of the ecclesiastical institution, however rudimentary it be'. He continues in more detail, 'It is your irenicism that has reconciled me, not with the Catholic Church – for that I did not need – but with the notion of Church in general, and with the Huguenot Church in particular'.[6]

Pursuing his reflection on this subject, Fallot, in a personal note, is led to this twofold affirmation: 1. *The Church will be Catholic or it will not be the Church*; 2. *The Christian will be Protestant or he will not be Christian.*

Thus both the Catholic conception and the Protestant seemed to him legitimate: and it was this conviction that led him to write the following letter to the Abbé Birot.

'You want, you tell me, to form the Protestant party in the Catholic Church. I would like, so far as my poor strength allows, to help in the formation of the Catholic party in the Protestant Church. We need no more than a hint to understand one another. It is not a matter of ecclesiastical strategy, nor of diplomacy, but of tendencies that have to be made stronger. In you, the tendency that has to be made stronger is the one which is over-pronounced in us; and similarly on our side, we have lost, or at any rate allowed to weaken, the secret of the power to mould. You know how to build, but the stone you use is sometimes very poor. We, on our side, often have fine granite ready to hand and do not know what to do with it.

'One thing, however: we must understand one another properly. If I think that I ought to help in creating a Catholic party inside Protestantism, I in no way mean by that to give my allegiance to certain schools of Protestantism which dream of some sort of

6. 26 December 1894. Several of the extracts that follow may be found in *La Vie et la pensée de T. Fallot*: I quoted them in a lecture given in Rome on 11 November 1964 to the Cercle Saint-Louis de France.

bastard Catholicism, a dream which makes them continually more intolerant of historical Catholicism.

'My conception is completely opposed to theirs. I am convinced that sooner or later God will reunite what men have separated. As my eminent friend M. Naville says, and as you also say, our task is to pave the way to this glorious return to unity by making it clear to both parties that *they must have mutual understanding and love*.

'The Protestants I hope for will be true Protestants, sharply aware of their special mission, which is to bring about the full development of human individuality in all its power; but these Protestants, extremely Protestant in attitude and temperament, will repudiate once and for all all the hateful prejudices which have prevented them from contemplating and admiring the work of God in the Catholic Church. What is more, they will understand that individual virtues cannot by themselves give piety its full breadth and depth, and that, if Protestantism has known the secret of those vitues, it is Catholicism which has retained the prerogative of the *social virtues*, those virtues made up of voluntary subordination which are the only effective bond of durable societies.

'When the time comes that Protestants understand all they can gain by contact with Catholics, and when Catholics, inspired by feelings such as yours, understand that Protestantism is more than a denial of Catholic faith, then heart will search out heart, and the angels will get ready to sing the hymn that welcomes the coming of peace in charity and regained unity.'[7]

Two notes dating from the same period are apposite in this context.

'It is indeed the ancient Catholic Church which will renew herself in order to receive her long separated children, and it is to her that we must henceforth direct our affection. It is her evolution that matters to us. If we cannot act upon her directly, let us at least help her with the full force of our sympathy to hasten the day when our children will worship at her altars.'[8]

And some months later:

'*Evangelical Catholic* – the phrase is Oberlin's. I am taking it

7. 3 November 1894.
8. December 1894.

over and making it my own. It is more than a name – it is a
programme that sums up for me thirty years of thinking and
working.

'Henceforth I look on myself as an evangelical Catholic sec-
onded by the will of the Head to the service of the Reformed
Church of France.'[9]

It is now sixty years since I was reading those pages, written
some ten years earlier. No wonder they came to me as a shock.
Who at that time, in the French Protestant Churches, would have
dared to write such words? What Protestants were sustaining soul
and mind with these ambitions, these visions, and prophecies?
And what an illumination falls on them from all that has been
lived through from 1910 until the morrow of the Vatican Council!
When, for the first time, their long echoes reverberated in the
depths of my interior life, it seemed to me as though a thick mist
that surrounded me was being torn aside, that glorious peaks were
emerging on the horizon, to be gained at the end of a magnificent
and perilous adventure.

It was on that day that I was born into the ecumenical life, and
the summons it contains was never more to leave me.

9. 23 April 1895.

CHAPTER 2

The Edinburgh Conference 1910 and the Origins of the Modern Ecumenical Movement

1910-1914

I. Teaching at the theological school of the Société des Missions évangéliques 1911-1914. John R. Mott and J. H. Oldham. II. The unity of the Church.

I

THE World Missionary Conference, which met in Edinburgh from 13 to 23 June 1910, has been regarded ever since as the cradle of the ecumenical movement. In 1960 when, with the Central Committee of the World Council of Churches meeting in Saint Andrews, the fiftieth anniversary of the Conference was being celebrated in St Giles's Cathedral, Edinburgh, none of those present had any doubt about the supreme importance in the history of the universal Church of that earlier gathering.

It is true enough that in the course of the nineteenth century other conferences, more restricted in scope, had brought together representatives of European and American missionary societies, together with a limited number of missionaries. Nevertheless it was in London in 1888, at the time of the centenary of the Protestant missions, that the full extent of the apostolic work carried out in the non-Christian world by the Reformed Churches was brought to public notice for the first time. A hundred and forty societies were represented by nearly fifteen hundred delegates. The object of the meeting was to spread information about missions, to promote fraternal co-operation between all the organizations engaged in the apostolate, and to help the Churches and their members to realize the importance of the missionary work carried out in their name.

Twelve years later, in 1900, a new conference was held in New

York, with 1700 representatives of 115 missionary societies, from 48 countries, and in addition 600 missionaries. The conference styled itself 'ecumenical', not because it claimed to represent all the Christian denominations, but because it was a conscious manifestation of the reality of the Christian apostolate all over the world. With the number of its members who belonged to American or Canadian Churches or organizations amounting to fifteen hundred, it could not claim to be truly representative.

In this respect the Edinburgh Conference gave evidence of considerable progress. From the start it was agreed that only official delegates of missionary bodies should participate, in the proportion of one delegate for every £2000 annual expenditure, plus one more for every extra £4000; and it is noteworthy that every missionary society availed itself of the seats allotted to it.

It was also decided that the Conference should study as closely as possible the various aspects of apostolic activity in the non-Christian world and the manifold problems it raises for the Churches. Eight preparatory committees were formed; and here we need only note that of these three were presided over by laymen of recognized competence. The first committee, concerned with studying the Church's apostolic vocation in the whole of the non-Christian world, had for its chairman Dr John R. Mott; the chairman of the seventh, dealing with relations between missions and governments, was Lord Balfour; and that of the eighth, responsible for matters that affected co-operation and the development of unity, was Sir A. H. L. Fraser.

I have just mentioned one name: that of the man who, more than any other, was for nearly sixty years the incarnation, in the Protestant and Orthodox Churches, of the summons to unity which Christ addresses to his Church – John Mott.

He was just forty-five when he was elected chairman of the Edinburgh Conference. Fifteen years earlier, while he was working for the Y.M.C.A., he had founded, with a number of friends of different nationalities, the World Student Christian Federation, at the castle of Vadstena in Sweden. As a result of his continual visits to universities all over the world, this had quickly expanded to a marked degree. It was thus that he came to Paris, where I was then engaged in my theological studies, and I shall never forget the evening he devoted to a small group of young people in the Protestant students' society. With incomparable spiritual force, he endeavoured to make us share the vision of the world that came to him from his close communion with Christ, of the world which the present generation had to 'win' for Christ: and this it could not do except through the obedience of all his disciples to the apostolic vocation fulfilled in unity.

I can see him still, in all the vigour of his forty years. I can see his look, to which his heavy eyebrows gave even greater penetration, and the gestures that were so characteristic of him. I can hear his brief, incisive speech. How often, later, did I not hear him speak again in similar terms, but always with the authority that comes from a faith that knows for certain whence it comes and whither it is going.

As chairman of the Edinburgh Conference, his quickness and precision, his intuitive guidance of the discussions, his firmness combined with great courtesy, and the vigour of his speech, often laced with humour, won him the recognition and respect of all. Among these was the principal delegate of the Paris Société des Missions évangéliques, its director Alfred Boegner. Mott could have had no more than a fleeting glimpse of him during these days which were filled to overflowing not only by his responsibilities but also by meetings, conversations that were always too short, and obligations that often conflicted with one another. Nevertheless he discerned the spiritual stature of the French pastor, the love of Christ which inspired his thought, his action and the fire of the words he so often used when he pointed out to the Churches their apostolic duty. Both men shared the same vision, and I can recall the warmth with which, when Alfred Boegner had just died (so prematurely, two years after Edinburgh) John Mott described to the Committee of the Paris Société des Missions the impression of sanctity he had received from our director.

Mott's closing address made his hearers look into their hearts: his first words were, 'the end of the Conference is the beginning of the conquest'. In another remarkable passage, he said, 'Has it not humbled us increasingly as we have discovered that the greatest hindrance to the expansion of Christianity lies in ourselves? . . . I make bold to say that the Church has not yet seriously attempted to bring the living Christ to all living men. Reality means that we will not only revise our plans concerning the Kingdom, but we will revise with even greater faithfulness the plans with reference to our own lives.'

Side by side with Mott, helping him in running the Conference, looking after every detail, making himself felt as an admirable worker both for the missionary cause and for its ecumenical requirements, J. H. Oldham had been chosen as secretary of this vast gathering. A Scotsman by birth, he had worked for the Y.M.C.A. for many years in what was still British India, where he had noted the lack of dynamic force in the apostolate and of the power to radiate Christianity, and with this the spirit of individualism and competition which was characteristic of certain Protestant and Catholic missions. Oldham had received the grace of humility. When, a year after the Edinburgh Conference, he went to Paris to consult with the Committee of our missionary society, we had the great privilege of receiving him and his wife in our home; and this was the first of many meetings, some of which will be recalled later.

As the discussions approached their end, some members of the Conference expressed the fear that the climate of understanding, collaboration and prayer in common which had gradually surrounded and permeated them, would lose its vitalizing power if some organization were not created to continue the work of the Conference in the same spirit. There was no difficulty in reaching agreement among all concerned and it was unanimously decided to set up a continuation committee, destined to become in 1920 the International Missionary Council. John Mott was its chairman until 1942.

The final decision of the International Missionary Conference did not arise solely from the wish not to allow the disappearance of a *spirit* whose effect had been felt by all. The report presented by Sir Andrew Fraser on behalf of the eighth committee, set up to examine all the possibilities of international co-operation, had forcibly emphasized the immense damage caused in all fields of the Christian apostolate by the incredible proliferation of missionary activities. Attached to societies or Churches who were alien to one another, who deliberately ignored, who suspected and denigrated one another, they wasted in ecclesiastical and doctrinal disputes energies that should have been wholly devoted to evangelization, and so doomed their apostolic work to sterility.

The Conference was greatly impressed by the Fraser Report, and realized that it had a double duty: first, to address an appeal to the Churches to seek, both in the home country and in the mission fields, for ways that would lead to mutual understanding and a determined and continuous collaboration in brotherly love: and secondly, itself to give an example by setting up an organization whose business, or still more whose duty, it would be to introduce into all the organs of the apostolate the spirit whose grace had been felt in the Conference.

All those present noted the part taken in the work and decisions of the Conference by the representatives of the Anglican Communion. Some even felt that at times Mott gave them preference in the discussions. However, good Methodist though he was, he knew what he was doing: he saw quite clearly that to make Anglicans and Episcopalians commit themselves to the work undertaken in Edinburgh was the most effective way of including them irrevocably in an international and ecumenical line of action which, being common to the various non-Roman Christian denominations, might well, through the power of the Holy Spirit, win the pagan world for Christ.

I have still to mention what was, in fact, the most important aspect of the Conference. While the overwhelming majority of those present in Edinburgh were white, the native communities of Japan, China, India and other countries, were nevertheless represented by a larger number of delegates than had been present in New York in 1900, delegates, moreover, of high intellectual and spiritual quality. Honda from Japan, Cheng Ching-yi from China, Chatterjee and Azariah from India, all spoke with authority in Edinburgh. They spoke of the gratitude felt by the faithful of their respective Churches for the sending to their people of men who bore the Gospel message, who had taught them to know, love and serve Jesus Christ; but at the same time they spoke of the almost insurmountable obstacle to the evangelization of their countries created by the scandalous divisions among the missions and Churches of Europe and America. What they said made extremely painful hearing. And the Conference, deeply moved and, maybe, with a sudden sense of humiliation, could not fail to heed so striking an appeal for unity.

Of those who listened to these Christians from Asia, one man in particular was more deeply conscious than any other of this burden of suffering, and more upset by the scandal it reflected: Charles Brent, a bishop of the Protestant Episcopal Church of the U.S.A. and a missionary in the Philippines. Edinburgh was a turning point in his life and made him into the first inaugurator of the modern ecumenical movement.

Like so many others of my generation, I am indebted to Bishop Brent for having, as early as the immediate post-Edinburgh period, made me realize the horror of the countless divisions, the shocking rendings of the Lord's coat without seam, but also for having shown me that it is only through love that a way can be found to the visible restoration of the unity of the Body of Christ.

He was no sooner back in the U.S.A. than he made it his business to see that his Church, and in the first place its bishops, shared the conviction he felt so deeply. This state of division in the Church could not be allowed to endure. It was the duty of Christians, realizing the scandal it caused, to meet it with a categorical *No*. The Churches, every one of them, must be keyed-up to readiness, invited to meet together in the persons of their bishops, their church leaders and theologians. A conference must be arranged, to enable them to know and listen to one another, frankly to expose their doctrinal and ecclesiastical differences (so often too trifling to be taken seriously), and, under God's guidance, to find out whether certain causes of their divisions could or could not be eliminated. Brent had some difficulty in obtaining the agreement of his own Church and, more generally, of the Anglican Communion; but as soon as he had done so, he threw himself wholeheartedly into the difficult and generous-minded work which in 1927 was to produce the Lausanne World Conference on Faith and Order.

From the very beginning, Brent received unstinting help, which proved highly effective, from a layman of great breadth of mind and vision, Robert Gardiner. I well remember the delight and hope with which one read the booklets – hardly more than leaflets – which Brent and his friend sent to those who they thought might be won over to the cause to which they were both devoted body and soul. Every one of them bore on the first page, in Greek or in Latin, or in one of the most widely used world languages, the words from Christ's prayer 'that they may all be one . . . so that the world may believe' (John 17:21). It was at that time that those words were adopted as the slogan of the infant movement. Until the war, these ever-welcome leaflets brought us, with news of the movement and of the Churches, messages from Brent and Gardiner, and from others too, who, by their appeal for perseverance in intercession, bound us ever more closely to the cause of unity.

It was thus that Charles Brent, in pain and labour, gave birth to the theological branch of the ecumenical movement.

The Edinburgh Conference made a great impact on the Reformed Churches, in which love of the foreign missions takes the practical form of generous donations, one need hardly say, but also of vocations among men and women who devote their whole life (as was then the rule) to the promotion of an apostolic work.

At the same time, one must ask whether these Churches had a clear understanding of the questions raised by the International Conference: were they fully aware of the scandal of their divisions, and were they really concerned to work *as one* to see whether they could find a way of healing them? Charles Brent and his friends set out to convince them, and we shall soon be looking at the fruits of their efforts. Nevertheless, it was only a very few of the leaders of Churches and directors of missionary societies who realized at that early stage the necessity of making contemporary theologians face the question of what *theological* bond unites the Church of Christ to the apostolate entrusted to it, and what is the goal of that apostolate. Can the Christian missions operating in the world regard themselves as permanent institutions, or should they be getting ready for the spiritual and ecclesial coming of age of autonomous native Churches, responsible for their own church life, for the training of their ministers and their apostolic work? In most places, it is true, something was being done about the training of a native ministry, but it was taken for granted by most of those who thought about it that it must remain under the authority of missionary conferences, themselves subordinate to committees at home. Few in those days would have foreseen that missionaries would one day be placed under the authority of indigenous directors.

The problem was how to give back to parish communities and national Churches a sense of the prime vocation of every Church of Christ. The Church *exists only* for the world, this world which 'God so loved'. Years and decades were to pass before an end was made of the contradiction between the attachment of a minority of the faithful to the missionary work of their denomination, and the absorption of a large number of parishes in the almost exclusive concern for their own local life or the life of the national community to which they belong.

II

At the beginning of the summer of 1912 the Committee of the Paris Société des Missions évangéliques sent me, through Alfred Boegner, an urgent invitation to become the principal teacher of theology for the 'missionary students' working in the 'Maison des Missions' before leaving for the field in which they were to practise their ministry.

The Maison des Missions in the Boulevard Arago had been the Society's headquarters since 1891; at this time, besides the chapel and the administrative offices, it contained quarters for the director, the teacher and their families, rooms for the students, a library that was also used as a lecture room, and other rooms to accommodate missionaries who were waiting to go abroad or were stopping in Paris while on leave.

After a great deal of hesitation, the very orthodox-minded Committee had agreed that these missionaries should take part of the courses given at the faculty of Protestant Theology, on the other side of the Boulevard Arago, by lecturers who did not arouse over-grave suspicions of 'liberalism'. Dogmatics, of course, the New Testament, pastoral theology, history and geography of the missions, would continue to be taught at the Maison des Missions.

When I received this invitation, I had just taken my examinations for my licentiate in theology, and, while still engaged in my ministry in the parish of Aouste, I was working on the first part of my *Vie et la pensée de T. Fallot*, as the main thesis for my

licentiate. I was deeply attached to my parish, but I was still
suffering from the after-effects of earlier illnesses, and these made
my work difficult; for my only way of keeping in touch with
very scattered homesteads was on foot or by bicycle, and this in
valleys that were often swept by the *bise noire* – the savage wind
from the north. After much painful interior wrestling I finally
decided to accept the invitation from Paris, and, with our three
eldest children, we moved there at the beginning of November
1911. It was understood that from the beginning of the next
year, the students would live with us and no longer with M. and
Mme Alfred Boegner, and that I would be responsible for the
teaching of New Testament studies, practical theology, and the
main branches of what was soon to be called missiology.

While we were waiting for repairs to be finished which would
enable us to accommodate the future missionaries at meal-times,
we were to receive transient guests. Thus it was that we had
hardly settled in before we had the privilege of offering hospitality to J. H. Oldham and his wife. As I have already remarked,
the secretary of the Edinburgh Conference continuation committee
was later to become a dear and valued friend. At that time Brent
and Gardiner's leaflets and other publications were giving a
vigorous impetus to the ecumenical tendencies aroused in me six
years earlier by Fallot's correspondence with Ernest Naville and
the Abbé Birot; and this meeting with Oldham helped to determine the bent of my mind. Various visits that John R. Mott
paid to the Société des Missions during the following years, gave
it final confirmation. It was this that led me to take as my subsidiary thesis for my licentiate in theology the problem of Church
unity. Since it had to be presented in a foreign language, I wrote
it in English, in the form of forty-six propositions, preceded
by a short introduction and followed by an even shorter conclusion.[1]

However, before the oral examination on my thesis, some great
changes had shaken the Paris Société des Missions. The sudden
death of Alfred Boegner had been quickly followed by the
nomination as director of the Society of Pastor Jean Bianquis,
the general secretary since 1898, the new general secretary being
Daniel Couve who for reasons of health had been obliged to come

1. Published by Coueslant, Alençon.

home from our mission in the Gabon. With these changes there was a new atmosphere in the headquarters in the Boulevard Arago.

Nevertheless, I got on with my work, happy at living at the centre of the apostolic work of French Protestantism. My horizon was continually growing wider and was gradually covering the whole extent of the missionary fields. At that time a cardinal problem was engaging the attention of Christian students of Islam: how was the amazing progress of Islam in black Africa to be halted? How could one build up a dam strong enough, if not to throw back, at any rate to contain the mighty Islamic tide? An international conference met in Paris to study the situation. Men of great scholarship such as Julius Richter, Dr Zwemer, and Dr Watson from Cairo, took part in this important meeting at the Maison des Missions. So many societies and different denominations were concerned that it was difficult to unite them in common action. Even so, great efforts were made to do so, for the warnings of the Edinburgh Conference could not be forgotten. Unfortunately, the war which broke out in the summer of 1914 put an end to this work, and the followers of Mohammed had the opportunity of turning to good account for themselves the fratricidal crime of Christian nations murdering one another with the help of black and yellow troops recruited in their respective colonies.

The thunder-clap of 2 August 1914 completely upset everyone's personal situation: it brutally suspended ecumenical work and in the belligerent countries threw the Churches back into an isolation that was often poisoned by Chauvinism. Some weeks before that day, I had just been orally examined on my theses for the licentiate, in particular the subsidiary thesis on Church unity. Of the three members of the examining board, two at least had often given thought to a subject whose grave importance and urgency had been brought to universal notice by Brent, Gardiner and others. These two were Jean Monnier and Wilfred Monod, the latter the representative of nascent ecumenism who was most widely listened to in the Churches of France.

In offering the Paris faculty of theology the fruit of ten years' incessant reflection, what plan did I have in mind? Not to put forward a solution to the problem of unity, but to affirm and, if possible, gain acceptance for, the proposition that unity must be recognized as the principle upon which the Church is built.

Founded on the teaching of Christ and the apostles, lived in the apostolic age, professed in the great ecumenical symbols and later in the Reformation's confessions of faith, the unity of the Church is not something that has to be established in the twentieth century: *it is a fact*.

The law of incarnation, which is the essential law of the spiritual life, demands that its unity, today invisible because of the successive schisms that have occurred in the course of the centuries, be made manifest in a visible organism. And this does not mean a *uniformity* which entails the absorption of all the Churches by one of them, nor a formless unity, producing doctrinal indifference and confusion, but an *organic unity*, in which legitimate differences do not impair the closest solidarity.

The great Churches which emerged from the sixteenth-century Reformation allowed themselves to be drawn into a distortion of the teaching of the Reformers and their confessions of faith, admitting no unity of the Body of Christ other than an invisible unity – that is a sad fact whose consequences lie heavy on the life of the Churches and their apostolic activity. We must, I said, have done with a proliferation of denominations which arises from the right claimed by their founders to shatter the unity of the Church in order to remain faithful to what they themselves regard as the truth. Irenics must take the place of polemics and be included in theological studies. Unfortunately, the Protestant Churches have largely lost the sense of the unity of the Church: they must learn again the meaning of the Catholicity without which hope of the Kingdom will always be stunted. No essential affirmation of faith, moreover, stands in the way of unity of the Churches of the Reform, whether founded on mutual recognition of their order, or on general acceptance of episcopal and priestly orders. Nevertheless, for all that, I said, the unity of the Body of Christ was not made manifest.

I adopted as my own the sentence I have already quoted from Fallot: 'The Church will be Catholic or it will not be the Church. The Christian will be Protestant or he will not be Christian.' And in my forty-fourth proposition I quoted Vinet's words, which have now been constantly in my mind for sixty years: '*Since freedom is only a means, Protestantism also is only a means . . . Separation is only a prelude to a new unity . . . Individualism must return to socialism, Protestantism to Catholicism, freedom to unity.'*

No doubt, I was asking a great deal of the theologians; but that does not lessen the responsibility of the Churches. They have all to realize their sins against truth and love, to confess them, to undergo the pain of repentance, and to be willing 'to grow less in order that the Church may grow greater'. Unity is a lovely flower which blooms only in a climate of humility and love.

Ten years, then, after my initiation into ecumenical life, and four years after the Edinburgh Conference and the vision of Bishop Brent which was born from his distress, such was my approach to the goal towards which the spirit of Christ leads so many of his disciples. The war of 1914-18 was to oblige me to slacken my pace, but it could not halt me.

CHAPTER 3

The First World War

1914-1919

I. Père Laberthonnière: the beginnings of an incomparable friendship 1912. II. The war: work for blinded soldiers 1915-1919. III. Invitation from the church of the Annunciation 1918.

I

AT this point I must retrace my steps. In 1912 there intervened in my life a critical event – I can find no other word for the meeting I am referring to – which was to have endless intellectual consequences for me. I was received by Père Laberthonnière in the modest quarters placed at his disposal by a Catholic lady, already very advanced in years, in the house she owned at 23 Rue Las-Cases, near the basilica of Ste Clotilde. How often, since that day, I have climbed the four flights of stairs up to Père Laberthonnière! At the third landing I used to ring and a maid, wearing the Breton head-dress, used to take me up to the study, littered with books and papers, on the floor above, where Laberthonnière was tirelessly writing.

In January 1907, having recently become a subscriber to the *Annales de philosophie chrétienne*, I had written to him, to thank him for his article on 'the witness of the martyrs' ('Le Témoignage des Martyrs'). 'It is a joy and a comfort', I told him, 'to see that at a certain spiritual level some disciples of Christ can feel themselves in a full communion of souls, in spite of their dogmatic or ecclesiastical differences, however deep those may be.'

At that time Laberthonnière was fifty-two. On leaving the Grand Séminaire at Bourges, he entered the French Congregation of the Oratory. The next year he became lecturer in philosophy in the celebrated college at Juilly, taking advantage of its closeness to Paris to follow the teaching of Boutroux. He was already becoming irresistibly convinced of the impossibility of separating philosophy and theology. Pascal and Maine de Biran were confirming him in this attitude, and St Augustine was increasingly dominating his thought. The publication in 1893 of Maurice Blondel's famous *L'Action* gave a new impetus to his reflections, and an admirable friendship grew up between him and the philosopher of Aix-en-Provence, the fruitfulness of which was visibly expressed in a constant correspondence mostly devoted to philosophic dialogue.[1] When I met Laberthonnière, this spiritual and intellectual intimacy was proving a source of strength and consolation to him.

Strength and consolation of which, in fact, he was sorely in need. Superior of the École Massillon, and later of the Collège de Juilly, he had been obliged in 1903, by the law governing religious congregations, to leave the college of which he was so fond. It was then that he moved into the Rue Las-Cases. In 1905 he took on, with Blondel, the editing of the *Annales de philosophie chrétienne*, which had got into very low water; with the assistance of contributors of outstanding merit, he had quickly made it into one of France's leading Catholic periodicals. Unhappily, the storm was soon about to burst on him.

What happened was that the movement known as 'modernist' drew upon itself a severe condemnation from the Holy Office, warning of which was given to the Catholic world by the encyclical *Pascendi dominici gregis* of 8 September 1907. Neither Laberthonnière nor Blondel had ever belonged to the group of exegetes, such as Alfred Loisy and Marcel Hébert, who were the main target. Nevertheless, by quoting in a distorted form some sentences from their publications, and by confusing notions that were in fact distinct, the intention was also to condemn *moral dogmatism*, two words which Laberthonnière had used as the title of one of his most important studies. Without naming him, the encyclical was an attack on Laberthonnière as well as on his friend. But worse was soon to follow.

It was thus five years after the encyclical that I first met Père Laberthonnière. The *Annales*, although conscious of the threat hanging over it, was nevertheless continuing its work, with Laberthonnière, vigorously supported by Blondel, the king-pin.

1. Maurice Blondel–Lucien Laberthonnière, *Correspondance philosophique*, Paris, 1962.

Sometimes under their own names, and sometimes under various pseudonyms, they were developing St Clement of Alexandria's and Origen's assertion, 'Christianity is our philosophy'. They rejected all *separate* philosophy. 'Christianity is my moral science and my philosophy', Laberthonnière was later to write. 'And my moral science and philosophy are Christianity. I mean to be philosophically a Christian, and Christianly a philosopher. The further I look, the more I realize that this is in all respects the attitude of St Paul.'[2] This was his fundamental intellectual position, and it was completed by the qualification, 'Christianity is a metaphysic of charity'.

I rather think that I had already read 'Le Dogmatisme moral' when I went to see Père Laberthonnière. In any case I brought back to the Boulevard Arago a copy, signed by the author, of the book in which it appeared;[3] and it is still in my library, in spite of the Gestapo's temporary theft of the latter at the beginning of the Second World War.

Laberthonnière and I had certainly met again on a number of occasions and a bond of mutual trust and friendship had already been formed between us when a new decree of the Holy Office, dated 16 May 1913, struck him a blow of the utmost severity. Two short papers bearing his name, *Le Témoignage des Martyrs* and *Sur le Chemin du Catholicisme*, were placed upon the index of forbidden books, and the same was done to the *Annales de philosophie chrétienne*. Shortly afterwards, without being given a hearing, and with no explanation, Laberthonnière received an order forbidding him to publish. This was an act of revenge on the part of the *Action française*, whose godlessness had been denounced by Laberthonnière with uncommon vigour and most remarkable clarity in his book *Positivisme et Catholicisme*.

I am not concerned here to explain Laberthonnière's thought nor to show how it influenced my own. I know, however, that frequent conversations about the Church and her authority initiated for me a line of thought which was not without effect on my intellectual approach to ecumenism. But above all, by being close to him and listening to him, I breathed in a Catholicism, a good many of whose doctrinal elements I no doubt rejected, but

2. Letter to Blondel, 6 April 1925.
3. *Essais de Philosophie religieuse*, Paris, 1903.

which was so deeply rooted in the Gospel and lived in so living a communion with Christ that it aroused in me the highest hopes for a Church which could produce children spreading, in St Paul's words, 'a fragrance' of Christ (2 Corinthians 2:16).

For, since the first years of our friendship, I met at Laberthonnière's and learnt to know and love, Catholics, both priests and laymen who were treading the path of light; and remembering the letters of Fallot to the Abbé Birot, I could feel a whole intellectual and spiritual ferment which, in spite of encyclicals and decrees, was heralding deep-seated movements from which our own ecumenical movement could not but acquire new dimensions.

II

The war, far from interrupting our relationship, made it even closer. I was called up at the outbreak of hostilities but almost immediately sent home. I would like to have been posted to the military chaplain's department, as my brother was, but a series of medicals confined me to auxiliary service. This was due to the after-effects of bad attacks of phlebitis and a serious pulmonary condition, when I was pastor in Aouste, which for more than a year had made it impossible for me to use my voice.

At the beginning of 1915 I was posted as a medical orderly to a hospital for typhoid patients in the Lyons area. Shortly afterwards I was appointed as military assistant to the director of the convalescent home for blind soldiers which the Ministry of the Interior had decided to open in the Rue de Reuilly, next door to the house of the Protestant Deaconesses, in the fine grounds of the former Sainte-Clotilde boarding school. The director, theoretically under the authority of the director of the Quinze-Vingts (the hospital for the blind), was a civil servant; military orderlies were given him for work inside the building, and I was put in command of them. For four years I lived in the Rue de Reuilly, in a deeply united community of service with some remarkable nurses, whose matron, Jeanne Lefebvre, was to become after the war one of those parishioners who are an inspiration and a tower of strength to their pastor. I shall mention only one other by name, whose face I cannot forget – Rose-Marie Michel, the young widow of the son of André Michel, the art historian, who was killed at Soissons at the very beginning of

the war. On Good Friday 1918, her passion for music took her
to the church of Saint-Gervais, where there was a concert of
religious music: there she was crushed to death, with a great
many others, when a shell from a long-range gun struck the
church, and the vaulting collapsed.

Shortly after my arrival at the blind soldiers' home the question
of the Catholic chaplaincy came up. The director was good
enough to ask my advice. I suggested Père Laberthonnière, who
had already told me that he would be willing to accept the position. The suggestion was approved, and accordingly twice a
week at least from 1915 to 1919 – in addition to Mass on Sundays
– Laberthonnière used to visit his cruelly maimed parishioners.
Thus I had the opportunity of seeing him and, when my duties
permitted it, having long conversations with him. We used to
discuss a great variety of subjects: the war, with its disappointments and hopes, its countless victims, of whom hundreds of
the most unfortunate enjoyed the hospitality of the home in the
Rue de Reuilly; politics, with all the confusion caused by the
continual prolongation of hostilities and the disappearance of
all prospects of peace; the great distress of our people, weakened
by the bloody toll of casualties, their future seeming so uncertain
in spite of all hopes of victory; the responsibilities of the Churches,
both the Roman Catholic and the others, when peace should
return with its vast problems, and their duty to be ready to fulfil
their primary vocation. It most often happened, however, that
Laberthonnière, whose mind was always in travail, came back
to the fundamental question of God's creative design in relation
to man, of the metaphysics of creation, of incarnation and salvation. 'God', he was fond of saying, 'not a problem, but the
solution of the only problem', the problem of man, his origin,
his being and his destiny.

It was during these years that a metaphysic of charity took on
definite shape in his mind: sometimes, indeed, the process was
held up by events, but at others it was stimulated by the conviction that, in spite of the silence imposed on him, he had a
message for his Church and for the world. And yet he was far
from foreseeing that for three years that message would be
taught from the pulpit of Notre-Dame to a vast crowd of
listeners, both visible and (drawn by the radio) invisible.

Would it, I wonder, be too much to say that our friendship, which was known to all at Reuilly and elsewhere but particularly in ecclesiastical circles, was in itself an ecumenical testimony? However, it was after the war that that testimony had the most frequent opportunities of making itself felt.

My memories of that distant time – now over forty years ago – are connected with the meetings of two distinct groups, at which Catholics, Orthodox, Protestants, and sometimes 'secular humanists' enjoyed meeting one another and discussing some main problem of Christian thought.

First, there were the meetings in the Rue Dupuytren, where there had been founded a Christian association of Russian students who had come to France after the 1917 Revolution. It was, I imagine, at the instigation of Professor Zander, a steadfast Orthodox pioneer in the cause of unity, that premises were made available to an interdenominational group; I forget the precise circumstances, but I remember that I joined them at the very beginning. It was a strange collection, of Catholics with violently opposed philosophical and theological views: Père Laberthonnière, Père Gillet (later Master-General of the Dominicans), Jacques and Raïssa Maritain, Stanislas Fumet; of Orthodox, suspecting one another of heresy, and dominated, in the vast sweep of his powerful mind, by the great Nicolas Berdyaev; and finally of Protestants such as Wilfred Monod, Édouard Soulier and myself, united in spite of our different theological shades.

At these meetings I witnessed the full flood of the orthodox Thomism of Père Gillet, the neo-Thomism of the Maritains, and the vigorous anti-Thomism of Laberthonnière: they clashed with such violence that on one occasion, when I was in the chair, I had to call out, 'One at a time, *please, mes Pères*, none of us can hear what you're saying.' Shortly after this explosive meeting, Mgr Chaptal, auxiliary bishop in charge of foreigners, forbade Catholics to attend meetings at which Père Laberthonnière was present. The Thomists gave up coming, and the group did not long survive their departure.

A further step was taken in this same post-war period by Frank Abauzit, a teacher of theology at that time on leave, whose translation of William James's *Varieties of Religious Experience* had gained him a considerable reputation in intellectual and religious circles. As in the earlier enterprise, Church unity was not the prime concern; nevertheless there was an ardent desire to bring together representatives of religious denominations, secular idealism, and spiritually conscious humanism. Édouard Le Roy, Bergson's successor at the Collège de France, Paul Bureau, recognized as an authority on social ethics, and Canon Viollet, a man of liberal mind and generous heart, were constant in attending the meetings of the Abauzit group; and other enthusiastic members included, in addition to a few Protestants, two chief inspectors of schools, Gustave Belot and Dominique Parodi. The presence of the two latter could not fail to add very considerably to the interest of these meetings. The most weighty metaphysical problems were discussed: in particular I remember a talk by Laberthonnière on 'God', which gave rise to a vigorous debate.

Meetings took place in the house of one or other of the members, Paul Bureau, Édouard Le Roy, or myself. At these I was impressed by the seminal quality of Laberthonnière's thought. He frequently intervened, and often with striking effect. Sometimes, when he was back in the Rue Las-Cases, he would try to put down in writing what he had said; but he then found himself involved in such lengthy developments of his subject that, without his always realizing it, it was a major work that he was sitting down to. Thus, for example, as they were leaving a meeting of the Philosophical Society, at which Jean Baruzi's *Saint Jean de la Croix* had been discussed, Xavier Léon asked Laberthonnière to make what he had said into an article for the *Revue de métaphysique*. Laberthonnière reeled off seventy-two massive pages for him, in which a conflation of philosophy and mysticism shed a decisive light on the teaching of the great Spanish Carmelite.

On another occasion I had asked him to speak on authority in the Church, to the 'captains' of the 'unionist' Girl Guides of Paris. He gave them a clear and lively talk which really got home to them. Back in his study, he wanted to make a note of its essential points, and for hours on end he wrote down what forms the main part of a book published many years after his death, with lengthy notes by Canet, under the title *L'Autorité de l'Église*.[4]

4. Paris, Vrin.

The ecumenical significance of this study has not as yet been sufficiently recognized.

III

I have just mentioned the 'unionist' Girl Guides. The youth movements inaugurated at that time in French Protestantism were an indication of an ecumenical tendency which aroused reactions of considerable force.

It was in the Federation of Student Christian Associations that this concern was most boldly asserted. Ever since my arrival in Paris, in 1911, I had taken part personally in its activities. The Whitsun meetings, in the domaine des Ombrages just outside Versailles, had contributed, during the immediate pre-war years, to the development of generous-hearted vocations. There a team of volunteers for the countries threatened with being submerged by Islam announced its decision, their spokesman being a theological student, Francis Monod, who, unhappily, was to fall during the opening weeks of the war, the first of the many in that sacrifice of our greatest hopes.

In spite of its irreparable losses, the Federation emerged from those tragic years with the firm determination to be faithful to the inspiration and vision of those who were no longer alive to lead the new generation. A congress, held at Montpellier in 1919, brought about an unforeseen change. Dean Raoul Allier, one of the founders of the Federation, who had been its president ever since, was replaced by Pastor Albert Dartigue. I was notified by telegram that I had been appointed vice-president. Three years later Dartigue, whose pastoral work was in Geneva, felt that he could no longer undertake the responsibility of his office at such a distance from Paris, and I was asked to succeed him. I decided to do so, because I was convinced that the ecumenical question was going to produce a crisis in which the unity of the Federation would be seriously jeopardized.

The women students in the movement were eager to accept the guidance of Henri Bois, who taught in the faculty of theology at Montpellier; he was the director, in the fullest sense of the word, of a number of these girls. His ecumenism inspired their thinking and their attitude; and they felt that the Federation should follow a similar line by including Catholics in its executive committee.

Suzanne de Dietrich, whose exceptional intelligence, scientific and biblical knowledge and culture, and contagious spirituality, gave her widely accepted authority, displayed an ecumenism which was bold and even, it seemed to me, at that particular time, rash. Pierre Maury, on the other hand, who had been working with me for a long time as general secretary of the Federation, was much more cautious. His good sense and authority prevailed; the crisis was overcome, and the Federation continued on its way, not, it is true, without having to get through some dangerous situations, but without any split and in the certain belief that the day of ecumenism would come.

At the beginning of this period, a decisive change was introduced into my life. During the weeks immediately before the Armistice of 11 November 1918, Jean Bianquis, director of the Société des Missions évangéliques, had come to the conclusion that with the restoration of peace there would have to be a radical reform in the training of our missionaries, pastors and layfolk, if they were to be able to cope with their duties: both their earlier and their new post-war tasks. The pastor-missionaries would do their theological studies in the faculties and, when the time came, would be ordained by their own Church. Then, with the future doctors, schoolmasters, nurses, primary school teachers and missionary craftsmen, they would spend a year at the Maison des Missions in missiological studies and practical training. Since the committee was evidently disposed to accept the views of the director, it was clear that there was now no reason for my teaching as I had been doing for the last three years, and that I should have to go back to a new parochial ministry.

This was the situation when, on the actual day of Charles Wagner's funeral, I received, by word of mouth, an invitation that could not but be worrying.

For reasons which I need not go into now, the parish of Passy, one of the eight parishes of the Consistory of the Reformed Church of Paris, had fallen into a lamentable state of disintegration. Several Presbyteral Councils, elected in succession, had found the responsibility too much and had collapsed. A great many families had left the church of the Rue Cortambert and sought refuge in the church at the Étoile, the Oratoire, and even further afield. How much longer was the war going to last? With long-range guns and other dangers still an active threat, it was impossible to send children to Sunday School or to any religious instruction at a distance from their homes. I was accordingly asked to take over the responsibility of giving biblical and catechetical teaching to the children whom the families would send me; this would take place in a hall in the Rue Lekain, just by the Place de Passy. The hall did not belong to the parish but to a property company whose directors were completely in agreement with the people behind the appeal I had suddenly received.

My reaction was immediate. If I accepted, what I should have to do would be to build up a new church, for it was impossible for a Sunday School, a catechism class and the training of a Christian youth, not to develop into a parish community, with its organic bodies, its mission to teach and bear witness and serve, and its communion with the other parishes of the Paris Consistory. Then came the question of what the 'ecclesiastical authorities' of my own Church thought of the plan, presuming they were already aware of it. It was impossible for me to consider such an invitation until I had discussed it with the pastors who exercised a real authority in Paris.

I was still extremely busy with my work at the home for blinded soldiers. A new building had been opened; workshops, a school of massage, and another school for telephonists and typists stood on a portion of the fine park of Sainte-Clotilde. I used the little leisure I had in making contacts, paying visits and having conversations in order to clear my mind and decide whether, in the absence of any other invitation, I ought or ought not to follow the undoubtedly difficult road that had just opened up for me.

After some months of uncertainty, indecision and prayer, with the situation cleared up by the assurances of colleagues I respected, I decided that in following this course I would be doing what God expected of me, and I accordingly accepted the invitation. This was in September 1918, and the end of the war was looming upon the horizon. It would be some months still before I was demobilized, but I was nevertheless installed on 13 October by Pastor Benjamin Couve, president of the Consistory, as pastor of the Reformed church of the Annunciation: a name, displayed on the corner of the Rue Lekain, which had seemed to us to carry a message of promise and hope.

Looking back after fifty years, I believe that I can say that I thus performed one of the *truest* acts of obedience in my pastoral ministry, and, in simple terms, of my faith as a Christian.

This is not the place to retrace the stages of a parochial ministry which was to last for over thirty-five years. For four and a half of these I was pastor of what was a real refugee church: and then the day came when, by a decision of the Conseil d'État, arbitration was refused and the building in the Rue Cortambert reverted to its legal owners. They moved back into it on the first Sunday of March 1923, with what emotion and thankfulness can be imagined. The years then rolled by, with their mixture of joys and sorrows; and in that time, with the help of such pastors as Georges Lauga, Charles Bonzon and Pierre Maury, and assistants like Jaques Courvoisier and André de Robert, I was able not only to fulfil my parochial ministry – with many shortcomings, it is true – but also to assume the national and ecumenical responsibilities I was asked to accept.

I may sum it up by simply saying that my acceptance of the pastorate of the church of the Annunciation had consequences for my ecumenical life that I can fully appreciate only today.

On my arrival at Passy I urged, and with success, that the new 'Church Association' should join the Union of the Reformed Churches of France, which at that time was separate from the Union of Reformed Evangelical Churches. I was soon invited to become a member of the former Union's General Committee, and later, to succeed J.-Émile Roberty, after his death, as one of the delegates of the Reformed Churches to the Council of the Protestant Federation of France. Shortly afterwards the Council chose me as the French member of the Inter-Church Aid Committee, directed by Adolf Keller, whose activities were unreservedly ecumenical. When I became president of the Federation in 1929, I was of course one of its representatives at the International Life and Work Council. At the Oxford and Edinburgh Conferences in 1937, I sat as one of the delegates of the Churches of France, and was elected as one of the presidents of the former conference and one of the vice-presidents of the latter. Chosen as one of the 'seven' from Oxford to take part in the meeting in Utrecht in 1938 from which emerged the World Council of Churches 'in process of formation', I had to accept the presidency of the administrative (in fact, the executive) committee of the new council until the general assembly planned for 1941. However, the war of 1939-45 intervened, and any meeting of the World Council was out of the question until 1946; and it was the two years' preparatory work for the Amsterdam assembly that led to my being nominated as one of the six first presidents of the World Council when it was finally set up. Had I not accepted the invitation from Passy, what would have happened to all that?

This quick summary of thirty years of my ecumenical life calls for some essential qualifications on a number of important points. We must go back to Bishop Brent and his plans, and meet another eminent pioneer in the ecumenical movement: Archbishop Nathan Soederblom.

CHAPTER 4

The Three Roads of the Ecumenical Movement
1910-1927

I. The doctrinal basis of Faith and Order. II. Practical
Christianity. Archbishop Soederblom. III. The Stockholm
Conference 1925. IV. Bishop Brent and the Lausanne
Conference 1927.

I

THE war obliged Brent and Gardiner to abandon one of the
most effective instruments in their activities; the distribution in
Europe and other parts of the world of the leaflets that were
always welcomed with gratitude had to be suspended. This,
however, did not prevent them from continuing with the
preparatory stages of their plan, which was the convening of a
conference, as ecumenical as possible in character, which would
face the doctrinal and ecclesiastical differences between the
principal Christian communions and investigate possible ways of
putting an end to them.

Moreover, they were witnessing the establishing in the U.S.A.
of a movement, also claiming to be ecumenical, which was in
origin and aims openly pacifist and received moral and financial
support from the Church Peace Union. Under the name of 'The
World Alliance for International Friendship through the Churches',
its beginnings came close to being tragic. The new organization's
message and programme had been favourably received by eminent
Christians of a number of European nations, and the intention
had been to hold an inaugural meeting at Constance in Germany,
from 2 to 4 August 1914. It was on the 2nd that war broke out
between Germany and France. French, English, German, Swiss,
Scandinavians, Americans, and other nationalities too, who had
already arrived in Constance, were asked to leave German
territory as quickly as possible. After a hasty consultation, all
they could do was to arrange a rendezvous in London for those

who could succeed in meeting there within the next few days, and hurry to catch the last train available for civilians. Among the few Frenchmen present was Pastor Jules Jézéquel, who for nearly fifty years was to be, with tireless devotion, the driving force behind the French Committee of the Alliance. A large number of Orthodox, Anglicans, and Protestants of all denominations became members, often at the same time joining in the ecumenical movement properly so called. While there was at times question of including the Alliance in the World Council of Life and Work, of which we shall soon have something to say, it maintained its independence until the end. The death of its most active workers seems to have robbed its activity of its drive.

The Alliance appealed to individuals. Brent hoped to win the adherence of *Churches*. He had therefore, either directly or with friends as intermediaries, to make contact with Churches and their leaders. As a bishop of the Protestant Episcopal Church of the U.S.A., he had no difficulty in explaining, or finding someone to explain, his plans to the episcopal Churches of Scandinavia, and the same was true with the Reformed, Lutheran and Methodist Churches and other Protestant communities. In the direction of the Orthodox Churches an extremely promising opening was available.

In 1920, the Ecumenical Patriarchate of Constantinople addressed a solemn appeal to the Christian Churches of the whole world to seek for measures that would put an end to their divisions and, on the morrow of the war, give witness to the world of the unity of the Church of Christ. In this ecumenical document, whose importance often seems not to have been recognized, Brent (and, as we shall see later, Soederblom) found immense encouragement.

Nevertheless, contact had still to be made with the Roman Catholic Church. A delegation from the bishops of the Episcopal Church of the U.S.A. expressed the desire to be received in audience by Pope Benedict X V. The audience was granted. This was in 1919.

In 1937, during the week between the Oxford and Edinburgh Ecumenical Conferences, I stayed for a short time with Archbishop William Temple at Bishopthorpe, near York. An American bishop, who had been included in the 1919 delegation, was good enough to tell me about their two visits, to Cardinal Merry del Val and to Benedict XV. Both had been distinguished by great cordiality. The Pope assured his visitors of the interest he took in their efforts and promised them his prayers. He said nothing, it is true, to raise hopes that the Church of Rome would be represented at the projected conference, if only by an observer. Nevertheless, the Protestant bishops, pleased by their welcome and grateful, left the audience with at least some glimmer of hope.

... However, as the door closed behind them, they were handed a memorandum which reminded them, somewhat drily, that the unity of the Church had been realized from the very beginning in the Roman, Catholic and Apostolic Church, and that those who sought this unity had simply to return to Rome.

For decades this meant that it was impossible to inaugurate any official dialogue. Less than ten years later, the encyclical *Mortalium animos* was to assert this with some bluntness.

Neither Brent nor his friends were men to lose heart. The years that followed were fully occupied in the delicate task of preparing for a conference in which there would be a confrontation, as they examined their dogmatic disagreements, between Churches so different (and, in addition, so wholly unfamiliar to one another) as the Orthodox and the Methodist or Baptist communities. By dint of correspondence, travelling, personal interviews, and meetings of national committees, obstacles were overcome, difficulties were ironed out, a programme was drawn up, and decisions were taken; with the result that in the summer of 1927 the World Conference on Faith and Order, whose necessity and urgency Brent had been continually insisting on since 1910, was finally able to meet in Lausanne.

However, there was the problem of what doctrinal 'basis' the Churches would be invited to meet one another on, to discuss the problems included in the agenda, to put forward solutions for them, and, if it should seem necessary, set up an organization to carry on their work. When the World Alliance of Y.M.C.A.'s was founded in Paris in 1855, it had taken as the basis to be accepted by all the unions a formula that has become famous. It ran as follows:

'The Young Men's Christian Associations seek to unite those young men who, regarding Jesus Christ as their God and Saviour according to the Holy Scriptures, desire to be His disciples in their faith and in their life, and to associate their efforts for the extension of His Kingdom among young men.'

I am uncertain whether this formula was known to Brent or other organizers of the conference, or whether it came to them from some other source. In any case it matters little, and I mention it here only because it attracted particular attention from a number of the Churches which had been invited, among others the Union of the Reformed Churches of France, a considerable number of whose pastors and faithful were liberal in tendency.[1] It seemed difficult to them, if not impossible, for their Union of Churches to accept a dogmatic statement which qualified Christ as God-Saviour.

There followed a correspondence between Pastor Wilfred Monod, president of the General Committee of Reformed Churches, and Bishop Brent, president of the Conference's Preparatory Committee. The former committee, after noting Brent's reply, decided, though not without serious reservations on the part of some of its members, to take part in the Lausanne World Conference.

Two years, however, before that meeting, another – the first of the great ecumenical assemblies in the twentieth century – was held in Stockholm, in 1925. It was concerned, not with doctrinal questions, but with problems of life and action. Its conveners had accordingly chosen for their movement the name 'Life and Work' (English was already becoming accepted as the unrivalled ecumenical language): the corresponding French name 'Christianisme pratique' (Practical Christianity) was not very satisfactory.

II

If ever a man gave the impression of having been predestined to the ecumenical life, it was Nathan Soederblom, Archbishop of Uppsala, and primate of the Lutheran Church of Sweden.

He was born in 1866, in a manse in northern Sweden, where his father was an incarnation of revivalist piety, combining a

---

1. In the ecclesiastical idiom of the time, *liberal* was opposed to *orthodox*, and meant the refusal to accept certain dogmas taught by the orthodox Lutheran and Reformed Church, in particular the literal inspiration of the Scriptures. Today the word would appear to be used with a new emphasis.

scrupulous devotion to the faith with a passion for the salvation of souls. Nathan's upbringing (his real name was Jonathan) was strenuous. His studies took precedence over everything: but as soon as they allowed him a little freedom, he would hurry off to the holding attached to the manse, take part in all the field work and, in spite of his tender years, lead the life of a farm-worker. This intimate combination of intellectual work and intense physical activity helped to make him a man of exceptional energy and drive. He took up the study of theology more out of deference to his father than from a sense of personal vocation. Nevertheless, after years of spiritual crisis and interior conflicts, the vocation asserted itself unmistakably. Unable any longer to accept orthodox dogmatic teaching, he sought for a long time before finding peace of mind and soul in a theology of Revelation that was closely associated with the history of religions, a subject in which he had long taken a passionate interest and of which he was to become a master. His eloquence, combined with the warmth of his heart, always receptive of human contacts, soon gained him a dominating influence in the student body of the University of Uppsala, and he became its president.

In 1890, as the representative of the Christian students of Sweden at the International Conference in Northfield, U.S.A., he came into touch with a number of people, and these meetings were to be decisive for a future that was still far distant. There he met again Wilfred Monod, whom he had seen two years earlier in Stockholm at the Y.M.C.A. conference. He made the acquaintance of John Mott, who later, in 1895, founded the World Student Christian Federation, and Mott was greatly taken by the young Swede, with his clear gaze and generous heart. Wilfred Monod, John Mott, and Nathan Soederblom: twenty-five years after their meeting in Northfield all three were to make their impact on the Christian world as pioneers of Christian unity.

Nevertheless, in 1890, there was still a long way to go before Edinburgh and Stockholm. Soederblom's realization at Northfield of the seriousness of the divisions between Churches, and the distress he felt, is apparent in this prayer which he jotted down in a note-book: 'Lord, give me the obedience and the wisdom to be instant in working for the unity, in free agreement, of thy Church.'

Twenty years later, when he was teaching at Uppsala, he went to Constantinople to take part in the ninth conference of the World Student Christian Federation. In Rome, in Athens, and then in Constantinople, he came into contact with Churches which he had never had the opportunity of meeting before. An audience with Pius X was a profound disappointment to him; still more so was the atmosphere of the Papal Court, which he found completely stifling. In Athens and Constantinople he was struck by the anti-Roman emphasis that was apparent to him in the Orthodox liturgy of the Passion. There, too, he met representatives of Christian communities which traced their descent to the most remote times, Copts and other Monophysites. At the same time there were some things which gave him great pleasure; his meeting with the future Archbishop Germanos, later elected one of the first presidents of the World Council of Churches, and with the Chinese Christian Wang, who appealed for close co-operation between all the Christian missions, and made plain to Soederblom the urgency of a union of the Western Churches. In this experience there was a strange similarity with that of Charles Brent at the Edinburgh Conference.

In May 1914 Soederblom was appointed Archbishop of Uppsala. He loved his Church of Sweden, and he loved it all the more from having learnt to know and love the Reformed Churchmen of France, the Anglicans of Great Britain and America, the Lutherans of Germany, the Orthodox of the Balkan nations and Constantinople, and so many others too. Then came the war, forcing the Churches into divisions that were no longer ecclesiastical but national, and bringing the vast problems heaped up month after month by such a mass of material, moral, and social destruction. When peace should be restored, a heavy burden of responsibility would fall on all the Churches without exception: and they would have to be persuaded to meet together and take counsel in a spirit of loyalty and mutual goodwill.

Thus Soederblom's position and his field of action were very different from those of Brent. It seemed to him an illusion to devote his efforts to paving the way for the restoration of doctrinal unity. Insurmountable dogmatic differences might be defined and examined in the light of Revelation, and the doctrinal traditions of each Christian denomination might be appraised as being either a softening-down or a hardening: but they would none the less remain as barriers that could not be crossed. And it might well be that the most obstinate would prove to be those that related to *ministry* in the Church.

Soederblom did not hesitate. There could be no mutual approach and no co-operation unless the Assembly he envisioned resolutely faced the concrete (which is far from saying the easy) problems to which war had given a special gravity: problems of war and peace, of race, of education, of capital and labour, of social order, of Church and State. By the contacts he made, by his correspondence, his reports to the preparatory meetings, by his massive influence and eloquence, the Archbishop of Uppsala convinced those to whom he wrote and spoke. From 1920 until 1925 he devoted himself entirely to the realization of his plan, to which many of his friends gave their enthusiastic support: and on 14 August 1925 the World Conference was opened at Stockholm with impressive ceremonial.[2]

III

The French delegation, chosen by the Council of the Protestant Federation of France, consisted of fourteen members, representative of the various spiritual families included in French Protestantism. Pastor Scheer, the deputy from the Haut-Rhin, was by way of being their leader. The most notable of the pastors and theologians were Wilfred Monod, Élie Gounelle, Henri Monnier, Jules Jézéquel, and Altorffer, from Strasbourg. A smaller group of laymen accompanied them, among whom was François de Witt-Guizot, who for many years had sat on the Councils of the Reformed Evangelical Churches.

There was a large German delegation. One of its members, Professor Deissmann, worked effectively to ease the unfortunate situation which arose from the French demand that before the Conference took any action the German delegation should recog-

2. One cannot but wonder what part the Swedish nation played in this great event. During these last decades Sweden has been the scene of a dechristianization so much more extensive, more rapid and more widespread than in the other nations of Western Europe that the future of Christianity must be viewed with the gravest anxiety. Nevertheless, at Christmas 1967 there seems to have been evidence of a remarkable Christian recovery in a section of the Lutheran youth.

nize their country's guilt in declaring war. Throughout the meeting Deissmann worked in fraternal communion with Wilfred Monod and George Bell (whose name occurs for the first time),[3] at that time Dean of Canterbury. They played a dominant part in drawing up the Conference's report, which Wilfred Monod used to say was finally passed for press by him during the night, with the printers waiting to run it off.

A number of men who were to have a marked influence on the World Council were first introduced in Stockholm to their future responsibilities. Of these I shall mention but two: Alphonse Koechlin,[4] a skilled translator in French, English and German, who took a leading part in the 1937 Oxford Conference, and whose wise counsel, based on a sure judgment, was of great assistance during the difficult years of 1939-45 to the World Council 'in process of formation'.

The second of these two was W. A. Visser 't Hooft, of whom we shall have a great deal to say later. At that time he was twenty-four and represented the Y.M.C.A. at the Conference. Some day, no doubt, he will record the influence that Stockholm had on the development of his ecumenical side.

Just as I gave no detailed account of the Edinburgh Conference, so I shall pass over the happenings in Stockholm. It has entered deeply into the memories of those for whom, close at hand or at a distance, it was a vital experience. Younger people, whose ecumenical thought and life seldom go back beyond the Second World War, can have little interest in encumbering their memories with events that appear to them antediluvian. By many Christians of that time, however, that event was recognized as capital. We were still very close to the war. The Treaty of Versailles was being vigorously contested; bitterness and rancour were far from being extinguished. That representatives of all the great Churches, with the exception of the Roman Catholic, should meet together in the name of Christ and endeavour to unite in putting forward Christian solutions for the gravest and most urgent problems, captured attention in the most diverse quarters and gave Christians strong grounds for hope.

3. Bishop of Chichester, and for many years chairman of the Central Committee of the World Council of Churches.
4. President of the Basle Mission and of the Reformed Church of Basle.

In Stockholm, as in Edinburgh fifteen years earlier, a Continuation Committee was elected, with Soederblom himself as chairman, and other committees were formed to continue the study of the principal subjects discussed at the Conference and, if possible, to put forward solutions that would meet the demands of the Gospel: this was with a view to a second conference on Life and Work; it was anticipated that this might be held ten years later, and, in fact, it was this that developed into the 1937 Oxford Conference on 'Church, Community and State'.

IV

In 1927 Bishop Brent could at last see the fruit of his long labours. What he could no more than glimpse when he was faced by a Christian Church whose divisions had reduced it to impotence was to become a concrete fact in the Lausanne meeting of church leaders and theologians from the most important religious bodies, with the exception of the Church of Rome.

Although the World Conference on Faith and Order did not arouse so much interest in religious intellectual circles as that of Stockholm, nevertheless it proved of exceptional importance, particularly for theologians and the clergy. Since the time of the Reformation, it is true, there had been a few discussions which had brought together scholars representing Churches that were separated by dogmatic disagreements; the door had sometimes been opened to dialogue, even though it had soon been closed again. This, however, was the first occasion on which there was to be not a clash but a meeting face to face, on the ground of doctrine and ministry in the Church, between the Orthodox separated from Rome and the disparate family of communities which had emerged directly from the sixteenth-century Reformation or as the result of later secessions. It was a meeting conducted by official delegates from the Churches which had accepted Brent's invitation, and not by adherents of the ecumenical movement who were acting in a private capacity.

The Reformed and Lutheran Churches had chosen as their delegates at Lausanne some men of high quality: the faculties of theology at Paris, Strasbourg and Montpellier were represented by their most eminent teachers. The ridiculously unimportant divisions within French Protestantism were, no doubt, publicly aired. Nevertheless, Lausanne was some years later to contribute to the acceptance of the principle of conversations between Evangelical Reformed and Reformed on the necessity and possibility of restoring the unity of the Reformed Church of France. One 'Evangelical', and by no means one of the least important, came back convinced by what he had seen and heard, that he could not avoid asking himself, before God, whether the maintenance of the breach finally made in 1905 was not in these days a sin which must be wiped out.

With Brent's energy behind it, the organizing committee had done a vast amount of preparatory work, with which a number of committees had been fruitfully associated. The most important of the doctrinal questions on which Orthodox, Anglicans, Old Catholics, and Protestants had to define their positions and thereby learn to know one another, were included in the agenda. Each particular one was entrusted, at the very opening of the Conference, to a committee instructed to report, after studying it themselves, to a full meeting.

One is justified, I believe, in suggesting that if, in Stockholm, the intellectual guidance of the Conference was in the hands of Protestants of every sort, in Lausanne the predominating influence was that of the Orthodox and the Anglicans, particularly the latter. Orthodox metropolitans and bishops, and bishops and theologians of the Anglican Communion took the leading part in the discussions. The Malines conversations, whose special character will shortly be dealt with, had just ended in failure. The Anglicans, who had once again been rebuffed by Rome and who had long been drawn to the Orthodox, must, I imagine, have been more or less consciously aware of the need to consolidate one of the piers of the bridge which they wished their Church to provide. However that may be, there is no doubt but that the Faith and Order movement aroused a constant and lively interest in both Anglican and Orthodox circles.

Following the precedent of Edinburgh and Stockholm, the Conference was not to break up without addressing a message to the Churches. This had to combine a hope of unity, and the expression of a brotherly affection received as a grace, with the acknowledgment of disagreements that it would be impossible to settle without more profound theological exploration. Here again a committee was formed, to continue through specialized theological sub-committees, the study of the dogmatic questions that were the subject of dispute. Under the unfortunately too short-lived chairmanship of Bishop Brent, the task defined by the Conference was taken up with great vigour. Edinburgh, following Lausanne in 1937, was to make apparent the value of the work done during those ten years.

Thus, seventeen years after the World Missionary Conference of 1910, which inspired the whole ecumenical movement of the twentieth century, that movement was advancing along three distinct roads.

The International Missionary Council, under the presidency of John R. Mott, was hard at work in studying, co-ordinating and organizing in a less confused and more coherent way the non-Roman Christian missions. Mott's numerous personal contacts with the Orthodox world were making possible the preparation for 1928 of a new world conference at Jerusalem, at which the work undertaken since the first would be examined, analysed and criticized in the fullest meaning of the word, and new plans would be drawn up for the covering of the whole world by the Christian apostolate.

The Stockholm Continuation Committee, established on the practical and social basis laid down in the Conference's message, was endeavouring to persuade the non-Roman Churches to agree, as a matter of obligation, to study the essential documents produced by the Conference, both in their synods and in their parishes. Soederblom, the chairman, and his co-workers were still convinced that the unity of the Church of Christ must be sought exclusively in the domain of the concrete realities of life and of the activities of Churches and Christian organizations.

Finally, the Lausanne Continuation Committee, announcing its conviction that there would never be any true Church unity without communion in faith and the acceptance of a common doctrine of ministry, was trying to direct the Christian denominations towards the examination, through their ecclesiastical organizations, their synods and theological institutions, of the problems on which they were in disagreement.

The question was whether, in the course of the coming years, these undoubtedly diverse roads would diverge from one another, or would they, on the other hand, come together so closely that they would find themselves irresistibly impelled to join up? The final and definitive answer was to be given in 1961 in New Delhi, by the Third Assembly of the World Council of Churches.

Then there was the question of the Roman Catholic Church. Was it standing by, indifferent to these activities, to the mutual approach, the meetings, the studies of all sorts, and the great gatherings which had been going on incessantly for the last seventeen years? It was true that in 1919 Benedict XV had clearly indicated the Catholic attitude to what non-Romans call the problem of Church unity. There was no sign that this had acted as a check to the vigour of the ecumenical movement. After Edinburgh had come Stockholm, and after Stockholm Lausanne; and afterwards it would be Jerusalem. The Orthodox too, who were only schismatics, were joining in a theological confrontation with heretics! There could not fail to be a Catholic reaction: Rome did not mince matters, and the condemnation of the Malines conversations provided the opportunity.

What exactly were these conversations? They had been started in 1921, with the approval of the Holy See, under the chairmanship of Cardinal Mercier, Archbishop of Malines, and brought together a number of Catholic theologians (none of them English) and Anglican theologians authorized by Dr Davidson, Archbishop of Canterbury. Their sole aim was to investigate whether, and on what conditions, the Church of England, the Church of the Thirty-nine Articles and the Prayer Book, could be reunited with the Church of Rome: 'united, not absorbed'. None of those who took part in the conversations brought to it the least concern with ecumenism, in the sense it had been given since the Edinburgh Conference by half a century of meetings, theological enquiries, common prayer, and communion in love and hope. It was only the Roman Catholic Church and the Church of England who were confronting one another. Or rather – since many English Catholics and Anglicans strongly repudiated the conversations – it was only a few Roman theologians (French and Belgian) and a few Anglo-Catholic theologians of the Anglican Communion, who in response to Cardinal Mercier's invitation, were studying (on the basis of statements of position that were sometimes surprising) problems that went no further than the possibility of an organic union of the Roman Church and the Church of England.

Behind Cardinal Mercier's initiative can be recognized the activity of two men who had long entertained the dream of the return to Rome of the 'Anglican' Church: a French priest, the Abbé Portal, and an Anglican layman of rare breadth of mind, Lord Halifax.[5]

It is highly possible that these two possessed an ecumenical spirit: but it was certainly not that which inspired them to suggest these important conversations to Cardinal Mercier.

On 6 January 1928, Pius XI, without mentioning anyone by name, condemned what some years earlier he had formally encouraged. The reason is plain enough. The encyclical *Mortalium animos* automatically included in its condemnation the ecumenical movement, then in its eighteenth year. The terms used were a grievous blow to a considerable number of Orthodox and Protestants, and of Catholics too, who were persisting in the hope that theological and spiritual contacts would soon be established in mutual respect, trust, and prayer. We believed that these hopes would be killed. We were soon to be surprised, and even amazed, when the contrary proved to be true. What follows will provide the explanation.[6]

5. For the former, a deeply evangelical priest, see Jean Guitton's *Dialogues avec les Précurseurs* (Paris, Aubier), which contains also a fine portrait of the other great servant of Christ, Lord Halifax.
6. See Appendix 1 for the passages in the encyclical which were directed against the ecumenical movement.

CHAPTER 5

The Fanö Meeting

1934

I. President of the Protestant Federation of France 1929. The Federation's ecumenical orientation. II. Inter-Church Aid in Europe. III. The Christian Life and Work Council and the Church revolution in Hitler's Germany 1934.

I

In December 1929, the Council of the Protestant Federation did me the honour of electing me as its president. Pastor Morel, who had succeeded the layman Édouard Gruner in 1927, was unwilling to remain in office after the General Assembly of French Protestantism, which had just met in Marseilles. As I was coming back from that meeting with Count Paul de Pourtalès, vice-president of the Council, he told me on the way that he and his colleagues intended to appeal to me: I had accepted his suggestion, without closing my eyes to the difficulty of the task but in the conviction that the position I was offered would enable me to do a great deal for French Protestantism by extending the work of the Federation.

The story of the thirty-one years of my presidency does not fall within the scope of this book. In writing of this period I shall dwell only on what concerns the relations between the Protestant Federation and the various branches of the ecumenical movement. I must, too, explain briefly what the Protestant Federation of France was in 1929, and how it proposed to deal with its responsibilities.

Various attempts had been made during the last quarter of the nineteenth century to persuade the Reformed Churches in France to throw off an ecclesiastical individualism which was gradually making them strangers to one another. 'Irenic' pastors, such as Auguste Decoppet of the Oratoire, and Roger Hollard of the Free Church of the Luxembourg, were the organizers of these attempts. Their goodwill came up against the 'ecclesiasticism'

of the orthodox Reformed,[1] from which Fallot had suffered so
much, and the distrust of the Lutherans, who were dominated by
a minority complex in relation to the Reformed. Their position
had been seriously weakened since the Treaty of Frankfurt had
made the Church of the Augsburg Confession in Alsace and Lorraine one of the Lutheran Churches of the new German Empire.

In 1903 a synod of the independent (free) evangelical Churches
was held in Clairac (Lot-et-Garonne), during which a sermon was
preached by Wilfred Monod, at that time pastor of the Reformed
Church in Rouen. His audience was deeply moved by his appeal
for closer contact between the different French Churches, for co-
operation, mutual trust and fraternal love. A number of pastors,
such as Roger Hollard and Léopold Monod, and of laymen, such
as Édouard Gruner and Raoul Allier, felt that it was imperative
to make a new attempt to set up a Federation of the French
Churches. The proposal was welcomed by the Reformed and the
Lutherans, and conversations were started which, not without
some difficulty, resulted in the drafting of provisional statutes.
Speed was essential, for it was known that the separation of
Churches and State was in the offing. Before the end of 1904 the
Statutes were adopted, although the first official meeting of the
Council did not take place until 20 January 1907. It was no doubt
the great dislocation of the life of the Churches produced by the
passing of the law of separation which accounted for the delay.

In the form in which it was set up, the Protestant Federation
did not meet the wishes of Wilfred Monod and its founders. Its
aim was strictly confined to developing a closer relationship
between the Churches, to affirming their solidarity and the
possibility of common action in the moral and social field. Though
still accepted at that time, the term *religious* was excluded from the
Statutes. It goes without saying that every member Church of
the Federation had to refrain from intervening in the doctrinal
or disciplinary life of the others.

The separation of Churches and State, by causing the Reformed
Churches (faced by the rejection on the part of the orthodox of
any plan for union) to set up three *distinct national* unions,[2]

1. See above, p. 29, note 6.
2. The Evangelical Reformed, the Reformed (known as the '*Reformées de
Jarnac*') and the United Reformed Churches.

resulted in the inclusion in the Federation, at the beginning, of six 'National Unions of Church Associations' (Unions nationales d'Associations cultuelles), a horrible name imposed by law: besides the three Reformed Unions, there were the Unions of the Lutheran Evangelical Church, the Free Evangelical Churches, and the Methodist Churches. The Statutes provided for a general assembly of Protestantism every five years, and it was decided that the first should be held at Nîmes in October 1909.

Odd though it may seem, the word 'Church' was scrupulously excluded from the name of this Federation, even though its members were Unions of Churches. The original intention had been to use the word, but on reflection it was decided that it was inappropriate and dangerous. The name finally chosen saddled the life of the Federation with an ambiguity: and so, without realizing it, the Federation was already making it possible to foresee that, fifty years later, it would include, side by side with the Churches, 'the movements, institutions and activities of French Protestantism'.

As one of the delegates of the Reformed Churches, I took part in the Nîmes General Assembly, acting as one of the secretaries. However profitable, thanks to Alfred Boegner, Élie Gounelle, Léon Marchand, and above all Charles Babut, the 'religious' meetings may have been, the Assembly left many of its members with a feeling of pessimism. They had hoped that its message to the Churches and the nation would affirm the spiritual communion of all French Protestants in love and scriptural meditation; and Charles Babut, who was asked to draw up the draft of the message, had included a passage of uncommon nobility, written on these lines. Unhappily, François de Witt was hurried to the rostrum to call, on behalf of the forty delegates from the Reformed Evangelical Churches, for the withdrawal of this fine plea. It was not de Witt himself, however, who had decided on this ultimatum, but Dean Émile Doumergue, who at that time exercised a sort of dictatorship over those Churches. Deep emotions were aroused; Babut could not disguise his disappointment, but he had to give way.

The war of 1914-18 wiped out the memory of this unfortunate beginning. The second Assembly, held in Lyons in 1919, eagerly welcomed the representatives of the Churches of Alsace and

Lorraine. Their adherence, which was confirmed at the Strasbourg General Assembly in 1924, was a reinforcement of the Federation whose value has ever since been appreciated by the Lutherans and Reformed 'of the interior'.

I had taken part in the Lyons Assembly as the representative of a number of Churches which had not yet joined any national union: Lyons, Bordeaux, Passy, Royan and two or three others. To my great regret I could not be present at Strasbourg; but since the parish of Passy had shortly afterwards joined the Union of Reformed Churches, I was invited, on the death of Émile Roberty, to succeed him on the Council of the Federation, and it was in that capacity that I took part in the Marseilles Assembly in 1929.

Great ecumenical events had taken place between the Nîmes and the Marseilles Assemblies, with four notable landmarks: Edinburgh, Stockholm, Lausanne and Jerusalem. As I have already said, the Churches of France had been present at those meetings. Their representatives at the Stockholm Assembly had been chosen by the Council of the Federation, of which I had recently become a member. I had been sounded about being one myself but had been obliged to decline. However, I remember very well the meeting at which some of those who had been to Stockholm gave their colleagues the impressions they had formed. From that time there was a very close bond between the Federation and the Life and Work movement. A similar situation did not arise after the Lausanne Conference, for this was attended by official delegates from Churches with whom the Faith and Order movement immediately maintained direct relations. That movement, moreover, was developing in a domain which the Protestant Federation had barred itself from entering.

This first, and extremely cordial, contact between the Council of the Federation and the Life and Work continuation committee was of great importance. It established what I might almost call a legal principle. As was confirmed by later contacts, it anticipated and ruled out the attempt of any person or body, whether pastor, layman, or church council, to maintain that there could be no question of ecumenism at the Council of the Protestant Federation of France. When, many years later, this claim was made by the representatives of one of the member Church Unions of the

Federation, I was to be able to show them in writing all the circumstances in which the traditional relationship between the Federation and the World Council for Life and Work (and, after 1938, the World Council of Churches) had been affirmed and strengthened.

A more special bond linked us with the Churches of the U.S.A. Before the end of the war, two of our military chaplains had visited America and received a most cordial welcome. The establishment in France of Franco-American clubs for the forces had produced numerous contacts with ministers and laymen of various denominations. Generous friends, among them the Revd. MacFarland and Mr Sloane Coffin, had the kindness and energy to provide the Federation with more secure quarters than those it was then occupying. The house at 47 Rue de Clichy was bought, and the Federation, the Reformed Evangelical Churches, the Protestant Committee for International Friendship (Comité protestant des Amitiés étrangères) – founded at Government request during the war – and other religious organizations moved in; and this concentration of similarly minded bodies was not without welcome results. MacFarland was a frequent visitor, as secretary of the Federal Council of the Churches of Christ in America, the slightly younger brother of the Protestant Federation of France.

Such, from the point of view of ecumenical relations, was the position of the Federation when I became president, an office which I never dreamt I would be holding for thirty-one years. Every day, since that time, except when I was away from Paris, I went to the 'Rue de Clichy', as we always called the headquarters of those various organizations. Long years, however, were to pass before the Federation found workers and the material organization to keep pace with the development of its work. Even so, in spite of the shortage of manpower and our limited funds, we were able to cope with essential needs.

Some years earlier, a course of lectures I had given on two occasions at the Academy of International Law in the Hague[3] had enabled me to get to know not only the leaders of the Walloon Churches but also of the Netherlands Reformed Church. The

3. *L'Influence de la Réforme sur le développement du droit international*, Paris, 1925; *Les Missions protestantes et le droit international*, Paris, 1927.

Church of Geneva had already invited me to preach in the cathedral of St Peter on the opening of a session of the League of Nations. In 1931, the fifth centenary of the edict of toleration granted to the Protestants of Bohemia brought me to Prague, where I was able to strengthen our ties with the Reformed Church of Czechoslovakia. Masaryk, who received me at the Hradschin Palace, assured me of his satisfaction at this welcome result.

II

Meanwhile, it was in the World Alliance for International Friendship through the Churches, of which, if I am not mistaken, I was the only French member, that from this time I was able to establish useful contacts with the representatives of many foreign Churches. Dean Choisy of Geneva, the president, was assisted by a vice-president of great experience, Professor Joergensen of Copenhagen. The soul of the enterprise was Adolf Keller, a pastor from German Switzerland, a man with an uncommon capacity for hard work; he wrote his reports as secretary-general in French and English as easily as in German, and he had the ability to focus attention on the most striking aspects of the often unhappy lives of the Churches which the Committee felt itself obliged to support by financial assistance. Every year he gave us an overall picture of Christian activity in Europe, and when the hour of trouble came upon the Churches of Germany he helped us to understand the significance of the struggles involved.

The Committee was very much concerned with Hungary and Spain. At all our meetings the Churches of those countries were represented by men who were in a position to give us the most reliable information. I can remember, too, the interest with which we listened to a Polish Lutheran bishop as he explained to us the great difficulties which Polish Protestantism had to face.

From 1934 until 1939 I was closely associated with the work of this Committee. Keller was familiar with our Churches and activities, and often proposed that substantial assistance should be given to them. On countless occasions during the Second World War, he helped us greatly. Nevertheless, when the World Council of Churches set up its own inter-Church aid section, the Committee decided to hand over its responsibilities to the new organization.

This marked the end of a generous undertaking on whose behalf I had had to travel to Copenhagen, Edinburgh, Vienna, Poděbrady and Basle. Everywhere I had the opportunity to speak about our Churches, and their special vocation in our country, and I tried to consolidate their moral and spiritual reputation. I can testify that the descendants of the Huguenots almost universally enjoyed a trust and esteem which caused our Churches, without their always realizing it, to be a powerful influence towards friendship and unity in the divided world of the Reformed Churches.

III

Of all the ecumenical meetings in which I took part during this period, the most important was without any doubt the Fanö meeting in August 1934.

Fanö is a small island, just off the western coast of Denmark, opposite the town of Esbjerg. It had been chosen in 1934 as a meeting place by three movements: the World Council for Life and Work, the World Alliance for International Friendship through the Churches, and an international Christian Youth Congress.

This was the first time, I believe, that I sat on the World Council for Life and Work. The Protestant Federation of France had chosen me as its representative, together with Wilfred Monod, who carried great weight in its deliberations. He was unable to attend the Fanö meeting, and Jézéquel and I were the only Frenchmen. Adolf Keller and Alphonse Koechlin, both German Swiss, could be classed as 'French-speaking'.

The chairman was George Bell, Bishop of Chichester, of whom I had had no more than a glimpse until that time; and it was a great joy to be able to learn to know him, to live in the light of his serenity, to see those intensely blue eyes of his fix themselves on one, as one walked up to him. To love him was indeed a blessing from heaven. The friendship he showed me during those crowded days on Fanö was the richest memory I brought back to France, and I still nurse it intact in my heart.

Besides the problems of the State and of preparations for a new conference, the great question to be debated by the Council arose from what was happening in Germany. The political revolution produced by Adolf Hitler's coming to power had had profound repercussions on the life of the Churches. A party of 'German Christians' had imposed an ecclesiastical revolution which a large number of pastors and of the faithful were determined to resist. A 'Reich Bishop' (*Reichsbischof*), Dr Müller, had been appointed by Hitler, supported by a legal representative – Hitlerite, needless to say – and an *Oberkirchenrat*, Dr Heckel, was at Fanö, as the representative of the new ecclesiastical power. Beside this man, the other Germans present could hardly open their mouths.

On my way to Fanö I had stopped in Berlin, where I had met Professor Deissmann. I have already spoken of the part he had played in the Stockholm Assembly, and he was obviously badly needed at Fanö. He explained to me his reasons for not attending, which were that he did not wish to argue with Heckel and his collaborators in front of foreigners. He was anxious to know what I thought about his attitude. I could not but approve of it, and events showed me that he was quite right.

Some long letters which I wrote from Fanö make it possible for me to describe with accuracy, not, indeed, everything that was said and done in the week we spent on the island, but what related to the situation of the Churches of Germany.

The Bishop of Chichester appreciated its extreme gravity. I had hardly arrived before he asked me to take part in a private discussion he hoped to have with some members of the Council in whom he had particular confidence. He told us of his concern to find 'the best way of handling the formidable question of the Church in Germany'. It was understood that the Council would raise this problem on the next day, and that the discussion would be closed that same evening. 'It appears', I noted shortly afterwards, 'that the majority of the members of the Council have decided to support a strongly-worded motion and to express their sympathy with the opposition.'

The opposition had not yet, in fact, taken the definite form of the Confessing Church (*Bekennende Kirche*), whose foundation we could not foresee at that time.

The discussion opened with an address by Bishop Bell. He told us what he himself and the executive committee of the Council had done to induce Bishop Müller to listen to the Churches' protest against the brutal policy he had inaugurated. 'We then had an interminable speech from Bishop Heckel, who made a most disagreeable impression. He was immediately answered, with great vigour, by Keller, who dealt with the principles behind which Heckel was constantly taking refuge, and then we went in to dine. By 8.30 we were back again in conference, and I was the first speaker. I said that Heckel could not but acknowledge that on each occasion on which we had met I had done my best to understand his views but that I really could not agree with him that at this moment the Council should remain silent. On the contrary I urged that it speak up, in loyalty to the message of Stockholm, and even more to Christ himself. I asked some very searching questions about things which I knew to have been said or done in Berlin. I was followed by Dr Leiper from the U.S.A., and he and a Swedish professor and bishop rammed home the point. Simons, a former president of the State Court of Germany, announced that the German delegation would not reply until it had considered the questions we have raised.

A smaller committee, meeting in between the general sessions, attempted on several occasions to steer the discussion in the direction the majority of our colleagues desired. At a public session, J. H. Oldham delivered 'a most remarkable address'. But 'Heckel keeps on repeating that we cannot understand the situation in Germany and shelters behind a political and religious philosophy which throws dust in the eyes of his audience'.

Other topics of study obliged us more than once to break off discussion of German affairs: Church and State, the Church and the International World. The pacifists of the Alliance, who were admitted to the meeting on this subject, vigorously defended their point of view. In private conversations, however, it was the German question that constantly occupied our attention.

On 28 August – we had been in conference since the 24th – the Bishop of Chichester asked me to take part in a conversation he hoped to have with Heckel. 'Poor Heckel', I wrote at the time, 'with whom I had a long interview after dinner, is in a dreadful position . . . He has been denounced on the telephone to Berlin for not having replied with sufficient vigour to the attacks (?) made on the government of the Church. Yesterday morning he was called to the telephone by the *Reichsbischof*, who gave him a terrible dressing down, blaming him in particular for not having answered a question of mine about a serious incident in the Church of Hesse-Cassel. I am extremely sorry for the poor man: and, at his request, I promised that he would have "fair-play"[4] from us, and that we would give him plenty of time to consider what his attitude should be this afternoon.

'10.20 hours. The pace is hotting up, and the position is getting worse. Heckel has just had a telegram from the *Reichsbischof* telling him that a man called Birnbaum has been sent from Berlin to Fanö with full powers. He thinks that this envoy has been told to give him instructions that will lead to a break. He sees himself on the point of being dismissed. I have just seen him alone for quite a long time, and I cannot help being sorry for him. I can see that this is going to be a difficult day.

'13.50 hours. Müller's precious envoy is just on the point of arriving. He will land right in the middle of the discussion on the resolution about affairs in Germany. A moment ago I was saying to Heckel "You must feel that we all sympathize deeply with you." "Yes", he answered, "but when I am back in Berlin I shall be all alone."

'Müller's messenger did in fact arrive early in the afternoon. It had been agreed that Bishop Bell should welcome him as a visitor during the evening session, and invite him to speak in the hope that he might have some useful news for us.

'This was done: Birnbaum got up . . . and we listened to the most incredible address you could imagine. There was not a single allusion to what we find so heartbreaking in life today and particularly in the government of the Church. There were platitudes about the spiritual revival, the increase in the number of marriages and baptisms, the development of Christianity in the proletariat as a result of the National-Socialist revolution . . . We just sat and gaped . . . The chairman told him in reply that we had listened to him with interest and that an opportunity would be provided today for questioning him on the matters that cause us such anxiety. We shall be seeing him this afternoon at an informal gathering.

'11 hours. We have just voted on the resolution about Germany, after a moving statement by Heckel. The representative

4. The author uses the English word.

of Austrian Protestantism sided with the Germans in voting *against* it, and what he said showed us that the religious *Anschluss* has been effected.

'30 August, 23 hours. The interview that five or six of us have had with *Oberkirchenrat* Birnbaum began at half past two. We asked him a number of straight questions. He then talked for over two hours. To hear him, you would think that everything was for the best in the best of all possible worlds.

'. . . Conversation with Heckel, who was nearly out of his mind after a new telephone call from the *Reichsbischof*. He had been reported to Berlin as having himself inspired a motion urging the overthrow of the *Reichsbischof's* régime.'

I may seem to have devoted too much time to the long hours we spent on Fanö in discussing the troubles of the German Churches; but they marked an important date in the history of the ecumenical movement. For the first time, one of the Churches affiliated to the movement (in both its branches, practical and doctrinal) was engaged in a battle that was at once religious and political, and was soon to become theological. Would it have been possible, or even conceivable, for the Christian Life and Work Council to remain silent? To do so would have been to sign its own death sentence.

Two days later, Bishop Bell and I were in Copenhagen with some members of our Council and of the World Friendship Committee. The Danish papers were full of more or less fantastic details about the Fanö meetings. As usual, I saw the Havas news agency man. On 2 September every Copenhagen paper published a solemn protest from the German Ministry of Church Affairs against the Fanö resolution. It asserted that our attack had been directed against the Government of Adolf Hitler himself!

During the evening of the same day, I suddenly saw the Bishop of Chichester enter the hotel bedroom I was just getting ready to leave. He was coming, in his wonderfully friendly way, to bid me good-bye. Before leaving – and this I can never forget – he asked me to give him my blessing. Rightly, indeed, I could write, 'This man has won my heart'.

CHAPTER 6

The Beginnings of a Massive Task
1928-1932

I. Lenten addresses 1928-1963. II. Cardinal Verdier. III.
Père Laberthonnière: the Notre-Dame addresses 1925-
1927; his death 1932.

I

DURING the years that followed the Stockholm and Lausanne
Conferences it was not only outside France that I had the opportunity to collaborate in the development of the ecumenical
movement and to bring out the concept of the Church I had put
forward in my thesis of 1914. In 1931, the fourth series of my
Lenten addresses gave me the chance of expounding the fruits
of my lengthy reflections on the unity of the Church.

When, in 1928, with the approval of the Presbyteral Council
of my parish, I embarked on these lectures, I had committed
myself to a formidable step in the dark. It was two years before I
was to be elected president of the Protestant Federation. I would
never, at that time, have dreamt of undertaking such a task;
indeed, as I look back, I ask myself how it was possible for me,
in spite of my parochial and national duties and the upheaval in
the world – and in my own personal life – to continue this
arduous task for more than thirty years.

I had conceived these addresses as an essay in apologetics which
I wished to put forward, on behalf of the church of which I was
pastor in the sixteenth *arrondissement* of Paris. The invitations
sent out to professors, teachers, and people connected with the
liberal and other professions, brought quite a number of accept-
ances. Nevertheless, I never felt that I was properly understood
or supported by a considerable number of my parishioners.
Starting with the second year, my lectures were relayed by
Radiodiffusion française from the church in the Rue Cortambert,
so that many Protestant listeners preferred to hear them at home,

and there was never a large audience in the church. But what an eye-opener was the 'invisible' audience, larger every year, and expressing itself in numerous, often moving, letters! Even today I cannot think without a feeling of gratitude of the messages I received from Catholics who had just been listening to me as I spoke about Jesus Christ.

'What is the Church?' This was the question I set out to answer in my 1931 addresses. I made no claim, it is true, to offer a doctrinal exposition which could satisfy all minds. But, as against the total vacuum which at that time took the place of Reformed ecclesiology, I wanted to emphasize the major importance of the question I was asking, and the duty of theologians to establish a reformed doctrine of the Church and its unity on the basis of the teaching of the New Testament and in harmony with the thought of Calvin.

After a lapse of thirty-five years, I have just been re-reading the sixth address, on 'The Road to Unity'. The essential elements of the problem, it seems to me, are correctly expressed, and the criticism of certain ideas of unity seems still to be accurate today. Nevertheless, while there are numerous references to the investigations inspired by Edinburgh, Stockholm and Lausanne, a great deal of time is given to the Malines conversations. The comments aroused by those conversations, particularly after their condemnation in the encyclical *Mortalium animos*,[1] could not but influence ecumenical thinking. The temptation to pave the way to the restoration of visible unity by bargaining and agreement had been a dangerous snare for the 'negotiators' of Malines. There had been violent reactions to this sentence from the report: 'Theologians, just as diplomats in similar cases from the secular point of view, must find a way of reaching their goal without sacrificing the rights or susceptibilities of either party.'[2] Looking at it in the light of Stockholm and Lausanne, how could one conceivably suggest such a road to unity? This, accordingly, led me to point out that 'only those Churches will advance along the road to living unity which have made up their minds to ask God for the grace of humility. This means that the Churches, conscious of having all sinned in different ways against the unity of the

1. See above, p. 68.
2. *Conversations de Malines*, p. 33.

Body of Christ, will together offer their repentance to God.' And I quoted in support (what, since Vatican 2, can seem prophetic) not only the act of repentance made by the members of the Lausanne Conference, but a too-little-known declaration by the papal legates at the Council of Trent:

'If we wish to confess the truth, we cannot but admit that not the least part of the responsibility for the evils we are called on to cure, rests upon ourselves. It is we pastors who must accept our guilt before the tribunal of God's mercy, taking upon ourselves, not out of pity but as a matter of justice, the sins of all.'[3]

The whole development of my thought led up to the great saying of St Paul, which I am never tired of quoting to those who listen to my lectures on the problem of Church unity today: 'Speaking the truth in love' (Ephesians 4:15).

'It is through love that we enter into truth', St Augustine also had said. 'Not through toleration; one single word contains the full measure of our obligation of catholicity, and that is the word love . . . The unity of the Church presupposes love, and love demands unity.

'Love does not resign itself to divisions . . . Without ever disguising the disagreements which prevent the unity of the Church from being made manifest, but at the same time without ever allowing itself to lose heart, love untiringly continues its work, effecting what is possible today, so that the impossible of today may be the possible of tomorrow.'

Would I speak differently today? No doubt I would. I would emphasize more strongly than I then did that the road to unity must run through the awareness of the essential apostolic vocation which the Churches must arrive at; and, by the grace of God, they have now all entered that stage together. But what would I change in the sentence I have just quoted? If the impossible of 1931 has become the possible of the day of Vatican 2, it is because those who truly serve the cause of the unity of the Church have striven never to sin against the apostolic charge: 'Speak the truth in love.'

On the very day on which I gave my first sermon on the Church, an ecumenical study group was meeting in Paris. At the French

3. Labbé, *Sacrosancta Concilia*, XIV, p. 738.

Protestant headquarters, I welcomed the prelates, pastors, and theologians – Orthodox, Anglican, Lutheran and Reformed – who had come in order to join together in examining the political and social problems confronting the Churches at that time. As their chairman they chose Martin Dibelius, the widely respected Heidelberg theologian.

II

At about the same time the news from Russia aroused great anxiety. The revolution of 1917 had overthrown a régime which for many centuries had reduced the human masses to appalling slavery, and in consequence Christians of the western world were uncertain about the religious and moral future of the Russian people, so long deeply rooted in the Orthodox faith. The brutal persecutions which struck at Orthodox, Catholics, Protestants, Jews and even Moslems, but particularly at the clergy of the Orthodox Church, gave rise in all quarters to a great upsurge of prayer on behalf of those who suffered from these attacks on religious freedom. The Council of the Protestant Federation thought that our Churches, even more than others, had the duty publicly to display their participation in the sufferings of the Russians, both Christians and non-Christians, who were living under a reign of terror. It instructed me to publish an appeal for prayer, and authorized me to try to organize a meeting at which representatives of the religious denominations engaged in this terrible struggle would join in intercession.

It was on this occasion that I first met Cardinal Verdier, Archbishop of Paris. Having already obtained the agreement of the Orthodox Patriarch Vladimir, Exarch of the Ecumenical Patriarchate of Western Europe, and of the Chief Rabbi of France, I put before him the plan for an ecumenical meeting in which we would all be associated, as a testimony to our unhappy brothers in Russia of our fraternal love and our sharing in their sorrows and hopes.

Without the least hesitation the Cardinal turned down my suggestion. He did not know, he told me, what attitude the head of his Church would take up towards these tragic events, and he did not wish himself to adopt one that might contradict the pronouncement the Holy Father could not fail to make. I could only note this refusal, which, in its own way, led later to the most loyal co-operation.

Instead of a meeting at the Trocadéro, we held a solemn service of intercession at the church of the Oratoire. The crowd filled it to overflowing. Every religious denomination was represented, except the Roman Catholic Church. Nevertheless, a considerable number of Roman Catholics were present and joined in the common prayer.

It was not long before I called again on Cardinal Verdier. One evening we learnt that, by order of M. Chautemps, Minister of the Interior, all religious broadcasts were to be ended. First thing the next morning, I saw the Archbishop and suggested to him that a united protest should immediately be made to the president of the Council by him, the Chief Rabbi of France, and myself, demanding the resumption of the cancelled broadcasts. The Cardinal immediately agreed to this step, but at the same time he raised some objections to the sending of a single letter signed by the three of us. 'Perhaps, then', I said to him, 'each of us might write a letter from the point of view of his own Church? Would you yourself, in that case, be willing to have them forwarded to the president of the Council?' This suggestion was readily accepted and shortly afterwards the broadcasts were resumed.

A much more serious situation again united the Archbishop of Paris, the Chief Rabbi and myself in common action. The 6th of February 1934 was a tragic day for Paris. After an evening of rioting, dead and injured were lying in the Place de la Concorde. Appeals to violence multiplied. The worst fears appeared to be justified, and the days that followed showed the difficulty of preventing their realization. Early on the morning of the 7th, I asked to be received by Cardinal Verdier. Relying on the agreement of Chief Rabbi Schwartz, I told him that I was convinced that we should approach the Head of State *together* and beg him to take or impose all the measures needed to prevent further bloodshed. The Archbishop accepted the principle of common action. At the same time a visit to the Élysée at such a juncture from representatives of the three 'cults' recognized until the law of separation, seemed to him (and rightly) inopportune. We accordingly repeated the procedure adopted at the time of the prohibition of religious broadcasts. With this Chief Rabbi

Schwartz was fully in agreement. Three letters were written and the Cardinal immediately forwarded them, enclosed in one envelope, to the President of the Republic. The answer we each received from Albert Lebrun showed how deeply he had been moved by our appeal.

After that agonizing day I often saw Cardinal Verdier again. We were continually being asked to give our patronage to some generous enterprise, in the field of social justice and work, or to join the honorary committee of some new undertaking. A sad disappointment, however, was in store for me. As time went on, our relationship had become increasingly cordial. In our last interview (though neither of us foresaw that it was to be the last) he gave me a proof of his affectionate trust by asking me to obtain, in connection with the requests made to us, all the information that would enable us to give an identical answer. A very few days later, the morning news on the radio announced that he had just died after a sudden operation. I immediately went round to the Rue Barbet-de-Jouy: and looked with deep emotion at the peaceful but solemn face of this servant of Jesus Christ who, prince of the Church though he always was, had ever remained the kind and humble Christian whom so many seminarists at Saint-Sulpice had loved as 'Monsieur Verdier'. It was a great joy to me to be able to pay tribute to him one evening when I was lecturing in Rodez, in that part of the Rouergue in which he seemed to be so solidly rooted.

III

Since the end of the war, and particularly since all the work I had taken on at Passy had been claiming all my time, my meetings with Père Laberthonnière had become less frequent; but I may make bold to say that they were all the more intimate. I delighted in seeing him again in his study in the Rue Las-Cases where I would always surprise him in the act of filling great white sheets of paper with his neat and elegant handwriting. Sometimes another visitor would have arrived before me, the Abbé Hemmer for example, *curé* of the church of the Trinité, who was one of the French participants in the Malines conversations. Those meetings, from the time they were announced until they were closed down by the encyclical *Mortalium animos* in January 1928, provided material for many conversations. Louis Canet, a true spiritual son of Laberthonnière and at that time adviser on Church affairs to the Foreign Ministry, often took part in these. His brilliant intelligence, his wide culture, his knowledge of canon law and his undisguised Gallicanism, gave an astonishing vigour to his conversation. His criticisms of the Roman Curia, and in particular of the Holy Office and its judicial practices, sometimes attained a vehemence that I have met later only in the words of a certain English bishop at the Vatican Council. It is to him, too, that we are indebted for editing, after Laberthonnière's death, numerous unpublished writings which contain some wonderful surprises for those who take the trouble to follow to the end the sometimes rather prolix elaborations in which he could not refrain from clothing his thought.

We used, accordingly, to discuss Malines, in the light of what the French theologians had to tell us when they were back in Paris between sessions. I must, however, emphasize again that there was never, in my presence, the slightest connection established between Malines and the ecumenical movement in which the Stockholm and Lausanne meetings were then being planned. These latter, it is true, were held before the encyclical which, some months after Lausanne, took the opportunity to condemn the movement for unity. In so far as the Catholics I met at Laberthonnière's during those years were interested in the cause of Christian unity, they always looked at the conversations from an Anglo-Roman point of view.

Meanwhile, at the beginning of 1925, an unexpected event intervened to revolutionize Père Laberthonnière's hard-working life. Père Sanson, who, after he made up his mind to leave the secular clergy, had on Laberthonnière's advice entered the community of the Oratorians, had just been invited by Cardinal Dubois, Archbishop of Paris, to succeed Père Janvier as the Lenten preacher in Notre-Dame. Père Sanson's fine voice and his great oratorical skill had greatly impressed Mgr Dubois, at that time Archbishop of Rouen, when he had heard him preach a retreat at Deauville as a young abbé. Sanson went straightway to see Laberthonnière and explained to him how hesitant he was to accept, and how incompetent he was as a theologian and a philosopher. Laberthonnière was most insistent that his young colleague should not dismiss this chance of exercising a magnificent apostolate. Sanson decided to accept but only if Laberthonnière would promise to help him. The two of them immediately got down to finding a subject. 'The Spiritual Burden of Mankind' seemed to them to allow the introduction of the essential problems. The scheme for the six Lenten addresses (to be delivered very shortly) was soon decided on, and Père Sanson began to prepare the first.

In the crowd which filled Notre-Dame on this first Sunday in Lent 1925 there seemed to be a great expectancy, stimulated both by the announcement of the subject and by the reputation Père Sanson had already won as a fine preacher. The audience seemed to be completely captivated – but Père Sanson was disappointed. Early the next morning he told Laberthonnière that he had made up his mind to send his resignation in to the Cardinal. By his warm-hearted encouragement and his promise of fuller assistance, Laberthonnière managed to dissuade him: and from that moment he devoted himself completely to Père Sanson's apostolic work.

'I wrote the whole of the third address', he wrote to Maurice Blondel, 'from the first sentence to the last . . . You must agree that it was a most unusual venture. This third one is the hinge on which those that follow will turn.'[4] 'Those that follow', right up to the end of the third and last series, were all to be written by the same hand, the spontaneous fruit of constant reflection.

For some time it was only two or three friends who knew the truth: Blondel, still at that time his intimate and trusted friend, the faithful Dernis, whose filial devotion never failed, Louis Canet, and, no doubt, the Abbé Magnin, *curé* of Saint-Séverin, to whom the text was sent by the Archbishop for his imprimatur. From the very beginning I, too, certainly knew that the sermons were the result of a close collaboration, for it often happened that on arriving at the Rue Las-Cases I found Père Sanson 'working' with his prompter. It was only later that through M. Dernis I learnt, not without some consternation, the whole truth.

In considering so 'unusual a venture', one should remember that pseudonyms were perfectly normal in the *Annales de philosophie chrétienne* at the time when Laberthonnière was the editor. It was important to hide the author's name from the Holy Office.

94. March 1925, op. cit., p. 325.

Similarly, Laberthonnière himself had written an important chapter in the *Histoire de l'Église sous Léon XIII*,[5] which was attributed to the author of that book, Père Lecanuet. And in December 1914, when the German bishops published a pastoral letter on responsibility for the war, Mgr Chapon, Bishop of Nice, asked Laberthonnière to write a reply: 'I know that you are so magnanimous and disinterested as to be willing to efface yourself under the name of the episcopate in order to carry out so opportune, so important and necessary a task.'[6] What was even more, between 1915 and 1918 Laberthonnière wrote a book entitled *Pangermanisme et Christianisme*, which was not published under his name and in its full form until 1945, with a foreword by Louis Canet: but the first two parts of the book were published in the *Correspondant* in 1915 and 1918, under the name of Mgr Chapon, who had the support of over sixty bishops.[7]

However that may be, all the hard work Laberthonnière put into thinking about, planning and drafting sixteen Lenten addresses had infinitely fruitful results, among which may be counted a number of conversions, without any doubt, and, what is more, of vocations to the priesthood. The preacher's voice had a penetrative power and a persuasiveness by which no one could be long unmoved. His voice, indeed, must have been one of the finest heard for many long years.

Sitting at the foot of the pulpit, in a reserved seat Père Sanson had been kind enough to send me, I noticed on countless occasions the reappearance of thoughts I had so often heard Laberthonnière express, it seemed to me, in just the same words.

'That God is Father, is the central idea of the Gospel . . . A true father desires his children in themselves and for themselves, so that they may be personal beings, as he himself is a personal being . . . It is a love by which instead of taking one's own self as end, one takes those who are the object of that love; in short, it is a love which loves them as beings in their being, in order, not to use them, but to be of use to them. It is by generosity, by the gift he makes of his own life, that a true father is a father . . .

5. Chapter IX; and later he wrote Chapters X and XI.
6. 20 February 1915.
7. Paris, Vrin. See Louis Canet's 'Avertissement', p. xiv, at the beginning of *Pangermanisme et Christianisme*.

From the moment God creates, the only motive he can have, the only purpose by which he can be animated in creating, is to bring about the existence of beings in a pure generosity . . . through the gift of his own self and his own love.'[8]

As I saw these thousands of men and young people so absorbed in the eagerness of their attention, I felt an immense sense of gratitude that my dear friend, imprisoned in unjust silence, could know the welcome accorded to his words. I could see him, an unrecognized figure sitting beside Louis Dernis, his head turned attentively towards the speaker, and I was wondering whether he was completely satisfied with the result of the 'collaboration'. Sitting close by were the canons of the chapter of Notre-Dame, some dozing, others looking surprised and even anxious. Were the preacher's attacks on Aristotle in fact aimed at that target?

The Cardinal never took his eyes off Père Sanson. Was the force of his enthusiasm getting through to him? He once said that he could not understand all the speaker was saying, but that he was delighted by the great amount of good for which the sermons were responsible.

The Pope, however, made no mistake. Fully informed about the series, he said to a French bishop in 1927, 'Behind Père Sanson stands Père Laberthonnière; Père Sanson will never again occupy the pulpit of Notre-Dame.' And, in spite of the distress it caused him, Cardinal Dubois was obliged in 1928 to provide a successor for the Oratorian whose words had for three years in succession produced such an impact.

What a mystery is the poor human soul! Shortly before his death Père Laberthonnière confided to me the painful emotions produced in him by a certain drifting apart from Père Sanson. The latter seemed to blame him for being the cause of the check to his career as preacher in Notre-Dame. And yet, without Père Laberthonnière, what would he have amounted to as a preacher?

Père Laberthonnière suffered another heartbreaking blow at a time when, already a sick man, he was spending many days and nights in agony. The publication of his correspondence with Maurice Blondel had made him, if I may use the words, public property. It was a shattering exchange of letters, in which could

8. Lent 1926, fourth sermon, 'The God of the Gospel', pp. 4, 5.

be seen the first outline and then the development in full depth of an intellectual and spiritual friendship that reached the heights of a pure brotherly tenderness . . . and suddenly, under the corrosive influence of misunderstandings that were not only philosophical but also psychological and moral, the seemingly indestructible link slackened: it had been worn away from within, and finally it snapped apart, in an outburst of sorrow and distress.

I do not wish to dwell too long on this ordeal, about which Père Laberthonnière took me into his confidence. At the same time, I must mention the last visit he paid me in the Boulevard Beauséjour, where we were then living. It was in March 1932. That same morning he had received from Maurice Blondel, after years of silence, a copy of his latest book, *Le Problème de la philosophie catholique*; with this dedication on the fly-leaf, '*Animae carissimae semper memor*'. He told me this with a look of suffering on his face that pierced my heart. 'Would you believe', he said, 'that he should make not the least reference in his book to his long collaboration with the *Annales de philosophie chrétienne*? He doesn't even mention it: and then he writes me this dedication!'

I have never forgotten his distress, which was aggravated by a more and more worrying state of health. He was unable to visit me again but I saw him on a number of later occasions in the Rue Las-Cases. From month to month his friends' anxiety increased. They felt, too, that enemies were prowling around his home who would have been only too pleased to get hold of some of his papers. The manuscript of the Notre-Dame sermons was put in a safe place, and Louis Dernis and Canet felt obliged to exercise extreme vigilance.

Père Laberthonnière fell asleep in God on 6 October 1932. Of the many griefs I have known in my life, that death was one of the greatest. And yet I could not but give thanks to God for this incomparable friendship and this revelation of the *metaphysic of charity* which is the real heart of his Christian philosophy. Fallot, Laberthonnière: both enabled me, each in his own way, to discern in the distance the coming of a Catholicism that would be freed of its egocentricism, of its falling back on an extravagantly centralizing post-Tridentine tradition, of its inquisitorial and inhuman Holy Office. And thus I received first from the one and later from the other, an impetus towards ecumenical life and work, new stages of which, shortly after 1932, I was summoned to enter.

Some weeks before learning the grievous news of this passing I had taken part in a true ecumenical week, in Muoterhouse near Niederbronn, in a house which the Dietrichs, through the good offices of Suzanne de Dietrich, had kindly placed at our disposal. Père Brillet, Superior of the Fathers of the Oratory, two Catholic theologians (one from Germany, and one from Austria), Orthodox such as Nicholas Berdyaev, Sergius Bulgakof, Zander and Vycherlatzeeff, an Anglo-Catholic monk from Mirfield, and a number of French Reformed and Lutherans (among whom were Suzanne de Dietrich, Pierre Maury, and I) made up the bulk of those present. All day long, except at meals, which were taken in silence (to the exasperation of Pierre Maury), we had long discussions on the various aspects of the problem of unity and the obstacles we were meeting in achieving it. There I learnt, in the most emphatic form, that in the service of this great cause joy and sorrow are inextricably interwoven.

It was a joy every day to kneel side by side for the recitation of the Creed and the Lord's Prayer; it was a joy to listen together and meditate on the Word of God, in one and the same oblation of hearts and minds to its demands and promises; it was a joy to live hours of wonderful spiritual communion and trusting friendship.

Sunday morning brought the hour of suffering. Père Brillet, with his co-religionists, went to say Mass in the village church and give communion to our friends; the Orthodox celebrated their Eucharist in a room which they had fitted up as a chapel; the Anglican monk had his morning service in his own bedroom, and received communion with an Englishwoman who was passing through; and the Protestants went to the Lutheran church of Muoterhouse to offer their worship to God, to hear a sermon by Pierre Maury, and to partake of the Lord's Supper.

I found this terribly distressing; I understood how Brent had suffered in Edinburgh from the scandal of our divisions, and once again I dedicated myself to the cause of bringing together those who were separated in their confession of faith, and of achieving the unity of the Church of Christ.

CHAPTER 7

Progress Towards the Unity of the Reformed Church of France
1933-1938

I. The Reformed Churches immediately after the war. The Synods of 1933. II. Paving the road to unity 1933-1938. The role of André-N. Bertrand. III. The General Assembly of French Protestantism: Bordeaux 1934.

I

MY ecumenical life developed along such different roads that, in recalling my memories, it is hardly possible to follow an exact chronological order. I found it necessary to devote rather a long time to Fanö, and from that point I had to retrace my steps. Meanwhile, a strong concern with unity was making itself felt in French Protestantism.

Since 1910 the World Conference in Edinburgh had been stimulating a great deal of thought among young French pastors. Some of them had been military chaplains during the war of 1914-18; they were distressed by the divisions apparent in our Churches, whose testimony they foresaw might well remain barren in a people which had been weakened by such huge losses; and they took the opportunity of a meeting to draw up a manifesto designed to awake Protestant opinion to the gravity of the position in the Church, and of its spiritual consequences. However, the impression produced by this document was short-lived. Fifteen years passed before the seeds, still living in some minds, began to germinate.

There were two National Unions of Reformed Churches existing side by side, or, I might well go so far as to say, confronting one another. Their delegates used to meet on the Council of the Protestant Federation of France: pastors or laymen of the two Unions sat together on the Committees of the Société des Missions évangéliques, of the central missionary society (Société centrale d'évangélisation), and of our other great active institutions. Nevertheless, they had very little direct contact.

Among the Reformed Churches known as *de Jarnac* there was a unanimous desire for an end to be made of the division, while in the Reformed Evangelical Churches fear of 'liberal' contamination meant that those who opposed any form of reconciliation could do so with a clear conscience.

A clear conscience? After Edinburgh, and then the war, Lausanne had come to disturb the 'clear conscience' of a number of French Reformed Evangelicals. One of their delegates at Lausanne asked himself on his return whether the maintenance of the division of the Reformed was not a sin. The atmosphere gradually changed, and after 1930 the possibility dawned of an agreement.

A decisive event took place in 1933. Two regional synods, each representing a different Union of Churches, brought together some neighbouring parishes in the Drôme and the Ardèche. On both sides, in the meetings of the synods arranged for the same date, a motion was proposed in favour of Reformed unity; and, after a moving meeting in Livron at which the two synods had affirmed that in them and in their parishes unity was already a living reality, both sides passed strongly worded resolutions. It was then for the two National Synods to pronounce on the statements forwarded to them.

There was one man then in the 'Reformed' Churches in whom was embodied the conviction that the time had come to put an end to the situation that had been created, immediately after the separation of 1905, by the decision of the 'Reformed Evangelical' Churches to constitute themselves legally as a National Union, without any preliminary discussion with the other Reformed Churches – these latter being thereby obliged to take a similar step. That man was Pastor A.-N. Bertrand.

After serving the parish of Castres, Bertrand had been invited to Lyons, where his ministry soon exercised a profound influence. When Wilfred Monod, pastor of the Oratoire du Louvre and professor in the theological faculty of Paris, decided to give up the presidency of the General Committee of the 'Reformed' Churches, Bertrand was almost the inevitable choice as his successor. It soon became clear that to combine all the work of a ministry in Lyons with the presidency of a national committee in Paris was altogether too much. When the death of Émile Roberty left a vacancy at the church of the Oratoire, the General Committee persuaded the Presbyteral Council to send a pressing invitation to Bertrand.

I well remember the meeting of the members of the General Committee, in Paris, with the delegates from the church of Lyons, who had come to plead with them not to deprive them of so well-loved a pastor. They had to give way to the general interests of the National Union and the requirements of the situation of French Protestantism.

Bertrand was thus at the head of the 'Reformed' Churches when the National Synod of the Oratoire met in the summer of 1933 to make a decision about the 'Livron resolution'. The Synod had no hesitation in accepting it, and asked Bertrand to convey to the 'Reformed Evangelical' Churches their ardent hopes that conversations between the two National Unions might be initiated without delay on the basis of the resolution. Some weeks later the National Synod of the 'Reformed Evangelical' Churches decided in turn, after some discussion, to take the resolution into consideration and to give a favourable answer to the request of the 'Reformed' Churches. Shortly afterwards it was agreed that the governing committees of the two Unions should meet in an 'Assembly', which would formulate the decisions that might result from the forthcoming conversations, and that their officials should form a 'mixed delegation' for the purpose of studying in detail and making the necessary preparations for the Assembly's deliberations.

As I shall very shortly be recording, in the course of the following years two other Unions of Reformed Churches joined in these conversations, the Free Evangelical Churches and the Methodist Church. Thus was made plain the existence within our Churches of an ecumenical urge directed to ending divisions between Protestants.

II

The direction of the deliberations was assumed in turn by the President of the permanent commission of the 'Reformed Evangelical' Churches (Pastor Maurice Rohr), and the President of the General Committee of the 'Reformed' Churches (A.-N. Bertrand). Maurice Rohr's complete loyalty, his great pastoral experience and his kindness were a great source of strength at difficult moments.

But what shall I say about Bertrand? Was he too much of a great friend and brother to me – as, moreover was Pierre Maury – for me to be able to speak of him with complete objectivity? However, those of our contemporaries who still survive will agree with me if I emphasize the greatness of his intellectual and religious personality, his moral courage, his ever-persuasive wisdom, his spiritual tact, his art of guiding a discussion towards a conclusion that would be acceptable to the great majority of his colleagues, and the contagious influence of his spirituality, whose source sprang from the innermost core of (in a favourite phrase of his) *la vie profonde*, the depths of the interior life.

All this was to make itself unmistakably felt in the course of the years 1939–44, during the occupation of France, with an authority we all unanimously bowed to. But already in those days, when he was presiding over or even simply taking part in the delicate discussions – often difficult and, indeed, painful – about Reformed unity, his serene greatness was evident to all. He, more than any other, was the artisan of the reconstitution of the Reformed Church of France in its historical unity.[1]

The task presented numerous difficulties, and on a number of occasions serious incidents threatened to jeopardize everything. Bertrand, with a liberal educational and theological background, was evangelical to the core. That perhaps was why some of the other party were suspicious of his persuasive charm. I can remember one meeting at which Bertrand was vigorously taken to task by one of the representatives of the 'Reformed Evangelicals', loaded with reproaches and unjust accusations, and denounced as a man of bad faith; he listened in silence and then answered with a self-control, a mastery of the inner emotional storm I could detect in him, that captured the respect and admiration of all.

I had the joy of being able to be by his side during these few years. Re-reading the reports of these memorable discussions, I

1. See Manen, *Le Pasteur A.-N. Bertrand* (published in association with the C.N.R.S.), in particular the chapter which the author was good enough to ask me to contribute.

have noted without surprise how constant was our agreement. In spite of the accumulation of work during this period, from my pastoral ministry, the presidency of the Protestant Federation and attendance at numerous ecumenical gatherings, I was able to take part in nearly all the meetings; and if some of them have left me with painful memories, from all of them I retain the picture of Bertrand's figure, as dear to me as that of a brother, his face often lit up by a mischievous smile.

This is not the place to explain in detail the drafting, discussion and final acceptance of the wording of a declaration of faith, an ecclesiastical constitution and subsidiary regulations, which, after the National Synods of the different unions of Churches, had to be passed by the constituent Assembly meeting in Lyons in May 1938. It was an arduous task, calling for much tact, but often absorbingly interesting, for example when the Declaration of Faith of the Reformed Church of France had to be worked out.

The Declaration, known as the Declaration of 1872, to which many pastors and layfolk of the 'Reformed Evangelical' Churches were deeply attached, was accepted as the basis of discussion.[2] A number of us insisted that the communion of our Church with the universal Church should be witnessed from the outset by express mention of the great symbols of the Councils of the first centuries. It seemed to us indispensable that the Reformed Church should from the very beginning take up an ecumenical or catholic position; and to our great joy this was agreed.

Another incident during the working out of the Declaration is worth recording. The Declaration of 1872, following the funda-mental principles of the Reformation, proclaimed 'salvation by faith'. On the authority of St Paul's most unmistakable teaching, I proposed the formula, 'Salvation by grace through faith'. At that moment François de Witt-Guizot called out, 'So you're going to drag us into theology!' It was then that Bertrand, to still these fears, proposed the insertion in the Declaration, as 'the central revelation of the Gospel', Christ's words in John 3:16,

2. At Guizot's request, Thiers's Government authorized the calling of a National Synod, which had been refused by earlier Governments. It was held in Paris in 1872, in the church of the Holy Spirit. After heated discussions it accepted the Declaration of Faith, known since that time by the date of the meeting.

'For God so loved the world that he gave his only Son . . .'
Both suggestions were unanimously adopted. For my own part,
I thought that John 3:16 bristles with theological problems.

The gravest crisis was produced by the consideration of what
is called the 'Preamble'. To work out and pass a declaration of
faith is all very well: but who has then to adhere to it? And how,
and in what terms, shall that adherence be given? I had some very
personal reasons for being closely interested in the examination
of these questions.

In 1905, some months before the passing of the law separating
Churches and State, there had been a meeting in Rheims of the
(unofficial) General Synod of the 'Reformed Evangelical'
Churches. Some of my friends and I, young pastors or 'candidates
for the ministry', had had the boldness – some said the imperti-
nence – to send a petition to the Synod advocating a modification
in the liturgy of ordination to the pastorate.

After reading the Declaration of 1872, and as he was receiving
the ordinand's adherence, the ordaining pastor said, 'Such, my
brother, is the wording in which our Church confesses its faith:
do you declare that you adhere to it?' Our petition pointed out
that 'it' referred, grammatically, to 'the wording' and not to 'its
faith', and we asked that the question we contested should be
replaced by another, which contained no ambiguity: for example,
'Is that faith your faith?'[3]

I was on the eve of the oral examination for my degree as
bachelor of theology, and less than three months from my
ordination. I went to Rheims to be present at the discussion of
our petition. It was, indeed, an exciting meeting. Charles Babut,
Louis Lafon, Émile Gautier (who was to preside at my ordination) and even Isaac Picard[4] supported our request. It was
vigorously opposed by Émile Doumergue, Benjamin Couve and
some pastors and laymen of the strictest church orthodoxy, and
was rejected. It was quite certain that thirty years later we could

3. The ambiguity is apparent in English only if the rather unnatural 'the
wording' is substituted for 'the words'. In French it is more obvious: 'Tels
sont *les termes* dans lesquels notre Église a confessé sa foi; déclarez-vous *y*
adhérer?' (*Translator.*)
4. Pastor Picard was some days later to ordain my friend Raoul Patry,
who declared that he could not adhere to the *wording* of the Declaration of
Faith.

not agree to a system of secret compromises and public declarations vitiated by hypocrisy.

How, then, were we to solve the question of the adherence of pastors to the Declaration of Faith? When, as I write these lines, I think of the 'conciliar oath' that all bishops of the Roman Church had to swear at the opening of Vatican 2, I am literally terrified by the thought of the 'reservations' behind which so many Christian consciences in such solemn circumstances take shelter.

In the matter of adherence, we tried to remove any danger or temptation of this sort, in a case where future pastors, feeling themselves unable in conscience to accept all the formulas of the Declaration of Faith, nevertheless are unwilling to lend themselves to a more or less disguised duplicity. Did the Preamble, by authorizing them to distinguish between the letter and the spirit of the formulas, satisfy this anxiety? Thinking about it once more, after an interval of thirty years, I must admit that I am uncertain. It would, I think, be better to confine oneself to quoting the authorization to receive ordination given by the Commission of the pastoral ministry after the candidate has declared his faith to it, and not to combine the demand for a public adherence with an authorization which inevitably robs the former of any substantial force.

I am well aware that our orthodox party of that time – whose orthodoxy, however, was contested by the great Calvinist theologian Auguste Lecerf[5] – rejected any preamble and insisted on a public, unreserved, adherence. They should have remembered how many of their young pastors, after loyally mentioning their theological reservations to the Commission qualified to authorize or refuse their ordination, had been encouraged to 'adhere to it' with a clear conscience.

Four years were thus spent in studies of all sorts, in discussions, in final drafts, in voting with or without reservations, and in synodal debates: they culminated in the unhappy National Synod

5. While still a theological student, Auguste Lecerf had undertaken, with his friend Émile Gautier, a new edition of Calvin's Catechism. When he joined the theological faculty of Paris in 1923 as lecturer and later as professor, he immediately made his mark as the initiator of a neo-Calvinism which paved the way for the influence of Karl Barth.

held in 1938 by the 'Reformed Evangelical' Churches. Before noting the importance of this Synod I must deal with an event that occurred at the same time, which also was evidence of the ecumenical hopes of our Churches.

III

The fifth General Assembly of French Protestantism met in Bordeaux in November 1934. After Nîmes, Lyons, Strasbourg and Marseilles, the capital of the South-West, in which Protestantism is so active, had been eager to be chosen. Months before the appointed date, I had been to Bordeaux and arranged with the Presbyteral Council the details of the organization, the main items of the programme and the public events which this meeting of the Protestant Churches of France would call for.

By its constitution, the Assembly (which was under the presidency of M. Gambier, the highly respected pastor of Dijon) included only official delegates from the member Churches, and the members of the Council of the Federation. Nevertheless, representatives of the great Protestant societies and youth movements had been invited. The subjects on the agenda were important, particularly that of education, which was at that time a matter of great public concern in France. This produced a discussion, at times extremely lively, in which two pastors Édouard Soulier and Jean Autrand, both parliamentary representatives, played an important part. It was odd, incidentally, to hear these two politicians (the only two in the Assembly) reproach their colleagues for introducing politics into their discussions.

On the Sunday afternoon a meeting for young people was very well attended. That same evening, I noted that the speakers (among the most prominent of whom were A.-N. Bertrand and Élie Lauriol) had led us to the highest peaks of the Christian life, in its interior aspect and in its incarnation in society. In spite of the restrictive wording of the statutes of the Federation,[6] a living communion was manifestly present among all: a tremendous advance since the Nîmes Assembly of 1909, and evidence of the desire to attain, and so later to bear witness to nationally, a true religious unity of French Protestantism.

6. The first statutes of the Protestant Federation, drawn up in 1908, had been at pains not to speak of the 'religious' unity of French Protestantism.

At the opening of the session, my report had raised the ecumenical question. It may be well to quote some extracts from
this.

'There are three ecumenical movements: what is known as the
Stockholm movement (the World Council for Life and Work),
the World Alliance, and the so-called Lausanne movement (Faith
and Order). To these three organizations must be added the
Central Office of Inter-Church Aid for the Protestant Churches
of Europe. The Protestant Federation of France is directly
responsible for the representation of our Churches on the Life
and Work Council and the Central Office of Inter-Church Aid.
Some of our colleagues have represented us, or still do so, on
the various international councils or committees, in which duty
they spare neither time nor trouble. By their good work in the
cause of ecumenical Christianity, they are at the same time faithful
messengers of the thought and spirituality of French Protestantism.

'. . . For the last four years I have been able to take part in
meetings of the Central Office of Inter-Church Aid which have
been held in Paris, Geneva, Copenhagen and Edinburgh . . . And
this year, with Pastor Jézéquel, I represented the Federation at
the World Council meeting on the island of Fanö.

'. . . At the last session of the World Council for Life and
Work, I was appointed as a member of the Council's administrative Committee . . . I shall thus be able to co-operate even more
closely in the great enterprise undertaken by the Stockholm
Conference, and thereby more continuously to associate with it
and the Churches it represents.

'I must not forget to add that during these last years several
international committees or conferences have met in Paris, at
our headquarters (the Maison du Protestantisme français).
Among these I need only note the World Conference on Church
and State, which met in April this year . . . This again emphasizes
the duty of French Protestantism, and those who are authorized
to represent it, always to attend meetings at which Christianity's
great responsibilities in the modern world are considered and
discussed.'[7]

7. 'Actes de l'Assemblée générale du protestantisme français, réunie à

We had invited representatives of Churches abroad to attend our discussions. A number of them spoke and assured the Federation of the fraternal esteem of their Churches. Professor Zilka, of the faculty of theology in Prague, delivered an address in French which brought home to all of us the value and significance of a truly ecumenical enquiry *within* the daughter Churches of the Reform.

The ecumenical movements were also represented. Henriod, secretary-general of the Life and Work World Council, and Adolf Keller, secretary-general of the Central Office of Inter-Church Aid, gave us a most impressive picture of the sufferings of the Churches in Germany and Eastern Europe. This was at the last meeting: the Assembly broke up on a great act of hope.

This simple fact was sufficient to establish that the Protestant Federation had maintained, since Stockholm, a firm connection with the ecumenical movement as a whole. The World Alliance for International Friendship through the Churches was also represented at Bordeaux in particular by Jules Jézéquel, secretary-general of the French branch; it enjoyed a cordial relationship with our Churches which was largely due to the reputation of Georges Lauga, president for many years of the French section.

An ecumenical event within the Protestant Churches of France was a cause of great satisfaction not only to the Assembly but also to a great number of layfolk. This was the preparation, followed by the publication, of a selection of psalms, chorals and hymns common to all the Churches. Six or seven different hymn-books were in use at the time when *Louange et Prière* (*Praise and Prayer*) was being put together. Members of our Churches who moved house, perhaps several times in a few years, had to obtain books with which they were unfamiliar, in which the music and words of their favourite psalms and hymns were changed in a way that they did not always think an improvement. In the long run it seemed impossible to accept this diversity. Theologians, pastors, composers, organists and choirmasters set to work. It took several years, but ever since the new book, which we wanted to be a real prayer-book, has done a great deal to strengthen the spiritual

Bordeaux du 16 au 20 novembre 1934', Paris, *Siège de la Fédération protestante*, 1935, pp. 50-2.

unity of French Protestants, whether Lutheran or Reformed, orthodox or liberal, in every part of the country, north, south, east or west. And even if some improvements seem to be called for no one will any longer dispute the need for the book.

The presidency of the Protestant Federation of France, a continually more engrossing ecumenical task, and the work involved in the Lenten addresses were obliging me to cut down on my parochial ministry. The Presbyteral Council of the church of the Annunciation accordingly decided to call in a second pastor. After the greatly appreciated service as an assistant of Jaques Courvoisier, the future rector of the University of Geneva, the parish had the joy of welcoming Pastor Georges Lauga. His long ministry in Rouen and the very many lectures he had given in France, Switzerland and the Netherlands on behalf of the *Cause*, had won for him a spiritual authority which was recognized in all quarters. Unfortunately, the excessive public speaking he had allowed himself to be drawn into had not only ruined the quality of his voice but had so affected his health that after a first period of enforced leave he had been obliged, in the autumn of 1933, to give up all pastoral ministry. The grievous ordeal he suffered then had a deep effect on our parish, for the warmth of his heart, his sensibility, his ardent sharing in the joys and sorrows of all and the force of his preaching gave his work an influence that radiated fraternal tenderness. We had just drawn up and obtained the approval of the Presbyteral Council for a plan for the evangelization of the Boulogne-Billancourt district, when a bad relapse forced him to leave us.

At the very moment when his departure was raising a serious problem for the church of the Annunciation and myself, my own home was struck by the cruellest of trials. If I allow a glimpse of the tragedy that upset my whole life, it is only in order to emphasize the relief brought to both the parish and myself by Pierre Maury's acceptance of our invitation to become our second pastor. His installation in the first months of 1934 was the beginning of twenty years of collaboration, one of unequalled mutual trust and fraternity; and in the many fields of my work it gave me unfailing support and freedom from anxiety.

I had known Pierre Maury for a long time. Since my election

in 1922 as president of the Federation of Student Christian Associations, he had for a number of years been its secretary-general. Later, as pastor of Ferney-Voltaire, he gave some series of lectures and addresses in Geneva which brought out the vigour of his theological thought. His *Trois Histoires spirituelles* made a great impression. To young people, he was teacher and guide; nor did they lose him as such when he came to Passy. And so for twenty years he was to form an intimate part of my life.

As was the case with the General Assembly in Bordeaux, the troubles in my own domestic and parochial life in no way diverted me from my collaboration in the unremitting work which was slowly paving the way to the return to unity of the Reformed Churches. I would prefer, however, not to dwell on the countless incidents which filled the latter part of this difficult period. Press and lecture campaigns, appeals to loyalty, endlessly renewed denunciations of pastors who were accused of 'tearing up the Bible', all that may remain shrouded in oblivion. The unhappy truth was that at the National Synod of the 'Reformed Evangelical' Churches, summoned to pronounce on the wording of the Declaration of Faith and of the Preamble included in the liturgy of ordination, a by no means negligible minority voted against acceptance, and this meant a split.

Again and again since that time I have asked myself whether it could have been avoided. Nevertheless, I do not believe that the minority, who wished to continue to include the 'Reformed Evangelical' Churches, would ever have agreed to giving the Pastoral Ministry Commission the right to decide whether the ordination of future pastors, without public adherence to the Declaration of Faith, should or should not be authorized.

If, on the other hand, the majority had surrendered the Preamble in order to prevent a secession 'to the right', they would have made a left-wing secession inevitable. Reformed unity could be achieved only on conditions that made it possible for certain liberals, pastors and laymen, to remain in or to enter the Reformed Church of France. The Preamble guaranteed them, and those who would succeed them, the same liberty of expression in a heartfelt fidelity to the great Christian tradition.

The progress towards unity could not be halted by these distressing incidents. It was decided that the Constituent Assembly of the Reformed Church of France should be held in May 1938. The meeting took place in Lyons.

I had the great honour of presiding. This office should have been held by A.-N. Bertrand, whose authority had been continually increasing in the intervening five years. It was thought, however, that neither of the presidents of Churches could be chosen, and my assistance was invited. The work was made easy for me by the fact that all the members of the Assembly had previously agreed on the documents submitted for their final approval. Only minor amendments could be proposed, discussed and voted on. It was thus – though I wonder whether it can be called 'minor' – that the fixing of a retirement age for Presbyteral councillors was rejected.

There was a lot of work to be done: the Declaration of Faith, the liturgy of ordination, and the Church Constitution, including all the regulations for the operation of a strictly presbyterian, synodal system, were all adopted. François Méjan who, as secretary-general of the 'Reformed Evangelical' Churches at the time of the separation of 1905, had been an enlightened adviser, showed extreme vigilance in scrutinizing the documents, and helped me untiringly in guiding the discussions.

The 'Constituent' Assembly had approved a discipline, and set up an ecclesiastical system; but, within its restored unity, the Reformed Church, through a national synod taking its place in succession to the synods that preceded the Revocation of the Edict of Nantes, had itself to inaugurate the new period of its life. Legal difficulties had to be overcome and many necessary steps taken. However, everything was settled in time, and the National Synod was able to meet in the church of the Holy Spirit in Paris during the second week of December 1938. By a strange historical repetition, the Reformed Church of France affirmed its refound unity in the same building as that in which the passing of the Declaration of 1872 had prepared and no doubt made inevitable the separation that was then ended.

On 13 December, after numerous decisions had been made under the firm authority of the Moderator, Jean Cadier, the Synod elected the first National Council of the Church; on the same day its members appointed me president, with Maurice Rohr as vice-president. Thus a most onerous duty was added to those for which I was already responsible. I was to carry it out for twelve years.

There are many things which thrust those years back into a distant past: national and international events, the war and the occupation of France, the wars in Indo-China and Algeria, the political crises which shook France and Europe, the coming of the nuclear age, the dominance of technology – and at the same time many great ecumenical happenings. But when I think of that period I am grieved by the thought that men like Bertrand were made to waste their energy, drain themselves of their spiritual life-blood, squander their intellectual powers, on arguments and corrections and definitive formulas that now seem quite ridiculous and absurd. On how many occasions, unhappily, did we not bring sorrow to the Holy Spirit? How much better it would have been from the point of view of Churches and faithful, had they been able to live in closer contact with the great political and social movements, Communism, Fascism, National Socialism, whose brutal impact was so close at hand.

It may be thought, perhaps, that the interior life of French Reformed Protestantism had no relation to what at the same time so profoundly marked the progress of the ecumenical movement; and in many respects that is true. Nevertheless, it is true that the restoration of Reformed unity, almost on the eve of the war, while a provisional World Council was inaugurating its work, had undeniable ecumenical consequences.

In the first place, for the Reformed Church itself. At the beginning of 1939, the new National Council, in response to the invitation to the Reformed Church to become a member of the World Council, instructed me to tell the secretary-general that 'the Reformed Church of France would be happy to collaborate even more closely in the great work whose primary aim is to induce the Christian Churches to examine together the causes of their differences and the possibility of eliminating them, and then to associate them more effectively than ever before in the domain of Christian life and work'.

The war, which broke out some months later, dealt many serious blows to our Churches. When so many of its parishes, institutions, homes and faithful were in such distress, the Reformed Church was able, with an authority recognized by all, to make known its needs to the Churches of allied or neutral nations, generally through the medium of the Geneva Council. The 'ecumenic' reputation our Church gained from the work of *Cimade*,[8] whose personnel was almost exclusively Reformed, was undoubtedly invaluable. The admirable generosity shown to the Reformed Church and its work by the Churches of Switzerland, the U.S.A., Great Britain and Scandinavia, was the fruit of contacts with the evangelical communities of many countries which its representatives established and continually strengthened from the very first months of the war.

At the same time, the World Council itself benefited from the re-establishment of our unity. The handful of Christians who in Geneva were working tirelessly to maintain ecumenical communion between the Churches of the warring nations and, with this in view, to establish secret contacts between gallant workers for Christian unity – this devoted handful found in the great majority of the pastors of the Reformed Church unfailing understanding and support: and when the 'provisional' World Council undertook a generous attempt to help refugees, of which there were so many in France, the Reformed Church proved its most prudent and effective helper.

However, I have gone much too far in anticipating the events that succeeded one another in the ecumenical movement from the meeting on Fanö to the declaration of war in September 1939. We must retrace our steps again, and I shall try to do this as briefly as possible.

8. See below, pp. 155, 173.

CHAPTER 8

The World Conferences of 1937

I. The World Conference on Life and Work: Oxford July
1937. II. A week-end with William Temple. The World
Conference on Faith and Order: Edinburgh August 1937.
III. A great book by Père Congar 1937.

I

THE Fanö meeting in August 1934 was concerned with more than
the troubles in which the Churches of Germany were involved by
the National-Socialist revolution. One of its principal tasks was
to consider whether a second Life and Work conference should
follow that of Stockholm and, if so, to arrange the date, the place
and the programme.

That a new conference should be held was soon agreed. Everyone was more or less convinced that it was most important to
introduce order into the prophetically-inspired plans that had
sprung from the enthusiasm of Stockholm. There were, moreover, many adherents of Life and Work who realized that all
their thinking during the last ten years about the Churches'
mission in relation to the world's problems always came back
to the same question: 'What is the Church of which we are
continually speaking? What is its nature, and its function? What
is its place in the nation, and what is its mission in relation to the
State?' It is this that accounts for the line of approach, different
from that of Stockholm, adopted by the research section which
had been set up in Geneva and was directed by a German theologian and economist, Dr Schönfeld, who made of it a most
effective tool. On Fanö, the essential theme of the projected
conference was recognized by all as being inevitably: Church,
Community, State. It was decided that the meeting should take
place in Oxford, in July 1937.

One man, J. H. Oldham, had at that time, by the force of his
conviction and the lucidity of his intelligence, won a dominating
position among the members of the Council meeting on Fanö.

They decided to entrust to him the direction of the preparatory investigations for the Oxford Conference. Schönfeld and Ehrenström assisted him, and the three immediately went to work.

Two years in succession, in 1935 and 1936, at Chamby above Montreux, the Universal Christian Council for Life and Work heard Oldham and his fellow-workers explain the programme worked out for Oxford, with its main divisions and subsidiary themes. They had suggested the names of the principal speakers, outlined the way in which the committees would work and emphasized the importance of the life of worship which was to give the conference the spiritual nourishment of meditation on Holy Scripture, of liturgical prayer and the sacrament. I still retain a vivid memory of those days during which, looking out on the lake and the Savoy Alps, we witnessed the building up of the framework of what in 1937 turned out to be a great and fruitful conference on Life and Work.

Wilfred Monod took part in the first of these two meetings. He spoke little, and drew a great deal, generally silhouettes of his neighbours. From time to time he passed me under the table a scrap of paper with some highly amusing comment. He gave me the impression that he no longer felt in complete sympathy with the leadership of the movement.

On each occasion the Bishop of Chichester was in the chair, with his tact, his feeling for the right direction in which to guide the discussion towards the desired end. It was always a joy to see his bright glance rest on one or other of us. Henriod assisted him, as secretary-general of the Council. Mme Soederblom, by whose presence we were deeply moved, sometimes spoke; and the faithful Jézéquels often, by their friendliness, won our affectionate gratitude.

The question was already coming up of what attitude the Conference would take in Oxford to the future of the ecumenical movement. It was known that Faith and Order, on their side, proposed to follow up the Lausanne meeting, and that their officials wanted a meeting as close as possible, in time and geographically, to that which we were organizing ourselves. Edinburgh was finally decided upon, and the date of the conference settled for shortly after Oxford. It was immediately apparent that something of importance was in preparation.

What this 'something' was was made unmistakably clear on the eve of the Oxford Conference, at a meeting of thirty-five representatives of the various branches of the ecumenical movement, held at Westfield College in Hampstead. All those invited were present, except Zilka of Prague who was sick, and three Germans, who were prevented from coming: Hans Lilje, Dr von Thadden, and General Superintendent Zoellner, who, unhappily, was to die a few days later.

Arriving a few hours late, I was surprised to learn from my friends that one thing had already been settled: the two Conferences were to draft the constitution of a new World Council of Churches, which, while continuing to carry out the particular programme of each of the two movements, would, in liaison with the other organizations, look after the future of the ecumenical movement. After three days of discussion, the members present unanimously passed a briefly worded resolution to this effect, together with a memorandum outlining the main features of the proposed organization. Both were passed on to the two Councils responsible for the meetings which were about to open.

It was a great joy to all to be in Oxford. And those of us who had not been there before were immediately captivated by the charm of the ancient city and of the colleges with their wonderful green lawns, so refreshing to eye and mind after hours of long and sometimes arid discussion. Little time, however, was devoted to strolling in gardens and parks, for our time-table was so crowded that we could allow ourselves only an occasional break.

I have no intention of 'covering' the Oxford Conference. Church and Community; Church and State; Church, Community and State in relation to the economic order and to education; the Universal Church and the World of Nations; in its five sections and in its full meetings it got through the work prepared in the books and documents published under the direction of J. H. Oldham.

Max Huber, former president of the International Court of the Hague, a humble and totally dedicated Christian layman, was chairman of section 2, Church and State. Some years earlier, when I was giving a series of lectures at the Academy of International Law in the Hague, I had admired the perfect skill with which he controlled the Court's discussions, and I had had the honour of being received by him. I accordingly joined that section. Huber impressed on our exchanges of views his own accurate mind and rigorous scientific approach, and the report he presented in the full meeting was a model of clarity and conciseness.

The chairman at the full meetings was John Mott, who had been the obvious choice at Chamby. As one of the six presidents of the Conference, I often sat beside him. What a master he was of the art of controlling a debate! Always an erect figure, his glance, his energetic features and his dynamic vigour imposing respect, he combined humour with a firmly based authority. He knew how to cut short the over-talkative who exceeded the time limit. He made a discreet selection from the names of those put down to speak, which allowed him to give a hearing, in what he considered the best order, to divergent or contradictory views. Mott was in large measure responsible for the success of the Conference.

I must not, I feel, fail to emphasize that the richest source of inspiration for the Conference was the morning and evening worship celebrated in St Mary's. This had been organized by Bishop (then Canon) Cockin with tact and liturgical efficiency; he had the art of introducing us, as our day's work opened and drew to a close, into a vitalizing atmosphere of communion with the Lord of the universal Church and of fraternal charity. No ecumenical gathering – I speak of those in which I took part myself – ever gave me such a feeling of contact with the 'things unseen that are eternal'.[1] Cockin, too, was among those to whom the Conference was greatly indebted.

Here, perhaps, I may be permitted a brief aside. Emil Brunner, the Zürich theologian, was one of the most popular and authoritative speakers. Nevertheless, it is not his address on 'The Foundations of Christian Morality' that I wish to recall here. He had arrived, preceded by the reputation of being very much involved with the 'Oxford Group' movement. The Oxford Groupers had, in fact, decided to hold a large 'house-party' during the meeting of the World Conference. It was said that Frank Buchman hoped that Brunner would be able to serve as a useful intermediary between the group and the ecumenical movement.

1. 2 Corinthians 4:18.

On the afternoon of the first Sunday of the Conference we were all invited to a meeting at which we would be told about the work of the Oxford Group, its growing importance and its universal vocation. Buchman, sitting on the platform, never opened his mouth. An address was given which deeply shocked the French who were present, by one of our compatriots who thought fit, on British soil, sharply to criticize French womanhood.

There has, in fact, been no other contact between the World Conference and the Oxford Group.

It would be difficult to name all those whose presence was a tower of theological, philosophical and spiritual strength to the Conference and gave each one of us the joy of extending earlier or making new friendships. But I cannot pass over the two primates, Cosmo Lang, Archbishop of Canterbury, and William Temple, Archbishop of York; George Bell, Bishop of Chichester; John Mackay, from the theological seminary of Princeton; W. Adams Brown, from that of New York; Archbishop Eidem, primate of Sweden; the Orthodox Archbishop Germanos, one of the old guard of Stockholm and Lausanne; Professor Zander of Paris, and Professor Zankov of Sofia; Bishop Azariah of Dornakal; Adolf Keller, secretary of Inter-Church Aid; William Paton, secretary of the International Missionary Council; Samuel McCrea Cavert, secretary of the American Federal Council of the Churches of Christ, and Visser 't Hooft, secretary of the World Student Christian Federation: there were too many for me to mention them all, but as I write these few names I can see again the faces of many dear friends and I thank God for having allowed me during those distant years to meet so many of his servants, whose friendship remains one of the most unalloyed joys of my life.

Our French contingent was only a small one, appointed, as for the Stockholm Conference of 1925, by the Council of the Protestant Federation: it consisted of Dean Strohl from Strasbourg, Élie Gounelle, Henri Monnier, Professor Clavier from Montpellier, and myself. I am uncertain in what capacity Pierre Maury was on one occasion enabled to speak, but he gave a vigorous address on 'The Ecumenical Nature of the Church and its Responsibility Towards the World' in which he showed himself to be a faithful disciple of Karl Barth.

The organizers of the Conference did not lose sight during those hard-working days of two matters of grave concern.

The situation of the Churches in Germany was becoming tragic. Pastor Niemöller, the soul of the resistance to Nazism, was under arrest. The absence of any representatives of the German Lutheran, United or Reformed Churches, created a void at Oxford that nothing could fill. Two or three delegates from the free churches did their best to explain their position and defend the new régime, but they were listened to in an icy silence.

At the very first full session, the Bishop of Chichester had read the message which Bishop Marahrens had managed to get through to him. On the next Monday he proposed the text of a reply which would bring our German brothers a token of our participation in their distress and their faith. The Conference adopted it without discussion, as they did a telegram addressed to Hitler calling for the release of Niemöller. I was assured later that when Hitler received it he threw it on the ground and trampled on it.

The future of the ecumenical movement, too, was a matter of major concern. We had discussed this at great length during a meeting of the 'Continental section' of the Life and Work Council, of which I had become president at Chamby on the resignation of Wilfred Monod. I had been asked to move, before the full meeting of the Conference, a resolution supporting the plan drawn up at Westfield by the 'Thirty-five' meeting. We asked that 'the specific character of Life and Work shall be closely preserved in the new organization, so that the latter may not be confined to theological study but may be directed towards action, in particular towards the ecumenical education of the Churches'. And we added: 'The majority of the section are of the opinion that there should be an organic connection between the Alliance [for International Friendship through the Churches] and the new organization, and that there should be a continuation of the close co-operation between the Alliance and Life and Work.' There was general approval for the whole resolution, and the Conference appointed seven of its members to study, as necessary, with seven delegates from the Edinburgh Conference, what further steps should be taken. I was one of them, and this introduced me to a new and important stage in my ecumenical life.

The Edinburgh Conference, 1910

*Milestones on the
Road to Unity*

Cardinal Bea at the headquarters of the World
Council of Churches, Geneva, 1965

The Faith and Order Conference, Edinburgh, 1937

The First Meeting of the World Council of Churches, Amsterdam, 1948

Like the earlier Conferences of 1910, 1925 and 1927, the Oxford Conference felt called upon to address a message to the world. I was on the committee which drew it up: I remember the hours we spent, with William Temple as chairman, in working out drafts, none of which satisfied us. Finally we asked Temple to do it. His version was widely approved, and Professor Clavier rightly described it as 'a charter of freedom in service and of service in freedom'.[2] The essential sentence, which engraved itself unforgettably on our minds, ran: 'The first duty of the Church, and its greatest service to the world, is that it be in very deed the Church, confessing the true faith, committed to the fulfilment of the will of Christ, its only Lord, and united in him in a fellowship of love and service.'

I cannot leave Oxford without mentioning the day of Sunday, 25 July. The Archbishops of Canterbury and York had decided that the Eucharist, celebrated in the morning in St Mary's and St Aldate's, should be open to those members of the Conference who wished to communicate according to the Anglican rite. Their decision was not strictly in accordance with the canonical regulations then in force, and this aroused some sharp criticism. To all of us – except the Orthodox, who could not canonically participate in a non-Orthodox Eucharist – it was a most gracious gift. The service in St Mary's, conducted by the Archbishop of Canterbury, was one of great beauty; and we felt that a new bond, stronger and more fraternal, was uniting us in Christ present at his Supper.

In the afternoon, again in St Mary's, we assembled once more, this time including the Orthodox. I spoke, together with John Mott and Archbishop Eidem. The occasion, the audience, and still more the place, were all calculated to move me deeply. I saw myself in the pulpit from which John Henry Newman had delivered his sermons during the Tractarian Movement which, in his case, culminated in his conversion to the Roman Church. For a number of years I had found strength in his thought, in the fine essence of his spirituality and in his suffering too; and his *Apologia* was always alive in my mind. Speaking in that place of the lesson of humility I had been taught and the summons of

2. *Report of the Conference at Oxford, July 1937, on Church, Community and State,* 1937, p. 57.

love I had heard, I lived one of the great moments, not only of
my ecumenical life, but of my life as a Christian too.

II

A solemn service in St Paul's Cathedral on 29 July was a public
demonstration of the extent and vitality of the ecumenical movement. Many of those present in Oxford had stayed on in London
before going home, and some members of the Edinburgh Conference had already arrived. There was a large congregation. I
had been invited to take part in the liturgy and read, in French,
the story of the calling of Isaiah. Archbishop Lang of Canterbury
preached a fine and vigorous sermon on Church unity which
made plain his attachment to the cause of ecumenism.

The Archbishop of York and Mrs Temple had invited my wife
and me to spend the week-end before the Edinburgh Conference
with them at Bishopthorpe. Temple had succeeded Lang at
York, but had not the same passion for flowers as Lang. Even so,
there was still a fine display, and it was a delightful solace to
eyes and mind to stroll through the lovely gardens of Bishopthorpe.

In his own home Temple was the least episcopal of hosts. A
warm humanity radiated from his whole being. Full of gaiety
and humour, interested in all life's problems, his dynamic force
gave sparkle to friendly conversations, punctuated by great
bursts of laughter, that would have been enough in themselves
to win him fame. I have never heard anything like it. The roar
of Dr Fry (chairman of the Central Committee of the World
Council), vast though it was, was nothing to Temple's Homeric
laughter.

Two or three bishops of the Protestant Episcopal Church of
the U.S.A. were enjoying, as we were, the bright serenity of those
lovely summer days. It was there that one of them told me about
the audience Benedict XV gave in 1919 to the delegation I
mentioned earlier, of which he himself had been a member.

We spoke about the Conference which was about to open but
also about the one which had just ended. Our satisfaction was not
quite unalloyed. None of us, it is true, had any complaint at
our having entered the theological field at Oxford, or about the
affirmation of the necessity for a Church doctrine, for this was

part of the logical evolution of the Stockholm movement, which had come up against the duty to provide a solid basis for Life and Work – and what basis could one find other than the Church? The problem, however, was how to define the Church, and in Oxford there had been a confrontation between different concepts of the Church, each with its vigorous defenders.

We could not, for example, but regret the disappointment and pain we had involuntarily caused to our Orthodox friends. All through the Conference they had felt uncomfortable, attached to a 'pan-Protestant' movement which could not disguise its rather patronizing sympathy for their ecclesiology and love of the liturgy. Worst of all, they had been wounded, in a way that took a long time to heal, by the Archbishops' decision to throw open an Anglican Eucharist to *all* the members of the Conference. They *must* have known that the Orthodox could not legitimately take part in it, and yet no steps had been taken to hold an Orthodox service at the same time so as to associate them with the Anglican service.

We regretted also the Conference's 'Western' complexion: Western, both because the overwhelming majority of its members came from Europe or the U.S.A., and because of the preponderance of Cartesian intellectual approach and logic. This was something which it was essential to guard against. Stockholm had plunged into the concrete and practical, and the fear of being lost in an activism without theological foundation had stimulated a salutary reaction. At the same time it was important that the reaction should not make the movement lose contact with human beings.

We went to Edinburgh wondering whether the second Conference could put things right. We arrived in miserable weather, cold and wet, and it was seldom to clear up. No one was tempted to walk in Princes Street gardens or to climb up to the old castle, the view from which embraces the whole of the city and its environs. There was nothing to do but work, and plenty of work was done.

We French members were thirteen in number, delegates from seven different Churches. Our three faculties were represented by some excellent theologians, whose contributions were listened to with attention. Élie Gounelle was also in our party. Wilfred

Monod, unfortunately, was unable to attend and I read his letter of apology. A well-earned tribute was paid to Pastor Merle d'Aubigné, one of the members of the Lausanne movement, who had been detained in France by sickness. From the outset, his charm and affability, and his mastery of English and German, had made him widely listened to in ecumenical circles.

William Temple, with John Mott, Dr Garvie and me as vice-presidents, presided over the discussions with an authority compact of good humour, courtesy and a complete familiarity with the problems involved.

At the opening of the first working session William Temple, deeply moved, informed us that one of our colleagues, a Negro bishop of an American Church, had been refused admission to the hotel at which his room had been booked. He added that he had asked him to share his own quarters. And so the capital of Scottish Calvinism came down on the side of segregation! It caused a great scandal; but there was a worse scandal, from the other side, when the wife of a leading British politician was seen in the streets of Edinburgh in company with the bishop's niece.

We held our full sessions in the huge Assembly Hall of the Presbyterian Church of Scotland, where the International Missionary Conference, cradle of the ecumenical movement, had been held in 1910. John Mott reminded us of this, and our youngest members no doubt learnt it then for the first time.

The work was divided into four sections. On the subject of grace, and of the unity of the Church in life and worship, there were exchanges of views which brought out differences of opinion at times profound, but at the same time there was a unanimous desire for agreement.

This was by no means the case in the section which studied the ministry of the Church in the sacraments. Contradictory views came into direct conflict, culminating in violent clashes in full session. I have never forgotten the encounter between a young Anglo-Catholic theologian and Dr Curtis, principal of the Presbyterian theological college of Edinburgh University. For the Anglican, the acceptance or rejection of the apostolic succession and a sacramental episcopate was a matter of life or death for the cause of Church unity. The *non possumus* with which Curtis, as a convinced Presbyterian, answered him, was given with an emotion and a firmness that shook the whole Conference.

Then there was the question of the Orthodox. Did they feel more at home than in Oxford? I should hardly dare to go so far as to say that they did. Their delegation, headed by Germanos, included some eminent theologians, one of whom, Professor Bulgakov, enjoyed great authority. When, on one occasion, he tried to explain in a section meeting what veneration of the Virgin Mary means for Orthodoxy, and how it is indissolubly tied up with the doctrine of the Incarnation, he felt that his Protestant listeners thought he was a mystical visionary.

All unwittingly, moreover, I upset the Orthodox delegation by an intervention at a full session in the discussion on Scripture and Tradition. An Orthodox theologian had said that 'tradition *completes revelation*', and I expressed my surprise at such a statement and, on behalf of the Protestant members of the Conference, asked that it might be explained more exactly. The next morning Archbishop Germanos asked to speak and read a statement which, I must confess, far from clarifying the position made it even more confused. He used the word *sumpleroun* which both in the New Testament and the papyri means to complete or finish, and includes many other shades of meaning patient of a number of interpretations.

In a general way, the Orthodox felt as they did about Oxford: they had had the feeling of being welcomed in a fraternal spirit but as strangers difficult to understand: and with an imperfect understanding of Western thought on their own side. 'Too many abstractions, too many arguments about words. In the absence of the liturgy, the Church could not be present.' Nevertheless, a salutary communion in our Lord Jesus Christ had brought together, in one and the same ardent desire for unity, Christians who taught Christologies with divergences that amounted to contradiction. Moreover, like all the members of the Conference, they voted for an 'Affirmation of Unity in the service of our Lord Jesus Christ'.

Some sentences from this are worth quoting:

'We are one in faith in Our Lord Jesus Christ, the incarnate Word of God. We are one in allegiance to him as Head of the Church, and as King of Kings, the Lord of Lords. We are one in

acknowledging that this allegiance takes precedence of any other
allegiance that may make claims upon us . . .

'Our unity is of heart and spirit. We are divided in the outward
forms of our life in Christ, because we understand differently
His will for His Church. We believe, however, that a deeper
understanding will lead us towards united apprehension of the
truth as it is in Jesus Christ.'

The Conference had left plenty of time for an examination of
the plan put forward by the 'Committee of Thirty-five' and the
Oxford Conference's proposal. Before coming up at a full
meeting, the question of the future of the Lausanne movement and
its close association with that of Stockholm had been studied by
a small committee of eight members, and later by a commission
of sixty. Faith and Order attached the utmost importance to the
maintenance of a certain autonomy within the proposed organization and to the continuance of a doctrinal study along the lines
followed since the 1927 Conference. Bishop Brent had died in
1929 and had been replaced as president by William Temple.
Since 1933 Canon Hodgson, a model of conscientiousness and
theological competence, had been acting as secretary-general. It
was he who had drawn up the 'guarantees' to be included, should
the Conference consider it necessary, in the acceptance of the
'Thirty-five' plan. Hodgson had no difficulty in convincing the
meeting of the wisdom of his proposals. The discussion was more
protracted than at Oxford. A constant opponent, the Archdeacon
of Monmouth, fought a long series of delaying actions. Defeated
on each of his amendments, he finally acceded to the unanimous
decision of his colleagues to call for the creation of a World
Council of Churches. Last-minute resistance from Bishop
Headlam of Gloucester, the distinguished chairman of the
committee on grace, only had the result of bringing out – subject
to the desired guarantees – the complete agreement of the two
Conferences.

Some days later, in a hotel in Northumberland Avenue in
London, the seven delegates from Oxford met the seven from
Edinburgh: so the name ought to have been the 'Committee of
Fourteen'. However, as each delegate had brought an alternate
one, it seemed best to the fourteen to co-opt these into a working
committee whose function would be to give the resolution of the

two Conferences the practical implementation it entailed. A number of delicate points had to be settled without delay. And first of all the member Churches of the two movements concerned had to be officially informed and, if necessary, invited to state their attitude towards the new organization. Who should do this, and in what terms? And how long should be allowed for their answer? And when the answers had been received, who should collate them? Again, the plan passed in Edinburgh already indicated the main lines of the future organization. Who should be responsible for examining it and producing a provisional working plan, since it was clear that only a general assembly of the Churches which had accepted the forthcoming invitation would have the right to give the World Council its permanent constitution?

These questions, and others with them, were studied during the meeting of the fourteen. Hodgson in Winchester, Henriod and Schönfeld in Geneva, and Leiper in the U.S.A. were instructed to contact the Churches, and all arrangements were made for calling a meeting in the spring of the next year, which would include the twenty-eight together with official representatives of the Churches which had accepted the invitation. This meeting would decide the question of a constitution and the problems of staffing and finance. In May 1938 this was realized as the Utrecht Conference.

III

In this same year of 1937 there occurred an ecumenical event of importance, which was all the more significant in that it took place within the Roman Catholic Church. I am referring to the publication by Éditions du Cerf of a study by Père Congar, of the Order of Friars Preachers, entitled *Divided Christendom: A Catholic Study of the Problem of Reunion*.[3] It should be noted that it came out before the Oxford and Edinburgh Conferences, and the author made it clear that they might have led him to modify some of his judgments.

At that time I did not know Père Congar, with whom I feel today (and have for a long time felt) a strong bond of respect,

3. The first volume in the well-known series *Unam sanctam* (Paris, 1937; English translation, London, Geoffrey Bles, 1939).

gratitude and affection. When, in 1934, Karl Barth came to give three theological lectures at the Institute of Art and Archaeology of the University of Paris, I had been struck by the intensity of the attention with which Père Congar listened to Barth. I soon learnt that in fact several of his fellow-Dominicans and he himself had felt themselves almost carried away by excitement at finding themselves in the presence of the man whom they regarded as plainly the greatest theologian of the day.

I in my turn was carried away when I opened Père Congar's book. In the first place, by its honesty. In the foreword he said, and rightly, that his book might seem hard to some readers. No doubt he was thinking primarily of certain Protestant readers. It is true: at times I did find it hard and, I think, unjust through lack of information. But what honesty! He opens his explanation of the success of the Reformation by describing it as 'in essentials a religious movement, an attempt to revive religion by a return to the sources'.[4] How many Catholic authors, moreover, would have had the generosity to quote on the same page St Clement Maria Hofbauer's magnificent words:

'Since I have had opportunity, as Legate in Poland, of comparing the religious state of Catholics in Poland with that of Protestants in Germany, I have understood that the schism from the Church came about because the Germans had and have still the necessity to be devout. If the Reform grew and maintained itself it was not through heretics and philosophers, but through men who truly aspired after interior religion.'

It is a great pity, however, that Père Congar relegated to an appendix an extract from the admirable instructions given by Pope Adrian VI to the nuncio Chieregati in 1522. Here is one short passage:

'You are also to say that we frankly acknowledge that God permits this persecution of His Church on account of the sins of men, and especially of prelates and clergy . . . We all, prelates and clergy, have gone astray from the right way, and for long there is none that has done good, no, not one. To God, therefore, we must give all the glory, and humble ourselves before Him . . . Therefore, in our name, give promises that we shall use all

4. Op. cit., p. 19.

diligence to reform before all things the Roman Curia, whence, perhaps, all these evils have had their origin.'[5]

I can well imagine that John XXIII and Paul VI have very often pondered on those words. Had Adrian VI lived, just think what disasters would have been avoided.

It is not possible here and now to analyse this great book or show how, before concluding, Père Congar indicates the 'main lines of a programme of Catholic ecumenism', and I must confine myself to a few remarks.

The first is a point that cannot be overlooked. The expression 'Catholic ecumenism'[6] used by Père Congar, was used twenty-five years later by the drafters of the first version of *De oecumenismo*, whose importance will be apparent later, and was rejected by Vatican 2 when it discussed the document. The phrase 'Catholic principles of ecumenism' was substituted. The reasons put forward by the majority of the Fathers of the Council will be noted later. What, however, was in Père Congar's mind when he chose his sub-title, is made abundantly clear by his foreword.

While recognizing that the word 'ecumenism' has a Protestant origin,[7] he gives it a connotation which even in 1937 the founders and leaders of the ecumenical movement found it impossible to accept. I am, it is true, very largely in agreement with Père Congar's criticisms of 'the Stockholm ideology';[8] but after Lausanne and the lengthy theological deliberations at Oxford and Edinburgh, how could he, even hypothetically, attribute to us the supposition that, in the eyes of the Churches associated in the movement, the different Christian bodies now in existence have all failed in some respect; that each, therefore, possesses only a part of the truth, and they must, in repentance and self-humiliation before God, negotiate on an equal footing, agree to certain sacrifices and unite in the profession of what they hold in common and in respecting their differences? Having made that assumption, Père Congar had no difficulty in contrasting with this illusory ecumenism the only true ecumenism which, concentrating on the problem of the reunion of the Churches, seeks theologically to

5. Op. cit., p. 277.
6. The words are used in the French sub-title (but not the English): '*Principes d'un oecuménisme catholique*'.
7. p. xiii.   8. Op. cit., Ch. IV.

determine 'the relations of the dissident Churches to the one true Church and its unity'.[9] That will be Catholic ecumenism, which it is not only possible, but a duty, to promote. Père Congar's effort, accordingly, was directed towards 'defining the possible roads open to a movement which seeks to restore dissident forms of Christianity to unity'.[10] The unity of the Church cannot be effected except by a return of the separated Churches – which in any case are not Churches – to the one true Church of Christ. Pius XII, in quite other words, on countless occasions invited the non-Roman confessions to this 'mass return', and I am among those who have clearly demonstrated its impossibility. Some lively differences in emphasis may be noted between the profound thought of Père Congar (whose fine book brought upon him such unmerited trials) and the appeals of the Sovereign Pontiff, but behind both lies the same conviction: unity *exists* in the Catholic Church, it *is* the Catholic Church; and all ecumenism built up outside the Catholic Church can only be built on sand.

I am quite sure that Père Congar's theological work since 1937 and his contacts with non-Roman ecumenical circles have taken him beyond the thought expressed in *Divided Christendom*. If the Vatican Council has given us at least a glimpse of other roads to unity than that proposed in Père Congar's seminal study, it is to him that we are in large measure indebted: and it is a great privilege to be able to express to him here our fraternal gratitude.

9. Ibid., Ch. VII.   10. Ibid.

CHAPTER 9

The Formation of the World Council of Churches

1938-1939

I. The Utrecht Conference 1938. II. The meeting at Saint-Germain-en-Laye February 1939. III. Last meetings before the war: Geneva, Zeist, Clarens July-August 1939.

I

IT was in Utrecht, from 9 to 12 May 1938, that the Conference was held upon which we had decided when we met in London during the August of 1937. It included seventy-five members, the 'fourteen' and their alternates forming the nucleus. In addition, over forty official representatives of different Churches in Europe, America and Asia, had answered our invitation.

On my arrival during the evening of 8 May, I had the pleasure of meeting some old friends, soon to be followed by others: William Temple, John Mott, J. H. Oldham, W. A. Brown, Koechlin, Guillon, Adolf Keller. Schönfeld, Ehrenström, Henriod, W. Paton and Visser 't Hooft were also there. On the Orthodox side, there were Germanos, Zilka, Metropolitan Eulogios from Paris, and Irenaeus, Bishop of Novi Sad, one of the most outstanding characters in the Church of Serbia. One absentee was much regretted: George Bell, Bishop of Chichester, had been invited to travel to Germany and then to take part in Sweden in the consecration as bishops of two sons-in-law of Soederblom, Brilioth and Runestam. His knowledge of people and his advice were greatly missed in our discussions of personal problems.

Temple was elected chairman. He managed our debates, often by no means smooth, with a smiling serenity, and knew how to wind them up within the time allotted. Two smaller committees were set up at the first session: one to produce a final draft of the proposed constitution, and the other to prepare the Council's budget, and fix the remuneration of the staff, a plan for whose appointment had been prepared with great care by Temple and some others of us.

There were any number of delicate problems to solve. Those which had personal implications aroused conflicts that were difficult to settle. Different conceptions of the Council's secretariat and its functions and responsibilities necessarily influenced our choice. Schönfeld, until then director of the research section of Life and Work, and Visser 't Hooft, whom the majority of us wished to see as secretary-general, did not see eye to eye. And, quite apart from the personal angle, the mission of the World Council of Churches was not envisaged in the same light by J. H. Oldham and some of our American colleagues. There was the further question of whether to allot seats on the Central Committee and at the Assembly to the member Churches by denominations or by continents.

The question of a doctrinal basis gave rise to a long discussion. Many members of the Assembly insisted that confessing Christ as our 'God and Saviour' should become the World Council's basis. Faith and Order claimed the right to reserve this basis for its own work. The Orthodox wished for clearer emphasis to be laid on the Trinitarian character, and simply proposed that the Nicene Creed should be adopted.

I had no objection to the first suggestion. At the same time I thought it my duty to draw the Assembly's attention to the feeling which the announcement of this doctrinal basis was already arousing among some members of the Stockholm movement; and I recalled the assurance given at Oxford that the Lausanne basis would not be imposed on the united movement; but the Conference overruled the objection.

The full sessions were preceded and followed by meetings of the two committees. As chairman of the committee for administration and finance, I had to have lengthy interviews with the staff whose services we thought it indispensable to retain, with those whom it seemed better to replace, and finally with those about whose appointment there was unanimous agreement. All this was finally embodied in resolutions which I put before the Assembly, where they were adopted.

Every morning at a quarter to eight, some of us would meet in Oldham's room for half an hour of recollection and prayer.

Mott was always with us, and the intensity of his spiritual life was unmistakable. We felt the need to prepare our day, our deliberations and decisions, by asking for the grace of humility, wisdom and love. These were precious moments of brotherly concourse, strengthened day by day in communion with Christ.

On the last morning the Council adopted the constitution of the new organization. It could only, of course, be provisional, and it would have to be completely re-examined or ratified at the first General Assembly, planned for 1941. Meanwhile, however, the Provisional Council would have work to carry on with or initiate, responsibilities to be undertaken, funds to be raised, and a staff to maintain, advise and perhaps control.

It was decided that the twenty-eight members (principals and alternates) elected by the 1937 Conferences should choose six others qualified to constitute with themselves the provisional Committee of the Council until it was fully established. This committee would appoint its principal assistants, draw up a budget and raise the necessary funds. Meanwhile, since it would be meeting only once a year (under the chairmanship of William Temple) it would appoint from among its members an administrative or executive committee which would meet several times a year and ensure that the work of the secretariat was efficiently carried out.

It was then that I was faced by a nice decision. I was asked to serve as vice-chairman of the provisional, and chairman of the administrative committees. Mott had already warned me of this the day before, urging me with great warmth not to evade the responsibility my colleagues were anxious to entrust to me.

The secretariat was to be set up in Geneva – except for W. Paton in London and Henry Leiper in New York – together with the research and financial sections, and it accordingly seemed essential that the administrative committee should be made up of Europeans. Moreover, it would only be in control for a short time, three years at the most, until the General Assembly arranged, as I have just said, for 1941. I yielded to the Provisional Committee's arguments and accepted the position they wished to entrust to me. I must confess that the prospect of working in close collaboration with the secretary-general, Visser 't Hooft, whose magnificent capabilities I could perceive, was one of the reasons for my decision. After all, I was committing myself for only three years, and the company of Bishop Bell as vice-chairman, of Koechlin, President of the Reformed Church of Basle (and so close to Geneva), and of Charles Guillon as chairman of the finance section, enabled me to look forward with confidence to this short period. The war and its aftermath were to extend it by seven years.

The World Council of Churches 'in process of formation' had hardly been set up when, as a sequel to a conference in Jerusalem, in 1928, of the International Missionary Council, a new meeting was held in Tambaram in India. There, Mott, the chairman, emphasized the importance, from the point of view of the evangelizing world, of the creation of a World Council of Churches, and how vital it was to the extensive efforts made in the missionary field since the Edinburgh meeting in 1910 that they should be supported by a solidly based community of Churches.[1] Thus the Tambaram meeting, foreseeing that the problem of the relationship between Church and Mission would inevitably arise, called for the immediate setting up of a joint committee of the two great branches of the ecumenical movement, the World Council of Churches and the International Missionary Council. This resolution was soon to be adopted by the Provisional Committee, at Saint-Germain-en-Laye, at its February 1939 meeting.

However, before Tambaram and Saint-Germain-en-Laye there came Munich. We little imagined what was going to happen when in the summer of 1938 the Inter-Church Aid Committee met in Basle. We met once more in the company of Dean Choisy, Joergensen, Keller, Koechlin and other great workers in the movement for inter-Church solidarity which had already done such excellent work. The great surprise was the unexpected arrival of Bishop Heckel, whom we had not seen since Fanö. I immediately asked him what was the truth about Niemöller's position; all he could tell me was that he was not believed to be in danger.

My colleagues, from whom he had a cool reception, and I asked him many questions about the situation of the German Churches. To listen to him, Berlin was the most Christian city in

1. See Le Guillou, *Mission et Unité*, Paris (Éditions du Cerf), Vol. 1, pp. 50 ff.

Europe: in the last four years, only ·2 per cent of children, Protestant or Catholic, had given up religious instruction!

Asked about the *Anschluss*, his only answer was '*Heimkehr!* Coming home!'[2]

The Munich meeting, after Chamberlain's fruitless visits to Hitler had brought the world to the brink of disaster, was an immense relief to some people in France and a source of shame and anxiety to others. In the Place de la Concorde I watched Daladier's triumphal return, when he had expected to be lynched; and when, the next day, he drove up towards the Arc de Triomphe I was intensely distressed at hearing the crowds bellowing the words of the 'Marseillaise': 'Let blood so vile our furrows drench' ('*qu'un sang impur abreuve nos sillons*'), punctuated by hysterical cries of '*Vive la paix!*'

At the end of October, on my way to Stockholm and Uppsala, I stopped in Copenhagen, where I had been invited to lecture. The Queen was present, and during the interview she granted me before she left, we spoke of the growing apprehension felt by our peoples. 'There is one of them who wants war', she said to me.

In Sweden, the warm welcome of Archbishop Eidem, of the professors of the University of Uppsala, of the pastor *primarius* of Stockholm and of the Swedish members of the Consistory of the Reformed Church of France, allowed me to strengthen the already long-standing links between the Churches of Sweden and France. Pastor J. H. Hoffmann, too, proved to be – as he still is today – the best possible channel of liaison.

II

As we moved into 1939, I had just been elected president of the National Council of the Reformed Church of France. In the opening weeks of the year, I had to visit a number of places in an attempt to solve some difficult problems which had arisen in them. The 'Ardèche revival', the challenging of infant baptism by a number of pastors in the valley of the Eyrieux and its neighbourhood, which at times went so far as a refusal to carry out the baptisms asked for by the parents, and the practice of re-baptizing adults who joined their movement – all this had

2. In English.

created a great disturbance in a number of parishes. I was able to discuss the matter at length with my colleagues and the best qualified of their layfolk, give evidence to them of the maternal presence of the Church, and pave the way to a less disturbed church life.

Meanwhile, at the beginning of February, the Provisional Committee of the World Council held its first regular meeting since its election in Utrecht of its officers, its nomination of members of the general secretariat and its definition of their principal duties.

I can still see myself welcoming William Temple on a winter's evening, at the Gare Saint-Lazare, whence a lady of our acquaintance had offered to drive us to the Pavillon Henri IV at Saint-Germain-en-Laye, which had been chosen as our meeting-place. The members of our committee were not a little surprised to be holding their meeting in the room in which Louis XIV had been born in 1638. A big log fire soon produced an atmosphere of goodwill and fraternal understanding, even though many minds were filled with gloomy apprehension.

Many 'current affairs' were dealt with during our meetings; I may note a number of important decisions.

Informed of the resolution drawn up by the Tambaram Conference, the Committee approved the proposal to appoint a Joint Committee of the International Missionary Council and the World Council of Churches. The General Assembly of 1941 would certainly take up the problem of Church and Mission and arrange for its examination.

Dr Schönfeld, to whose work as head of the research section of the Stockholm movement I have referred, gave us the result of his reflection on the situation and responsibilities of the Churches in a profoundly disturbed world. The Committee asked him to undertake a full-scale enquiry into 'the living Church in modern society' – an enquiry which circumstances were to make uncommonly comprehensive.

We discussed the future. Gloomy though it seemed, we were unwilling to believe that there would be a new conflict. The forces of peace seemed to be having a positive influence on public opinion, and even on the political direction of some nations. Unfortunately, however, Great Britain's blatant policy of appeasement, we feared, could not but serve to convince Hitler that she would never declare war on him. However that might be, and whatever might happen, we wished the World Council to carry out the plan proposed in Utrecht, and we decided to make preparations for the first Assembly of the World Council of Churches, to be held in the U.S.A. in 1941.

My 1939 Lenten addresses began shortly after this. On the morning of the day when I was to speak about the parable of the Good Samaritan, the world learnt of the entry of German troops into Prague. I branded this action as shameful at the beginning of my talk, which as usual was broadcast: and it is probable that my words helped to fabricate the charge of fomenting a Church crusade against the Third Reich of which I was accused by the Gestapo agents in July 1940 when they searched my papers, and in January 1941 when they rifled my library – though some weeks later they returned most of my books to my daughter, after being ordered to do so. They had kept any that dealt with the ecumenical movement.

III

In the course of my various duties I had, during the spring, to make a number of journeys. In May I represented the Reformed Church for the first time at the General Assembly of the Church of Scotland in Edinburgh: and what a wonderful example it was of fidelity to ancient traditions and of devotion both to Protestant individualism and to democratic rights. In Scotland, ardently in favour of peace, there seemed to be no anxiety; though maybe there were rather more signs of it a month later, when I returned to receive the honorary doctorate of divinity which the University of Edinburgh was kind enough to confer on me. On our way there, my wife and I had the pleasure of spending a couple of days with our friends the Bells in Chichester. We talked at length about the work of the World Council, its general secretariat, of the favourable attitude of many Churches towards the new organization, and also of the steps that should be taken if anything really serious should happen. The administrative committee, moreover, was due to meet in July in Zeist, Holland, and we would then be able to make definite plans.

However, before going to Zeist I had to be in Geneva to take part in new conversations. The international situation was rapidly deteriorating. What action could, or should, the Churches take in an attempt to still the threat whose imminence could not now be disguised? Requests for this meeting had come from various quarters, and a number of eminent men were anxious to attend: John Foster Dulles; the Oxford professor Sir Alfred Zimmern, with whom I had long maintained a relationship of mutual trust and friendship; Édouard Rist, the highly esteemed French economist; the Revd Cockburn, who was soon to take on, with great success, the direction of the Reconstruction section of the World Council of Churches; Emil Brunner; Dean Matthews of St Paul's; and of course Visser 't Hooft and his associates.

From the very first session there was profound disagreement on some essential questions. Brunner said that it would be madness to expect states to conform to the Christian law; it would be wonderful enough if they practised justice. 'But what', we asked him, 'is justice according to the state which claims to practise it?'

Zimmern and Rist gave clear expositions, full of good sense, of the causes of the present situation. At the Sunday morning religious service, Dr Palmer, who officiated, asked each one of us to say what was our most profound inner reaction to the thought of war and peace. Adolf Keller, in answer to two ultra-pacifists, declared that his faith could never come to terms with an idealistic optimism which did not recognize the tragic reality of sin.

I was due back in Paris before the end of the meeting. Zimmern and Paton were responsible for the abandonment of the plan for a Conference which could no longer serve any useful purpose.

On 20 July the administrative committee was again in Zeist, with nearly all its members present: William Temple, John Mott, Nörregaard, Mrs Pierce (the only woman to be a member of the committee), and our colleagues, Visser 't Hooft, Schönfeld and Ehrenström of Geneva; W. Paton, of London; and Henry Leiper, of New York. After we had settled some minor questions, our exchanges of views did nothing to relieve our pessimism. When, we wondered, would the storm break: it seemed impossible that we should have to wait much longer.

During these anxious days, I had to preside over a last ecumenical conference at the English College of Saint George, above Clarens. In spite of everything, my wife and I had been able to have a few days' rest in Adelboden, but we had to be in Clarens on 22 August. William Temple had asked me to take his place as chairman of the Executive Commission of Faith and Order, of which I was one of the vice-presidents. After stopping in Geneva (where we had the opportunity of admiring the treasures of the Prado, then on exhibition in the museum), we arrived at Saint George: and I so well remember on the morning of 23 August, before the meeting started, opening the *Gazette de Lausanne* and reading the news of the Nazi-Soviet pact signed the day before by Ribbentrop and Stalin. Shocked beyond words, we all realized that this meant certain and undoubtedly immediate war.

Dr Flew, chairman of the commission for the theological study of the problem of the Church, nevertheless presented his report, and I took the chair at an animated and interesting discussion. One very vivid memory remains with me: Charles Merle d'Aubigné, who was on holiday at his chalet in Chexbres, visited us during the afternoon. As he came into the room, everyone rose and applauded him, as a tribute to the services he had rendered the Lausanne movement for fifteen years, and still more to his inexhaustible kindness.

The evening session was a sad business. Visser 't Hooft, who was listening to the radio, came in and told me that the international situation was developing so rapidly that he thought it best to close the meeting immediately so that everyone would be able to get back to his own country as soon as possible. I consulted my colleagues, who agreed to the suggestion. However, I proposed that before we said good-bye to one another we should go up to the chapel together and pray in common. That was an unforgettable moment of communion in prayer. Our countries were about to become enemies or to shelter in an uneasy neutrality: at all costs ecumenical communion had to be preserved by the power of love and faith in the grace of the Church's one Lord. As we broke up, our feelings were almost too much for us. We had the certain assurance that whatever might happen we would remain members of one another because members of the same Body.

Early the next morning, my wife and I left for Paris; and the morning after that we were saying good-bye to the Leipers, on their way back to the U.S.A. My three sons and my son-in-law reported to their mobilization centres. A new period, whose duration no one could foresee, was opening in our family lives, in the lives of our parishes and in the life of the young World Council of Churches, for a long time still to be 'in process of formation'.

PART TWO

The Maturity of the Ecumenical Movement
1939-1959

CHAPTER 10

The Second World War and Ecumenical Work from September 1939 to May 1940

I. Accumulation of responsibilities in the first months of the war. II. Strange meeting in De Zilven January 1940. III. Continuation of ecumenical work in anxious times.

I

AT about midnight on Thursday, 31 August, I was woken from my first sleep. 'Hallo! Hallo! We have a call for you from Berlin.' It was my son Jean-Marc, attaché at our embassy in Berlin, who felt that he must make this personal contact. He knew, though he did not tell me, that Poland would be attacked a few hours later, and that nothing short of a miracle could prevent France and Britain from being involved immediately in war. And, in fact, on Sunday, 3 September 1939, after several fruitless diplomatic moves, our two nations announced that they were at war with Germany. Threatening though the international situation had been for some months, we had been persisting in saying that a new war was unthinkable, that the war-mongers and aggressors would back down in the end. They had not backed down, and one man's diabolical ambition had suddenly flung us into a life that reversed everything it had meant to us the day before, into a chaos of problems, personal, domestic, professional, national and international, which contradicted and clashed with one another; problems so numerous that we could only move from one to another and apply solutions which were themselves bound to be contradictory.

A much longer book than this would be all too short if I yielded to the temptation to record all that I heard and saw, all that I said and did, during the years of the war and the occupation, as president of the Reformed Church of France, of the Protestant Federation or of the administrative committee of the World Council of Churches. It is by design, then, that I shall refrain from speaking of important problems, of actions which had to be carefully weighed and of personal interventions which called for nice judgment, but which had no direct connection with the ecumenical work I had to carry on in France or with which I was associated abroad. The years 1939 to 1945 were exceptionally fruitful in expanding the ecumenical movement and strengthening its roots. It is this which I wish to bring out, even if I give the impression of refusing to discuss some sensitive matters, in connection with which my own personal activities, in any case, may well have been criticized.

The first weeks were fully, and even more than fully, occupied in the study of a great variety of questions all of which called for an immediate answer. No one had any idea that there was going to be eight months of a 'phoney war'. The supply of military chaplains had to be organized, and first of all, in addition to those appointed beforehand, new pastors, over forty years of age, had to be found to carry out this ministry. There was the painful question of conscientious objectors, of whom a number had immediately been arrested. Substitutes had to be found to fill the gaps left by the calling-up of many pastors. It had to be decided whether it would be opportune or not to set up at a distance from Paris an administrative echelon of the Reformed Church. A newspaper had to be started for officers and other ranks. The reception of refugees had to be organized, for their number, considerable before the declaration of war, was continually increasing and called for our constant attention. Negotiations had to be opened with the controllers of news and radio with a view to securing the broadcasts we thought necessary. Help was needed for the youth movements (which were then setting up *Cimade*)[1] to send teams of volunteers into parts of Poitou and the Limousin, where we learnt that whole villages of Alsatians, who had been obliged by the French authorities to evacuate their country and abandon their farms and stock, were living under terrible conditions in places where no preparations had been made to receive them. This tangle of problems represents only some of the anxieties that accumulated for us day by day. Others, often tragic, were to be added as the war developed.

I was greatly worried, too, about the church of the Annuncia-

1. See below, p. 371.

tion. Pierre Maury had been called up on the first day of the war as a captain in the Army Service Corps, and was about to leave the Paris area, though we had the joy of seeing him there once again. I was accordingly the only one available for the Sunday services, religious instruction, public worship, making and receiving visits. On Sunday mornings the church was still practically full, and every evening at half past six a few of us met there, sometimes only two or three, to read a page of the Bible and pray.

I could not shelve my responsibilities in the World Council of Churches. Its literature might well include the qualification 'in process of formation', but it was none the less almost universally regarded as being called on to maintain ecumenical communion between all the member Churches, whether the countries in which they were established were at war, were allied or hostile, or anxious at all costs to preserve their neutrality.

Further, Visser 't Hooft and his fellow-workers, Guillon on behalf of the Y.M.C.A., and Keller on behalf of the Inter-Church Aid Committee, did not delay in taking measures from a number of which we benefited. In Geneva they were already concerned to persuade the Churches of the U.S.A. to make a financial effort on behalf of our Churches and their pastors.

In another sphere, I had been asked to induce our Government to agree to the World Council and the Y.M.C.A.'s being authorized to provide spiritual and material relief to prisoners of war already held on French soil. It was the skeleton of the great work to be carried out, when the 'real war' started in Western Europe, by the Ecumenical Commission for prisoners of war.

In November, Russia declared that it was threatened by Finland and had no scruples in attacking that little country, great in the courage it drew upon.

The Council of the Protestant Federation thought that our Churches should show their sympathy with Finland, almost the whole of whose population is Lutheran, not in speeches and messages, but by as generous an offering as possible. On two occasions I was able to hand the Finnish minister considerable sums from French Protestants.

At the same time I received from the Ecumenical Press Service extracts from speeches by Scandinavian Lutheran bishops, saying

that their Churches and their peoples should work for the reconciliation of the belligerents. This, it was true, was before Finland
was the victim of Russian aggression. I wondered whether those
prelates would say the same after that attack. I was soon to learn.

On 6 December, to be exact, I received a telegram from Visser
't Hooft telling me that William Temple had agreed to a meeting
of the administrative committee in Holland at the beginning of
January. Some days later I received through William Paton, an
invitation from Bishop Berggrav of Oslo, primate of the Church
of Norway, to take part, after the meeting of the administrative
committee, in conversations which would include the four
Scandinavian primates, the Archbishop of York, the Bishop of
Chichester and myself. The discussion would be 'chiefly concerned with the concept of peace put forward by the Scandinavians'. I wondered what was in the offing.

The date was then 22 December, the day when Finnish resistance seemed to have won the day – unhappily, only for the
moment. On the same day I had a long conversation with M.
Champetier de Ribes, Under-Secretary of State to M. Daladier, the
Prime Minister. The latter had instructed him to come to a decision, with me, about conscientious objectors at the front. He was
a most upright man, an authentically Christian Catholic, of whom
I retain a memory full of respect and gratitude. He understood
perfectly the problem of conscientious objection, and the extreme
gravity it could suddenly assume in the firing line. We solved
together a number of serious problems which I put before him
on that actual day.

I then went on to speak about the meeting I was to take part in
in Amsterdam. Had our Government, I asked him, determined its
attitude about the method to be followed – after victory – in
making peace? 'There are only two ways of making peace', he
answered, 'either to exterminate all your enemies, or to be reconciled with your adversary. We cannot do the first, and so we must
choose the second. And we must not repeat the mistakes of
Versailles . . . I may tell you, in complete confidence, that at the
Cabinet meeting on Tuesday, M. Daladier explained the reasons
why he is not anxious to have war aims discussed in the Press.
But he said that, even if France had no territorial guarantee in
mind, she would demand material guarantees that would ensure

her complete safety during discussion of the peace treaty. We shall demand the Rhine bridgeheads.'

Such words make strange reading, spoken, as they were, a few months before France met with the greatest disaster in her history. She recovered from it, it is true, thanks to the help of her allies, to the courage and sacrifices of her troops and her resistance workers, and to the indomitable will of General de Gaulle. But how, at the end of 1939, could our Government have been so blind to the vast superiority of the German army and nourish such fatal illusions about the true condition of our own and that of Great Britain?

On St Stephen's day, in thick fog, I went to see Cardinal Verdier. We decided to make a joint approach to the broadcasting authorities in order to secure the retransmission of the Notre-Dame and Passy Lenten addresses. The Cardinal's great cordiality allowed me to hope for a fruitful collaboration during the war, but alas, some months later he was called home to his God.

That same evening I noted, 'Letter from my dear friend the Bishop of Chichester. His attitude in favour of negotiations as early as possible seems to me most dangerous. He sends me the report of a disconcerting meeting of the House of Lords during which he spoke in support, on the whole, of accepting the offer of the good offices of the King of the Belgians and the Queen of Holland . . . Chichester says that he has a sense of reality, but I fear that he may be allowing himself to be over-influenced by German refugees.'

A new year began. On 2 January, Visser 't Hooft stopped in Paris, on his way to Holland, to have a talk with me. The conversations about to open in Amsterdam were very much in our minds. How would we be able, in a message to the Churches on peace and war, to agree on a text that would be anything more than a theoretical exposition or a lamentable compromise? And at that very moment I had just opened a splendid letter from Pastor Lauriol of Nîmes asking for the World Council at last to speak out!

That same evening I received the Archbishop of Finland's appeal to the Christian Churches. I was about to discuss it with the Finnish minister. 'Whatever happens', he told me, 'the Finns have shown that the Soviet army is a giant with feet of clay.'

Re-reading those words now, I cannot help wondering whether we were all struck with blindness.

II

On 5 January I left for Holland with Charles Guillon, chairman of the finance committee of the World Council. Koechlin joined us at the Gare du Nord. A long day's journey. Having arrived in Amsterdam, we were driven to a hotel, where Schönfeld welcomed us. He sent me a message that because of the Gestapo it would be better if he did not dine with me. To my great surprise we drove off again, over often icy roads, in an easterly direction. A hundred and twenty kilometres from Amsterdam, near Apeldoorn, we stopped in front of a hotel to which, apparently, we had been invited by some Dutch friends of the Bishop of Oslo, who wanted our conversations to be as undisturbed as possible. It was about 10 in the evening when, gathered round a fine log fire, I met the Archbishops of York and Uppsala, the Bishops of Chichester and Oslo, Visser 't Hooft and Paton.

Our first conversation led me to think that I should have some rather strange proposals to listen to. Several of my colleagues thought that the first thing to be done was to cease hostilities.

It was only the next morning that I learnt that we were in De Zilven, at a hotel the whole of which had been hired by some wealthy Dutch people, very much involved, as was Berggrav, in the Oxford Group (which was not yet using the name 'Moral Rearmament'). Our hosts were two middle-aged couples, and, as Temple said, they entertained us 'munificently'.

In fact, two different meetings developed, each attended by different groups: the administrative committee, regularly convened and with a very precise agenda, and – not later, but simultaneously – the conversations planned by Bishop Berggrav. It was in this situation, incidentally, that the latter was introduced into the circle of those who directed the World Council, in which, after the war, his influence was to be continually more pronounced.

However, first thing the next morning, 6 January, he put before us 'an account of the origins of our meeting, the extraordinary circumstances which dictated the choice of meeting-place, and the Churches' duty to work effectively for peace. All this led up to the conclusion that there should be no delay in urging governments to declare their peace aims and the conditions under which they would be willing to open negotiations.

'From 14.30 hours to 19 hours, there was an animated discussion of the question whether the Church should demand the immediate opening of negotiations and if so on what conditions. I spoke first, in an attempt to explain the development of public opinion in France since Munich, pointing out what a shattering victory it would be for Germany if negotiations were opened which led to a bloodless peace, soon to be followed by another war. York, Koechlin, Berkelbach, van der Sprenkel and Visser t' Hooft on the whole supported this view. Chichester, the pacifist Carter, and Uppsala adduced their own arguments in favour of negotiations as soon as possible.

'The general discussion was followed by a private conversation, at which was considered the possibility of entrusting to Berggrav an Anglo-French text which he could show to the Germans (Heckel, Weizsäcker!). I immediately pointed out the extreme danger of such a document. Again and again I repeated that I could not, in accepting the views of some, run the risk of supporting a peace that entailed so many formidable dangers. I reproached them for not looking at the facts, and for passing over in silence Hitler's lies and aggressions and all that went with them.'

In the evening, Gulin, who represented the Archbishop of Finland, described to us in moving words the unhappy situation of his country, whose army was now falling back under heavy pressure. 'He then went on to say that if Finland was to be saved, the western powers must make an immediate peace, that Germany, France, and Britain should come to terms in order to save the Christian faith from Bolshevism, and moreover that Germany had been thrown into the arms of the Russia whom Britain and France wanted to force into war with her. In spite of the presence of Schönfeld I felt it my duty to press home the point I had made.

'At 22 hours, there was a meeting of the "War Cabinet". I refused to sign a document that could be handed to the Germans. I drew the attention of the English to the grave situation they might well be placing themselves in in relation to their Government . . . York had drawn up a statement which I was unable to sign. And even so, it went nowhere near so far as Chichester's.

'I arrived full of great hopes that we would be able to join together in telling the Churches and the world what our conscience as Christians has been forced to accept. I am asked for a document – subject, admittedly, to my consent – to be shown to the Germans. And public expression of sympathy with Finland is refused!'

On the morning of the next day the administrative committee was at last able to start on its agenda. The Scandinavians had decided not to take part in its meetings! If they were to remain as 'intermediaries' between the committee and the Germans, they thought they should dissociate themselves from our activities. We had a discussion about whether we could and should draw up a statement about the present situation and the Church's duty. Visser 't Hooft prepared a draft. Some hours later I learnt that the Scandinavians vigorously opposed its adoption.

Was not one of them, and by no means one of their lesser men, soon to say to us, 'I have no sympathy with Hitler, but he is the greatest man the world has ever seen, greater than Napoleon and Julius Caesar'?

A further exchange of views with the Scandinavians and the English led me to confirm 'my refusal to be associated with any paper whatsoever which is to be handed to Weizsäcker, Heckel and others'.

The truth of the matter is this: shortly before his arrival in Amsterdam, Berggrav had been to Berlin. He called on Weizsäcker, Ribbentrop's Under-Secretary of State, and allowed him to see how eager he was to serve the cause of peace . . . and he arrived in Holland with a very full document in his pocket which detailed the conditions on which Hitler would be disposed to make peace. After he had read it to us, I asked him whether he would be good enough to lend it to me, so that I could think it over. I cannot think why I did not make a copy of it.

The possibility of addressing a message to the Church was once again considered by the administrative committee. 'Three drafts were put forward, by Visser 't Hooft, York and Chichester. In the end, with the Scandinavians refusing to be associated with our deliberations – which exaggerated still further the Franco-British predominance in the committee – and, balancing this, the anxiety of Chichester and York to mention nobody by name and to judge nobody, we had to recognize the impossibility of saying anything that would not immediately be frowned on or would not be a vague string of words.

'It is a distressing set-back, which many friends will feel with as much pain as I do. No doubt God wishes to teach us some new lesson by thus forcing us to be silent.'[2]

In my notes of 8 January I read: 'York left at 8 a.m.' He had to return to England before the end of our meeting. I was most anxious to say good-bye to him. Was this a presentiment? His image stays in my mind, getting into the taxi to go back to Amsterdam . . . I was never again to see him in this world.

A final meeting of the administrative committee was occupied by an interesting discussion of the part to be played by the Church in the preparation of a new international order. Schönfeld spoke with great feeling about the silent work being done in Germany and the consolation it was to the faithful of the *Bekennende Kirche*[3] to know that ecumenical work was still continuing.

An amusing detail about this extraordinary gathering: as Visser 't Hooft was leaving the hotel the manageress asked him, 'Who is paying for the detectives?'

Some days later, in Paris, I received a letter from Hoffmann, from Stockholm. He gave me some remarkable details about what our legation in Sweden had learnt, through Oslo, about Berggrav's activities and the proposals he was to show to York and me, which, we saw, originated from Ribbentrop's office.

Naturally, I gave M. Champetier de Ribes a report in writing of what, in our conversations in De Zilven, was of direct concern to the French Government. The Germans found this report in the mass of diplomatic and military documents they captured in an abandoned railway truck at La Charité-sur-Loire. This probably accounts for the Gestapo's search of my papers, in my flat, immediately after the German entry into Paris; and similarly for the accusation of organizing a crusade of the Churches against the Third Reich.

III

The uncertainty of a morrow which everyone anticipated would be one of terror, was suddenly made even worse for our family

2. 7 January 1940.   3. The Confessing Church.

circle, by the gravest and most cruel of anxieties. At about 11
o'clock on the evening of 1 February, Third Army Headquarters
telephoned me to say that my son-in-law Jacques Berthoud,
attached to the Deuxième Bureau, had been taken to the hospital
in Peltre, just by Metz, that his condition was critical and that
my daughter should go to him with all possible speed. She was
just back in Paris with her four children after staying for some
months with an old friend in the Tarn-et-Garonne. We left the
next morning, my daughter and I, after endless comings and
goings, and after being met in Metz by an officer from Headquarters and a chaplain of the Third Army, we were immediately
driven to Peltre.

The position was, in fact, extremely grave. Influenza, developing with startling rapidity into meningitis, had given rise to the
keenest anxiety. Fortunately there was in Peltre a team of very
highly regarded specialists, among them Dr Garcin and Dr
Guillaume. Their immediate treatment had warded off a fatal
issue, but the prognosis was still doubtful.

Family sorrows and trials cannot hold in this book the place
they occupied in my own life and the lives of those dear to me;
but even so I cannot refrain from recalling them. At a time when,
day after day, I was surrounded by cares and anxieties in which
mind and heart had not a moment's respite, their impact was felt
in the inmost depths of my life and came to be, I might almost
say, one of its permanent factors.

The weeks that followed were extremely hard, with their
constant alternations between hope and fear. Several times it
seemed as though the doctors had lost the battle. Their skill,
devotion and determination to beat the disease finally drove
death from the field. Jacques was convalescent for a long time,
until just before 10 May.

During these burdensome months there was an unending
succession of tasks and cares. Four times I made the journey to
Metz, on one occasion to visit the pastors of Lorraine and the
chaplains of the Third Army; one evening, at Bar-le-Duc station,
I met Père Congar, then a lieutenant in a light infantry regiment,
on his way back to the front. Some quick visits to a number of
churches were a welcome relief during those harassing days in
Paris. Even the National Synod of the Reformed Church, which

met in February in Montauban, was a rest, spent in the living fraternal communion of pastors and elders from all parts of the country.

My parochial ministry, too, was a source of joys in which I found new strength. My former assistant, Professor Jaques Courvoisier, came to help me with the Passion and Easter services. Some flying visits from Pierre Maury gave me the opportunity of comparing his views with mine and of calling on his great love for our parish and the Church. At that time he was in command of a hospital company.

The Lenten talks that year brought me many contacts with listeners on the radio, although it was a great distress to have to write them too quickly, often in the most unusual places; and week after week, from all parts of France, I had letters of thanks or encouragement.

Some of my time was taken up by the refugee problem: visits to internment centres to look for an alien whose position had been noted as being particularly hazardous, interviews with the chiefs of screening boards or with the director-general of the Sûreté Nationale, who was in fact very understanding. As early as 1938, together with Louise Weiss (who was always ready for any generous undertaking) I had persuaded Georges Bonnet to set up a committee which, with him as chairman, brought together representatives of public authorities and directors of private organizations, both Church and lay, which were concerned with refugees. We used to hold our meetings in the Salon de l'Horloge at the Quai d'Orsay. Cardinal Verdier, the Chief Rabbi Schwartz and I sat side by side. We did useful work, I believe; but during the first months of the war the private organizations soon exhausted their resources, and it took endless representations to secure Government assistance for them.

A redoubling of our efforts was all the more necessary in that we had been the target of some strong criticisms from abroad. An American paper, for example, printed an article entitled 'From Hitler's Concentration Camps to France's'.

Foreign pastors, serving French parishes or anxious to lend us their support, were also a serious anxiety. I was just leaving for Montauban, when François Seydoux, at that time attached to the Political Affairs Department, telephoned me: *'Someone'*, he said, 'has asked me to say that *someone* thinks that it is not desirable that Swiss should run French parishes'.

'There again', I noted, 'you have a senseless attitude. If we close the frontier to the young Swiss pastors who are offering us their services – and this is even more true of those already working here – there will be an outcry in Switzerland against our Government – and rightly so. A stupid way of doing things – to offend, to fly in the face of, the public opinion you ought to conciliate.'[4]

When I was received, after some preliminary representations, by M. Henri Hoppenot, head of the Political Affairs Department, he told me that before the war bishops had introduced Belgian, Italian, Irish, Spanish and even German priests into the country. Several had been arrested for espionage. The Government had decided not to allow the entry into French territory, during the war, of ministers of foreign Churches.

I urged upon him that the application of this measure would make it impossible for our parishes to be anything like normally served, since many of them had lost their pastors to the armed forces, as chaplains or combatant troops. A lengthy discussion followed, at the end of which M. Hoppenot asked me to send him a written explanation of our difficulties and of what we wanted. He led me to hope that some pastors might be authorized to return to France, but that no new admissions would be allowed. It was the latter that we were most in need of.

Two months later the invasion, the return to their parishes of demobilized chaplains (a considerable number were prisoners), and more serious difficulties swept aside this problem.

In spite of all this, my ecumenical life did not come to a halt. Visser 't Hooft made several journeys from Geneva to Paris, where he stopped on his way back from London to discuss things with me. He saw quite clearly that as soon as the 'real' war broke out it would be almost impossible to maintain contact with all the member Churches of the World Council, while at the same time the Council's responsibilities would be considerably increased. As I listened to him and felt his piercing glance rest on me, and saw his almost childlike smile, I used to thank God for

4. 23 February 1940.

having given us, to meet a situation so bristling with dangers, this man of faith, intelligence, initiative and courage.

On Good Friday we had the joy of celebrating an ecumenical service in the Anglican chapel of the British Embassy. The vicar, the Revd Mr Wade, had suggested this to me some weeks before and I had accepted with gratitude. Needless to say, he invited all the Anglican clergy in Paris to take part in this service of intercession. The priest of the Anglo-Catholic community in the Rue Auguste-Vacquerie wrote to him that he would not commit the 'mortal sin' of praying with French Protestants, who had, themselves, committed the 'sin of separating themselves from the Church of France'. Many of the faithful, British and French, took part in this service, in which I opened the prayer of intercession by an address on the words: 'Lest the cross of Christ be emptied of its power' (1 Corinthians 1:17).

Visitors from abroad often came to see me, bringing me news of their country and their Church, and discussing the responsibilities of the universal Church in the warring world. Where, however, was the universal Church? Visser 't Hooft and I had fought in order that the World Council might speak to the world in the name of the non-Roman Churches, but not a word had been said! This remained a heart-breaking disappointment to me.

On 15 March, I paid a long visit to Cardinal Verdier; we had both received exact information about the deterioration of morality in the army. We examined the possibility and opportuneness of a joint representation to the Prime Minister (at that time Paul Reynaud) or the Commander-in-Chief. We agreed to meet again, after having put out some feelers, to make a final decision.

At 8.30 a.m. on 9 April, the radio, after announcing that Copenhagen and Denmark had been occupied the day before, gave us the news of the sudden death of the Cardinal after an operation whose seriousness nobody had realized. Deeply moved, I hurried to the Archbishop's house, to which the dearly-loved Archbishop's body had been brought. Standing by his bier, I thought of the difficulties in our first contacts, and then of how we came to have a better knowledge of one another, which introduced us to a relationship of continually greater trust, and to a cordial co-operation when our Churches recognized their duty to join together in giving a Christian witness in the nation.

The grief of the vicars-general, of the fellow-workers and nuns who served him was a heart-rending sight; M. Champetier de Ribes and I were the first to witness it.

The last month before the storm broke began in an uneasy atmosphere which was heightened by the news each day brought. In Norway we found grounds at once for fear and hope. We were assured, and we believed it, that 'Hitler had missed the bus'. Churchill announced the imminence of important developments by land.

It was at this moment that two Scottish friends, the Revd Mr Hagan and the Revd Mr Hamilton, who had been sent by the Church of Scotland to assure the Reformed Church of France of its fraternal communion, arrived in Paris. The Government, the Army, and most of all French Protestantism in Paris, did all they could to make them welcome. Both were eminent in their own Church. Their visit, in the weeks when tragedy was looming up, brought us, with extra work, a wholesome encouragement.

I accompanied them to Metz, where pastors and chaplains met and talked with them. The next day, they were invited to visit one of the strongest fortifications in the Maginot line, the Haekenberg. They received an impression of impregnable strength and solidity. Alas for our hopes!

Other days were spent in the bustle of the most diverse activities. I went to visit the Church in Toulouse; I returned once again to Meaux, where I had been so often to discuss with Daniel Monod questions raised by the functioning of the chaplains' department. Many hours we spent working in his little office, which I then saw for the last time.

Refugees called for more of my time and attention than ever. With Louise Weiss and Mgr Courbe, representing the archbishopric, I called on M. Roy, Minister of the Interior. We explained to him that private organizations were still assuming the responsibility for 12,000 refugees, and that Government assistance was indispensable. He admitted the principle but, as a new Minister, he told us, 'I have far too many foreigners around me.'

We also saw the Finance Minister, who did not seem to us over-anxious to provide the millions for which we were asking to keep the refugees in our care from dying of starvation.

Whitsun was close at hand: it would be on 12 May, and the twenty-four catechumens who were to be confirmed on the 5th would communicate for the first time. On 3 and 4 May we had our usual retreat at Bièvres. Was it, I wonder, by presentiment that I decided, with our Presbyteral Council, to celebrate the two ceremonies on the same day, Sunday the 5th?

On 8 May I was noting, 'Paris is wonderful these days! The trees are wearing their spring shoots, dazzling in their freshness. Foreigners are impressed by the complete calm.'

The next day there was talk of nothing but Paul Reynaud's imminent resignation and a coalition under the leadership of Marshal Pétain.

On Friday, 10 May, at 4.45 in the morning, the air-raid warning sounded. The attack had begun.

CHAPTER II

Days of Distress

1940

I. The invasion. We leave Paris. II. First contacts with
Vichy. III. Move to Nîmes and trip to Geneva.

I

THE storm that raged in the weeks that followed will find little
echo in these pages. They were the most distressing weeks I have
ever lived through. Every day brought a stream of contradictory
news in which glimmers of hope lit up for a moment the dark
night of our agony. As one woke up in the morning, one's heart
was torn by the shock of reality. But one still had duties and
responsibilities, and it was impossible to stand idle.

The unhappy stream of refugees from Belgium or the Nord,
their pastors, with their families, in particular, anxiously seeking
advice and sometimes material assistance, obliged me to spend
long hours in our offices in the Rue de Clichy. We had to welcome, listen to, try to comfort and provide a fraternal atmosphere
for the people who came to us, still terrified by the menacing
scream of the stukas and shattered by the horrifying sights they
had witnessed. It was thus that there arrived one Sunday morning
a party of chaplains who had been cut off from their units and
had lost everything, including their sacred vessels; it was a great
comfort to be able to take them into our parochial house.

There was a constant succession of such incidents, and at the
same time there were other pressing duties. Long hours of discussion had to be spent on the Council of the Protestant Federation, the National Council of the Reformed Church, the Missions
Committee (of which I was chairman in the absence of Merle
d'Aubigné), and in studying with Daniel Monod, who had come
from Meaux, the many problems connected with the chaplains'
department.

On 18 May, I noted, 'Yesterday morning I arranged a meeting of the presidents of the Reformed and Lutheran Consistories, the president of the Paris Synod, the directors of the main organizations – and Rohr. We examined the various possibilities and considered what we should have to do. Bertrand, most nobly, and Berton, said that in any case they would stay in Paris. All were agreed . . . that I should remain where I could keep in touch with the public authorities.'

During the morning of the same day what claimed to be well-informed circles were greatly depressed; but in the afternoon there was a complete change of atmosphere. It was learnt that 'Marshal Pétain was willing to enter the Cabinet as vice-premier'.

Already, three days earlier, the news that the Germans would be arriving at any moment had decided many Parisians to leave for the south. Masses of documents had been burnt in the garden of the Quai d'Orsay. Meanwhile the direction of the fighting had changed, and the race for the sea was on.

Nevertheless I did not forget the responsibility of the World Council and its directors, and I was not resigned to its remaining silent. 'I have written to 't Hooft about this once again since 10 May. Yesterday I had his answer. He has sent an excellent cable to W. A. Brown, and suggests that I do the same today; it is only the Christians of the U.S.A. who can take steps in this direction. York, 't Hooft and I are belligerents, and anything we said would lack authority. Nevertheless, the ecumenical movement must be saved, and to do so it must be prevented from enclosing itself in complete silence.'[1]

Since the death of Cardinal Verdier, we had enjoyed uninterrupted relations with the Catholic side. Mgr Suhard, the new Archbishop of Paris, took over his see on 31 May, 'solemnly dedicating France to the Sacred Heart' in a ceremony that was broadcast by all national stations. We were assured that 'many bishops testified by their presence to the unanimity of France'. I was among those who expressed fears that this might be the prelude to a sinister reaction.

The Council of the Protestant Federation met once again on 21 May, the ill-starred day on which we learnt that in less than a fortnight the German armies had overrun Holland, Belgium and Luxemburg, and cut through France from Sedan to the sea. I

1. 19 May 1940.

proposed to the Council the election of Bertrand as a vice-president, in place of Merle d'Aubigné, who was ill in Switzerland and had sent in his resignation. If I should have to leave, we needed a man in the prime of life, who enjoyed the respect and affection of all, to exercise authority. My colleagues accepted the suggestion unanimously. They then asked me 'whatever happens, to remain in touch with the government and churches in the unoccupied areas'. Nobody at that time foresaw what the occupation would mean.

Tragic though the position of our forces seemed to be, the appointment of Weygand as commander-in-chief brought a resurgence of confidence. The moral and material means at his disposal, however, were not up to the measure of his military skill and his determination to save his country; and he was to experience many hours of bitter distress.

I was trying to make it possible still to maintain contact with our Churches by means of the radio. The Sunday service, started in 1939, was broadcast by station Radio-37, now closed down. By the good offices of Bondeville and Duhamel, we were able to have it transmitted from Radio-Paris II, the first transmission being on 2 June. Without this already established concession I do not think that, so soon after the disaster, I would have been able to secure the almost immediate resumption of the broadcasts.

Every evening a group of us used to meet in our church to pray in common. On Sundays the communion of the faithful who had remained in Paris, in spite of our sufferings, was a great boon. On 2 June I took as my text a passage from the Book of Job (29:24) which I had noted at the beginning of the war: 'I smiled on them when they had no confidence; and the light of my countenance they did not cast down.'

On Monday, 3 June, at about lunch-time, there was a bombardment of Paris, directed primarily at the Citroën factories, opposite Passy and Auteuil on the left bank of the Seine. The XVIth *arrondissement* also came under fire. Some hours later I was able to visit some of our parishioners in houses that had been partly destroyed. The news was heartbreaking: Dunkirk and the fighting continually closer. We realized then, without any doubt, that the battle for Paris was being fought. I have no words for the anxiety we felt when we thought of one or other of our children.

On Saturday, 8 June, I was able (in a cable sent to John Mott) to send a message to American Protestants who had just issued a fine statement calling urgently for the Allies to be assisted in every possible way. I was asked to read my message again on the Paris-mondial station the following night, at 3 a.m. What a strange hour it was that I spent there! I found the band of the Garde Républicaine there, for a concert broadcast to the U.S.A., which had not been cancelled. I read my message, and made my way back again through a Paris plunged in total blackness. At 10 o'clock I preached for the last time before we left, on St Paul's admirable exhortation to the Ephesians (6:13), 'Take the whole armor of God, that you may be able to withstand in the evil day, and having done all, to stand.'

On Monday, 10 June, in the evening of a day crowded with incidents which have left me with the most painful memories, with the Government already gone from Paris and the Germans about to enter the city, I was urged with the utmost force not to delay our departure. There was time for just one more moment of prayer in our church, and as we entered it we learnt that Italy had just declared war on us. A little after 22 hours we left our flat in the Rue de Boulainvilliers, which we were never again to see, and set out on the Orléans road. I would rather not recall the horror of the hours spent between Paris and Étampes.

II

At Limoges we had a warm welcome from my brother Pastor André Boegner, to whom we had handed over the care of the parish for the time being, and his wife. The town was packed with thousands of refugees, camping in the streets, around the station, and on the quays, access to which was made difficult by the crowds. There was an endless stream of vehicles, handcarts, horse-drawn carts, and cars. I tried without success to telephone Bertrand.

I was then assured by my friends the Jacques de Bethmanns that they were putting their house in Bordeaux at our disposal; it was in Bordeaux that, after endless comings and goings, Albert Lebrun and his ministers had just installed themselves. The headquarters of the Protestant Federation would accordingly be set up in that city. We arrived during the afternoon of Sunday the 16th, just when the drama was about to be staged which ended in the coming to power of Marshal Pétain and the request for an armistice. Marshal Pétain's speech, at midday the next day, cast us into the deepest gloom. My wife was by herself when she heard General de Gaulle's first appeal, and on coming in I found her in tears of emotion and hope.

We received from the Church in Bordeaux a welcome that was fraternal and comforting. M. Brunet, secretary-general of the Reformed Church, had joined me. We were uncertain, however, whether we should remain in Bordeaux. The German advance could no longer be held. The departure of the President of the Republic and of a part of the Government for Perpignan and then North Africa was considered, then decided upon, and then postponed, in view of the formal opposition of Marshal Pétain and General Weygand, now Minister of War. Nobody knew what the German terms would be. The news from foreign stations, which were still listened to, raised the gravest apprehensions.

In instructing me to keep in touch with the Churches in the south of France and with the public authorities, the Council of the Federation had also had in mind the necessity of maintaining contact with Churches abroad and with the general secretariat of the World Council of Churches. There could be no question of my remaining in Bordeaux. But where could I go? We learnt just then that the Berthouds and their children had found somewhere to live in Lavilledieu, in a house right out in the country, some kilometres from Montauban, and that they could take us in. Montauban! A Protestant town which could be an excellent centre for my work. On Monday 24 June, in pouring rain, with Bordeaux already surrounded by the German army, we set out for Agen and Montauban.

Two days before that, at the time of the communiqué which, we thought, would at last give us the German terms, I had spoken on the radio to the people of France. Never, I am sure, did I have such an audience. At the beginning of the week, Mgr Feltin, Archbishop of Bordeaux, who later replaced Mgr Suhard in Paris, had delivered a bewildering appeal. With M. Pomaret, Minister of the Interior, I was the last to be able to use the

Radiodiffusion nationale, before its temporary disappearance. I did not imagine then that I would be using it again, and would continue to do so throughout the occupation, thanks to the unfailing courtesy of its directors, and in spite of the absurdities of the censorship.

In these terribly sad days, it was deeply moving once again to see our children and grandchildren. Other surprises were in store for us. General Headquarters had ended their miserable withdrawal in the Montauban area, and Daniel Monod was there. Then Pierre Maury arrived, too, shattered by the scenes of cowardice and selfishness he had witnessed. Parishes and pastors were a continual source of great anxiety to me.

Every day brought me appeals for help. On all sides I was asked for visits that might help to make the faithful understand the necessities of the time, and the responsibilities of the Churches in our cruelly mutilated country. Sad though it is to relate, a pastor said to me about his parishioners, 'Money is coming in. That's all they care about. They are selling their potatoes at 4 francs instead of 2.50. Their hearts have turned into solid cash.'

Political passion was coming back into its own. When, on 11 July, the inhabitants of the Midi learnt of the 'revolution' effected the day before in Vichy, they were seized with terror. 'You'll see,' I was told, 'we are going to be governed by reactionaries, by the croix de feu or the Cagoulards.'

I had lost no time in visiting the various parts of the unoccupied zone: Albi, Castres, Mazamet, Pau, Agen and Toulouse were the first towns at which I stopped. However, I was being urged to go to Vichy, where Marshal Pétain and the Government had just established themselves. It was rumoured that a concordat was in preparation between the 'French State' and the Holy See, and that at the very least a clerical régime was in process of being set up. On 26 July I arrived in Vichy.

Before leaving, I had called a meeting of the Committee of the joint youth movements, now definitively established as *Cimade* (the Comité inter-mouvements d'aide aux évacués),[2] in order to obtain its views on the plan for the organization and civic education of French youth, which the new Government was about to

2. See above, pp. 106, 136.

publish. This was a matter I should certainly have to raise in Vichy.

I did in fact discuss there all the subjects that forced themselves on the mind of a Frenchman, a Protestant Christian, and a man who had been entrusted by the Churches with a weighty responsibility. Here I shall refer only to some essential points.

Everyone I saw in Vichy, with a few exceptions, believed in the urgent necessity, in this national defeat, of a 'national revolution'; and, for reasons that often differed, they were ready to co-operate with it.

There was such a congestion in the corridors of the Hôtel du Parc that it was not easy to obtain an interview. On the very first day, nevertheless, I was able to speak with Pierre Laval, the vice-premier, and, should circumstances require it, designated as successor to the Head of State. As soon as I entered the room I spoke to him of what was described as the 'Catholic character' of the national revolution. He stopped me, to say that this tendency might be present in some of the Ministers, but that the Government would vigorously maintain religious freedom: far from being persecuted, Protestants would have their rightful place in the nation. And he immediately went on to say, 'As for the Jews, they have done such harm to the country that they deserve collective punishment'.[3]

I told him of our feeling of shame at the clause in the armistice convention which obliged us to hand over to the Germans any refugees they should demand. On this point, Laval referred me to the Minister of Justice, Alibert, who, on the same day, had

3. I have been told that this remark, which was no doubt found in the report I presented to the General Assembly of French Protestantism in Nîmes in 1945, was quoted in a book published in 1967 and used against Pierre Laval's policy towards the Jews. The long interview I had with Pierre Laval in September 1942, extracts from which will be found in the next chapter, confirmed the attitude he expressed on 27 July 1940. I have seen with my own eyes sworn evidence establishing the fact that Laval did his best to save a number of Jews and I have no reason to dispute it. At the same time, nothing can ever persuade me that when he spoke to me, in July 1940 and September 1942, in the terms I have quoted he was trying to disguise from me a secret sympathy with the Jews. Had that been so, would he have told me to obtain from M. Bousquet, in charge at Police Headquarters, details of the application of the measures decided on against non-Aryans of the southern zone?

the effrontery to assure me that 'there have not been many requests, and they seem to have been satisfied . . . among others there was a pastor from Alsace whom we hesitated about handing over, and who exclaimed "Don't make such a fuss about it, I'm a German." '

Pierre Laval made a note of some questions I asked him about our pastors and their return to their parishes in the occupied zone. He told me that in no circumstances could they re-enter the 'reserved' zone. He promised to keep an eye on the position of pastors who were unable to return to Alsace or remain there.

With Alibert, I raised the question of the concordat that, it was said, would probably be signed. He assured me that no plan was under consideration in the ecclesiastical field. Some days earlier, Cardinal Gerlier, Archbishop of Lyons, had given him to understand, moreover, that the Holy See would never accept a concordat which would restrict the exceptional freedom the Catholic Church had been able to extract from the law of 1905, in particular in the matter of the appointment of bishops.

In the very first days of the new régime a savage law had stipulated that all officials, magistrates and officers must be born of French parents. Those who could not satisfy this requirement were simply regarded as having resigned. I put before the Minister of Justice the case of an Alsatian pastor, the father of five children, but himself the son of a Swiss citizen. Could not an exception be made in his favour? 'It is impossible', was the answer, 'sad though it be, to consider individual cases. The man you speak of must rely on charity.'

On the other hand I was assured that we could ask for help from Swiss pastors.

Other problems came up during this lengthy conversation. Here I shall note only the matter of gifts and legacies to Churches, whose competence to receive them was not recognized by the law of separation. I had already discussed this with Paul Reynaud before the war, and he had shown himself willing to consider a modification of the law. Alibert took a similar view: in the administration of their 'temporalities' the Churches should be able to rely on the right to receive gifts and legacies, not in virtue of a special right created for their benefit but as a matter of common law.

General Brécart, my friend René Gillouin, and M. Arnal, deputy director of Political Affairs – all three Protestants – gave me some valuable information. They were not alone in thanking me for coming and establishing the contacts that were so indispensable. There were others, it is true, pastors and laymen, who criticized me; but the Council of the Protestant Federation had instructed me to remain in touch with the public authorities; and, whatever authorities might be in control – or might believe themselves to be in control – in unoccupied France and were maintaining normal diplomatic relations with the majority of countries in the world, it was therefore my duty to go to Vichy – only thus could I bring home to all the living reality of French Protestantism, insist on respect for the rights legally recognized for our Churches, win a hearing for their protest when occasion demanded, and, most of all, present their evidence in circles where there was too marked a tendency to be blind to it. It was these reasons that caused me to be often in Vichy during the years 1940 to 1943.

During this first stay, I was greatly taken up by matters that affected our youth movements. There was a Minister of '*Famille et Jeunesse*' (Family and Youth). I saw his principal private secretary and informed him of our essential requirements, in connection with the actual existence of our movements, their representation in the efforts that were being made to organize and re-group French youth, and with the appointment of chaplains to the '*Jeunesse et Patrie*' (Youth and Fatherland) camps which were planned. I was given assurances about these various matters, and these were confirmed by Jean Borotra, whom I met there, holding an important position in the same Ministry. He promised to get hold of Jean Gastambide as representative of Protestant youth movements.

As we were crossing the park from one interview to the other, I had a sad encounter. The Chief Rabbi of France, M. Schwartz, and his wife were wandering, apparently aimlessly, along the paths. We sat down and had a long talk. He was a man who commanded unbounded respect, an ardent Frenchman, and he had been wounded to the depths of his being. He was in Vichy because that was where the Government was. He had asked for no interview for fear of being refused. He had asked to speak on the Bordeaux radio, knowing that I had done so. He had had an evasive answer. I was deeply sorry for him and could not hide my apprehensions. I promised him that I would sound General Brécart[4] and Olivier de Sardan[5] about the possibility of an interview.

The former, when I asked him the next morning, told me that he would see the Chief Rabbi and would advise him to leave Vichy. All the latter said to me was, 'Tell him to advise the Jews who are here to leave and go into hiding.' Later I heard that after waiting a long time M. Schwartz was received by Marshal Pétain. For my part, I did not think it well advised to ask for an interview during this first visit.

III

In the middle of these manifold spiritual, ecclesiastical and temporal matters for which I was responsible, there was one question that insisted on an answer. The return to Paris of our Berthoud children meant that our staying in Lavilledieu was pointless. Montauban had not proved to be an effective centre for work and contacts. The question was, where to go? I finally settled on Nîmes, and told my colleagues in that Protestant capital that I would like to come and discuss the matter with them. It was decided that I should stay in Nîmes from 10 to 14 August in order to meet the Presbyteral Council, the pastors of the Reformed Church of France and of the local parishes, and to preside at the Sunday worship. In addition, the members of the National Council of the Reformed Church of France, living in the unoccupied zone, would be meeting at the same time. There were enough of them to enable us to make the decisions the situation required.

The National Council decided in fact to transfer to Nîmes for the duration of the war the direction and administration of the Reformed Church, and asked me to move to Nîmes as soon as possible.

There was no doubt that Nîmes, where we lived for two and a half years, offered great advantages. It was near Montpellier and its faculty of theology, and Marseilles and the Churches of

4. Secretary-general to the Head of State.
5. Principal private secretary, *Directeur du cabinet* to Pierre Laval.

Provence, and from it one could easily reach Valence, Lyons, the Savoy, and also Clermont, where the Strasbourg faculty was installed. Nîmes made it possible to maintain continual contact with the regional synods, the parishes and the youth movements of unoccupied France. Moreover, a through train enabled me to go to Vichy whenever necessary. Finally, and perhaps most important of all, I was not far from Geneva, from the headquarters of the World Council of Churches, from Swiss Protestantism, whose generosity meant so much to us, and from friends through whom, so long as the frontier remained open, I could communicate with foreign countries.

I could not for long resist the repeated invitations of Visser 't Hooft, Adolf Keller, Charles Guillon and Henriod. I decided accordingly to go to Geneva, after a quick visit to the headquarters of the Churches of Alsace and Lorraine, in Périgueux, and I arrived in Geneva on 30 August. I received an unforgettable welcome from the Church authorities, from Visser 't Hooft and his colleagues, and, two days later in Berne, from the Council of the Federation of Swiss Protestant Churches.

When I saw Schönfeld again, to have a discussion with Visser 't Hooft, Koechlin and him, I was profoundly moved. From the very first words spoken, I knew that, come what may, the 'communion of saints' is still a wonderful reality. What he told me of the feelings of some of his fellow-countrymen towards me, and of the threats I would be unwise to ignore, confirmed me in my conviction that for the time being my place was in what was still unoccupied France.

It was a unique opportunity to obtain complete and reliable news about the Churches in the belligerent and in the neutral countries and in still hesitant America, and about the ecumenical movement all over the world. There were contacts which ensured the exchange of news between Geneva and any places which sought or could give information. What a blessing it was to be able to write at length from Geneva to Bishop Bell in Chichester!

Since the armistice of June, an immense burden of work, whose importance the Churches appreciated only later, had fallen upon Visser 't Hooft and his colleagues. This was the responsibility for the spiritual and intellectual relief of prisoners of war, shared with the Y.M.C.A., which had already interested itself in the problem. It was then that the Ecumenical Commission for Prisoners of War was founded, under the presidency of Professor Jaques Courvoisier. We discussed the difficulties involved in the work: a sense of its urgency took precedence over every other consideration. The work that was done in the course of five years of war, through visits that were authorized all too seldom, through the publication of booklets of rare spiritual substance, and through innumerable parcels, was the first great assertion of the World Council's self-identification with the distress and suffering of a mankind that had been flung into the black night of hate and death: the prelude to so many similar gestures in the years to come.

The refugee situation called for lengthy discussions. It was a matter of urgency to co-ordinate and, if possible, reinforce a great variety of efforts. I must confess that the measures decided were not to prove to be the best. Further, the setting up of the over-notorious 'camps' in Gurs and other places was to raise problems for us of quite a different dimension.

I left Geneva, thankful that the Council 'in process of formation' had decided to show itself an active and ever-present centre of love and brotherhood and a messenger of hope to all the victims of the war, and particularly thankful that I had consolidated the liaison between the Churches of France and the ecumenical movement, with which was combined my delight at being able once again to share in the work.

Some days later, after stopping in Valence and Lyons, where I saw a great many pastors from the Drôme, the Ardèche and the Lyonnais, I was back in Vichy; and on the same day I was received by Marshal Pétain.

I had met him only once, before the war, when the Council of the Protestant Churches had asked me to express to him our desire that our Churches might be granted their own shrine at Douaumont. It did not seem reasonable to us that the Catholic Church alone should be present. The Marshal's reception, in his office at the Ministry of War, had been icy. He had said no more than a few words, and I had left without obtaining the least satisfaction. I had no reason, therefore, to expect a cordial reception: but it was courteous. As I entered the Marshal's vast office, I saw

René Gillouin working with him; so the interview was three-cornered.

What were the questions I thought it necessary to raise with the Head of State? There were several matters of which he had spoken during recent pronouncements on which it seemed to me desirable that he should know our views: alcoholism, the family, youth, and public morality. At the outset I quoted as my authority one of his own sayings, 'I hate the lies which have done such harm', to draw his attention to the disastrous effect produced in France and among our friends abroad by the vulgarity and excesses of the State Radio, in particular its Anglophobia. I added that the most serious aspect of this was that, since it was impossible to refer to Hitler's responsibility and there was an incessant emphasis on that of certain Frenchmen, France appeared to the whole world as pleading guilty.

The Marshal answered, 'I am inclined to think that I shall have to do something about it.' And he added, 'There is a saying which I am constantly repeating: dignity towards Germany, silence towards England.' 'Yes', I said, 'so long as the Press and the Radio conform.'

The same day, I saw Admiral Darlan, with whom I had in the old days been a candidate for the Naval College, and asked him for a full-time chaplain on the Navy's peace establishment. He was good enough to let me have two, one of whom would be for North Africa. I took the opportunity of mentioning the radio to him; he made some notes and said, 'The Government is neither Anglophobe nor Anglophile. It is Francophile.' 'But its radio is Anglophobe', I answered.

Since my first stay in Vichy, the wish to see England win had made itself unmistakable. A sailor said to me, 'There's only one Anglophobe at the Admiralty – Admiral Darlan.' It was, of course, an exaggeration; nevertheless, an admiral, speaking to me of the British resistance, said, 'It's our only hope.'

The sailor I mentioned was none other than Admiral Platon, Colonial Minister since the crisis of the preceding week. I met in him a former parishioner of mine and I knew of his magnificent work as governor of Dunkirk. I went to him, too, to ask for a chaplain for the Malagasy troops stationed at Fréjus, waiting to return to Madagascar: they were constantly said to be on the point of leaving but in fact did not do so until after the end of the war. Platon sanctioned my request without hesitation.

What a fine look that man had, warm and true! I soon learnt that he described me as the 'leader of the Protestant Gaullists'. None the less, he treated me with the utmost cordiality until the day when, after he had decisively come down on the side of Germany, he refused to listen to me after the persecution of non-Aryans had broken out.

It was thus that the Vichy régime was established, shaky though the foundations may have been. In January 1941 I was appointed to represent the Protestant Churches at the 'National Council', where I had countless opportunities of practising the policy which I had adopted of being on the spot; there, too, I witnessed the succession of crises which undermined the régime from within and the increasing pressure from Hitler's Government which threatened to strangle it. All this side of my work lies outside my present scope, and I shall speak only of the chief matters in which I was personally concerned.

CHAPTER 12

The Defence of Religious Freedom
1940-1943

I. Continual negotiations in Vichy. II. The refugee problem. Cimade in Gurs. III. Persecution of the Jews. Interviews with Marshal Pétain and Pierre Laval.

I

IN the course of one of the many visits he was kind enough to
pay me in Nîmes, Charles Guillon told me (the date was 15 March
1941) that Dietrich Bonhoeffer,[1] one of the leaders of the Confessing Church in Germany, had said to him that 'our Churches were
for collaboration and were betraying the cause'. It may be well at
this point to recall what part our pastors and Churches played
during those melancholy days in order to show how completely
without foundation was Bonhoeffer's accusation.

Had he, I wonder, read the indictment of our Churches and, I
must admit, of my own self, which appeared in a study on French
Protestantism during the war (*Französicher Protestantismus im
Krieg*)? There he would have found that the Church leaders
appointed by the Nazis made no mistake about the fundamental
and unchanging attitude of the vast majority of French Protestants.
There were, it is true, some Protestant collaborators who were
content to remain silent in face of the shocking treatment in-
flicted on the Jews. Nevertheless, the multiple problems raised
by Hitler's policy towards occupied France found French
Protestants loyal to their noblest traditions: some, I agree, as a
result of their strong democratic instinct, but the great majority
of them from a clear appreciation of the Gospel commands.

It was, let me repeat, a blessing from heaven that the Reformed
Church of France had been enabled to re-establish its unity some
months before the war broke out. On countless occasions, since
those distant days, I have found myself reflecting (as I have for

1. See below, p. 346.

other reasons of which I shall be speaking later) on the reciprocal relationship between *event* and *institution*. Those who, from 1939 to 1944, bore the spiritual and ecclesial responsibility of the Reformed Church, knew that their most important duty was to offer a Christian witness to the nation, to the French authorities and the occupying power, and to the Churches: both those associated in the World Council and the Catholic Church in France. Our Churches and, above all, their pastors and Councils fought a continual battle to save non-Aryans and to defend religious freedom, for respect for the fundamental rights of the human person, to combat the political enslavement of youth movements, to resist the sending to Germany of a large proportion of working youth, and to assert the close communion of the Christian Churches in their refusal to accept the triumph of the powers of darkness. This battle inspired and directed the most practical manifestations of the work of our Churches, work which, moreover, was carried out in constant communion with the World Council, of which they were nearly all members. At the same time this was possible only because the institution – by which I mean the Protestant Federation of France or the Reformed Church of France – was always actively concerned to support and co-ordinate the prophetic message and to make it heard where it needed to get home – even if it were to be immediately rejected.

One source of strength to the Reformed Church was that at that time it had at the head of its regions, regional presidents who, in unoccupied France in particular, formed a team of men of character, of living and contagious piety, not afraid of responsibility, fully alive to the spiritual mediocrity of many parishes, and yet with the ability to make them recognize that their pastors felt it was their duty to co-operate in every form of relief work and in the defence of freedom and justice.

During the last months of 1940, and later in 1941 and 1942, I travelled constantly through the so-called free zone, taking part in all the regional synods, and also in meetings of presbyteral councils or pastors of many consistories, and preaching in small villages as well as in towns: starting in March 1943, after my return to Paris and until the end of the war, I carried on with the same travelling ministry in the occupied zone: always and everywhere, I became convinced that the presence among French

Protestants of authorities entitled to speak in their name and, at all levels, to initiate the necessary action, to denounce when circumstances so required, to the State or the occupying power, their attacks on freedom, on the dignity of persons or human communities, was for the Churches and their pastors a most valuable reinforcement to their own efforts at simply being faithful to the Gospel of Christ.

On many occasions one had to recognize that the defence of French Protestantism was a matter of duty. It was the target of accusations, at times inept. In a booklet whose purpose was to eulogize Joan of Arc, it was stated that if the English had not been thrown out of France, France would have become Protestant and heretical, and that would have been the end of western civilization. A sharp protest brought in reply a promise 'to consider ways of soothing the susceptibilities of Protestant circles'.

More serious was the charge, retailed throughout unoccupied France, that Freemasonry had been founded by French pastors. It should be borne in mind that at that time Freemasons were hounded out of the public services, the magistrature and the army, and that the *Journal Officiel* published every day the names of Freemasons who had been dismissed. M. Fay, former administrator of the Collège de France, who had accepted the position of director of the 'secret societies' department, prepared a lecture in which he sought to spotlight the misdeeds of Freemasonry, and gave his 'first performance' in Vichy, in the presence of Marshal Pétain. He brought up the accusation against French pastors I have just mentioned, and was careful not to point out the radical difference between Anglo-Saxon masonry, which has never renounced its religious basis, and the 'Grand Orient' masonry of France, which long ago deleted from its statutes the belief in a 'great architect' of the universe, and boldly proclaimed its atheism.

I was immediately informed of M. Fay's crusade and his insidious attacks on French Protestantism. The letter I wrote to the Marshal was immediately, by his orders, forwarded to the lecturer. The latter asked for an interview with me, and we arranged a meeting. It was a distressing and at times violent conversation. The names of 'Pastors' Dides and Desmond were hurled at me, and I was told that a number of French pastors were at that moment Freemasons. I challenged M. Fay to give me their names; but I was never told them, and I noted his silence on this point.

The most interesting and, in some ways, the strangest incident came about in connection with a secret circular sent to certain police units in the unoccupied zone, instructing them to keep under observation the activities of pastors, particularly in the Drôme, the Ardèche, and the Gard, and to obtain the information they needed from the *maires* – and the parish priests. I was told of the existence of this document but did not know its exact wording, and was anxious to get hold of a copy. Wherever I asked I was met with a blank denial. In Vichy and in Nîmes, no one knew of the existence of this instruction. The commandant of the *gendarmerie* of the Gard formally denied it.

One day, when I was visiting a parish in the Ardèche, my colleague Brémond told me that the *gendarmerie* headquarters in Le Pouzin, where he carried on his ministry, had received the circular in question, and that I might perhaps be able to read it. The sergeant was a parishioner of M. Brémond, and so we called on him. The register in which official telegrams were entered was lying – by chance? – on the table. The *sous-officier* was called out of his office and left the room for a moment. I leapt on the register and soon found the message I had so patiently hunted for, and quickly noted the contents.

I immediately drew up a carefully worded note addressed to the police authorities and, more important still, to the Ministers concerned, the text of which will be found in Appendix 2.

When I informed Nîmes and Vichy of the success of my enquiries, there was great (if simulated?) surprise. One thing is certain, and that is that there was no more talk of a general check on pastors. Some of them, and I myself most of all, were subject to special and constant surveillance; but on the whole it did not amount to much.

Nevertheless, a number of arrests in both zones obliged me to make urgent representations to the Vichy authorities.

The news that Pastor Freddy Dürrleman, one of the preachers and lecturers with the largest audience in the inter-war years, had been arrested on 22 January 1941, in Carrières-sous-Poissy, by the German authorities, aroused great feeling in Protestant circles in the unoccupied zone. On being told of it by his son Patrice, I immediately wrote to the Minister of Justice, asking him to intervene without delay with the occupying authorities; but I had already learnt that he had been handed over to French jurisdiction.[2]

Later, having heard no news, I spoke to Darlan about Dürrleman at the end of a long interview with the Admiral, and earnestly begged him to make representations about his case. He took the note I gave him, and undertook to do what he could, although he warned me that he was doubtful of success. I have never found out whether these interventions hastened Dürrleman's release or not; his son Valdo, who had moved to Montpellier, had become, to my great satisfaction, a regular contributor to our Protestant broadcasts: his talks, I may add, gave rise to some serious incidents.

Pastors André Trocmé and Theis were also arrested in Le Chambon-sur-Lignon, where the former served one of the finest parishes in France and the latter was in charge of the international and pacifist college of Le Chambon. Both were conscientious objectors. Taken to an internment camp, they found themselves surrounded by internees of every political and religious colour, and were filled with admiration for the brotherly spirit, the generosity and loyalty of their communist companions.

As soon as I had heard of their arrest I had, of course, made the necessary representations to Vichy. Some months later, about 15 March 1943, they were released, and I rather believe that they were sorry to leave the fellow-prisoners whose splendid moral bearing had so impressed them.

During the years of the occupation, youth problems engrossed a good deal of my attention and called for approaches on my part, to the earliest of which I have already referred. The directors of our movements decided to form a Protestant Youth Council, whose presidency I was asked to accept for the time being. This 'time being' lasted five years, and brought me the great joy of living through these troubled years in close communion of heart and mind with the leaders of our youth.

It goes without saying that on every occasion I resisted with the utmost tenacity the intention – barely disguised, and some-

2. See Appendix 3.

times openly avowed – to form a *single youth organization*. I had countless interviews on this matter with the ephemeral Ministry of Youth, then with the Youth Headquarters, directed with great zeal by M. Lamirand (himself opposed to the single organization), then with the successive Ministers of Education, and finally with the 'National Council', on which Joseph Darnand and some others were supporters of the single organization. The Catholic movements, backed up by Cardinal Gerlier, were engaged in the same battle. It proved impossible ever to carry out the plan. An attempt was then made to exact from our movements an undertaking to give their members a course of civic (i.e., in fact, political) instruction imposed by the authorities: in other words, to force us to give a political bias to the education of our young people. Here again our answer was a flat refusal.

A further, and most emphatic, refusal was called for again, when we were warned that we were going to be forbidden to retain or admit 'non-Aryan' young people into our movements. The prohibition of the admission (or retention) of foreigners, no matter what their nationality, was also under consideration. At various junctures the Protestant Youth Council had to make a choice with potentially serious consequences; and it always chose the line of unswerving fidelity to the Gospel. When, in June 1943, the Government decided to cancel all the concessions made to the youth movements, we were on the verge of a formidable conflict. It was prevented from erupting by the governmental crises which brought continual changes of personnel and, with them, ideology.

II

I can say that since I left Paris in June 1940 until I went back in February 1943, and even later, there was hardly a single day on which the refugee problem did not force itself on my mind and call for some action on my part.

The problem of political refugees claimed by Germany necessitated some of the most unhappy interviews I had in Vichy. One of the clauses of the armistice convention stipulated, it will be remembered, that we were to hand over to Germany those of its nationals who were regarded as guilty of having fomented hatred of National Socialism in France and encouraged the war mentality. Our representative had protested, it is true, against this humiliating demand. On Field-Marshal Keitel's assurance that only 'a few' individuals were concerned, they had finally consented.

These 'few' Germans, whose right to asylum we had recognized, soon became numerous, and even extremely numerous. There were many cases of disgraceful collusion between Vichy and the Gestapo. The Vichy police had no hesitation in assuring eminent people that it had to take them into protective custody because the Gestapo had discovered their hiding-place. These unfortunate people followed their 'rescuers', who then immediately handed them over to their hunters.

I saw an unending succession of Ministers and high police officials on this subject. The answer would be, 'Reasons of State', or, 'To save French citizens, or to get them back, we hand over a few Germans'; or, 'It's a Government matter'. Darlan listened without interrupting me, but would make me no concession. I ended the interview by saying to him, 'Our defeat will have been forgotten for a long time, when France's betrayal of the men who placed their hopes in her loyalty is still remembered.'

The name of the town of Castres is still sadly renowned in the memories of many Germans. It was there that some of their relatives waited in prison for the time when one after another they were handed over to the Gestapo.

These political refugees, victims of the armistice convention, were a group apart. The problem of refugees in the mass had a number of different aspects. When the anti-Jewish persecution broke out in Germany, a considerable number of non-Aryans, Jews by religion or Christians with three Jewish ancestors, had sought refuge in France, often in order to arrange a passage across the Atlantic. The majority of these had not yet had time to reach America when the war broke out. In addition to those who had to stay behind there were the non-Aryans whom Germany forced the Vichy Government to receive in the unoccupied zone and intern in camps, where no preparations had been made to receive them in large numbers and give them food and shelter. It was thus that the over-notorious Gurs camp, where Spanish refugees and later French troops had caused almost irreparable damage, had to provide shelter at a moment's notice for thousands of non-

Aryans from Germany, Austria, and Czechoslovakia 'entrusted' by the occupying power to the French authorities. We shall soon be meeting Gurs again.

I have already spoken of the depressing effect produced on me, during my first stay in Vichy, by the avowed anti-Semitism of certain Ministers and by the threat pronounced against the Jews: Jews who were not refugees or recently naturalized French citizens, but French Jews who were regarded as 'having done so much harm to the country that they deserved collective punishment'. It was these who were the first victims of the 'racial' law of October 1940. Shocking acts of injustice were perpetrated at that time in both zones, and not under the pressure of the occupying forces. Men and women employed in the public service, many of whom had done valuable work for France, were simply retired or 'struck off the strength'. When the National Council of the Reformed Church met in Lyons before the end of the year, André Bertrand, whose arrival was a great blessing to us, asked on behalf of the Council of the Protestant Federation that a written protest should be submitted without delay. I was asked meanwhile still to continue with verbal representations. To detail these would be a lengthy matter. A Minister assured me that, 'it is a defensive law, and will entail terrible injustice, but it must be absolute'. On the same day the Head of State's principal private secretary confided to me that 'that had not been the Marshal's intention'. That, I am convinced, was true: but what a tragic admission of impotence!

During the winter the position grew continually worse. That was why, when there was a new session of the National Council of the Reformed Church in March 1941, it was unanimously agreed that the Church's position should, without any further delay, be made plain in writing. This would meet the wishes of the Protestant Federation of France.

In accordance with the instructions I received on that day, I wrote two letters, dated 26 March, one to Admiral Darlan (then deputy Prime Minister)[3] and the other to the Chief Rabbi of France.

This second letter had a curious history. The newspaper *Le Pilori* which was read by many French people in the occupied

3. See Appendix 4.

zone – much though they hated it – published it in full, under the heading 'French Protestant Leader's Unacceptable Letter'. Later, in Nîmes, a 'non-Aryan' told me that it had brought the Jews of the occupied zone their first glimmer of hope – that Christian Churches should share their distress and seek for means to alleviate it! In the southern zone tens of thousands of copies of the letter were circulated; how this came about I have never been able to discover, but it brought the National Council of the Reformed Church and its president warm approval from some and bitter reproaches from others. In an interview which I agreed to have with some Protestants in Montpellier, I was attacked with incredible violence. I was blamed for not having consulted (consulted, indeed!) Protestants before writing to Chief Rabbi Schwartz. I was denounced to Marshal Pétain. From various quarters, and often in anonymous letters, I was called on to resign the responsibilities entrusted to me by the Churches. Needless to say that when, in addition, it was learnt in these circles which were so eager to follow the Marshal's 'leadership' that two of my sons had gone over to 'the other side', their attacks were re-doubled. All this is best passed over in silence.

My letter to Admiral Darlan brought no written reply, but he asked me to go and see him in Vichy. I had a long interview with him at the end of May. A new law concerning Jews was being drafted. 'I must warn you', he said, 'that article 1 is extremely severe. But have a look at article 8, thanks to which, I believe, all Jews who have been French citizens long enough and all who have had war service can escape the law.' Apart from that, all he wanted was to see the recently arrived immigrants 'clear out'.

The law of 3 June – which was the law in question – proved a bitter disillusionment. I informed the Marshal, through René Gillouin, of the strong feelings aroused in our Churches. During August I wrote a long letter again to Gillouin, for the Marshal to see; Gillouin forwarded it to him together with a letter of his own which, I cannot but say, did him the greatest credit. Shortly afterwards, Cardinal Gerlier promised me that as soon as he had the opportunity he would raise the question of the racial laws with the Head of State. This he did some days later; and it was on his return to Lyons that the Marshal, impressed by the united protests of the Christian Churches, sent for Xavier Vallat, the High Commissioner for Jewish Affairs – whose weakness was denounced by the Germans – and ordered him to apply the law with moderation.

The situation was continually growing worse. The Churches had the duty of making every possible effort to prevent a real persecution. Bertrand had once again authorized me to act on behalf of the Protestant Federation of France. I tried to do so during the visit I paid to the Marshal on 18 January 1942. Here I can only repeat what I told the General Assembly in Nîmes in 1945: it cannot be denied that what the Marshal learnt of the evil effects of the racial measures caused him real distress. He could see quite clearly that great injustices were being committed; but it is equally undeniable that he was bitterly conscious of his impotence to prevent or remedy them. Moreover, he was in no way astonished that the Churches should communicate to him their indignant protests; it was, rather, their silence that would have surprised him.

At this same time, the internment of alien non-Aryans was calling for the opening of new camps. What we learnt of the terrible conditions to which these unfortunate internees were reduced moved us to lively indignation. I discussed this with Darlan. He did not deny that serious mistakes had been made and he sincerely hoped to put them right. He told me that an inspector would be appointed to look closely into the position of each camp, to propose essential action, and to oversee the work of those in charge. I took advantage of the opportunity to ask him for authority to visit such camps as I thought it necessary to inspect, on the understanding that I would report to him on what I had seen: and to this he agreed.

It was thus that I came to visit the camp in Gurs, near Oloron. Jeanne Merle d'Aubigné and Madeleine Barot were installed there, and had every intention of ensuring, on behalf of Cimade, a fraternal and ecumenical atmosphere, in spite of all the difficulties they had come up against. I knew beforehand what I should find in Gurs: Jeanne Merle d'Aubigné has described it in the moving pages which contain some of her memories.

I retain an unforgettable impression of two meetings with the internees, held in one of the huts. The first introduced me to some of the camp's distinguished personalities: and distinguished is indeed the word for them. Eminent surgeons and doctors from Berlin or Vienna, celebrated musicians or singers from Bayreuth, Munich or Vienna, university professors and any number more of similar eminence. It was heartrending to see the physical and psychological condition to which many, if not all, of them had been reduced. There were complaints, it is true, and not without excellent reason, and amply justified demands, but at the same time it was a wonderful example of courage under trial, and deep in their hearts could be discerned the hope that still looks to the future.

The second meeting, confined to Protestants, took the form of a very simple service, but, with the assistance of a choir which included some of the great singers I have mentioned, one of great beauty. I left Gurs filled with shame for the negligence of the authorities, and with thankfulness for the presence of the two representatives of Cimade.

In other camps there were living other members, both men and women, of Cimade, an organization which the Protestant Federation energetically supported in its dealings with the Vichy or occupying authorities. Several incidents obliged me to intervene with the inspector of camps. He was one of the Vichy officials who understood their responsibilities and the *human* side of their duties.

The year 1942 was drawing to its close. The great battles in Russia and North Africa, with their alternations of advance and retreat, brought us long hours of suffering and hope. We were all eager to listen to foreign stations. Then suddenly the news burst upon us that the 'Jew-hunt' had begun in the occupied zone; revolting scenes had taken place in many parts of Paris; thousands of Jews, including women and children and the aged, had been dragged from their dwellings and crammed into the Vélodrome d'Hiver, forced into a shameful promiscuity and living from hour to hour in the most terrible uncertainty for the morrow.

There was immense feeling in Paris and throughout France. The disgust which these measures aroused was publicly demonstrated, and often, in the occupied zone, with a courage whose memory fills me with gratitude and pride. My noble friend

Bertrand who, as I have mentioned, was president of the Council of the Protestant Federation, was instructed by the Council to inform the Head of State directly of the distress felt by the Churches of the northern zone. He wrote the Marshal a letter which, as a precaution, I was careful to deliver to him by my own hand, and which I read to him on 27 June.[4] The Marshal was visibly moved, but from the interview that followed I gained the same impression of complete impotence.

I need hardly say that during these tragic events (and constantly, moreover, in connection with refugees and camps), I was closely in touch with my friends in Geneva who were responsible for the work and witness of the World Council. These problems concerned more than ourselves. In Holland the determination to exterminate the Jews was made vilely apparent. Mussolini, with some hesitation, was feeling himself obliged to imitate the example of his powerful ally. The Jewish problem had become a world problem, like that of refugees and prisoners of war. That was the reason for the establishment in Geneva at a very early date of an Ecumenical Committee for Refugees. We have always worked in close contact with it, and I can pay unreserved tribute to the intelligence which a German pastor, Dr Freudenberg, brought to the organization of this service.

A liaison committee for the relief of refugees was operating in 'free' France with great efficiency. It met regularly in Nîmes and on several occasions I took part in its meetings. Our American friend Lowrie was the chairman and made great efforts on behalf of the hunted Jews. The committee's ecumenical character was emphasized by the part taken in its work by the Abbé Glazberg, who was one of the outstanding figures in the battle, started and continued with such tenacity and courage, to save foreign Jews in the unoccupied zone.

When the first trains were made up into which the police crammed the arrested Jews, filling them with lies about their destination, revolting scenes took place in many stations. In Vénissieux, near Lyons, Madeleine Barot, the Abbé Glazberg and Père Chailley fought furiously to rescue at least part of their prey from the police. In Aix, my colleague Manen, chaplain in the Milles camp, in spite of his most desperate efforts, could only

4. See Appendix 5.

succeed in removing from the train five hundred-per-cent Aryans. He telephoned to the Abbé Glazberg in Lyons, who managed to release them as the convoy passed through.

Since it was apparent that there must be the closest possible agreement between the Christian denominations, I went back to Lyons to see Cardinal Gerlier once more. He received me on 18 August. On that same morning he had protested to the Prefect of the Rhône about the lack of humanity with which the Jews under arrest were treated. A trainload of these unfortunate people had just gone through Lyons, without the Chief Rabbi Kaplan being allowed to distribute any food to them. All that could be done was to throw a little bread through the openings made in the trucks for the horses' heads – when the occupants were horses.

We agreed that it was impossible for the Churches to remain silent. It was decided that we should both write to the Head of State.[5] The Cardinal thought it would be useless to write to Pierre Laval, but I felt it my duty to do so, on 27 August, in my capacity as vice-president of the World Council of Churches.[6]

It was thus that I wrote to Marshal Pétain the letter which will be found in the appendix. It had such a strange story that I shall recount it here.

In order to avoid indiscreet use of the letter, I had only three copies made: one for the Head of State, one for Cardinal Gerlier and one for myself. Being in Vichy a fortnight later, I was anxious to discuss with Mr Tuck, the American chargé d'affaires, the possibility of obtaining from Laval authorization for the departure to America of some hundreds of Jewish children, forcibly separated from their parents. To my great surprise, he thanked me for my letter to the Marshal. I could not believe that he meant my last letter, and made a reference to an earlier one. 'No, no,' he exclaimed, 'I mean the letter you have just sent him; I have cabled the text to Washington.' There was no necessity for me to ask him how he had come to see it.

Some days later, at the railway station in Nîmes, a clergyman who was a stranger to me, came up to me and told me that the day before Cardinal Gerlier's secretary had read my letter to a large number of priests, meeting in Lyons. And another traveller

5. See Appendix 6.   6. See Appendix 7.

told me that on the same day copies were being distributed in the flower-market in Marseilles. My colleagues in that town had read it from the pulpit the Sunday before. Édouard Herriot had spoken about it to Louise Weiss, and Éric Barde, arriving from Paris, assured me that 'everybody' knew it in the capital. I myself heard a French version of it, translated from English, on the Swiss Radio, and several foreign periodicals reproduced the full text of this same version, which differed considerably from the original.

It was no surprise to me, accordingly, to learn the next year that the Franco-German Paris periodical *Je suis partout* described me as the 'champion of Jewry'.

III

The Assembly of the Musée du Désert, which for many years had met every summer on the first Sunday in September under the ancient chestnuts of the Mas Soubeyran, near Anduze, had been called for 6 September. I had been asked to preside, to preach at the morning service, and to wind up the afternoon speeches. Some four thousand Protestants assembled at this stronghold of Huguenot resistance, the majority fired by the desire, in face of all the threats which hung over us, there to affirm their faith. In the sermon I preached on the words 'Be faithful unto death' (Rev. 2:10) I spoke as forthrightly as possible on our duty to act as good Samaritans to the Jews suffering in our midst. In the afternoon (with the Radiodiffusion Nationale broadcasting van in attendance, as it was every year) I dealt with the problem of the Church's vocation in its relation to the State.

Sixty-seven pastors took part in the Assemblée du Désert, several of whom belonged to Churches other than the Reformed Church of France. I gathered them all around me, when the crowd was dispersing, in order to bring them up to date about the situation, to obtain exact news from them, and to consult them. Some of them had already taken Jews into their presbyteries or were hiding them in hamlets in their parishes. Such was the beginning of this ministry, which, until the liberation of France, enabled thousands of Jews, both French and foreign, to escape the searches of the French and German police and to find shelter in convents and Catholic presbyteries, in Protestant presbyteries or in humble farms belonging to the faithful of our parishes, until the day when they could finally regain their freedom.

Two days later, I saw Cardinal Gerlier again. He gave me details of his recent interventions with Vichy. We were anxious that the emotion aroused should be expressed exclusively in a Christian act. We had both, moreover, agreed to become honorary vice-presidents of the Amitiés chrétiennes run by Père Chailley and his friends: some time afterwards their premises were visited by the Gestapo, and the Cardinal and I came close to spending some awkward moments. Meanwhile, on the day on which I saw him, we decided that our main effort should be directed towards the children.

The next day I arrived in Vichy, and was immediately received by Pierre Laval. Through his private secretary I knew that he did not understand the reaction of the Churches. Disturbed at the turn events had taken, Jardin had wisely advised him to see Cardinal Gerlier and myself. As soon as I entered I reminded him of my visit in July 1940 in the course of which he had spoken to me about the Jews. From there I went straight on to what I had to say and wanted to say about the surrender of arrested Jews, the hunting out of Jews in hiding, the disregarding of the exceptions provided for, the handing over of men who had served in our army, the condemnation of the political offenders, and the position of the children.

He answered: 'I cannot act otherwise, and what I am doing is a prophylactic operation . . . I do not want a single foreign Jew to remain in France. Some countries take a high moral tone with me, but when I say to them, "All right – *you* take them", they back out of it . . . I am paying for the mistakes of others, of a government which allowed them in . . . they are Gaullists, operating on the black market; if there was trouble, you'd find them leading the gangs.'

I asked him some straight questions.

'Will you organize man-hunts?' – 'They will be searched out wherever they are hiding.' 'Will you allow us to save the children?' – 'The children must remain with their parents.' 'But you know perfectly well that they will be separated from them.' – 'No.' 'I tell you that they will be.' – 'What do you want to do with the children?' 'French families will adopt them.' – 'That I will not have. Not one must remain in France.'

Laval told me that he had given orders that everything should be done humanely. 'There have been some abominable incidents', I answered. 'See Bousquet: I do not know all the details of this business.'

I cannot reproduce the whole of our conversation. At the end I said to him, *'Monsieur le Président*, it is my duty to point out to you the gravity of the situation. The Churches cannot be silent in the face of such happenings.' 'The Churches? They have done plenty of the same sort of thing themselves. I said as much to the representative of the nunciature who came to see me. They can do as they please, I shall continue to do what I have to do.'

I left him, convinced that there was nothing to hope for in that quarter.

It was then that I went to see Tuck at the U.S. Embassy, a visit to which I have already referred.

Laval had told me to 'see Bousquet'. I lost no time in taking steps to meet him. He was in charge of the Police Department. I found him to be an intelligent man, who explained just what he was doing and why, and was ready to listen to what I had to say.

I can mention only a few points about that conversation. In the first place I asked him what was the reason for the measures taken in the unoccupied zone. 'In July, the Germans had decided to deport all French Jews to Poland, where they claim to be establishing a Jewish State! The trains were already standing by. It was a matter of urgency to counter this threat. In order to save the French Jews, Laval offered to hand over the foreign Jews sent to France at the end of 1940, whom he had no desire to keep, and other Jews with them, who had been expelled from Germany in 1941 and 1942.'

'Once the decision had been taken', Bousquet went on, 'it had to be implemented. Cases for exemption were allowed for.' 'Why was no notice taken of that?' I asked. 'People over sixty years of age, women eight months pregnant, war-wounded, and even Aryans have been sent.'

Bousquet denied these facts. 'Another thing', I said 'the methods used in carrying out the decision. Some vile things have been done.' This was met by a formal denial, followed by this reservation: 'Obviously an operation of this nature cannot be carried out in kid gloves, particularly when time is short.'

'What are you going to do about all the Jews hidden in the towns or in the country?' 'We shall search for them.' 'So it will be a man-hunt, with police dogs and all the rest?' 'We shall pick them up from their hiding-places. We have to search for them. The Germans know everything that goes on here. They know that we have to give them so many foreigners, that they have received only so many, and that the others are hidden in convents, and farms. Only yesterday night I had a battle with them to save some French Jews.'

On more than one occasion, Bousquet said to me, 'The role of public opinion is to get excited. The role of the Government is to choose. It is easy enough to criticize when you are not the person responsible. I would say as much to Cardinal Gerlier if he were here.'

We spoke about the children and the possibility of the parents relinquishing their parental rights in favour of private relief organizations. I then raised the grievous problem of the political refugees. 'You are handing over people condemned for political reasons', I said. 'I am familiar with everything that has happened in Castres; I forwarded to M. Romier the list of Germans who had been held there in solitary confinement. I spoke about it to your predecessor, M. Rivalland. And now all of them have been handed over, except four. You have sent these men to the gallows.' Bousquet looked at me, and after a silence, answered, '*Monsieur le Pasteur*, there are reasons of State. And then, at the last minute, there is a Frenchman's life to save. Every State has had to do the same, all nations at war have done the same.' 'That may be so', I answered, 'but it does not make it any the less abominable.'

He made one final remark, 'The Government's unpopularity today will be one of its finest claims to glory in the years to come.'

On the same day I saw Admiral Platon again. He was no longer Colonial Minister, and was concerned with Freemasons, Jews, and the family. It was a long time since I had unburdened my heart with such feeling. All that I had suffered in the last weeks came out in my words. I told him how shocked public opinion was and how the consciences of Christians were reacting. 'You ought to be proud, you a Huguenot, that this is the reaction of the Huguenot conscience to the terrible sights of which we are all witnesses.' 'I keep my pity for the prisoners. And what is more, France has to be purified of all that mob. I agree with you in principle, but the job has to be done. And all the Churches do is to increase the chaos; this is simply not the right time . . . the Churches are playing de Gaulle's game.'

I cannot describe the misery of the hours I spent that day. I left even more strongly convinced that in this night of terror and in face of this unbridled hate and violence, the Churches had the duty of continuing their policy of making their commitment felt.

The events of the following weeks may be briefly summarized. Cimade teams, of men and women, under the ever-tireless Madeleine Barot, young Pastor Morel, and others, spent their time guiding Jews hunted by the police along routes that were kept secret, to the Chamonix valley; from there they helped them to reach the Franco-Swiss frontier and, if possible, to cross it – carrying the few precious bundles they had salvaged with vast difficulty from the disaster. Morel was arrested, and imprisoned in Bonneville; at his trial, Pastor Eberhard, called as a witness to his good character, made a magnificent speech in his defence; the court was completely won over by the eloquence of the courageous pastor from Lyons, and Morel was acquitted. In this way many Jews escaped being sent to the death-camps. Their arrival on Swiss soil was not always without its share of bitterness for them.

I found it necessary at this time to go to Berne and see the Swiss Police authorities. The Swiss policy towards these unfortunate Jews asking for asylum was still undecided, and at times contradictory. The reasons for this may perhaps be deduced from the singularly disturbing pages of the book which came out in 1966 under the catchy title *La guerre a été gagnée en Suisse* (*The War was Won in Switzerland*). However that may be, I was anxious to come to an understanding with the Swiss authorities, and, thanks to Alphonse Koechlin, my valued colleague on the World Council, I was received by M. von Steiger, head of the Confederation's department of Police and Justice. With his colleagues, we had a real conference on the refugee problem. I learnt that Switzerland had officially closed its frontiers. Refusal of entry was formally ordered. Nevertheless allowance was made for numerous exceptions. During those last weeks only 2,500 Jews had entered the country. What had happened to the thousands of others whose hopes had died when they met the barbed-wire of the frontier?

I discussed with the Swiss Red Cross the possibility of the acceptance, thanks to the understanding of Colonel Reymond, of five hundred children. And the next day, to my great satisfaction, M. Rothmund, chief of police for aliens, drew up with me a procedure that allowed the entry into Switzerland, in spite of the official closure of the frontier, of political refugees and of persons sponsored by representatives of Catholic, Protestant and Jewish relief organizations. We estimated the number at eighty: but I am sure that that eighty became several hundreds. Henriod was appointed as our representative, and discharged his responsibility with intelligence and skill.

Have I, perhaps, devoted too much space to this aspect of our work during those grim years? I believe that, compressed though they are, these sad stories show with what a concern for fidelity to the demands of the Gospel, with what a consciousness of their vocation and with what an ecumenical vision the Churches humbly endeavoured to unite in bearing witness to their Lord, Jesus Christ. They had faith in the power of prayer and in the sovereign work of God's grace.

CHAPTER 13

Return to Paris and the Liberation
1942-1944

I. Visits to Geneva and ecumenical work in France. II.
Return to Paris. Meetings with Dr Reichl. Deportation of
pastors. III. The liberation of Paris. Death of William
Temple, Archbishop of Canterbury and President of the
World Council of Churches.

I

WE have just seen how during the years of war, of the Vichy
régime and the occupation, the Protestant Churches of France
faced situations of extreme difficulty. They did not withdraw
into themselves, concerned only with their own spiritual and
material life, but made plain their presence in the life of the nation,
taking a world-wide view of their fidelity to their vocation as
Christian Churches. My own ecumenical work, as already described, was always carried out in agreement with the Councils
whose spokesman I had the honour of being. There were, however, other aspects of it, and it is of these that I now propose to
speak.

The Radio, the censorship (often annoying and ridiculous),
the Chantiers de Jeunesse (work and agricultural camps for young
people), the chaplains, the prisoners in Germany, and the distressing business of the *Relève* (forced labour for Germany) which,
starting in 1942, was a dreadful blow to the spiritual and material
life of our parishes – all these, not to mention my journeys, my
visits to other Churches and to regional synods, and the preparations for the National Synods in Alès (1941) and Valence (1942),
brought me endless anxieties, and demanded a great deal of
thought and hard work. All this, however, lies outside the scope
of this book, and I shall not write of it now.

From the very beginning of my stay in the unoccupied zone, I
had recognized my duty to carry out, so far as possible, my work

as chairman of the administrative committee of the World
Council. My first visit to Geneva, in 1940, was a way of meeting
this obligation. It was, however, essential to maintain uninterrupted contact. Until the moving in of the German army and
the Gestapo meant the complete closing of the frontier, I made
several journeys to Switzerland; and these enabled me to keep in
touch with the Churches whose unfailing generosity to us needed
exact information on which to work. They gave me the opportunity, too, to discuss things at length with Visser 't Hooft and
his colleagues, and with others who came to Geneva to help us
in getting ready for the work the 'provisional' Council would
have to do as soon as hostilities were ended.

The small house in the Avenue de Champel had become too
cramped for the new services. The research section was continuing the vast enquiry ordered at Saint-Germain-en-Laye in
February 1939: numerous works had appeared under its sponsorship during the war, such as William Paton's *The Church and
the New Order*. Staff and offices, however, were needed for
the Committee for Refugees, and then for the sections and
committees which dealt with the spiritual well-being of prisoners of war, and with international church reconstruction and
assistance; but it was not until 1945 that the general secretariat
and all the Councils' services moved into the Malagnou road,
where, later, huts and a second house made it possible for the
next fifteen years to carry out a task which of its nature inevitably became continually more demanding, both in scope and
intensity.

News used to arrive in Geneva, brought from Germany,
Scandinavia and the Netherlands by brave men and women who
did not shrink from taking great risks. On several occasions one
such messenger came to see me in Nîmes. From Geneva, moreover, we could correspond with William Temple, Bell, Oldham
and our friends in America. These last soon felt the necessity of
personal contact. They sent to Geneva one of their best qualified
ecumenical workers, Dr Sam McCrea. At that time Cavert
was general secretary of the Federal Council of the Churches of
Christ, and was therefore familiar with the problems concerned
with closer relations between the Churches and Christian unity.
The two days we spent with him in Geneva – Visser 't Hooft,

his colleagues, Koechlin and I – were extremely useful in assisting the Churches of America and Europe to reach a mutual under-standing. We were able to tell him all about the immense damage already caused by the war, of the efforts that would be required to put the Churches back on their feet on the material plane, but still more in the domain of theology and spirituality. Visser 't Hooft and Schönfeld gave him the most reliable news about the Confessing Church in Germany, and of the resistance of the Churches in Holland, which enabled him to see from within how the Churches of our various nations were living, suffering, and bearing their witness. Needless to say, I, too, did my best to do the same for our Churches of France. Through Cavert, again, we obtained a picture of an evangelical American Christianity united in a common determination to come to our help in concerted practical action. Cavert, when back in the U.S.A., most effectively laid the foundations of the generous combined effort made by the Churches of his country, from which the first to benefit were the Churches of France, the Netherlands and Belgium.

The future of the World Council of Churches 'in process of formation' was also one of our principal topics of discussion. Cavert was a great help to us in considering the question that was always in our minds, of what steps we should take with a view to the future.

Visser 't Hooft's journey to England in 1942 was also the occasion of some valuable contacts. Both going and returning, he stopped in Nîmes, where we spent many hours in exchanging views, receiving news from one another and sharing our ecu-menical cares. We had visits, too, from Adolf Keller, Henriod and Charles Guillon. In November the invasion of unoccupied France by the German army put an end to these possibilities of keeping in touch, of meetings in the Avenue de Champel and conferences with representatives of the Swiss Churches. For-tunately there were other, and less public, ways open to us.

In those parts of France to which I then had access, I never missed an opportunity of speaking about the ecumenical move-ment at meetings of pastors and at regional synods. At the National Synods in Alès (1941) and Valence (1942) I emphasized the duty of the Churches of France to remain in close contact with the World Council, the importance the Council attached to their presence, and the authority they enjoyed in it.

By means of talks I gave in town and country parishes, I tried to start the ecumenical education of the Protestants of the southern zone. Were they, I wonder, more influenced by my explanations than they seem to be today?

For a number of reasons, contacts with the representatives of the Catholic Church became more frequent in those sad years, franker too, and more cordial. I need not refer again to the relationship which grew up between Cardinal Gerlier and myself. It proved, I believe, really effective. Our agreement on the problems of youth, education and refugees enabled us, in difficult circumstances, to demonstrate the coincidence of views of the two faiths. There were times when the intimate intellectual sympathy which the Archbishop of Lyons and I could each rely on finding in the other added even more persuasive force to the presence of the Church of Christ.

I have retained a lasting memory of a visit I paid to Cardinal Saliège, Archbishop of Toulouse. He could hardly manage to produce more than a few hoarse sounds, occasional syllables of which I could distinguish: but what a courageous Christian he was! His pastoral letters, with their short, incisive sentences, brought him a load of trouble; but reproaches or threats could never intimidate him.

It may well be that it was two articles which Pierre Brisson asked me for, which, in 1941 and 1942, won me the confidence of many Catholics. The first, on 'The Responsibility of the Churches', came out in December 1941; the second, on 'The Great Problem of the Twentieth Century', brought me a voluminous correspondence and, wherever I went, I found people who wished to discuss it with me. But another article brought more positive repercussions.

I had made the acquaintance of the Abbé Couturier, the saintly priest of the Lyons diocese, who had suddenly emerged from the obscurity in which he lived to become the apostle of prayer for Christian unity. His influence was constantly making itself felt in new circles. As the time approached for the week of prayer for unity in January 1942, he suggested to me that I should write an article on ecumenism, to appear in *Le Figaro*, in the column next to the one in which would be printed a piece of his own inspired by the same event. I immediately agreed. There was, however, some difficulty in obtaining what he wanted. Later, he told me that he had had to go right back to Rome to obtain permission for our two names to appear side by side on the front page of a newspaper. The time was not yet ripe for Vatican 2.

Although I was not concerned with it myself, I cannot refrain from mentioning the splendid enterprise of Mgr Théas, at that time Bishop of Montauban, who was one of the great bishops of the Resistance. For several years in succession, during the period in question, he held meetings in bishop's house for the parish priests of his diocese and the pastors of Tarn-et-Garonne, where a doctrinal question would be studied in common. Mgr Bruno de Solages, Rector of the Catholic faculties of Toulouse, expounded the Catholic doctrine on the basis of a statement of the Catholic faith; Pastor Hébert Roux, later to be an observer at the Council, who came by a more or less secret route from Bordeaux, explained the Reformed doctrine. A discussion followed over coffee – which was not actually coffee. This ecumenical work of Mgr Théas contributed to a closer relationship, cordial and even fraternal, between priests and pastors.

II

I may well say that during this time my life was overburdened with responsibilities, with representations to be made, with journeys, sermons and lectures, with visits to be made or visitors to be received, and sometimes, too, with serious personal anxieties. And while it was opening out into ever wider fields of ecumenical work, I little thought that our exile, for whose end I had so often hoped, was drawing to a close, and that in a few weeks' time we should have the joy of being home in our parish. It was in Vichy that I learnt this.

On 19 February 1943 I called on M. Bousquet, the head of the Police Department, for a meeting with whom I had made an urgent request, in order to discuss the arrest of Pastors Trocmé and Theis, the seizure of the Quakers' possessions and of the Y.M.C.A. (which was on the point of being decided) and the blow that had just fallen on the Salvation Army. I was about to leave Bousquet when he told me that the demarcation line would be abolished on 1 March, and that, if my ministry required it, I would be free to travel from Marseilles to Lille.

My delight, which I shared some hours later with my wife when I joined her in Chambéry, was beyond words. We lost no time in taking the necessary steps for our departure. I arranged with Pierre Maury,[1] who had come to Nîmes on 22 February to bless the marriage of his elder son, that on 7 March I would preach in Paris. The days that followed went like a flash – they were occupied by the session of the National Council of the Reformed Church, meeting in Nîmes for the last time, and by the conference of Protestant youth-camp leaders held in Valence. We promised several dear friends that we would return before the end of March to say good-bye to them. As we set off for Paris, I experienced one of the most profound emotions of my life. I have no words to describe what I felt when we arrived, and met our dear children and grandchildren, and held our first service in our church in Passy. There are some moments of such grandeur that one can speak of them only to God. And in any case those hours we lived then do not belong to my ecumenical life or work.

The next day, the Council of the Protestant Federation asked me to seek an interview with Pierre Laval, in order to reach, if possible, a solution to the sensitive problems connected with the Quakers, the Salvation Army, and the Y.M.C.A., and to discuss the forced labour contingents and a new law proposed for the Jews.

When he received me the next day, I opened by raising the question of the Salvation Army.[2] Laval told me that M. Pichat, deputy Prime Minister and head of social welfare, had already been to discuss it with him. The matter had been pending for some weeks. Admiral Platon had proposed to the Cabinet that the Salvation Army should be dissolved as an 'English organization in France and a centre of de Gaullism', and its property handed over to the social welfare funds. The wearing of the uniform and the holding of public meetings were already forbidden by the occupation forces. On hearing this, I had written to Platon;

1. At that time in sole charge as minister of the church of the Annunciation.
2. As early as 1938 the Salvation Army had been included in the World Council 'in process of formation'.

his answer, the tone of which was unusual for him, had brought a letter from me which put an end to our relationship. The heads of the Salvation Army had been to see me in Nîmes, and Bertrand had made strong representations in Paris. Nevertheless, the solution was still delayed and great anxiety was felt.

Pierre Laval, after listening to me politely, immediately decided to place the Salvation Army under the care of the Association of Deaconesses in the Rue de Reuilly. It was a strange solution at first sight, but one that M. Pichat, informed of it by the Baron de Neuflize, had welcomed as satisfactory. Accordingly I was assured that the Association of Deaconesses, whose president was Georges Lauga, would be authorized to administer the property of the Salvation Army and look after its work, and I was asked to deliver urgently to Vichy a note about the Association of Deaconesses drafted the same day by Lauga and Christian Monnier.

The conversation turned to other matters. Here I shall simply note that Laval told me emphatically that he had no intention of adding to the severity of the anti-Jewish legislation, which he was being urged to do by the extraordinary personality at the head of the Commission for Jewish Affairs.

Anxious to establish with the Catholic hierarchy of Paris relations as cordial as those I had enjoyed in the southern zone, I went to see Cardinal Suhard. This first meeting came up to my hopes. Fragile in appearance, and with a keen intelligence, the Cardinal had a reputation for sanctity. All the questions I used to discuss with Cardinal Gerlier were examined in the same atmosphere of Christian fellowship. Some months later, when the question of civilian workers transported to Germany had become one of extreme gravity, I suggested to him that we should make a joint approach to Pierre Laval. He did not agree that this would be opportune, but made the counter-suggestion that each of us should ask for an interview on the same day and that we should agree on the nature of our protest. I shall shortly be recording its result.

On various occasions we were thus in contact with one another, and always in a spiritual atmosphere. I was surprised that in June 1944 he agreed to conduct the funeral service for Philippe Henriot in Notre-Dame. He suffered for this, and unjustly,

I think, when the liberation came. In spite of the attacks of some extremist Catholic resisters, he remained unmoved in his post of Archbishop of Paris. His unexpected death moved us deeply.

One of my first duties, as president of the National Council of the Reformed Church, was to visit the parts of the country from which I had been cut off for three years. It was, indeed, poignant once again to see, though often now in ruins, our town or country parishes and to meet their pastors, their presbyteral and regional councils, and to talk at length with such men as Babut, Namblard or Bouvier, whose authority was recognized by all.

I took advantage of these journeys to spread news about the ecumenical movement in public lectures and private meetings. In the Latin quarter of Paris, which had a truly sinister appearance at night, I had the satisfaction of meeting the Christian students again, still faithful to their ecumenical vocation.

It was at this time that Wilfred Monod died, one of the great figures of French Protestantism, one of the most contagiously influential and evangelical of Christians – in spite of what were called his heresies – and also one of the most ecumenical men of his generation. On terms of intimate friendship with Soederblom, Bell and Deissmann, he had played at Stockholm the leading part which I have described, and, until 1936, he had had a considerable share in the activities of the Faith and Work movement. Shortly before the end, I had seen him in his sickroom at the House of Deaconesses, and I treasure this picture of the prophet ready to go home to his God. How sorry I was that at his funeral service, since he had asked that nothing should be said about him personally, instead of reading long passages from his works, they did not simply give us the Gospel of the Resurrection.

Some days later, the National Synod of the Reformed Church was held in Paris. Pastors and layfolk representing all our ecclesiastical regions except Algeria were able to take part. I mention this meeting because it was marked by the ordination to the ministry of ten evangelists, and so the problem involved therein of authority in the Reformed Church was for the first time unequivocally raised.

I cannot pass over in silence an event which took place at this same time and had unexpected consequences for our Churches and for myself.

An important German official, behind whom could be discerned the power of the Gestapo, Dr Reichl, had been installed in Paris, his assignment being to keep an eye on the religious authorities and in the first place to establish contact with them. As soon as he learnt that I was back in Paris, he expressed a wish to call on me, and sent me a message to that effect through a neutral friend, a doctor, who had been called in to treat him. I had no reason not to agree to his request, and arranged a meeting in my office at the Federation, on 26 May 1943. As soon as he sat down, he said to me, 'I wanted to meet you, because I have heard a great deal about you'. 'Good or bad?' I asked. '*Gut und schlecht!* A person like you cannot escape criticism.' He told me that in Germany I was regarded as a 'radical democrat'. When I asked him what place democracy held in a totalitarian state, he confided to me that the metaphysics of National Socialism had not yet been worked out, and that a 'spiritual' concordat between it and Christianity was not ruled out. I retorted that there must inevitably be conflict between the Christian Churches and a totalitarian state, in the first place because the Christian teaching about man, society and the family is diametrically opposed to the National Socialist concept, and secondly because Christianity is totalitarian.

He told me that he would like to see me again in order to discuss the ecumenical movement. Before arranging another meeting, I informed him of our grave anxiety at the arrest by the Gestapo of four of our pastors. He promised to enquire into the matter, in particular into the case of Charles Roux, arrested in Marseilles.

Roland de Pury and Schwendener were arrested in Lyons some days later. The news had hardly reached us, when I had another visit from Dr Reichl. Before raising any other matter, I protested vigorously against the arrest of my colleagues, particularly that of Pastor Roland de Pury, who had been 'picked up' in his church, just as, already vested, he was about to confirm his catechumens. To this Reichl answered, 'Cardinal Suhard has protested to me on several occasions about the arrests of priests. Each time I have made enquiries at the Gestapo, and each time the arrest has been justified.' 'It may be', I told him, 'that the arrest is "justified" in your eyes; but I am protesting against the *how*, the *where* and the *when* of the arrest.'

He asked me to explain to him the aims of the ecumenical movement. I tried to make him understand its purely religious origins and its world-wide development. Then came the question I was expecting: 'Would not your contacts and your sources of information enable you to keep me posted about the attitude in religious circles, particularly in Great Britain and the U.S.A., to Bolshevism, peace and international reconciliation?'

My answer was, 'I have no information about what is going on at this moment in those countries. And as it has been impossible for me, since November, to go to Switzerland, I no longer see my colleagues on the World Council who used to keep me in touch.' A further suggestion made me sit up: 'If you wish to go to Switzerland to discuss Bolshevism and peace, the technical difficulties you are meeting at present would soon be got round.' 'Yes', I thought, 'but I should have sold my honour.' Reichl left me, his offer rejected.

I was doubtful of the effectiveness, and even of the reality, of an intervention with the Gestapo on the part of Dr Reichl, in the matter of the pastors they had arrested. I accordingly decided to go to the Avenue Foch, the headquarters of Hitler's political police. There I was received by one of the heads. I requested the release of Charles Roux and of the pastor of Morlaix, both of whom I knew had arrived in Compiègne, and in the first place authorization to visit them. I was told in reply that a section to deal with religious bodies had just been set up, and that I would be able to see the head of it on the Monday following. I accordingly went back later to that sinister corner in the Avenue Foch, and insisted that Charles Roux, who was in an extremely delicate state of health, should be released, and that in any case I should be allowed to see him in Compiègne. Alas, I very soon heard from the head of the S.S. that I could not be authorized to speak with Roux, who in any case had already left for Germany when I received the refusal.[3]

We soon heard of a new arrest. Juteau, former national commissioner of the *Éclaireurs unionistes* (scouts), who had recently

3. 29 January 1944.

been appointed director of the Institut de Glay, was thought to have been involved in an affair of which he was completely innocent. I thought it my duty to make immediate application to Dr Reichl.[4] He accepted a note I had prepared for him and promised to make enquiries first thing in the morning at the military headquarters and the Gestapo. He maintained that he had been extremely busy during the preceding week, on the occasion of the meeting of cardinals and archbishops, and that he had met some emiment church dignitaries at agreeable luncheon parties.

A further and more insistent personal application a fortnight later brought no result.[5] The next day we heard of the arrest of Yann Roulet, pastor of Mougon. This was on 10 March. On the 15th, while the National Synod was sitting in the Chapelle du Luxembourg, I was told that Dr Reichl wanted me urgently at the Grand Hotel. Thinking that I was going at last to receive an answer to my applications, I immediately went round. What I heard quite astonished me. Reichl asked me 'officially, on behalf of Berlin', whether the National Synod could not issue 'a statement on bombing and terrorism' similar to that which had just been published by the cardinals and archbishops, and which, to believe Reichl, it had taken him six months to obtain. 'It would make an enormous impression if a similar statement were issued from your side.'

Noting his request, I pointed out to him that the Reformed Church, to which I would lose no time in reporting it, would hold that only the Council of the Protestant Federation was qualified to do what he asked. 'But surely you, as president of the Federation, can issue the statement?' 'I am not in the habit of making personal statements', I answered, 'nor have I the right to do so; I can speak only when authorized by the Council and in complete agreement with it.' 'And when will the Council be meeting?' 'Shortly', I replied. 'You understand, Monsieur le Pasteur', he said, 'that in this matter there is less difficulty with the Catholics. If it were the same on your side, we might come to the gentleman's agreement[6] we were considering the

4. 23 February 1944.   5. 9 March 1944.
6. In English. Reichl was referring to his agreement with the Cardinal of which he had spoken to me on 9 March.

other day. And *then we would be able to talk about the arrest of the pastors.*'[7]

I need hardly say that after thinking it over the Council of the Federation decided to answer Dr Reichl by a blunt refusal.

The wording of the Council's resolution, drafted and signed by me, annoyed Reichl immensely. He had the effrontery to maintain that he had spoken to me only in a private capacity, and called on the Council to withdraw its resolution. A fresh refusal on our part had the unhappy consequence that the matter of the deported pastors could no longer be raised between Reichl and me. On two or three occasions he asked me for an appointment, and though I agreed to meet him, he never came. I learnt that after leaving Paris hurriedly during the night of 16-17 August, he stopped in Strasbourg, and had told a Lutheran pastor that his only regret was that he had not had me arrested.

III

Meanwhile the war was still being fought on all fronts. Beaten in Russia and North Africa, Germany was hoping to be able to withstand any Allied landing in France until the secret weapon which her scientists were working on with feverish energy was at last perfected. On the morning of 6 June the foreign radios told us of the tremendous happenings in Normandy. From that moment it was as though we lived in a state of suspended animation. I shall not describe the months that followed. Contrary to our fears, there was no taking of hostages at that time. Later, from telegrams sent in June 1943 by the German ambassador to Ribbentrop and found in the archives of the Wilhelmstrasse, I learnt that I had been included in a list of hostages to be arrested in the event of an Allied landing.[8]

The days that preceded the liberation of Paris beggar description. We lived those days with an intensity, an ardour, an impatience and a gratitude whose thrill has never left us. How could the Churches fail to urge their faithful to join together in order to offer thanks for their liberation? On 27 August, just as I was going to the Oratoire to take part in the service conducted by Bertrand, I was told that William Temple was addressing a

7. My italics.   8. See Appendix 9.

message to French Protestants on the B.B.C. I can hardly describe the emotion with which I listened to him: by the kindness of the French radio service, I was able to thank him immediately. In the Oratoire, after an admirable address by Bertrand, I passed on to the crowds crammed into the church the message, instinct with fraternal affection, which Temple had just sent them.

Nevertheless, our joy was not unalloyed. All over France, the execution of collaborators, and often the settling of personal accounts, were proof that violence and hatred had been let loose. Pierre Brisson was again insistent that I should let him have some articles. I had just written one about William Temple. Without delay, I wrote another which I called 'The Aftermath of the Te Deum' ('Lendemains de Te Deum'); Brisson preferred to give it the title 'Against Violence and Hatred' ('Contre la violence et la haine').[9] While this article brought me some warm congratulations, it also aroused violent criticisms. My views were distorted by any number of leader writers, one of whom accused me of urging a policy of 'kiss and be friends'.

It was apparent that it would soon be possible to resume ecumenical contacts. Temple, who during the war had been elevated to the see of Canterbury, after the resignation of my old friend Cosmo Lang, wrote to invite my wife and me to spend a few days at the end of October in Canterbury: an invitation that was eagerly accepted and warmed our hearts.

On 5 October Visser 't Hooft arrived in Paris. We spent many hours that evening and the next day in discussing the urgent problems raised by recent events for the leaders of the ecumenical movement. He wished to be in London at the same period as we would be there; and we lost no time in telling Temple that we all approved this plan.

On the morning of 27 October a telephone call brought me the news of the sudden death of the Archbishop of Canterbury. I was utterly crushed by the mystery of this passing, which robbed us of the leader who was not only essential to us, we thought, but irreplaceable. I could not stop thinking of the dear friend whom God had taken back from us, of 't Hooft, who was shattered by this blow, and of our common task which still had to go on without him.

9. 31 August 1944.

The next day I was told by the British Embassy that the British Government was agreeable to my attending the Archbishop's funeral. My departure was arranged for the afternoon of 29 October. At 18.15 hours, after an easy flight in a Douglas, I arrived in Croydon, where I was met by the Revd Mr Williams, from the Ministry of Information.

CHAPTER 14

London, New York, Geneva
1944-1946

I. Ecumenical meetings in London October 1944. II.
Discussions in Geneva. III. Visit to the U.S.A. May-June
1945. IV. The Stuttgart Declaration October 1945 and
the Geneva World Council February 1946.

I

THE death of William Temple, so shocking in its suddenness,
launched me without warning into the full flood of ecumenical
work. During the next six years it was always to demand a
considerable part of each day's working hours. Meanwhile, it was
in London, whither I had been summoned by the grievous blow
to the World Council, that I obtained a new outlook on this
domain of my life.

This return to London, in the poignant setting of the war and
the death of Temple, was profoundly moving. Before the Revd
Mr Williams dropped me at the hotel in which my room had been
booked, he took me through some of the most severely bombed
areas. What ruins! And what courage and what heroic patience,
what confidence in ultimate victory had been displayed and was
still being displayed under the assault of the V1's and the V2's by
the population of this huge city! Seeing St Paul's, severely hit but
still standing, brought back to my mind the ecumenical service
conducted by Cosmo Lang in 1937; I was about to meet the
former primate again at the funeral of the much younger man in
whose favour he had retired.

I learnt from Williams, to my dismay, that the meetings
planned by Temple, 't Hooft and myself, instead of being brought
forward as I had hoped, would not be beginning until Sunday,
5 November. My visit would accordingly have to be extended
until at least the 10th. Although so long an absence from Paris,
in such uncertain and anxious days, seemed impossible to me, I
had no alternative but to agree.

There was a large gathering at the funeral service of William Temple, which was conducted in Canterbury Cathedral. It was pelting with rain all the time. Archbishop Garbett of York, Bishop Fisher of London and Dr Hewlett Johnson, the well-known Dean of Canterbury – the 'Red Dean' as he was later known – went up to the altar in their brilliantly coloured copes. Everything was a proclamation of the glory of the Resurrection. Could not, I thought, an address, however short, have perhaps been introduced into the middle of the liturgical service, to bring home to us the message of Easter and the triumphant life of the world to come?

In the sad gathering at the house of Mrs Temple, an unaffectedly charming and welcoming woman, I met again many dear friends: the Bishop of Chichester and Mrs Bell, Archbishop Germanos, Visser 't Hooft, Dr Flew, J. H. Oldham and many others. Deeply grieved as we were, we shared with one another our grave anxieties about the future of the World Council, which now seemed to us to have been sadly mutilated. The sudden death, not long before, of William Paton, the associate secretary in London, had already been a severe blow, involving a loss which it would be difficult for us to make good. How were we to organize things, carry on with our researches and work in such a way that the 'institution', on which the war had forced so many accretions, would not be swamped by the 'event'? The days still available before our official meetings lent themselves to numerous 'private' conversations, which helped us to envisage the situation more clearly.

On the day after the funeral service in Canterbury, I attended a meeting of the House of Lords in which a number of tributes to Temple were paid by the leaders of the parties in the House, the Archbishop of York and Cosmo Lang. Everything that was said was both worthy of the dead man and true. Immediately afterwards Lang took me into the Archbishop's room where we had a long talk. He was greatly concerned about Temple's successor. His own preference was for the Bishop of London, Dr Fisher. He believed that he possessed better judgment than Temple, in whom he saw primarily a prophet. As did many others, he told me that Bell's speeches in the Lords condemning the Royal Air Force bombing of German civilians had ruled out the possibility of his appointment to Canterbury. Public opinion at that time was indeed hard on the intrepid Bishop of Chichester.

The meeting of the 'provisional' Committee of the World Council was fixed for 6 November. On the 4th, Bell, 't Hooft and I met in the austere Athenaeum Club, in order to make our preparations for it as carefully as possible. The presence of the American Bishop Oldham of Albany, 't Hooft, Ehrenström and me, gave the meeting an international character which ensured in advance that its proposals would be authoritative.

On Sunday the 5th, I had the joy of taking part in the service in the French church in Soho Square, which had become a sort of Protestant annexe of Free France. After an 'all-French' luncheon, at which I was bombarded with questions about our Churches, their pastors, our work, and the situation in France, I was driven to Kew Gardens, where Lang had retired to a royal 'grace and favour' cottage. There he was living in the midst of the floral beauties of the gardens, walking every day in fragrant avenues, thinking nostalgically of his beloved gardens in York and Lambeth.

I had heard a great deal since my arrival about the 'empty pews' in the English churches. The Archbishop told me in this connection that he had been struck by a strong reaction 'against the mistakes, the premature innovations and the over-hasty changes introduced by the Anglo-Catholics'. He himself fels great sympathy with them, while retaining serious reservationt about a closer approach to the Catholic Church. 'So long as it is a question of Rome', he said, 'I am a Protestant. But when I plunge into the great Christian tradition, I am a Catholic.'

To take the chair, in English, during the long meetings of the 'provisional' Committee was an exhausting ordeal. We got through some solid and useful work, I believe. Oliver Tomkins was appointed assistant general secretary, centred on London. It proved an excellent choice, and was to lead to Tomkins's becoming secretary and later chairman of Faith and Order, and to the episcopate, of which he is one of the most distinguished representatives.

Further meetings were planned. We were all agreed that it was essential that as soon as possible 't Hooft and I should visit the loyal supporters of the ecumenical movement in the United

States and Canada, and in a more general way the Churches of America. Shortly afterwards it was decided, in answer to American requests, that Bishop Bell, 't Hooft and I should accept their invitation for the month of May 1945.

Again and again during those days I was asked to explain the situation of French Protestantism after four years of a war that was still not finished, and of an occupation that was still effective in the eastern part of France. The Committee for the Reconstruction of the Churches of Europe, Press representatives, the Anglo-French Fellowship, the ministers of the Free Churches and other religious organizations, gave me the opportunity to dispel many misconceptions, to clear up points of obscurity, and to make plain the attitude of our Churches to racial persecutions. This did much to strengthen the links between the Churches of Great Britain and our own.

I was back in Paris on 10 November, shortly before the arrival of Winston Churchill, who, far from being hissed as he feared, was wildly cheered by a vast crowd. I saw him walking on foot down the Champs Élysées with General de Gaulle in the middle of an enthusiastic mob shouting out their gratitude to each of the two leaders. We were all in tears of emotion and joy.

Visser 't Hooft spared us two days on his return from London. We drew up together the programme for a forthcoming ecumenical meeting in Geneva, and reached final agreement about the date of our visit to the U.S.A.

Nevertheless, France was not yet clear of her troubles; there was still an evil spirit abroad in the most diverse and most antagonistic circles. The tide of violence, against which I had written on 31 August, was not yet on the ebb. I went to Pierre Brisson to suggest an article entitled 'The Truth Must be Told' ('Silence Impossible'). He at once fell in with my idea. I wrote my article immediately and it came out two days later (30 November 1944). In the days that followed many readers thanked me for having spoken out, but at the same time I received some violent criticisms. For several weeks I continued to get letters from which I was able better to understand the true state of public opinion.

Demanding though my ecumenical duties were during these last weeks of 1944, they were only the smaller part of my daily work. The Protestant Federation, the Reformed Church and its relations with the 'dissident' Churches, my rounds of visits and sermons in the country, the Society of Missions, numerous committees (among others, the committee concerned with general interests of French Protestantism,[1] which I was trying to re-vitalize), serious problems in the pastorate, and parochial questions, engrossed a great deal of my time. Every morning I was available in my office in the Rue de Clichy; it was icy cold, and visitors from the country were often astonished to see us working in such conditions.

And quite apart from all that there were the domestic cares with which so many French people were familiar at that time.

It was thus that we moved from 1944 into 1945. General de Gaulle invited the Archbishop of Paris, the Chief Rabbi of France and myself to visit him on 1 January. He was just back from Moscow, where he had signed a treaty of alliance with Russia. We each saw him alone. From our conversation I remember his conviction that it would be long months before the war was over. Our grave fears for Strasbourg were gradually allayed. For some time, the rejoicings at its liberation had given place, unhappily, to cruel anxiety.

Visits of quite another sort, which I made on Sunday afternoons to the Prefecture of Police, and to the Conciergerie prison, to which I was accredited as a chaplain, were a weekly source of spiritual contacts. I started by conducting a service for the women, whose numbers were increasing week by week; then I saw the men, among whom were many Parisian police superintendents and policemen whom their communist colleagues had imprisoned in the depot as soon as they thought victory was certain. What was my surprise when, hearing a voice calling me from some dim cell, I found myself face to face with one or other of Marshal Pétain's former Ministers.

II

On 18 January I left in Jean Weidner's car for Lyons and Geneva. Weidner had been one of the daring secret messengers who crossed the lines in spite of great difficulties and kept alive the ecumenical communion of the Churches of the nations who were at war or shut up in their neutrality.

1. The Comité des intérêts généraux du Protestantisme français.

In the crowded programme I had to get through in Geneva and Lausanne, the most important items were the meetings of the administrative committee, the Reconstruction Department and the Swiss reconstruction committee. It was sad to find Adolf Keller unwell, but he was still full of confidence. There was a great deal of work to be done, calling for much care and tact. We decided that it was essential that before going to New York 't Hooft and I should stop in London to arrange matters with our British friends.

Driving back through snow-bound roads, we were several times held up. I can see us now, trying to get the wheels to grip and pushing the car up difficult gradients, such as the Rochepot.

A load of work was waiting for me in Paris. Councils were followed by committees, committees followed by visits and big evangelical meetings in the Salle Wagram and Salle Pleyel; in spite of the admirable assistance of Mme Joseph, the correspondence was more and more difficult to deal with. And the preparation of a sixteenth series of Lenten sermons added a further task which was made no easier by having already done it so often.

On 15 February a cable from Henry Leiper, our secretary in New York, brought my wife an invitation from the World Council of the U.S.A. to accompany me on my coming journey. I was as delighted as I was relieved. Her perfect knowledge of English made her better equipped than anyone to make the Christian women of America understand the hardships of so many of our presbyteries in the aftermath of the occupation; and the presence of a Christian French woman, the wife of a pastor, could not but be a reinforcement to our delegation.

In the midst of all this, I was invited by a Catholic family in Paris to an interdenominational meeting in connection with the starting of an organization called *Ad Lucem*, whose founder, the Abbé Prévost, was anxious to work for ecumenism. Cardinal Liénart, Bishop of Lille, was to be in the chair.

When the time came, he was the centre of a large gathering of well-known Catholics, Orthodox and Protestants. The Abbé Prévost's ecumenism seemed to me extremely vague. Cardinal Liénart was amiable and cautious, leaving it to Rome to make the decision about a plan which he seemed ready to sponsor. 'The

Pope', he said in conclusion, 'is the instrument of the Holy Spirit.'

I had a conversation with him on my own. He thought that even before starting doctrinal discussions in private meetings of theologians, we should continue to develop a favourable atmosphere by making the faithful feel the painfulness of the divisions of the Church, and pray for unity.

This reminded me of what a prince of the Church once said to me, 'You are closer to us than the freethinkers.' What a different world we live in today!

The ecumenical life continued to develop. On 10 March, Bishop Bell of Chichester arrived in Paris, delegated by the new Archbishop of Canterbury to visit the Protestant Churches of France. We were overjoyed to welcome him in our home, more than four years after Mrs Bell and he had welcomed us in theirs. He preached in Passy on the Sunday 11 March, and on the same day in the Anglican church in the Rue d'Aguesseau. Several meetings gave him an opportunity of talking with the Parisian pastors. It was a great essay in ecumenical education, made particularly fruitful by his infectious serenity and his great knowledge of the Churches. We were able to have a really heart-to-heart discussion of the interests we shared, including our forthcoming journey. Although vice-president of the administrative committee, Bell had never yet been able to be present at our meetings in Geneva. Since the London meetings he had been closely associated with our work. Already I could foresee in him the man who would one day inherit the responsibility of piloting the World Council of Churches through the reefs it would be bound to encounter.

The date of our departure was approaching, and difficulties appearing in various quarters were causing us grave anxiety. Should we, or could we, travel by the Dakar-Trinidad-Puerto Rico route? Could we hope for a priority passage? Would I perhaps be obliged to make this long journey on my own?

It was only in London that all these questions could be answered, and we accordingly decided, come what may, to go to London, where meetings were planned for 23-30 April. During the preceding days the return of many deportees had united us with our whole people in an ecstasy of joy. We had received into our home our dear friend Pastor Tirel and his wife.

On Sunday 22 April we left Paris for England. The week we spent in London from 23 to 30 April was fully occupied with ecumenical meetings, visits, dealings with the security services, the police and our embassy. We were still, after all, at war! Finally we obtained the 'priority', without which we could not travel, on the clipper flying-boat from Shannon to New York by the southern route – Dakar, Latin America and the Bermudas.

The British Council of Churches – corresponding in Britain to the Protestant Federation of France – gave me a cordial welcome and was good enough to invite me to take part in its discussions. I was impressed by its determination not to reopen relations with the Churches of Germany until the latter had completely dissociated themselves from the crimes of their nation.

At meetings of the provisional Committee of the World Council and of the Church Reconstruction Committee, I had an opportunity of seeing again some English friends. We also met Sir Alfred and Lady Zimmern whose departure from France had deprived me of an always rewarding intellectual contact. At Kew Gardens we were guests of Lord Lang of Lambeth, ever paternal in his welcome. Time was too short to allow us more than a quick look at the gardens in which the old Archbishop was so fond of walking.

I was never to see him again. A few months after our visit he came out from his cottage, ran to catch the London bus he saw at the bus-stop nearby and collapsed in the street. He had had the satisfaction of seeing his own candidate as successor to Temple, the Bishop of London, appointed to the primatial see of Canterbury.

I had a profitable conversation with the new archbishop, Dr Fisher. The provisional Committee had, as it happened, instructed me to invite him to fill the place left vacant by the death of William Temple. I was able to talk at leisure with Fisher after a lunch he invited us to at Lambeth Palace. He agreed without hesitation to join us. We also discussed the Orthodox Church of Russia. It would shortly afterwards be sending a delegation to England. I asked the Archbishop if he would sound them about their attitude to the World Council, and he promised to make discreet enquiries.

III

It was a long journey from London to New York from Tuesday 1 May to Saturday the 5th. Our principal stops were Lisbon, Dakar, Trinidad and Bermuda. On the second day out, when we were flying over the desert, practically on the edge of the Atlantic, under an intensely blue sky, the vastness of the three elements made an impression on me such as I had never known before. I could never tire of gazing at them. 'The heavens are telling the glory of God; and the firmament proclaims his handiwork' (Psalm 19:1).

George Bell and Visser 't Hooft were with us in the powerful flying-boat. We were particularly fortunate in our stop in Port of Spain on the island of Trinidad. The night arrival, under the brilliance of the Southern Cross, the welcome of the black maids in a comfortable hotel, a morning drive with two French fellow-travellers through the luxuriant vegetation – of these I retain a memory I can never forget.

The approach to New York, the first view, from a great height, of Manhattan and its skyscrapers, the emotion of meeting my eldest son and his family, of seeing Henry Leiper again and other dear friends, were the introduction to weeks during which an abundance of work still left time for some greatly appreciated relaxation.

Here again I shall refer only to what concerns the ecumenical side of my life; and yet it was during these days that we had the news of the armistice of 9 May and of so many other events which it was a disappointment to us not to be at home to share with our own people.

The first contacts we made were a great delight to us. The Leipers, Henry van Dusen, the new president of the New York Theological Seminary, John Mott, and John Mackay, president of the Princeton theological faculty, let us feel the warmth of a truly fraternal welcome. Two days after our arrival a meeting of the provisional Committee, with Mott in the chair, gave me the opportunity to describe the activities of the administrative committee during the past months. The date, place and agenda for the first Assembly of the World Council were discussed, together with questions of staff, finance, theological research and church relief work. This, I believe, proved a useful start to later sessions, which went on for many hours.

Two other meetings had important consequences, the one for the World Council and the other for myself.

On one of the first meetings of our visit we were at the house of Mr and Mrs Thomas Lamont, with the John D. Rockefellers and others of their circle. After dinner, Bell, 't Hooft and I were asked to explain as clearly as possible what the World Council was and what would be the advantages of supporting its work. 'T Hooft spoke brilliantly, and John D. Rockefeller was so impressed that he asked him to call on him later at his office. The result of this meeting was the generous gift that enabled us, as early as 1946, to open the Institut de Bossey. Everyone knows how remarkably, in the last twenty years, Bossey has become, and still remains, one of the outstanding centres of ecumenical research, and in the education of those of all denominations and races, who seek for ecumenical unity.

On the next day I was to entertain Dr Roycroft, secretary of the Latin America Committee. John Mott was anxious to accompany him. After giving me comprehensive information about the religious and denominational position in that 'mission continent', they both begged me urgently to visit it the next year, and to stay for six to twelve weeks! Several times, during my time in New York, Mott returned to the attack, pointing out to me that the population of South America was *Latin*, and the Protestants of countries he had himself visited, now becoming more and more numerous, were intensely eager to have closer contacts with their *Latin* fellows in Europe. I could only give him an unqualified agreement – but the problem was when would I be able to do what he wanted? It had to wait, in fact, until 1949.

Various denominations had expressed a wish to see me and hear me talk about French Protestantism. In Newark, Baltimore, Washington and Indianapolis, in the universities of Yale and Princeton, and to former students of a number of theological colleges, I used my talks as an occasion to bring out the *prophetic* significance of the ecumenical movement. In addition there were many profitable conversations with such men as Bishop Dun of

Washington, Professor Niebuhr of the New York Union Theological Seminary, or the Methodist Bishop Bromley Oxnam, President of the Federal Council of Churches. Thus, in addition to official committees, I had many opportunities of serving the cause of Christian unity. It is true that sometimes I met a certain reserve and reticence, but there was, nevertheless, a general interest shown. Many Christians were more or less alive to the fact that in the presence of a Catholic Church which had made up its mind to 'win' the United States,[2] the closing of the gap between distinct denominations must be of prime concern to Church leaders.

A number of ecumenical services were held in the towns on my itinerary. The most impressive, in the Episcopal Cathedral of New York, St John the Divine, had attracted the largest gathering. I spoke after Mott, Chichester and Visser 't Hooft. There again I bore witness to French Protestantism.

On 2 June, sad to leave people of whom I had grown so fond and to say good-bye to new and old friends, but impatient to get back to France, we left by flying-boat. Travelling by Newfoundland and Shannon, we were back in London the following evening. As we had to wait twenty-four hours before going on to France, I had time to call on Archbishop Fisher and tell him about our conversations in New York.

We arrived in Paris on 5 June. It was high time for me to get back to work and prepare for the National Synod of the Reformed Church of France. The most important subject, based on a masterly report by Pierre Maury, was the problem of Protestant strategy.[3] Once again I realized that the agenda for our synods are so voluminous that, with the best will in the world on the part of those concerned, it is almost impossible not to deal superficially – or in my case incompletely – with the most serious questions of doctrine or work.

Other cares were also clamouring for my attention. The trial

2. The word was used in the title of a series of articles which came out in the United States during the spring of 1944: 'Can Catholicism win America?'
3. This word *strategy* (*stratégie*), used in a rather unusual way by the Churches, embraces the working out and application of principles on the basis of which, taking into account the means they dispose of in personnel and material resources, the Churches should endeavour to meet their vocation to evangelize, to bear witness and to serve.

of Marshal Pétain was about to open, and the defence appealed to me to appear as a witness. Cardinal Liénart declared that, as a prince of the Church, he could not appear in court; the Chief Rabbi of France, cited after a great deal of hesitation, was obliged to undergo an urgent operation and asked to be excused. I asked the Council of the Federation for a clear decision to which I would have no alternative but to conform. The Council thought it my duty to appear in answer to the summons: and this cost me some of the most painful hours of my life.[4]

IV

Ecumenical affairs could not be allowed to sink into the background. At the beginning of August letters from the Archbishop of Canterbury, Chichester and 't Hooft were a reminder to me of their urgency. I went to Geneva to have a discussion with the people working in the Reconstruction Department, under the presidency of Alphonse Koechlin. Keller spoke to me sadly about the Inter-Church Aid Committee which was to be replaced by our Department of Inter-Church Aid. These conversations took place immediately after Hiroshima. The whole world, reeling under the shock of horror and fear, was hoping for an immediate end to the war. It was more urgent than ever that the Churches should come together and, if possible, unite in bearing a common witness to the one Saviour of the world.

Nevertheless, the Churches of the Allied nations were cut off from the Churches of Germany by an agonizing gulf. Visser 't Hooft and I discussed the possibility of bridging it. I shall shortly be describing how this was done. Meanwhile, the arrival of Cavert from New York brought the assistance we needed in preparing for the coming ecumenical meetings.

I was unwilling to leave Geneva without seeing Max Huber again, the president of the International Red Cross, who had been the efficient and respected chairman of one of the committees at the Oxford World Conference. I knew that he was very unwell. He received me most kindly, and spoke to me about the work to which he was devoting what was left of his strength. Already very close to his death, he was hoping that God would grant him the time to write a 'lay theology'.

4. The text of my evidence was published in the *Journal Officiel*.

A few days after my return to my work in Paris, Pierre Laval, at the conclusion of a scandalous trial, was condemned to death. It happened that General de Gaulle had received me in audience on the evening of the day on which, as was customary, he had seen the condemned man's counsel. The Council of the Protestant Federation had asked me to raise with General de Gaulle on its behalf the question of prisoners of war, of internees, of our occupation of Germany, and finally of French legislation in Alsace. I thought this was a providential coincidence, and took the liberty of speaking to him as one Christian to another.

Although I had long been opposed to capital punishment, I was not, I told him, going to protest at the sentence. What I did protest against was the travesty of justice, which many of us felt as a shameful and grievous defilement. French justice should not make a mockery of itself before the world. Such judicial clowning could not be capped by carrying out a death sentence. It must be stayed, and a proper trial of Laval opened.

I was listened to in dead silence, filled, I do not doubt, with unexpressed thoughts. The sequel is well known: how Pierre Laval, saved at the last moment from his own poison, died with a courage before which even his worst enemies could only bow.

In the conversation that followed I welcomed with interest effects of the meetings between General de Gaulle and the German pastors he had received wherever he had stopped during his recent journey, and whom he had asked to tell him frankly what were their complaints. We thus moved on to a discussion of the situation of the German Churches and of the influence of the Confessing Church.

This interview was on 13 October 1945. Pierre Maury went to Stuttgart instead of me, where, with Bell, Visser't Hooft and some others, he was to meet the delegates who had been appointed by the Synod of the Evangelical Church in Germany to communicate to them the document that was known as the 'Stuttgart Declaration'. It was a great disappointment to me not to be present at this meeting; but the imminence of the General Assembly of French Protestantism, fixed for 23 October in Nîmes, made it impossible for me to think about anything but the necessary arrangements. On his return, Maury gave me a detailed account of the Stuttgart meeting. He read me the noble statements, drafted by the theologian Asmussen and addressed to the World Council by the new Council of the Evangelical Church. In it the German Churches affirmed their complete identification with the sins of their people and their duty to share the same repentance. They made no demand or request but their attitude in itself made possible a new starting-point.

This declaration created a great impression on the world, and in particular among the member Churches of the World Council. The General Assembly of Protestantism, which opened in Nîmes on the date arranged, heard it read by Visser 't Hooft in person, in the course of the talk we had asked him to give us on 'The Great Post-War Ecumenical Problems'. On the next day, Paul Conord presented a report on 'The Protestant Churches of France and the Ecumenical Movement'. The discussion that followed led to an exchange of questions and answers between members of the Assembly and Visser 't Hooft. The agenda included a resolution expressing the desire of the representatives of our Churches closely to associate the life of these with ecumenical research and work.

The importance of this Assembly, which was the first to be held since that in Bordeaux in 1934, should be emphasized. It heard reports from Bertrand and myself on the life of the Churches of France under the occupation, and also, among a number of comprehensive expositions, a definition of the essential tasks of the Protestant Churches of France, presented with great persuasive force by the layman Jean Courvoisier and the pastor Pierre Tirel; both had given a great deal of thought to this subject during their long years of imprisonment in Germany.

A journey to Morocco, Algeria and Tunisia was an opportunity for me during the following month to give the Protestants of North Africa, and their pastors in particular, full information about the World Council and its work during the war years. I was hardly back when I was off again to Geneva, where I took part in the discussions of the Reconstruction Department. With Koechlin, Visser 't Hooft and Cavert, I made preliminary arrangements for the meeting of the provisional Committee planned for the beginning of 1946, and we drew up the programme of work until 1948. The nice question of a successor to William Temple as president of the World Council was another matter that called for much thought.

As an introduction to the Week of Prayer for Unity, in January 1946, and in order to make the importance of the coming meeting of the World Council appreciated in both believing and non-believing circles, I wrote a new article on the urgency of rising above the divisions of Christendom ('Au-dessus des divisions chrétiennes').

It was on that same morning that General de Gaulle resigned as head of the Provisional Government. A new page was turned in the history of post-war France. The interview I had had with the General on 1 January had made me foresee the imminence of a crisis. In the disturbed climate that followed from his departure all we could do was to go on with our work and help our Churches and the faithful to act as a guiding force towards justice, freedom and peace.

The Week of Prayer produced some encouraging demonstrations of the ecumenical spirit. Some eminent Catholics – Édouard Le Roy, for example, and Mgr Calvet – signed a declaration affirming the agreement they recognized between Catholics and Protestants on a number of fundamental points. After a liturgical service of great beauty in the Romanian Orthodox Church, Père Congar and I, each with the emphasis proper to his own profession of faith, tried to make plain the urgency and the importance of prayer in common. There was not, however, universal approval for what was said, and my address during that service had a curious echo in South America of which I did not learn until 1949.

Shortly afterwards I left for Geneva, in order to join a group of members of the World Council in making preparations for the meeting to be held in the following week. John Mott and Henry Leiper had already arrived. We were at a loss to find a successor for Temple. We had been warned against selecting any too ardent partisan of the U.N.O. The Swiss Telegraphic Agency put out the news (reproduced in three Geneva papers) that my nomination seemed probable. I had immediately to issue a statement that the question was still completely open. I may as well say immediately that at the Council's last meeting, on 23 February, there was a complete change of mind. Five co-presidents were elected:

Archbishops Germanos, Fisher and Eidem, with John Mott and myself; and I was asked to remain as chairman of the administrative committee until the next Assembly.

Immediately on the opening of its first session, the Council decided unanimously that it should reply to the Stuttgart Declaration by once more solemnly receiving the Churches of Germany into ecumenical communion. Bishop Wurm, President of the Evangelical Church, and Martin Niemöller,[5] released from his long imprisonment after the surrender of Germany, were introduced and I welcomed them in the name of all of us. It was an occasion that aroused deep emotion, thankfulness and hope. Both Wurm and Niemöller took their places beside us.

More overwhelming still was the ecumenical service held the next evening in Saint-Pierre, in the presence of a most impressive crowd. Bishop Berggrav of Oslo preached in German, and Niemöller in French. This was an ecumenical *act* of wide import.

The greater part of the Council's time was devoted to preparations for the Assembly. The place was definitely fixed as Amsterdam and the date, the summer of 1948. We did not then foresee that the Assembly would coincide with the accession to the throne of Princess Juliana, on the abdication of Queen Wilhelmina.

Two or three recent events led to our discussing the establishing of contacts with the Catholic Church. The Bishop of Fribourg, Lausanne and Geneva had sent a cordial letter, to be forwarded to us, to our colleague Bishop Brilioth of the Lutheran Church of Sweden, assuring us of his prayers. At the same time, Visser 't Hooft had received numerous requests for invitations to the Amsterdam Assembly, from priests and religious, some of whom were regular contributors to the Press. What answer, we wondered, should we give them? What would be the views of Rome, or of the Archbishop of Utrecht? It was only during the months that followed that we received the necessary clarification. To put it briefly and frankly, I may say that no priest or religious, Dutch or foreign, was allowed to be present in any capacity at the Assembly. It was forbidden by a *Monitum* from the Holy Office.

5. Martin Niemöller, pastor of the church of Dahlem in Berlin, was one of the founders of the Confessing Church in the days of Nazism. His courageous preaching led to his arrest, and he was not released until 1945. He was one of the presidents of the World Council of Churches from 1961 to 1968.

However that may be, the discussions at the World Council produced a clear picture of the subjects with which the Amsterdam Assembly would have to be familiar, and, first among these, the main theme of investigation, 'Man's Disorder and God's Design'. The composition of the Assembly was decided, together with the names of those in charge of its work and of the principal speakers. From that moment the World Council 'in process of formation' was in sight of the fulfilment of its mission. The road was open to its permanent establishment, giving the Churches of the world the certain assurance that the movement towards Christian unity was irreversible.

CHAPTER 15

From Amsterdam to Evanston
1946-1954

I. The Bossey Ecumenical Institute. *Le Problème de l'Unité chrétienne*. II. The Buck Hill Falls preparatory meeting 1947. III. Amsterdam. IV. Visit to Truman. The Toronto Declarations 1950. World Tour 1952-1953: the Lucknow Central Committee; Pandit Nehru. V. The Evanston Assembly.

I

THE session of the World Council of Churches in February 1946 opened a year which, in a number of different ways, had a marked influence on my ecumenical life.

Our discussions on the international situation, characterized by the growing antagonism between the two great powers, the U.S.A. and Soviet Russia, brought out the necessity for the World Council of setting up a committee qualified to follow the development of the cold war and the threats to religious freedom. This committee would suggest to the Council or its administrative committee such representations to governments, the U.N.O. or other international institutions as seemed desirable.

A conference held in Cambridge during the following summer discussed this resolution at length, and after finally adopting it proceeded immediately to appoint the new Committee. Kenneth Grubb,[1] an Anglican layman and a well-known businessman, was appointed as chairman, and Dr Nolde, professor at a Lutheran theological college in the U.S.A., as director. In the course of the next twenty years, both were to render services to the World Council and the whole world whose value cannot be exaggerated.

The chairman of the conference was John Foster Dulles. Deeply involved in the work of the Churches of the United States, he had not yet reached the peak of his political career;

1. President of the Anglican Church's Missionary Society: later knighted.

nevertheless the troubled waters of international life were of constant concern to him. As vice-chairman of the conference, I had to take his place when he explained to us American policy towards the Soviet Union. I must confess that I was greatly surprised. The year before it was practically forbidden in the United States to offer even the mildest criticism of Stalin's policy. There had now been a complete change of attitude and Russia had become enemy No. 1. Dulles made no attempt to disguise his real feelings about Russian Communism.

Reinhold Niebuhr took part in this meeting. I remember him particularly, both for the clarity and vigour of his contributions and for the stupefying rapidity of his speech. The stenographers gave him up in despair. In Amsterdam, in 1948, he gave a similar performance, which could only be a disappointment to those in the audience who were not completely at home in English.

It was at this same time that the Bossey Ecumenical Institute was started. Thanks to John D. Rockefeller's gift, it was able to obtain quarters spacious enough for a beginning and lending themselves to extensions that later gifts made possible. Remembering that the Château of Bossey was in the canton of Vaud, but close to Céligny, in which part of the estate lay, we had invited the authorities from the cantons of Vaud and Geneva. The ceremony was simple and heart-warming. I had the pleasure of conducting it. We felt that we now had a valuable tool, and were confident that Hendrik Kraemer, who had left his university in the Netherlands to be the director of the Institute, would use it for the greater glory of God and the unity of the Universal Church. With him, Suzanne de Dietrich was invited to be the director of studies. Henriod looked after the administration.

I then took a holiday, and devoted it to writing a book on the problem of Christian unity,[2] which had been the subject of my Lenten sermons that year. In various quarters I had been insistently urged to publish them. I rewrote them entirely. This little book, which gave notice of the 1948 Amsterdam Assembly, did something, I believe, to waken the minds of a certain number of readers, both Protestant and Catholic, to the importance of the forthcoming meeting.

Two of the chapters seemed to me to give a good picture of the

2. *Le Problème de l'Unité Chrétienne* (Paris, Berger-Levrault, 1946).

current situation of the ecumenical movement. On the one side there stood 'impassable barriers' whose solidity and height I made no attempt to disguise, and which it would take a very long time to tear down or scale. On the other side was the 'new climate' which, to our joy, was already surrounding and colouring the relations between Catholics, Orthodox and Protestants, clergy and laity, and giving rise to theological discussions, lay groups for biblical studies and prayer and even ecumenical retreats in many parts of the world. More than any other enterprise, the Week of Prayer for Unity was contributing to the spread of this climate. Today, there is a readiness to believe that it should be attributed to the Vatican Council. It is true, indeed, that the Council gave it a great impetus; nevertheless, in 1946, those who had served the ecumenical movement from its beginnings, as I had, and had suffered from the repeated condemnations and re-fusals of the Roman Church, were filled with gratitude and hope when they saw that the wish expressed years before by Fallot was gradually being granted, with irenics taking the place of polemics and mutual trust that of suspicion.

In this same year, 1946, I went to the Netherlands and Belgium, two countries with which France had a special bond in their common experience of the ordeal of occupation. I was able to talk with the chief officials of their Churches about the prepara-tions for the Assembly of the World Council. I did the same in Sweden, where, moving on from Stockholm and Uppsala, I was delighted to visit the ecumenical centre of Sigtuna. In Copen-hagen, through the kindness of Bishop Fulgsang-Damgaard, I met Danish people interested in strengthening the ties between the Lutheran Church of Denmark and the ecumenical movement. From Denmark I went on to Berlin, where Georges Casalis, at that time a military chaplain, put me in touch with Bishop Dibelius and the Brandenburg consistory. What an apocalyptic vision I still retain of Berlin, and of Hamburg and Frankfurt, bombed into ruins: what a picture, too, of the scores of women working to clear away the rubble in order to hasten the work of rebuilding!

Similarly, I had to re-visit Hungary, not only in order to see the Reformed and Lutheran Churches again, but also to meet their

National Ecumenical Council and investigate with it the best way of strengthening the communion of study and work between the Hungarian Churches and the other members of our ecumenical family.

II

In spite of all the hard work put into it, under the direction of Visser 't Hooft, by the various sections of the World Council, arrangements for the Amsterdam Assembly could not be made entirely by correspondence. It was the occasion of a remarkable exchange of theological memoranda, circulated in a number of languages throughout the whole ecumenical world; answering memoranda would arrive in Geneva and again be circulated, and these in turn would bring new comments on the theme chosen for the Assembly, 'Man's Disorder and God's Design'. I could only marvel at the work done by our secretaries and their fellow-workers.

However, there were numerous questions of personnel, procedure, and organization for which personal contacts were indispensable. Since the Assembly was to be held in Europe, and the Churches of America had their own views about what form it should take if we Europeans, Orthodox or Protestant, were to be able to harmonize our views with theirs on many points, the World Council decided to hold a meeting in the United States. This took place during the summer of 1947 in a delightful place called Buck Hill Falls.

The hotel at which we held our meetings, and which was admirably adapted for such purposes, seemed to me to be chiefly frequented by young married couples on their honeymoon, by congresses of Christian women engaged in the social work of their respective denominations, and by conferences such as our own. I remember a very large feminine gathering which invited Niemöller and myself to talk to them about the life of our countries and their Churches.

I had been asked to take the chair at the meetings, of which I retain painful memories. From morning until late in the evening I was enveloped in clouds of smoke, which attacked my eyes, mouth, nostrils and throat, and caused me real distress. Scandinavian or American pipes, German and Swiss cigars, and endless cigarettes of all nationalities were constantly being re-lit, and, of course, with no consideration for the few non-smokers who were suffering from them.

All this consumption of tobacco, however, seemed to have made our work easier, of which there was, indeed, plenty. The discussion on complete freedom to hear and report, which the American Press claimed in advance, was highly charged. Among other questions was that of deciding whether the speeches of delegates from Churches in the satellite countries could, without danger to the speakers, be broadcast all over the world. It was decided that they could, and I must admit that Hromádka, the Dean of Prague, was not hampered by any personal fears when, in Amsterdam, he set out to justify his decision to go at least half-way with the authorities of revolutionary Czechoslovakia.

A special committee to make arrangements for the Assembly held many meetings. Thanks to Bishop Bell of Chichester, van Dusen and Visser 't Hooft, we were able to see more clearly what our main task in Amsterdam was going to be. John Mackay of Princeton, Father Florovsky of the faculty of Orthodox theology in Paris, and Koechlin played an important part in our discussions. 'T Hooft's authority was more and more impressive. One evening I noted, 'He leads the Committee wherever he wishes.'

On that same day I summed up my impressions as follows: 'Our American friends are strangely different from us; but their welcome is so cordial, their participation so generous, and their piety so sincere, that our communion makes itself felt through all our differences.'

An annoying incident deprived us of the presence of Archbishop Germanos. His ship broke down and was several days late. He arrived, accompanied by the Metropolitan Athenagoras (now Ecumenical Patriarch), on the day when the Conference had just finished its work. It must be admitted that in spite of the universal goodwill the World Council was over-dominated by the representatives of the Protestant Churches and the Anglican Communion.

Great progress was made in Buck Hill Falls in the direction of closer co-operation between the World Council of Churches and the International Missionary Council.

On several occasions already, at meetings of our provisional

Committee, we had recognized that such a move was essential.[3] It is true that in those days the three words, *Church, Mission, Unity*, were not seen so clearly in the light of the theological basis of their interdependence as they are today. At the same time, we were convinced that by failing to co-ordinate the responsibilities of the two great branches of the ecumenical movement, we would be doing a disservice to the cause which we both claimed to forward. With the same purpose in view, our two Councils had joined together, the year before, to call the Cambridge Conference and had been co-founders of the Commission of the Churches on International Affairs. Earlier we had already decided to set up a joint committee, in which some delegates from the World Council and the International Missionary Council would study together and endeavour to solve questions that were common to both. This committee had held several meetings in Buck Hill Falls, with Dr Goodall as secretary, released for the purpose by the International Missionary Council. He was one of those who, with patient wisdom, paved the way for the final integration of the two, which was announced in 1961 by the New Delhi Assembly.[4]

I was unable to be present at the World Conference of Christian Youth, which was held in Oslo, in this same year of 1947. As president of the Paris Société des Mission évangéliques, I had been obliged to make a prolonged stay in Madagascar, where political troubles, resulting from an independence movement, were raising serious problems for our missions. Oslo was the sequel to the youth gathering in Amsterdam, in September 1939, which had almost been broken in on by the declaration of war. On this occasion our youth section, set up by the World Council in 1946 at its Geneva meeting, gave abundant proof of its wisdom and efficiency. Reading the signs of the times, it saw the urgent necessity of an education in ecumenism for Christian youth, destined to become the men and women who in the next generation would have to assume control of the ecumenical movement.

III

For me 1948 will always mean Amsterdam. Before the delegates from over a hundred Orthodox, Old Catholic, Anglican and

3. See above, p. 125.   4. See below, p. 283.

Protestant Churches met in that large and lovely city, there was an important gathering in Geneva of the World Presbyterian Alliance (which French-speaking Churches know as the 'Alliance Réformée Universelle'). Protestant Churches of the Calvinist school, as is well known, are all attached to the system of government through the presbytery and the synod: while the Churches of France, Switzerland and Holland prefer the name 'Reformed'.

For the 'Reformed' who attended this was a prelude to the Amsterdam Assembly. An attempt was made to reach agreement on the position to be taken up in relation to the chief questions that would come up later. I shall pass over those discussions, which were a disappointment to me, in spite of John Mackay's valuable contributions. What has remained much more vividly in my memory is a trifling incident, which marked the beginning of a new friendship.

I had stayed until I was the last at the end of a meeting and was just about to leave the Maison du Consistoire in Geneva where we met; a 'young man' (I thought) was running up the stairs as I began to go down. I noticed his youthful appearance and his vivacious look, but as he came closer I saw beneath the clerical collar the episcopal purple. 'A bishop', I thought, 'but who can this youthful bishop be?' He introduced himself, saying that he wanted some Swiss money to pay his taxi. It was Bishop Newbigin of the Church of South India, the future secretary of the International Missionary Council and, after the New Delhi integration, the director in the World Council of the Division of 'World Mission and Evangelism'. He is now the Bishop of Madras.

From the first moment, I was completely won by him. In the course of the next twelve years we were present together at many ecumenical conferences. To me he is still the young man in whom, in Geneva, I found a bishop, the Bishop Newbigin whose ecumenical thought and word have given me so many reasons for gratitude.

Amsterdam! I do not propose to tell the whole story of this assembly at which the World Council of Churches acquired a clearer vision of its mission in the cause of unity, in serving the Churches too, and of its prophetic vocation in the service of Christ. With my co-presidents, I had to preside at a number of full sessions, in particular the session attended by Princess

Juliana, who had for some days been regent and next week was to be Queen of the Netherlands. In addition, at lunch every day I gave a guiding hand to the conversations between the members of the business committee, which was appointed to arrange all the problems which emerged as the Assembly proceeded.

Many of those taking part were full of praise for the organization, to which Dr Cavert and his colleagues had for many months devoted all their efforts. I must, however, admit that on one most important point I felt disappointment – the place allotted to meditation and prayer. Sometimes, it is true, in the church where we met each day, we listened to admonitions full of biblical and theological substance – essential nourishment for our spiritual life – but too often we were put off with alleged meditations which consisted largely of anecdotes. In this respect Amsterdam was inferior to Oxford in 1937, when, thanks to Canon Cockin, our morning and evening services were a rich inspiration to our Christian life.

The full sessions were held in the fine concert hall in which Mengelberg used every year to conduct the Bach Passion. For the first time we used the new system of simultaneous interpretation, which enabled us to listen through earphones to English, German or French translations of the speaker's words.

On the first evening I gave the Assembly an account of the work of the provisional Committee of the World Council during the period 1938-48. As I was speaking the Council was still 'in process of formation', but the next morning I proposed a resolution putting an end to the provisional status and recording the definitive existence of the World Council of Churches, formed in Utrecht in 1938. Before the voting took place, an Anglican priest, always the odd man out in our meetings, made his final protest. The Archbishop of Canterbury, who was in the chair, quickly silenced him. The Assembly unanimously (for the dissentient concurred at the last minute) affirmed at the same time both the decease of the provisional Committee and the birth of the World Council, to which over a hundred Churches had already given their adherence. This was the end of the 'formation' period with which I had been so closely associated.

Theologians, who had been eagerly awaited and were listened to with rapt attention, spoke during the opening days on the subject 'Man's Disorder and God's Design', their expositions revealing some profound divergences of view. Karl Barth, at the meeting which was attended by Princess Juliana, criticized, from the dogmatic point of view, the order of the two terms used. In his view, and he carried many of his listeners with him, the correct form should have been, 'God's Design and Man's Disorder'. His speech made all the members of the Assembly search their hearts: I saw some who said that they were 'shattered'.

The clash between John Foster Dulles and Dean Hromádka was, in the opinion of most people, the second great moment of the Assembly. Two worlds confronted one another: one, dominated by capitalism which claimed to be the champion of freedom, and the other, a communitarian socialism, basing its power on a rigorous planning. The limelighting of this opposition, foreshadowing the political and social conflicts of the morrow, made a deep impression.

The scrutiny of the constitution and rules of the World Council, its central committee, executive committee, assemblies and sections was entrusted to a commission under the authoritative chairmanship of Alphonse Koechlin; I took part in most of its meetings. At the same time I was anxious to share in the work of section 4, which dealt with questions of peace and war. Sir Kenneth Grubb presided at these discussions, from which I learnt the vehemence, and even the violence, the extreme pacifists sometimes brought to the defence of their cause. I remember that one day, disgusted by their rabid tone, an Englishman, a former M.P., who had been badly wounded in the war, got up and proclaimed to his pacifist colleagues his conviction that he had been a faithful witness to Christ when, on the first day of the war, he resigned his privileged position in the Commons and asked to be sent wherever the danger was greatest.

The opening passage of the message which the Assembly took the occasion of addressing to 'all who are in Christ and all who are willing to hear' are worth quoting: they mark the starting point of a common journey in which the next stages were to be Evanston and New Delhi:

'We bless God our Father, and our Lord Jesus Christ, Who gathers together in one the children of God that are scattered abroad. He has brought us here together at Amsterdam. We are

one in acknowledging Him as our God and Saviour. We are
divided from one another not only in matters of faith, order and
tradition, but also by pride of nation, class and race. But Christ
had made us His own, and He is not divided. In seeking Him we
find one another. Here at Amsterdam we have committed ourselves afresh to Him, and have covenanted with one another in
constituting this World Council of Churches. We intend to stay
together . . .'

Indeed, it was *together* that we undertook to maintain between
ourselves and between our Churches the new bond whose
comforting strength was already such a solace to us.

To digress from the Assembly for a moment, if I may: a reception in the Rijksmuseum, where I had to reply to a speech in
French by the extremely Catholic Minister for Church Affairs,
gave us an opportunity to examine at leisure our favourite
paintings. A luncheon given at the royal palace, by the Regent and
Prince Bernhard, for the presidents of the World Council and
their colleagues, an audience granted to me by Queen Wilhelmina,
more loyal than ever to the faith of her ancestor, Coligny, and to
her interest in youth. And finally, in Amsterdam's huge stadium,
the ceremony which recalled the fifty years' reign of the sovereign
who was about to surrender her power to her daughter, with their
joys and their sorrows, and with the great hopes, too, that were
rising over the nation in the dawn of a new reign.

On the last day, a thanksgiving service marked the close of the
Assembly. Sockmann of New York, Pierre Maury of Paris, and
Otto Dibelius of Berlin, came up to our expectations, and we
broke up, grateful for the days we had just spent in a vast fraternal
communion, and confident in the future of a movement now entrusted to our steadfastness.

The next day, in Woudschoten, at a country house allotted to
the youth movements, the presidents of the World Council, the
members of the new Central Committee elected by the Assembly,
and the leading workers in the Secretariat General, headed by
Visser 't Hooft, held the first meeting of the Central Committee.
Their first concern was to invite George Bell, Bishop of Chichester, to act as chairman. This choice was inevitable. The part
played by him in Stockholm in 1925 and since that time in the
development and consolidation of the ecumenical movement, his

work on Fanö and during the war, the universal appreciation of the richness of his interior life, and experience of his kindness all made us instinctively turn to him as the man in whom the cause of Church unity, in undiluted Gospel fervour, was incarnate.

Twenty years were soon to pass since the Amsterdam Assembly, a name unknown today to the majority of Christian youth. If I were asked whether it was really a great event, adding an unforgettable date to the calendar year of the Church's history, I should be tempted to answer: Yes, and No. *No*, because, unlike the 1910 Edinburgh Conference, it did not produce a creative outburst, almost agonizing in its intensity, of prophetic inspiration and work; Amsterdam did no more than mark the end of thirty-eight years of ecumenical research, contacts and prayer. But at the same time *Yes*, because it forcibly proclaimed the determination of over a hundred Churches to work for the fulfilment of Christ's prayer, 'that they may be one even as we are one'; and because, in the face of the Roman Catholic Church, Orthodox, Anglicans and Protestants affirmed the dedication of their Churches to the service of Christian unity; yes, finally, because it was the starting-point of new ecumenical events which, each in its own way, have attested the continuity of the prophetic message which the pioneers of the movement received from God.

It is that point which I wish to emphasize. It is true that at Amsterdam much time was taken up by the constitution and the rules; nor could it have been otherwise. On the other hand, since Amsterdam the institution has developed more rapidly even than during the ten formative years; and can one surely not say that it has sometimes threatened to stifle – at times, indeed, has stifled – the message which has been entrusted to the World Council?

I believe that I have always been aware of the danger, and there have been times when I have felt most anxious. The proliferation, particularly since the 1954 Evanston Assembly, of divisions, departments and services, has been a matter of concern to a number of us. And yet the 'institution' has not triumphed over the 'event'.

And to whom is this due? I will, I am sure, be forgiven if I say what I think. It is due to a few men: to Bell of Chichester,

Berggrav of Oslo, Niemöller of Hesse-Nassau, Germanos of London, Dun of Washington, Fry of New York, but most of all to the man who from 1938 to 1966 has been not only the secretary-general of the World Council, but its very soul; to the man whose vision of the *Una Sancta* has never been dimmed by the fog of an unceasing daily administration burdened with problems of personnel, organization and finance. At all times, and in all circumstances, he has wished the World Council to be the prophet of the living God. With fellow-workers of unparalleled quality, he has maintained the life, the testimony and the work of the World Council of Churches faithfully in line with the expressed ideals of a Brent, a Mott, a Soederblom, a William Temple. I give thanks to God, as do many others, for giving us Visser 't Hooft, and for having allowed him to remain to serve the World Council of Churches for twenty-eight years.

IV

Six years separated the Amsterdam Assembly from that in Evanston. The latter had been planned for 1953 but was postponed until 1954. Each of those six years saw a meeting of the Central Committee and two meetings of the executive committee. Before recalling some memories of that time I should mention my two months' visit in 1949 to South America. I had been invited to take part in the first Evangelical Conference of Latin America, in Buenos Aires, not on behalf of the World Council of Churches but as president of the Protestant Federation and the Reformed Church of France. After the Conference, I was to visit Uruguay, Chile and various parts of Brazil. My original programme included Bahia and Recife, but the Churches of those two towns refused to receive me because I was one of the presidents of the World Council.

The year before, a fortnight before the Amsterdam Assembly, and actually in Amsterdam itself, a Presbyterian minister, McIntyre, had set up an 'International Council of Christian Churches' which he intended to use as a weapon against the World Council and the ecumenical movement in general. And now he had turned up in Buenos Aires, attacking the president of the Conference, John Mackay of Princeton, and trying to induce me to take part in a public debate on the threat to Protestantism from ecumenism. I need hardly say that I refused to debate in public with an American pastor in a great Catholic city, on realities which hitherto he had never done more than caricature. However, by a strange reversal of events, wherever I went later, and in the numerous theological colleges I visited, I was constantly asked to explain 'just what the World Council of Churches is, and what it is not'. Recorded in a number of colleges, my words were sent on tapes to Bahia and Recife, from which towns I shortly afterwards had invitations to stop and visit them. It was too late to change my programme, and I have always regretted my inability to accept.

A curious incident occurred which is worth recalling. Mr Myron Taylor, President Truman's personal representative at the Vatican, came to Paris one day from Rome and asked me to see him in order that he might give me an important communication. He told me of a wish that Truman entertained, which he had already discussed with Pope Pius X I I and for which he asked my earnest attention. According to Myron Taylor, the President of the United States hoped that a crusade might be mounted by the Pope himself and the World Council against *immoral forces* (i.e. Communism) with a view to ensuring lasting world peace. I was quite unprepared for such a message, and immediately informed Visser 't Hooft and my fellow-presidents. All were in favour of cautious reserve. I told Myron Taylor of our uncertainty about the exact meaning of the plan and of our serious reservations as to the possibility of implementing it. I saw him again, and he urged me to visit Truman as I passed through the U.S.A. on my way to Toronto. In agreement with my colleagues, I applied for an audience with the President through M. Henri Bonnet, the French ambassador.

Truman received me in the White House on Wednesday 28 June. On Sunday 25 June, in blazing heat, I had preached three times in Washington; it was the day on which the U.S.A. went to war against the North Koreans: it was a severe shock to public opinion. We were assured that in this operation the American forces were working on behalf of the United Nations, and the majority of people in the West accepted this in good faith. I thought that my audience would be cancelled; but it was not so, and Henri Bonnet and I arrived at the White House at the appointed time. The waiting rooms were packed with high officials and journalists.

President Truman welcomed me cordially. As soon as I entered the room, I raised the question of the proposed crusade, which Myron Taylor had come to tell me about. I told Truman that the Churches were as much attached as anyone to the cause of peace, but that it was their policy to serve it in the domain that was proper to them, and only with the weapons of enlightenment which it was permissible for them to use. I had the impression that in the President's view Myron Taylor had committed himself too deeply. He confirmed his conviction that the *immoral forces* must be fought by all who believe in the value of Christian civilization, but recognized that the Churches must use their own weapons on the side of peace. The Korean war soon dismissed the proposed crusade into the background, and I heard no more about it.

Toronto, the great Canadian city on the shores of Lake Ontario, gave the members of the Central Committee the friendliest of welcomes in its many colleges. Crowded though my days were, I had time nevertheless to visit the Pontifical Institute, to which Étienne Gilson has devoted so much learning, perseverance and love.

I have mentioned the two 'Toronto Declarations'. The first was concerned with recent events with which I had been in touch almost at first hand in Washington. Certain members of the Central Committee wished us to adopt a definite position in the Korean affair. The text on which we finally agreed indicated our desire to support the action of the United Nations, which the United States claimed to represent.[5] The 'blue berets' had not yet been thought of, and the United Nations, having taken, in accordance with its charter, a very strong line in the Korean dispute, had, we were told, appealed to American force in order to impose obedience to its decision. This declaration aroused severe criticism, particularly in Europe. The World Council was blamed in the Protestant Press and in Church assemblies of a number of countries. When I got back to France I found myself being accused of war-mongering. How meaningless that all seems to-day!

5. See *Report*, p. 91.

The second declaration marked the end of a discussion, far-reaching and lively, introduced by a paper given by Visser 't Hooft on 'The Ecclesiological Significance of the World Council of Churches'.[6]

The question of the Council's essential character had already been raised in Amsterdam, although the examination had not been carried to any great depth. The World Council is a phenomenon without precedent, and it is essential to define it. A first draft was submitted to some theologians and Church leaders, whose comments led to a second version, itself again revised on behalf of the Central Committee. It was this third draft which was to be the basis of the discussion, one of the most important I witnessed.

Are the member-Churches of the Council justified in holding that none of them possesses in their fullness the 'notes' of the Church which Christian tradition has determined with increasing vigour in the course of history? The World Council has no desire to play the part of a super-Church; but can the Churches associated in the Council on a common doctrinal basis pass judgments on one another which deny to some the quality, recognized in others, of a true Church? It would not be possible to summarize all the contributions to this discussion. Fr Florovsky emphasized strongly that much more was at stake than a form of words to be accepted, modified or rejected. It was obvious that the Central Committee was deeply divided on this question. Was it possible to preserve ecumenical communion in spite of the divergences? Or were they so serious that the member-Churches no longer spoke a common language? Pierre Maury expressed his surprise that such questions should be asked. He did not hold that his own Church, or any other Church, possessed the fullness of truth and order to which the Church is called. The document under discussion marked a stage or moment in the progress of the Churches' quest for unity. It recognized a factual situation, and should be communicated to the Churches in order to help them in their attempt to define their own position and that of the World Council.

After a sub-committee's final redrafting, the following resolution was adopted: 'The Central Committee has taken note of the

6. *Report*, pp. 13 ff, 84 ff.

document entitled "The Church, the Churches, and the World Council of Churches", and recommends it to the Churches for study and comment.'

This declaration was an important landmark on the road to unity. It was studied with keen interest by the Catholic theologians who were already interested in ecumenical thinking. Until the New Delhi Assembly in 1961, it was the most authoritative approximation on the part of the World Council to a common definition of unity.

In 1951 the Central Committee held its meeting in Rolle, in Switzerland, a delightful little town not far from Geneva. It was the last ecumenical meeting at which I had the company of my wife. The constant help she had given me for fifteen years by her readiness always to place herself completely at the disposal of the Church, her support in the many different duties for which I was responsible, her spiritual tact, her great gift of receptiveness and intercession, were suddenly to be withdrawn from me. It was always a delight to her, at meetings of the Council, to find again such friends as Frau Niemöller and Mrs Bell, who also accompanied their husbands. The blow that struck me in the following December has forced many memories into the background; and for me Rolle is still wrapped in gloom.

Some long journeys helped me to take up my ecumenical life again. In the spring of 1952 I left for South Africa. I visited our mission fields in Lesotho and what is now Zambia.[7] The sight of Livingstone's statue near the Victoria Falls, the simple tombs of François Coillard and his wife in Séfula, and my arrival at Morija or Thaba-Bossiou were the highlights of memorable hours. From South Africa I had to go on, through Nairobi, to Madagascar, where the situation of our mission called for my presence.

In December 1952 I left again for a real world tour. At Beirut I had an ecumenical meeting with Orthodox, Catholics and Protestants. In what was still Indo-China I visited Protestant chaplains, officers and troops in the principal towns and also in the combat zones. I was pleased to be able to talk with pastors and future pastors of the indigenous communities coming under the Christian Missionary Alliance. I gave lectures and sermons. The

7. The Churches of Lesotho and Zambia are now independent.

Catholic bishops received me in a spirit of ecumenism, and, through the kindness of the High Commissioner, I had the joy the day before I left for India of paying a long visit to the temple of Angkor, and to the numerous smaller temples, almost completely overgrown by baobabs, of the 'Grand Circuit'.

The meeting of the Central Committee had been fixed for Lucknow in January 1953. We were offered hospitality by the co-president whom the Council had added to our group of five in place of T. C. Chao, who had resigned. This was Sarah Chakko, the headmistress of a large girls' school.

For a long time Sarah Chakko had been a dynamic worker in the youth movements of independent India. We were pleased that she should be the first woman to be appointed as a president of the World Council of Churches. She was a woman of prayer, but at the same time a scholar and an organizer. Unhappily, it was only very shortly after she had entertained us in her school that she was suddenly taken from us. Her death was a personal grief to each of us. I retain the memory of her upright figure, in her sari, with her penetrating look, instinct with the purest love; and I can still hear the words in which she spoke to me of my own loss, with the sensitive understanding which brings with it the blessing of peace.

Lucknow, the last meeting of the Central Committee before the Evanston Assembly called for 1954, was primarily a preparatory session. Following the method adopted for Amsterdam, a large number of theological studies on the chosen theme, 'Christ, the Hope of the World', had already been written, translated and circulated. Since Evanston is in the U.S.A., it was natural that our American colleagues should urge acceptance for their point of view on a number of important questions. And this was how it turned out.

Pandit Nehru came to visit the World Council. I saw him again shortly afterwards when I was in New Delhi. Very 'Oxford', he told me of his wish to see a French university established in India – once our French possessions had been surrendered to his country.

v

The second Assembly of the World Council of Churches opened

in Evanston on 14 August 1954. A meeting of the Central Committee had been held in the preceding days at the University of Chicago. The Northwestern University, situated in the north-western outskirts of the huge city, had given us the freedom of its colleges, campus and gardens. The heat was intense and Pierre Maury, like a number of others, suffered greatly from it.

The Americans were anxious that this great ecumenical gather-ing, held for the first time in their country, should serve in the education of their fellow-citizens. They had chosen as the centre for the full sessions a vast hall which made it possible for thous-ands of spectators, apart from the considerable number of members and secretaries invited to the Assembly, to be present at our discussions. The six hundred delegates from the Churches had perfect accommodation, each at a small table. But in the huge hall the acoustics were sometimes terrible. I remember being in the chair at the last meeting, when the Assembly had to decide on an amendment to the message proposed by Dr Ramsey, the future Archbishop of Canterbury, and having the greatest difficulty in hearing what van Dusen or Visser 't Hooft was saying from the rostrum only a couple of yards from me.

Normally, that is when they were not in the chair, the presidents sat on a raised platform, well above the members of the Assembly, from which they gave the impression of a row of venerable busts. They did not, however, bother very much about the respectability of their appearance: overcome by the heat, they would sit in their shirt-sleeves, and I can still see the Archbishop of Canter-bury in his sky blue shirt under his purple stock.

In spite of these inconveniences the Evanston Assembly worked hard. This was true of the full sessions but even more of the sections and committees. The main theme, 'Christ, the Hope of the World', was expounded at the opening by a German theo-logian and an American, who both overran by at least a third the time allotted to them, putting to flight many of the 'visitors'. The theme was resumed in all its aspects at the section meetings, providing abundant material to sustain theological enquiry and spiritual life.

At that time the World Council was entering into a period of growth. Many new responsibilities were claiming its attention: close contact had to be kept with the member-Churches, whose number had considerably increased since Amsterdam; inter-Church aid had to be organized; the refugee services had to be supplied with the means they lacked for carrying out their work; research and study requirements had to be met, and the needs of the Bossey Institute, of theological meetings and of youth had to be seen to. To meet all these responsibilities, and heaven knows how many more, the very structure of the Council had to be re-thought and re-designed. It was decided that the presidents should not be eligible for re-election. My four co-presidents and I had accordingly to retire. A number of serious problems were left to various committees, and the Assembly moved on to a far-reaching revision of the apportioning of duties and responsibilities operative until that time. The departments were grouped into divisions, each with its own committee. When I was back in Paris, I learnt from Visser 't Hooft that on the day after the winding up of the Assembly the Central Committee, without having had the opportunity of telling me in advance, had nominated me as chairman of the Committee on Ecumenical Action.

Meanwhile, there was a certain amount of excitement to punctuate these days. It was the time when McCarthyism was rampant. One of my co-presidents, the Methodist Bishop Bromley Oxnam, had won the admiration of American televiewers by standing up to the notorious senator with indomitable vigour during long hours of interrogation. Among the members of the Assembly who had, fortunately, been able to come from the so-called satellite countries, there were a number who were denounced in the American Press as communists in disguise. Interviews and Press conferences were demanded. How had they obtained their passports? Had they not come to spy? It was useless to say that the behaviour of our Czech and Hungarian colleagues was faultlessly correct, but the way in which they were treated (verbally, at least) left us with an uneasy feeling.

Two demonstrations are well worth recording.

On the evening of the first Sunday, over 120,000 Christians, from the whole surrounding area, assembled in Chicago's Soldier's Field. Visser 't Hooft undertook the task of making them understand why we had come from all parts of the world to affirm that Jesus Christ is mankind's sole hope. Songs and dances, representing the themes of the creation, the redemption and the one hope, then provided an animated sequel for this mass meeting. One regrettable fact – the procession of members of the Assembly, in their robes, mitres or academic caps, was so long that much of it, advancing slowly below the stands, was only entering the huge arena just as the performance was coming to an end.

President Eisenhower visited us, and made a speech on the problem of peace the religious tone of which was warmly acclaimed.

On the last day, as we were breaking up, I saw John Mott again. He was then nearly ninety years of age. At each full meeting he had come and sat next to me on the platform I have mentioned. He had difficulty in putting a name to some faces that were, nevertheless, familiar to him. He often asked me to help him out, and it was with some anxiety that I noticed this increasing confusion. The moment came for us to part. His final 'Good-bye – God bless you' echoed for a long time in my heart. Some weeks later God called back to himself this valiant servant, granting him the grace of a painless end.

It may seem surprising that I should make no mention of the presence of Catholics at the Evanston Assembly. In Amsterdam, Père Boyer, founder of Unitas in Rome, had entertained some of my friends in his hotel: the Bishop of Chichester, for example, and Fr Florovsky. At Evanston, even so slight a contact was impossible. The Archbishop of Chicago had forbidden any Catholic, American or foreign, to be present in Evanston while the Assembly was meeting. He took it very badly when Père Dumont, editor of *Istina*, and Père Lialine thought that, as journalists, they could call at our lodgings without being seen. They were reported on their arrival in Chicago and relegated to another suburb. Nevertheless, the Assembly had hardly finished its work before they could be seen hurrying to Evanston to obtain exact news of what had been said and done.

I have just found notes I made from day to day in Evanston, with some impressions left on me by this second Assembly of the World Council of Churches. From these I extract what follows.

'It is a great mistake to have added to the main theme (Christ, the Hope of the World) six subjects described as subsidiary, two of which would have been enough by themselves to stimulate fruitful discussions. In spite of their excellent preparatory work, we have been forced to be superficial in our work. Neither the groups (the main theme), nor the committees (departmental reports), nor the sections (subsidiary subjects) have sufficient time to get to the bottom of the problems.

'The opening session should not have been as it was. In the first place, I had been asked not to speak because of the crowded time-table, so that there was no welcome given to the thousands of people who turned up. And then Professor X expounded the main theme for fifty-seven minutes, in German! Thousands of the audience gradually slipped out. This undoubtedly made a bad impression.

'Most of the speakers at the full sessions *read* what they had to say, without attempting to *speak* to their huge audience. They did not *hold* their audience; they simply read out what they had to say without addressing themselves directly to the thousands who had come to listen to them.

'The morning and evening services were, with certain exceptions, much better than those in Amsterdam . . . On the whole, the spiritual quality was excellent. The recollection, and the atmosphere of prayer were most beneficial.

'I believe that, in spite of weaknesses which every one has commented on, of theological and ecclesiastical differences that no one could fail to notice, Evanston marks an advance on Amsterdam.

'The first part of the "message" is bad, because it purports to be addressed "to the world" and speaks a language the world cannot understand. The second part, which takes to task the parishes and their faithful, is excellent.

'There is much valuable material in the reports from the sections to the Assembly. It is in these that progress is most noticeable. In particular, there is much food for thought for our Churches in the conclusions of the section on "the responsible society". The social problem is treated much more boldly than in Amsterdam.

'I could say as much about several other reports. Section 1's report (*Faith and Order*) ends, "We dedicate ourselves to God anew that He may enable us to grow together". In spite of the opposition of the Bishop of Durham,[8] these words were retained by a large majority, and that is a good sign.'

A last word about Evanston: we suffered from the absence of four theologians, Barth, Brunner, Mackay and Niebuhr: unhappily, sickness at times nullifies the firmest intentions.

8. Dr Ramsey, now Archbishop of Canterbury.

CHAPTER 16

First Meetings of the World Council
in Eastern Europe and in the Orthodox World

I. The Division of Ecumenical Action. Meetings of the
Central Committee in Hungary and Rhodes. Andrews.
II. Pierre Maury takes over as president of the Reformed
Church of France. Meetings in North Africa. III. Develop-
ment of the ecumenical movement in France. The great
return. Catholic friendship. Taizé.

I

THE office of chairman of the Committee of the Division of
Ecumenical Action, set up at Evanston, had the great advantage
for me that, although I was now a 'retired president'[1] I could
attend the annual meeting of the Central Committee. Thus from
1954 to 1961, I was associated with the work of implementing
policy, dealing with information, and making decisions, with
which, it is true, I had long been familiar, but which increased
greatly in the days after Evanston.

In addition, before each session of the Central Committee there
was a meeting of the chairmen and secretaries of the four departments which made up the Division of Ecumenical Action. For
three or four days we would be receiving and discussing their
reports, and this allowed me to draw up my own for presentation
to the Central Committee.

Finally, I frequently made use of my right to attend, in Geneva
or Bossey, the regular meetings of secretaries of departments. It
was there that I was privileged to know the details of the work of
Madeleine Barot, of young men such as Hans-Rudi Weber and
Philip Potter, and of Dr Wolf, director of the Ecumenical
Institute. The memory of these meetings, businesslike, frank
and, above all, fraternal, is one of the most gratifying of that
period.

1. By virtue of the retirement rule for presidents.

A number of meetings of the Central Committee have left a lasting impression on my memory.

In August 1956 we met in Hungary, in Galyatetö, more than 120 kilometres east of Budapest. We had all travelled together by coach from Vienna to Budapest, where we had stopped in a huge square from which a colossal bronze statue of Stalin seemed to dominate the city. In all the villages we had passed through, having come from the 'West', we had been cheered by the children and by their parents, too; and some of us had felt an indefinable thrill of anticipation. Looking at the statue of Stalin, I wondered to myself whether it might not be overthrown one day. Less than three months later, it was lying on the ground.

The next day, which was a Sunday, after settling ourselves in Galyatetö, we went back to Budapest to take part in the services held in a number of churches. With Dr Fry, president of the Lutheran Church of the U.S.A. and the new chairman of the Central Committee of the World Council of Churches, I preached in French in a large church of his faith. A luncheon followed, in a vast hall in the parliament building, and the President of the People's Republic treated us to a long eulogy on religious freedom.

In Galyatetö, our Committee was welcomed by Bishop Bereczky, president of the General Synod of the Calvinist Church. We felt both esteem and gratitude for him, and for the dignity with which he carried out his burdensome duty. He suffered a stroke while we were in the middle of our work, so that we saw too little of him to make real contact.

The 1948 revolution, which had established a people's socialist democracy, had involved serious changes for the Churches. Their estates were seized. There was said to be complete freedom of worship. Nevertheless some bishops were either arrested or closely watched. Bishop Ravasz, who had received me in 1936 and 1946 with kindness and affection, was able even so to spend a few moments with us. In spite of the assurances we were given, we suffered from a persistent feeling of uneasiness.

For the first time I explained the work accomplished during the preceding year by the four departments of Ecumenical Action: the Ecumenical Institute of Bossey, Youth, Laity, and Co-operation of Men and Women in Church and Society.

As in all our meetings, the whole range of the Council's responsibilities and activities was reviewed. The reorganization decided on in Evanston was gradually being introduced, and the necessary action to prevent the ultimate predominance of the institution seemed to have been taken.

I retain a very vivid memory of our meeting in Rhodes in 1959. It was a greatly appreciated privilege to have the opportunity, dreamed of for so many years, to visit Athens, to gaze on the Parthenon, the Acropolis, the Agora and so many other beautiful sights, but also to have a close-up view of the Greek Orthodox Church, to meet its archbishop, a number of bishops, and the professors of theology in the University: and, after a smooth voyage through the islands of the Dodecanese, to land in Rhodes, intelligently restored under the Italian occupation, and to reach the place where we held our meetings by ascending the magnificent Rue des Chevaliers, its houses blazoned with French names; and then in the evening to go back to our hotel beside the sea, and rest after the exhausting heat of the day, was a delightful relaxation.

In Rhodes fruitful contacts were established, though not without a number of obstacles to be circumvented, between the Central Committee and a considerable number of Orthodox prelates. The problem of the relations between the Orthodox Church and the Holy See was not raised. On the other hand, there was much discussion of the attitude of the Orthodox to the World Council. We came to understand the extreme sensitivity of Orthodoxy and the hesitancy of its approach to the Protestant Churches. Indeed, putting ourselves in their place, it would have been impossible not to understand them. Some of them, often moreover in disagreement with one another, spoke with authority: Professors Alivisatos and Constantinides of the University of Athens, and Professor Florovsky who had moved from St Sergius in Paris to Harvard, where he was professor of Orthodox theology. In Rhodes, indeed, they were no longer guests, a little cut off, as they were in Oxford or Edinburgh. They felt at home, and wished us to enter into the mystery of their liturgical and theological life.

I mention our meeting in Nyborg, in Denmark, only because for most of us it is still closely associated with one of our greatest

sorrows. Although no longer a chairman of the Central Committee, the Bishop of Chichester had been anxious to attend. We
were struck by his tiredness. Nevertheless he was present at our
meetings, making numerous notes, as he always did, in the little
notebook that never left him. On the Sunday he preached at the
solemn service we all attended in Odensee Cathedral. How sad it
seems to have left him, like this, with a commonplace *'au revoir'*
without a thought that our next meeting must lie outside the
confines of the visible world and will only come true in the City
of God! His death, which occurred shortly afterwards, created a
void in the World Council of Churches that, in human terms, can
never be filled, and in the whole ecumenical movement, too, of
which he was one of the pioneers most devoted to the cause of
unity, the bravest in difficult times, the most thoroughly imbued
with the gospel of peace and love. In him I lost a friend, in the
fullest sense of the word, of whom I can never think without
feeling the warmest gratitude.

St Andrews, the home of golf, was the scene of our meeting
in 1960. From the window of my room I could watch the coming
and going of golfers of every social stratum, repairing to the
links before or after their day's work to satisfy their passion. The
nearby university had placed the necessary halls at our disposal;
and thanks to the unhurried despatch with which Dr Fry managed our discussions we were able to meet the demands of our
agenda.

St Andrews had been chosen as our meeting place because
we wished solemnly to celebrate the fiftieth anniversary of the
1910 Edinburgh World Conference, and the Church of Scotland
had associated itself with us in this plan. The service which
brought us together, on the first Sunday of the session, in St
Giles Cathedral, was a fervent act of thanksgiving. After Visser 't
Hooft had read a sermon by John Baillie, who was seriously ill,
there were a number of short addresses. J. H. Oldham's went
straight to our hearts. Since the death of John Mott, whose loyal
and intelligent co-worker he had been for many years, Oldham
was our patriarch. I have already recalled what a tower of strength
he had been to us in making preparations for the Oxford World
Conference. He was now completely deaf, but the sweetness
of his smile was still enough in itself to assure us that the

ancient bonds of friendship which united us still held as firm as ever.

Every summer, the annual Edinburgh Festival attracts large numbers of music-lovers. The festival is opened by a religious service celebrated in St Giles, for which the preacher is chosen by the Lord Provost of the city. Several months earlier I had been approached about taking on this duty, and had agreed to do so. On the second Sunday of our session, accordingly, I returned to Edinburgh. While a long procession of city officials, magistrates, and teachers in the various branches of education was proceeding down the 'Royal Mile' to St Giles, I was waiting in the vestry with the Dean of the Thistle, the president of the Council of Elders and the Anglican Bishop of Edinburgh, who was taking part in the service. I am not ashamed to admit that to proclaim the word of God in the presence of such a gathering of worshippers, in a language other than my own, is always an ordeal.

French readers would be surprised if I were to make no mention of the meeting of the World Council in Paris in 1962. The presence at the opening session of M. Couve de Murville, the Foreign Minister, and his address, were a sign of interest which made a great impression on visitors from abroad. And, in addition, it showed that the French language was being accorded a less niggardly share than before in the Council's discussions. This was because representatives of French-speaking Africa and Madagascar were present. Like their fellow-countrymen in the United Nations they preferred to speak in French. All the members of the Council were glad on several occasions to hear the impeccable French of Jean Kotto, general secretary of the Church of the Cameroons, and, since the New Delhi Assembly, a member of the Central Committee.

A few hours' relaxation had been arranged for the last day of the meeting. They ended in Saint-Germain-en-Laye, in the same Pavillon Henri IV in which the World Council 'in process of formation' had met in 1939. I was able to show our guests the room in which Louis XIV had been born and William Temple had presided at our discussions. Speaking to them at the end of the meal, and not being required at the later sessions, I made a

With Fritz Kreisler in New York, 1945

With Albert Schweitzer in Africa, 1955

The Central Committee of the World Council of Churches, Toronto, 1950

At the Evanston Assembly, 1954

*French
Academicians
Together*

Addressing the
Académie
Française, 1963

With Cardinal
Tisserant, 1964

With Cardinal Bea at Geneva, 1965

point of expressing to them my gratitude for the friendly trust they had been so kind as to show me for so many years.

In conformity with the rules adopted in Amsterdam, I was no longer chairman of the Ecumenical Action Committee. The link which, since Evanston, still connected me with the World Council of Churches, was now broken.

II

During this period when my remaining responsibilities in connection with the work of the World Council were becoming less heavy, I was also released from the most burdensome of my duties in the service of French Protestantism.

Since the end of the war, the Reformed Church of France had been engaged in a difficult programme of rebuilding. Churches, presbyteries and institutions had been destroyed or severely damaged. It was impossible for us, without outside help, to meet the great expenses involved, and we were obliged to appeal to the generosity of our friends abroad. Numerous donations reached us from the Churches of the United States, Sweden and Canada, through the medium of the World Council, whose Reconstruction Department was alive to our great needs. The Church World Service sent large sums of money to Geneva from which during the first post-war years Europe derived great benefit. Substantial assistance used to come to us regularly from the Swiss E.P.E.R.,[2] whose French-Swiss secretary, Pastor Freundler, showed the kindest and most practical interest in our Churches and our work. The Lutheran Churches, on their side, had solid support from the Lutheran World Federation, which year by year became the most powerful denominational organization. We were thus enabled gradually to restore our ruins.

Other questions were a matter of justified concern to the Reformed Church. In spite of my warnings, I do not think the Synods paid sufficient attention to the problem of the material existence of French Protestantism. My reports to the National Synods show to what a degree this subject filled my mind. By contrast, problems of the Church's ministry, of the various parochial ministries, of the Reformed Church's 'strategy', of

2. Entraide protestant aux Églises: Inter-Church Agency of the Swiss Protestant Churches.

liturgical reform, and of baptism, gave rise to lengthy discussions at the National Synod, these discussions being based on the earlier investigations of speakers at the Regional Synods, themselves based on the opinions of the presbyteral councils of our parishes.

The time came when I felt that I must in conscience resign the presidency of the National Council to a younger man. In 1950 I was approaching the end of the last extension which, according to the regulations then in force, the National Synod could grant to a pastor. No parochial minister may continue beyond the age of seventy-one, and I was to reach that age in 1952. Accordingly I told the National Council and the National Synod, when they met in Nîmes in 1950, that I did not wish to be elected again to the National Council, due to be reappointed that year. As soon as it was formed, the National Council gave me as my successor the man I earnestly hoped would take my place, Pierre Maury.

The next year's National Synod did me the great honour, when relieving me of my parochial ministry at the age fixed by the regulations, of keeping me, with no age limit, on the roll of active pastors. This evidence of trust and affection has undoubtedly helped to give me the strength which, during the sixteen years which have passed since that time, I have had the blessing of using in the service of all the Churches.

At the Nîmes National Synod I have just mentioned, there was a most serious question to be decided: did the Reformed Church of France, in taking over from the Société d'évangélisation des Colonies (a name that takes us a very long way back) agree to accept responsibility, spiritually and to some extent financially, for the French Churches of Dakar, Tunisia, Morocco, Indo-China and New Caledonia? The Synod agreed to do so and appointed a General Commission for French Reformed Churches overseas; it then asked me to accept the presidency. I did so, without, I must confess, much enthusiasm, and without foreseeing the serious events in Indo-China and North Africa that were soon to disturb the life of our Churches.

Thus, while I laid down one heavy responsibility, I was called on to accept a new one which I was soon to find burdensome.

I already knew the French Churches of Dakar, Tunisia, and Morocco. I visited those of what was still French Indo-China in

1952: Saigon, Hanoi, Haiphong, of which the last had been almost wiped out by the war. In 1952 I saw the French community of Noumea, served by one of our missionaries from New Caledonia. Later Jibuti, Tananarive and Banghi, where I opened the chapel, joined the Commission.

Each of these Churches had its problems. Different legal arrangements guaranteed them, in the countries in which they were established, rights which could, on occasion, be jeopardized. The problem was how to associate these communities scattered far and wide, with no common bond, and how to strengthen their union with the Churches of France. The Reformed Church was giving them practically all the pastors they needed, and our regular visits to the less remote of them brought them some encouragement. But did they really want solidarity with one another?

In 1950 North Africa was a source of great uncertainty for France, and therefore for our Churches. Troubles in the Sétif had aroused dangerous unrest in Algeria. In the two protectorates there was a constant demand for independence. I proposed to the Council of the Protestant Federation that it should inaugurate 'North African days', at which, in Tunis, Algiers, Rabat or Paris, representatives of the Council and of the North African Churches would once a year exchange essential information, study common problems, and, in the light of political developments, draw up the necessary proposals.

I derived great personal benefit from these 'days'. They bore the stamp of frankness, trust and fraternal communion which made sure of their standing, in particular with the French or indigenous authorities with whom we were at pains to consult.

One of these meetings was the occasion of a remarkable surprise. I had stopped in Bône on my way to Tunis, where we were meeting that year. In conversation with the commander of the garrison, I heard him prophesy that with Indo-China lost and North Africa inevitably going the same way, Alsace and Brittany would soon be demanding self-government. 'And what remedy do you see for this very dangerous situation?' I asked him. 'There is only one: France must reconquer Indo-China as soon as possible and then everything will settle down.' I expressed my doubts that any government would ever take the decision to call up several age-groups for an expedition to conquer Vietnam.

That was on 30 October 1954. Less than forty-eight hours after that conversation, we had the outbreaks in the Aurès Mountains. Of those, indeed, my colonel can have had no presentiment.

The last meeting in which I took part required my going once again to Algiers. I had pleasant memories of my first visits to that city, in its magnificent situation, dazzling white, and rising up in terraces over the blue Mediterranean. When I had come to set up teams of Cimade in Médéah and Sidi-Namane, I had spent some time with our gallant team from Le Clos-Salambier. I had mentioned torture to the military leaders without obtaining anything but flat denials. In this month of January 1960, however, the atmosphere had considerably deteriorated. We were anxious for accurate news. One of the best qualified representatives of the F.L.N. came, not without danger, to talk with us and answer our questions. The next day two senior officers gave us an impressive lecture on 'psychological warfare'. One of them horrified us by putting forward a doctrine of 'hurting in a good cause', i.e. torture designed to extract secret information about attacks, which could then be prevented before they caused the death of French soldiers. An evil atmosphere was about.

From the outset those North African 'days' had a markedly ecumenical character. Representatives of the Methodist Church, the Anglican and other missions, were invited to join in the conversations. The Christian Committee for Help to Algeria (Comité chrétien de secours à l'Algérie) was not to be founded until later. When that time came, our Cimade teams combined their work with that of the Committee.

The Algerian war had profound repercussions on the mass of the people in metropolitan France, and especially from the time when the Government decided to use the new intake. The feeling in Christian circles arose from other reasons. It was forcefully expressed at the General Assembly of Protestantism, held in Montbéliard in the autumn of 1960. Already in 1955, at the Montpellier Assembly, I had been instructed to forward to the Head of State and the Prime Minister the text of a resolution protesting against the methods and torture used against those who were regarded as 'rebels'. In 1960 public opinion had been shocked by the stories brought back by soldiers on leave or sent by newspaper correspondents. A long and impassioned discussion followed. Agreement was finally reached, just before the end of the Assembly, on a badly drafted text in which a number of separate questions were run together: conscientious objectors, refusal to report for military service, condemnation of torture, and the invitation addressed to me to co-operate with the authorities of other denominations with a view to making urgent representations on all these matters to the Head of State. Back in Paris at midnight, I learnt that messages from the Press agencies had arrived before me, and that attempts had been made to interview Cardinal Feltin and Chief Rabbi Kaplan, neither of whom had up-to-date knowledge of the facts. I was in a difficult position, and I am still thankful that the two eminent religious authorities I have just mentioned so quickly agreed that a letter signed by the three of us should be sent to General de Gaulle, strongly urging the necessity of ending the war and of immediately putting a stop to the tortures.

I soon learnt that our letter had created a stir. Nevertheless, when I was received by General de Gaulle on the next New Year's Day, he showed no signs of displeasure, and was good enough to tell me that it was 'perfect in form and substance'.

III

In the years which preceded the calling of the Vatican Council, the ecumenical movement developed in France both in scope and depth, to a degree that raised great hopes among the most ardent supporters of the cause of Christian unity.

Groups concerned with research, with meditation, with the study of theology, and with prayer, multiplied not only in Paris but in a number of other parts of the country. In Paris there were regular meetings of Christian women, Catholic, Orthodox and Protestant. The general procedure was for a theologian of one or other faith to introduce the subject for discussion, and this was followed by an exchange of views. Thus was strengthened a living communion of souls.

Theological conventions, such as that at Les Dombes, enabled religious and priests, teachers of theology and pastors to study, Bible in hand, one of the aspects of Christian truth, and to compare the dogmatic expression of their respective faiths; thus they were able to glimpse, beyond differences which may have appeared to them insoluble, a road by which the Churches could emerge from themselves in obedience to the Holy Spirit and attain unity of faith in a plenitude of communion with Christ.

Ecumenical exhibitions were also organized, under Protestant sponsorship, and attracted a large public. Diagrams of organization, and genealogical trees of the many different denominations gave visitors a clear and intelligible picture. I visited several of these, and found they helped me to understand better how we should meet the requirements of ecumenical education.

The Week of Prayer for Christian Unity was taking an increasingly important place in the life of Catholic and Protestant parishes. There were, it is true, some reservations and abstentions, and I shall be referring to these again later; but, when reading our local Protestant Press, I noticed that as the week approached it devoted a great deal of space to the ecumenical movement, and to the duty of bringing it to the notice of the faithful in every parish. Interdenominational meetings provided an opportunity for a communion in prayer in Catholic or Protestant churches.

I did all I could myself to contribute to the ecumenical education of as wide a public as I could reach. It was at this time that I began to deal with the problem of unity in lectures organized by local ecumenical groups or religious organizations. In some articles I wrote, in particular on the occasion of the appeal for 'the great return', I made it my duty to give a warning against deceptive illusions, against what I called sentimental ecumenism. And there were some pressing invitations which, on behalf of the Churches of the Reform, I thought it right firmly to decline. However, when at the end of the Holy Year, which was the year of the dogma of the bodily assumption of Mary, the celebrated door in St Peter's was solemnly bricked up, I wrote another article entitled 'The Door Is Still Open'.

On a number of occasions I spoke about the ecumenical movement to a narrower circle, but one which provides an excellent sounding-board for one's words. I read two papers on this subject to the Academy of Moral and Political Sciences, to which I had been elected in 1946. I had already, before the war, spoken to the Academy about the significance of a movement which was beginning to be talked about in the most diverse circles. My papers, after I had become a member of that illustrious company, gave rise to numerous conversations which confirmed my conviction that wherever a Christian faith is proclaimed it stimulates a common focusing of hopes and expectations.

It was during this same decade of 1950-60, when I made some of my longest journeys, that my Lenten sermons (which I continued until 1962) gave rise to Catholic friendships, some of which proved extremely valuable. I had long known from what depths some Catholic souls, in daily meditation on the Bible, draw the rich substance of an authentically evangelical piety. I came then to understand better what rich fruit it can bear in times of trial and suffering.

As I write those last words I am thinking of the almost maternal affection shown to me, during the last years of her long life, by a fervent Catholic lady of Grenoble. One day, after having heard the first two Lenten sermons, she wrote to tell me of her disappointment. Many years earlier, she had seen me about the streets of my first parish, and for half a century, without ever having spoken to me, she had been praying for me every day. The later sermons cured her disappointment and a regular correspondence grew up between us. She was a woman of the keenest intelligence, and of wide spiritual culture: as I sometimes wrote to her, she had 'the theology of the Holy Spirit'. As soon as I had the opportunity, I went to see her in Grenoble, where I was deeply moved by her welcome. I returned a number of times, to find her sitting in her armchair, surrounded by her souvenirs, her favourite books of piety ready to her hand, lovingly cared for by two of her daughters. Her son, Père Étienne Girardon, at that time spiritual prefect to the scholastics in the Jesuit theological college of Lyons, soon became a friend. I knew that from day to day I was borne up by the prayers of his venerated mother. She loved her Church with the love of a daughter. She had some difficulty, it is true, in accepting the reform of the liturgy, but her will to obey was strong enough to win her to it. I am sure that had she lived long enough she would have had the joy of reciting the Lord's Prayer with me in its ecumenical text. She fell asleep in the peace of the Lord: I have often said, and I think of it with immense gratitude, that in my life she was a miracle of God.

My bond of friendship with Mme. Philippe Hoppenot has no connection with my broadcast sermons. I learnt one day of her intense and deep-rooted passion for unity, and expressed a desire to meet her. We immediately experienced the reality of communion in God and of one and the same vocation to the ecumenical cause. At that time she was in charge, as she still is, of the diocesan Women's Catholic Action Group. In the course of the last fourteen years, I have had the joy of finding gathered around her a family of souls in whom the driving force of faith is directed, not in the first place to action, but to a deepening of *being*, of being what God wishes us to become in order to love him and serve him. To be, to be love, and to incarnate love in service: in that may be seen the union of the active and the contemplative in all its power and fruitfulness.

Three short books, *Vers le Royaume (Towards the Kingdom)*, *Midi sur le Monde (The World's Noon)* and *Le temps du Feu (The Age of Fire)*, which appeared a little before the Council opened and after its end, are full of a daughter's love for the Catholic Church without excluding regret for its shortcomings and delays; they express, too, the ardent hope of a soul which leaps out beyond our sorrows and divisions and clings, by faith, to the fulfilment of unity in the kingdom of God. I often wonder how it can be that so great a force of spirituality and witness is not better supported by those who are responsible for guiding the Church towards the fulfilment of its mission.

Other friendships, less vocal because farther from home, steadfastly envelop me in a prayer which is a gift from God: friendships with pastors and priests, laymen and laywomen, with whom I live in the communion of saints. How shall I ever be able to thank God sufficiently for my having so loved and been loved!

Now, however, I must introduce my readers to Taizé. I cannot mention it without repeating that God granted a great blessing to French Protestantism – and not to French Protestantism alone – when, back in 1940, he inspired the young pastor Roger Schutz to found the community of Taizé. When the twenty-fifth anniversary of the foundation was celebrated in 1965, I remembered the criticisms that for a long time were aimed at the brothers of Taizé, the refusal to take them seriously, the suspicions with which they were regarded. A regrettable lack of good faith was too often to accompany the understandable puzzlement and legitimate anxiety aroused by this restoration in Protestantism of the monastic life, with its vows of poverty, chastity and obedience.

There can be no doubt that, in the face of the Reformation tradition, solidly established since Luther, it called for great initiative, and great courage, too, to go back beyond the sixteenth century to the origins of monasticism, and so to recognize that the Reformation turned away from a rich source of spiritual treasure. Was it not a rash enterprise to seek to reveal again to our Churches, in an age when technology is dehumanizing man, the value and necessity of communities of prayer, study and work, completely devoted to waiting upon God in the love of the poor and the joy of ecumenical life?

The ecumenical aspect of the community is congenitally linked to its fundamental inspiration. The spirit of poverty has true being only in love, the one love which the Lord gives and inspires; and love invites, and demands, unity. Lived in the community, unity is a summons to universal reconciliation, and particularly to that of the Christian professions of faith which, in their divisions, nevertheless proclaim their faith in the one Lord. Taizé has the profound sense of its vocation of universality, catholicity, ecumenicity.

I know very well that, on one cardinal point, Taizé's position comes up against vigorous Protestant contradiction. According to Roger Schutz, the prior of the community (and here I am in complete agreement with him), visibly restored unity will never be able (any more than the smallest Protestant denomination) to dispense with an authority, be it but the president of an episcopal synod. The Orthodox, like the Churches of the Reformation, reject the personal infallibility and universal primacy of jurisdiction of the Bishop of Rome: but the question of the nature of the head of the universal Church is one to which we must return later.[3]

I am very fond of the Taizé community. Every time I go back to it, I feel myself welcomed, enveloped and animated by an atmosphere of prayer, of praise, of joy and of love offered to all

3. See below, Chapter 24, for further references to Taizé.

and lived with all. The liturgy introduces me to the mystery of
the Body of Christ, and I thank God that there is in France a
place in which prayer and love do not recognize any denominational barriers, and which one cannot leave without feeling certain
that 'when and how God wills it', Christ's prayer will be granted,
'that they may be one even as we are one' (John 17:22).

CHAPTER 17

A Look at French Protestantism

I

IN the French Protestant Churches nothing could yet console a great many of their pastors and laity for the sudden death of Pierre Maury on 13 January 1956. His absence from church life, from the theological and ecumenical life, left a gap which seemed to us impossible to fill. His friends and disciples, in particular the young pastors who had been his pupils, were lost in a confusion from which they had difficulty in recovering.

The parish in which for twenty-one years, since 1934, we had worked side by side, was deeply shaken by this unexpected blow. It was true that for some time, after he had had a serious operation, we had noticed in him a lowered power of resistance and a certain tiredness. Nevertheless, he was carrying on his pastoral work with the same love for his catechumens, the same concern to proclaim the word of God in all the power of its truth, and the same joy in meeting Sunday after Sunday the many parishioners who filled our church of the Annunciation.

To me the shock was terrible. A few days before his death we were together in Morocco, taking part with some other friends in the January 1956 North African days in Casablanca. The Sultan had received us and we had told him about our anxieties in connection with religious freedom. The day before Maury had preached in Rabat on the text 'My times are in thy hand' (Psalm 31:15). And then we exchanged impressions with our North African colleagues of the great political and social troubles from which this part of the world was suffering. What was the Churches' duty in this anxious situation?

On the last evening (a Tuesday, I think) at the end of the meeting, as we were all hurrying back to our hotels to have a few hours' rest before the flight to Paris, I asked Maury whether he was proposing to go back with me. He said that he was going to Marrakesh and would be home on the Thursday or Friday. I left him with a warm handshake.

On the Friday morning my colleague Gagnier, who had succeeded me at Passy, came into my office. 'Pierre Maury has just died', he told me. He had come back from Morocco the day before, disturbingly lethargic. A diabetic coma had suddenly raised a wall of silence between him and those dear to him, and the end had come painlessly. This was on 13 January 1956.

For many long years Pierre Maury had been not only the colleague sharing with me the responsibility for serving a large parish, in whom I had absolute confidence and to whom I had handed over the church of the Annunciation, its faithful and its youth, without the least reserve, but also the friend, the brother, the trusted partner in all my parochial, national and ecumenical cares, in my joys and my trials. After the death of A.-N. Bertrand, he had filled an even larger place in my life. His human warmth and his unbounded kindness gave the affection with which he returned mine a power to encourage, and sometimes to console; and always with a brother's tenderness, on which I knew in difficult times I could always rest with assurance.

His passionate devotion to the Reformed Church of France made him sensitive to the mistakes and excesses that are always possible in an ecumenism without a sufficiently solid foundation in indisputably apostolic teaching. This had not prevented him, when still very young, from taking part in the most ardent ecumenical life. While he was general secretary of the French Federation of Student Christian Associations John Mott had more than once made him his travelling companion. His intimate connection with Visser 't Hooft introduced him to the very heart of the ecumenical movement. I wonder what he would have thought of the Vatican Council, of its ecumenism, its debates, and of the constitutions and decrees which emerged from them.

There is no doubt that at the outset he would have expressed many reservations. I am convinced that later he would have recognized, and found great grounds for hope in, the will to reform which is to be found in a number of the Council's pronouncements and in some of the Pope's addresses.

Nevertheless his strongest interest lay in the Reformed Church of France. It was a grief to him to see so many spiritual potentialities lying dormant, and to note how the parishes were wrapped up in themselves and how their witness and their work was often hastily improvised. He wished his Church to have the boldness and the patience to adopt a strategy which, in spite of the smallness of its numbers, would enable it to fulfil its vocation as a Church of the word of God. As early as 1945 he induced the National Synod to inaugurate the study of such a strategy.

While president of the National Council of the Reformed Church (from 1950 to 1953), he had carried out the further task of teaching dogma in the theological faculty of Paris. Just as Calvin had made a shattering entry into the faculty with Auguste Lecerf, so with Maury it was Karl Barth who was swiftly introduced into the lecture-room. The prestige of the courses in theology which he gave to several generations of students contributed very largely to the wave of Barthianism which, following Auguste Lecerf's neo-Calvinism, broke upon the pastoral body and even on some of the Protestant laity. Thereby the personal effect of the president of the National Council on pastors was undoubtedly increased.

II

This is perhaps the appropriate time to stop and consider this Reformed Church of France. Like Pierre Maury I had tried to serve in the highly responsible position entrusted to me by that Church in 1938.

When, at the beginning of the century, it had ordained me as one of its pastors, it was dominated by the Church policy, and suffered from the fragmentation which Fallot denounced with the vigour of which I wrote earlier. The flight from the country to the towns was already weakening what some pompously called 'the Protestant people' of the Cévennes, the Dauphiné, Languedoc and Poitou. Free thought, inspired by such orators as Sébastien Fauré, was abusing the credulity of the under-educated. And the political climate was almost completely alienating them from their churches, except on great festivals – and when they were buried. The assertion that a 'republican' could only be a free-thinker was widely accepted as the truth. Dechristianization was in full swing.

I must add that no authority was in force either in the parishes or in the national Church. The pastors were their own masters. The elders concerned themselves with little more than the necessary repairs to the church or the presbytery – if there was a presbytery. The life of the consistories, especially of those where 'orthodox' and 'liberal' sat side by side, was practically non-existent. From the spiritual point of view, it was rock-bottom.

Had this state of affairs lasted, Père Rouquette would not have been mistaken when, much later, he wrote in the Jesuit periodical *Études* an article entitled, 'Agonie ou résurrection de l'Église réformée'. I hasten to add that it seemed that in many parts Catholicism, too, was almost in its death agony.

The law of separation, in 1905, came to the Reformed Church as a crack of the whip, which forced it to mobilize its forces and get back on the road. It had no alternative but to move into a period of forced organization, in which many of its pastors and laity were obliged to open their eyes and take note of the worst of their wounds. 'Protestant avarice', which goes hand in hand with so much admirable generosity, was put to a searching test. It could no longer be disguised that the financial question is a spiritual question, and that the Churches' budgets must be based on the authentic Christian life of the faithful and their communities. In addition, the vast expenses incurred by the Society of Evangelical Missions as a result of the conquest of Madagascar and the Treaty of Versailles (which set up a French mandate in the Cameroons and Togoland) focused attention, with fruitful effect, on the fundamental vocation of every Church: the apostolate.

The unity of the Reformed Church, effected in 1938 on the eve of the Second World War, was, as I have already said, a real blessing to it. It was spiritually in a position to make the Gospel message heard in all circumstances. It could do so, however, only because the new *institution* could assert authority in freedom, and solidarity in the face of diversity. Since 1938 there has been astonishing progress in this regard. A simple example will serve to illustrate my point. When I took the initiative of holding regular meetings, outside the sessions of the National Council, of the presidents of regional councils (who alone were in a position to give competent advice on the filling of vacancies and the creation or suppression of pastoral posts or parishes), there was talk of an episcopal college. Indeed, it was the necessity of having an episcopal college, more powerful than certain prejudices, which had to be accepted. At that time it was unofficial; today it is official, and it is a great gain to the Reformed Church of France which, most wisely, has recently granted the president of a regional council personal authority over the consistories, parishes and pastors of his region.

The Vatican Council, of which I shall soon be writing, will make us face the crucial problem of authority in the Church, the problem, therefore, of the 'event' and the 'institution'. But I would like, without waiting for that, to emphasize now the efforts made during recent years by the Synods of the Reformed Church to legitimize the exercise of authority where its introduction is indispensable. A great deal, of course, depends upon the way in which those who hold authority make use of it. Unhappily we are poor human beings, whose authority will always depend on their humility and love.

It would be difficult, after having spoken about the Reformed Church, not to add something about the Protestant Federation of France. I did not give up the presidency of the latter until ten years after I had retired from that of the former. Comparing the Federation as it was yesterday with what it is becoming today, how, I wonder, should I appraise the change?

In 1929, at the time of the Marseilles Assembly, the Protestant Federation was unknown to the general public and had only a limited audience. The social and political events of the following years, and above all the war of 1939-45, obliged it to take a definite stand, to make representations, and to address messages to French opinion which won it a place and a mission in the life of the nation. Let me quote a single example, taken from the strictly religious field. Since 1939 the Sunday radio services, organized by the Federation, have made its name known in all quarters, with its addresses, the names of its pastors, and, most important of all, the evangelical character of their teaching. The question of whether the positions it adopted and steps it took were in line with its tradition, is one that I shall have to discuss in my concluding chapters.

Two of the recent General Assemblies of French Protestantism,

Montbéliard in 1960 and Aix-en-Provence in 1963, introduced important modifications into the structure of the Federation. It is no longer the Federation of Churches which was created in 1905 and used the name only with hesitancy. It is the Federation of the Churches, the societies, movements, and communities of French Protestantism, and so justifies its name. At Montbéliard, the institutions, movements and communities invited by the Council of the Federation applied for and were granted one hundred per cent participation. At Aix-en-Provence the statutes gave constitutional standing to their inclusion in the Council. 'Departments' were set up, among them a Department of External Relations, which gives me the impression of taking on heavy commitments which are, perhaps, rather too much for the means available to it. On the other hand, I cannot but acclaim the efficiency of the Protestant Information Office, whose influence, both inside and outside Protestantism, is continually on the increase.

Moreover, it has certainly not won its authoritative position by disguising its Protestant character in any way. Quite the reverse. And here again it is a pleasure to see that the growth of the institution is not causing the message to be lost in a fog of concessions and compromises. As during the occupation of France, the policy of commitment has enabled the Federation (in connection with the wars in Algeria and Vietnam, with nuclear armaments, and the Suez affair) to remonstrate on the solid foundation of the plainest New Testament teachings.

Audio-visual methods are a constant aid in this many-sided work. Protestant Radio-Television, directed for over ten years by Pastor Marcel Gosselin with a competence which has earned him an increasingly authoritative position in Radiotélévision Française, is continually doing excellent work. The programme 'Présence Protestante' and the service broadcast on Sunday mornings, have an audience that undoubtedly exceeds by far the total of all the faithful assembled at the same time in the Protestant churches of metropolitan France.

It is a great pity, however, that this radio-television service, as, moreover, the Protestant Federation in its work as a whole, is financially supported by only a small minority of Protestants, those who realize, for their part, the outstanding value of the witness offered by radio and television.

It is not, I think, uncharitable to point out that in the Federation the Reformed and the Lutheran Churches represent the vast majority of French Protestants. There are four of these Churches, divided between the provinces of Alsace and Lorraine returned to France and the other parts of the country. I have long hoped to see them closely linked, co-ordinating their witness and moving resolutely together towards the establishment of one great evangelical Church of France. How often, when I have been suggesting various possibilities, have I not been told, 'Oh yes . . . but . . .!' Before I leave this world I shall not see what I long for with all my ecumenical French soul. And yet, an important step has been taken: the four Churches I mentioned meet regularly in the persons of the presidents of their respective councils: there is an exchange of information, common problems are studied, and if possible solved, and the fundamental tasks of the Churches are seen from a similar point of view. Moreover, Lutheran and Reformed theologians have agreed to prepare a common liturgy for the ordination of pastors, which has already been accepted by the four Churches, and the text of a common declaration of faith. On this last point, it would seem that the Colmar General Assembly in 1966 showed some hesitancy. We can only be patient and persevere.

There are some who persist in reproaching the Council of the Protestant Federation for allowing the concern for ecumenism to have weight in its discussions; and the Union of Churches, which in 1903 accepted the indispensability of a Federation, even withdrew for this reason.[1] I have already said that before and after the 1925 Stockholm Assembly, the Council and the General Assemblies continually showed lively interest in the ecumenical movement and wished to keep in touch with it. I had reminded all the member-Churches of the Federation in writing. But none are so deaf as those who will not hear.

III

In the preceding chapters I have not commented on the ecumeni-

---

1. The reference is to the Union of Free Evangelical Churches (l'Union des Églises évangéliques libres). How different things are today from what they were in 1903, at the time of the Clairac Synod, the cradle of the Federation. Cf. above, p. 70.

cal value of two societies which play their part in French Protestantism: one with excessive modesty, the other much more in the limelight. These two are the Société biblique française and the Paris Société des Missions évangéliques.

In 1818 a group of Christians, familiar with the work of the British and Foreign Bible Society, decided to found the Paris Bible Society. In several provincial towns, such as Strasbourg and Toulouse, associations with the same ends were already organized. Their task was to translate, revise, edit and distribute Holy Scripture. Later, there was a doctrinal dispute between the members of the committee, and it was decided to break up. This brought the foundation of the French Bible Society.

Immediately after the last war the two organizations had to decide to resign their work to a new body, the Alliance biblique française, now called the Société biblique française, of which, since its foundation, I have been the president.

Its ecumenical importance derives in the first place from the fact that all the theological shades of French Protestantism are represented on its committee; secondly from its inclusion in the United Bible Societies, a group which brings together all the Bible Societies in the world in the work of the Bible and its distribution; and finally from its close association with the British and Foreign Bible Society and the American Bible Society. These two powerful associations which have by themselves produced translations of the Scriptures, in whole or in part, into more than eleven hundred languages, give us the most generous collaboration: without their help biblical work in France would inevitably have disappeared.

I know that the biblical revival which is taking place in the Catholic Church has shown its vigour in a rich harvest of Catholic translations of the Bible. In various editions, the 'Jerusalem Bible' has enjoyed, as it still continues to do, remarkable success. I know too, and am glad, that a large team of biblical scholars has undertaken an ecumenical translation of the Bible which will no doubt be complete in ten years' time. Some Protestants accordingly ask why we want to make a new 'Protestant' translation into French: why not all use the Jerusalem Bible?

There is an excellent reason. There are many French and French-speaking evangelical communities, and many faithful in our Churches, who are in no way prepared to introduce into their worship and their teaching a Catholic Bible, containing introductions and notes which are often based on an interpretation of the text which the Churches born of the Reformation are far from accepting. It would, indeed, be surprising, to say the least, if Churches which purport to be 'Churches of the Word' were to leave it to another Church to provide them with the Bibles their faithful and their catechumens need.

Bearing that in mind, it is amazing that a large number of our parishes, certainly the majority of them, and the greater part of their faithful, take practically no interest at all in the persevering work of the French Bible Society and its indefatigable secretary, Jean Blumenthal. 'Bible Sunday' is almost universally ignored on the pretext that 'every Sunday is a Bible Sunday'. In short, the Protestant Churches of France, who proclaim so loudly that they are Bible Churches, are showing themselves incapable of keeping alive a French Protestant Bible organization. The unexpected death of Jean Blumenthal is a sad blow to the work he embodied. His successor, Pastor Pierre Marcel, is taking over with competence and resolution the great task he has just inherited.

In any case, do French Protestants still read the Bible? I would say that the majority do not. I have known the time when in many parishes collective Bible study was rightly regarded as one of the pillars of church life. And it is now over sixty years since I witnessed the energy with which Fallot, already a sick man, applied himself during the last three or four years of his life to teaching his parishioners, with the aid of booklets giving valuable introductions and short commentaries, how they should read the Bible day by day. One of my greatest sorrows is to see how the Bible study groups have disappeared in many places, and, where they still survive, how pitifully small is the attendance at them.

I know, and find it entirely praiseworthy, that the Reformed Church has given its approval to an attempt at reviving biblical study, and that Bible teams and other groups are working on the same lines. But who is going to benefit from these researches whose method appears to have a novelty of such interest? It will undoubtedly be educated parishioners, students, intellectuals. As for the mass of the faithful, will it ever be able to accommodate itself to this 'modern' method of reading the Bible which is now recommended to us, and receive from it the life-giving nourishment it needs? I leave the question for my readers to think about.

The ecumenical aspect of the Paris Evangelical Missionary Society cannot but impress itself on the mind of anyone who studies its work and, still more, sees it in action.

Its origins were ecumenical. It was not the child of a decision taken by the Protestant Churches of France but, outside the Churches, of the prayer and faith of a number of evangelical Christians, French and Swiss, of different religious denominations. From the first day of its existence, in 1822, it has been international and interdenominational, and it has never allowed this twofold character to be challenged.

Its history and the extension of its field of work in Africa, to Madagascar and in the Pacific, need not be recorded here. What it is essential to point out is that it has always been intimately associated with the apostolic work of the foreign missionary societies. Before the 1914-18 war, when the German Missionary Conference met each year the Paris Society would always accept the invitation it never failed to receive. The Society was present at the Edinburgh International Missionary Conference in 1910, and since then its director has always sat on the International Missionary Council.

Since the integration, at the 1961 New Delhi Assembly, of the World Council of Churches and the International Missionary Council, the Paris Missionary Society has shared in the evangelizing and missionary activities of the Division of World Mission and Evangelism. It was there that for years Charles Bonzon, the director of our work, met Bishop Newbigin, who took great interest in the activities of our Society.

The World Council, in fact, could not fail to be interested in the intelligence and tact which paved the way, in all our mission fields, to the autonomy of the indigenous Churches which, as soon as their independence was announced, asked to be admitted as members of the World Council of Churches. If today the evangelical Churches of the Cameroons, Togo, Gabon, Lesotho, Zambia, Madagascar, Tahiti and New Caledonia (I am speaking of those which were born from the preaching of our missionaries) can share in the work of ecumenism; if Jean Kotto, of the Cameroons, is a member of the Central Committee, it is to the apostolate of the Paris Society and the missionary labours that preceded it in one or other of its fields, it is to its selflessness, and to the humble and trusting devotion of its missionaries, that the World Council is indebted.

The Missionary Society is ecumenical, again, in the part it takes in the implementing of a 'common apostolic work', inter-racial, intercontinental and interdenominational. The fruit of Jean Kotto's prophetic vision, this project has received the unanimous approval of the Churches concerned. There can, it is true, be no denying that its realization in Dahomey is raising difficult and delicate problems connected with its establishment, with personnel and with finance. Nevertheless, this is the first time that an apostolic undertaking of this sort, conceived by a Negro pastor, has been thought out and entrusted to God's care by such a united body of Churches and missionary societies, whose extreme racial and denominational diversity unmistakably emphasizes its ecumenical significance.

At the moment, then, when the Assembly of the World Council of Churches was about to meet in New Delhi and when in Rome preparations were being made for the assembling of all the bishops of the Catholic world, this was the picture presented by the Protestant Churches of France and by the missionary work which brought them into communion with the apostolate of the universal Church.

PART THREE

The Extension of the Ecumenical Movement
1959-1967

CHAPTER 18

The Eve of the Vatican Council
1959-1961

I. The bombshell of 25 January 1959 and the project of Pope John XXIII. Père Congar and Catholic reform movements. II. The Reformed Church of France and Catholicism. The General Assembly of French Protestantism October 1961. Pastor Charles Westphal, President of the Protestant Federation of France. III. The New Delhi Assembly 1961. A new doctrinal basis. The old Orthodox Churches, the young Churches of Africa and Asia.

I

LIKE a bombshell the news broke on 25 January 1959 that Pope John XXIII had just announced to several cardinals his intention of calling an ecumenical council. The impact was as profound in the Vatican as it was in the various parts of the Christian world. 'It was perhaps', wrote the Catholic theologian Hans Küng shortly afterwards, 'the greatest surprise sprung on the Catholic Church, from within, in this century.'[1] Had not the centralization of the Church reached its zenith at the first Vatican Council? Had not the plenitude of power been accorded henceforward to the Pope? A new council was regarded as superfluous. 'In the life of the Church and its theology, the council was a dead letter.'[2]

There was great uncertainty about the plan behind the papal initiative. The first messages from the news agencies were extremely confused. Since it was an ecumenical council that was in question, some said that it would include representatives of all the Christian Churches; others said that the meeting envisaged would be the Council of Unity. Nevertheless Pope John's intention was soon perfectly clear. The Church's face was old and lined, and an *aggiornamento* would give it back its freshness and beauty: and then, perhaps, the 'separated brethren' would be more

1. Hans Küng, *Structures de l'Église*, 1963, p. 13.   2. Ibid.

susceptible to her charms. This latter was, if I may say so, only a secondary aim. The first was simply a bringing up to date; a new infusion of youth, a renewal of the Catholic Church was essential for the Church itself. The word 'reform' was soon to be used, and it made me think of what the Abbé de Tourville said, at the beginning of the century, to a Protestant theologian: 'The Church will reform itself and make your reform unnecessary.'

When Pope John disclosed his plan, could some aspiration other than his be distinguished behind it? Was a *reformist* tendency making itself felt in the thought of Catholic theologians and in the piety of the faithful? These were questions which I had for many years been asking myself, led to do so by my intimacy with Laberthonnière, by my reading and by correspondence and contacts that resulted from my Lenten sermons. There is no need, however, to go so far back in time. The decade which was just ending, had seen the publication of two great books, the first of which appeared in 1950 and the other a few years later. The first was Père Congar's book on true and false reform in the Church (*Vraie et fausse réforme dans l'Église*),[3] and the second was by another Dominican, Père Le Guillou, entitled *Mission et Unité*.[4] I cannot mention them without remembering the debt I owe to their authors; both have given a powerful impetus to my ecumenical thought, not only about the Church of Rome but also about the *essence* of the universal Church and the impossibility of *thinking* of it divorced from the apostolate.

According to Père Congar 'the Church has always been actively reforming itself'.[5] What, however, struck him most at the time he was writing, when no one was envisaging the calling of the Council, was the wide scope of reformist aspirations immediately after the last war. As early as 1947 he was writing, 'the Church has continually been in a state of self-reformation; it can live only by reforming itself'.[6] Pius X's famous summons 'Instaurare omnia in Christo' gave a reform movement its necessary orientation. In 1946, a bishop described his impression in the words, 'There is a feeling that we are at the beginning of a great revolution.' No doubt that prelate had felt, as I myself had, the shock which, even

3. Paris, Éditions du Cerf.   4. Paris, Éditions du Cerf.
5. Op. cit., p. 21.   6. Ibid.

before the end of the war, had been shared by the readers of a shattering little book by the Abbés Godin and Daniel, *France: A Mission Land?* (*La France, pays de mission*).[7] In that book, whose truth cannot be impugned, and which is written with love and respect for their Church, these two priests did not hesitate to expose its wounds: to show its blindness to its increasing weakness in a world which ignores it more and more completely without even bothering to despise it, and to emphasize its neglect of its fundamental duty of witness and service. I can recall the emotion with which I read their book, and the surge of gratitude and respect which made me share the distress and hopes of these Catholic brethren. Père Congar, in his book, has no hesitation in saying that it has a permanent place in history.[8] Did Pope John read it, I wonder? If so, this prophetic message must have sown a rich harvest in that humane and loving heart.

'At the root of today's reformism', Père Congar writes, 'there is, it is true, a crisis, a sickness; but it is not a crisis of loyalty.'[9] Large numbers of clergy and laity want 'real actions, which have a real correspondence with what they claim to signify . . . This is an irrepressible demand on which modern sincerity insists . . . Too many things have become "rites" for us, that is to say they are things presented to us ready-made.'[10] There is no concern to find out 'whether they are truly the actions of some *real person*. From all this it will be seen that what is really at stake is the truth of Christian being, the truth of man's relation to God . . . Beneath Church reformism, is it indeed a religious reform that is required, a reform such as Christianity makes a permanent duty as soon as it is fully itself?'[11]

It need hardly be said that, in considering the nature of 'true and false reform in the Church', Père Congar comes up against the Reform of the sixteenth century; indeed, he devotes a great part of his book to it, and I recognize that his examination of the ecclesiological position of the Reformers, and more particularly of Luther, is of very great interest and calculated to stimulate

---

7. Published in 1943; Eng. trans. in Maisie Ward's *France Pagan?*, London, Sheed and Ward, 1949.
8. Op. cit., p. 43.   9. Ibid., p. 40.
10. Ibid., p. 50.   11. Ibid., pp. 51, 52.

fruitful discussion. Nevertheless, it was not this that held my attention. For Père Congar, as a theologian of the Roman Church, the Protestant Reformation can necessarily only be a false reform: detached from the Roman stem, it is robbed of the plenitude which the Catholic Church claims to possess, it is infected by a *lack* which falsifies its teachings, even when they contain certain elements of Christian truth.[12] But it is a false reform, again, because it adopted an aggressiveness which rules out every movement that seeks to promote a true reform of the Church. Such a movement, whatever criticisms and demands it may include, is an expression of love and respect for the Church. 'Never, perhaps', writes Père Congar, speaking of the position as he sees it just before 1950, 'has there been seen in the Church a reformist movement with more respect for the demands of Communion and the prerogatives of the central authorities: never, perhaps has a reformist movement developed with so strong an attachment to the Church and with such filial trust in her, in order to serve Christ better. The modern reformist movement derives much more from the purity of the Church than from its impurity.'[13]

I read, and re-read, these and similar passages. And as I copy them out, I cannot help seeing the Council Hall and hearing the Fathers, with an uncommon reformist vigour, denouncing the scandalous methods of the Roman Curia and its methods of investigation, judgment and condemnation. What were those Fathers of the Council trying to do, if not to make 'impurity' make way for 'purity'?

This, however, in no way detracts from the greatness of Père Congar's book. All the reservations I could make, and all the questions I would like to ask, make no difference. Rich in substance, its ecumenical importance is undeniable, and in its own way it served as an introduction to the Council. Small wonder that Père Congar should have been one of the great theologians of Vatican 2.

With Père Le Guillou, Père Dumont's colleague at the Istina study-centre, we get to the heart of the ecumenical movement.

12. See on this, Père Bouyer's *The Spirit and Forms of Protestantism*, London, Harvill, 1956.
13. Op. cit., p. 571.

His *Mission et Unité*, finished in 1959, was prompted by his wish to raise what he calls, 'the key problem of the situation of the Christian communions in the world': what, in Protestantism, is the relation between Church and Mission? and why cannot 'the confrontation between the Catholic Church and the ecumenical movement be expressed in missionary terms?'[14]

With remarkable objectivity, Père Le Guillou describes the modern ecumenical movement at its birth in the Edinburgh Conference of 1910, and follows its growth as I have done in the opening chapters of this book. At every point in its development he notes an internal demand which is gradually brought home to the leaders of the two great branches of the movement, the World Council and the International Missionary Council. 'Born of mission', the ecumenical movement 'has a progressively stronger orientation towards mission'.[15] From Edinburgh in 1910 to New Delhi in 1961, the wish for closer contact, the necessity of association and finally the duty of complete integration make themselves felt in the resolutions of the joint committee (constantly referred to by Père Le Guillou), which in 1961 was to be superseded by the Division of World Mission and Evangelism of the World Council. As Père Le Guillou was finishing his book, that final goal had not yet been reached: it would still have to wait for one more year. Nevertheless, he had no doubt of its ultimate realization, since, in his view, 'the ecumenical movement does not derive simply from a passion for unity; it sprang from a passion for unity that is completely fused in the mission'. It came, in fact, from a rediscovery of the Church's mission and its nature and is therefore a summons to make manifest 'the integrity and plenitude of the Church of Christ . . . Its goal is the *plenitude of the Church in mission and fellowship*, in the organic unity of the different aspects of its life'.

It is impossible, therefore, to divorce Church and mission. Often found independently of the Church, the mission has long been regarded as a subsidiary activity; but the theological thinking stimulated by the ecumenical movement has led to the affirmation of its being part and parcel of the very being of the Church. 'The

14. M.-J. Le Guillou, *Mission et Unité*, Paris, Éditions du Cerf, 1960, Foreword.
15. Op. cit., Vol. 1, Ch. 3.

mission *is* the Church', wrote Pierre Maury;[16] and Roger Mehl goes so far as to say that 'the fundamental tendency of Protestantism is to define Church by mission'.[17] This implies that it should be defined by its relationship to a world in which it is only a minority and to which it is sent by the Lord as an ambassador: 'The field is the world' (Matthew 13:38); 'You are the light of the world' (Matthew 5:14).

Père Le Guillou also devotes several chapters of his first volume to Orthodoxy, of which he has a profound knowledge. In his examination of the position of Orthodox theologians in relation to the World Council of Churches and to the ecumenical movement in general, he detects an awakening to a concern for missionary work. Père Florovsky, whom I always found it most rewarding to meet and listen to on the Central Committee of the World Council, 'sees in Orthodox participation a step with missionary significance. The Orthodox Church bears . . . the heavy responsibility of making the universal truth known to all who lie outside it'.[18]

Until the Evanston Assembly in 1954, the delegates of the Orthodox Church refrained from taking part in the doctrinal discussions at the full meetings of the ecumenical assemblies. Immediately after Amsterdam, Mgr Michael, Metropolitan of Corinth, had thought it a great mistake that representatives of Orthodoxy should have accepted the ecumenical reports and the constituting charter.[19] No participation in the World Council seemed to him possible. However, from 1948 to 1954, the attitude of a section of the hierarchy and the theologians had changed, and I well remember even now hearing Mgr Michael say in Evanston that he had changed his mind, and that the Orthodox Churches should take part in doctrinal discussions in order that their witness might be heard.[20]

It is true that during the last centuries those Churches have not shown an apostolic zeal that can compare with that of the Catholic Church and the Churches born of the sixteenth-century Reformation. Nevertheless it must be recognized that the position is not the same today. All that the Orthodox Churches are asking is that

16. *Le Monde non chrétien*, 1955, p. 280.   17. Le Guillou, op. cit., p. 85.
18. Op. cit., Vol. I, p. 163.   19. Ibid., p. 164.
20. Ibid., p. 169.

there should be an end in all evangelical and missionary work to the proselytism from which they complain they have suffered at times. Their conflict, in Russia and elsewhere, with a rabid atheism obliges them, in their concern to be true to their surest tradition, to give witness of their faith in a dechristianized world. Thus their sense of the apostolate gains an added sharpness. And this painful road, again, leads Orthodoxy to an appreciation of the incorporation of the mission in the very being of the Church.

'It is an absolutely unique opportunity for a truly ecumenical dialogue', writes Père Le Guillou. 'The Orthodox Churches, like the World Council, are thus drawn into a movement that one might describe as a sort of power-house of Catholicity. Thus the problem is raised, in its full extent, in a missionary context . . . We are living in a time when the Christian mission is incessantly at grips with an essentially non-religious concept of human society . . . And to serve that mission, Orthodox, Protestants and Catholics, must in spite of the differences which separate them, meet together as men who share this "remarkable particularity, that they all acknowledge Christ as their Master, believe in his word and profess to live by it".' And Étienne Gilson, from whom Père Le Guillou quotes those last words, continues, 'The more the world around them differs from them, the closer they resemble one another . . . It is no small thing to share a common love of Christ, the saviour of mankind, and a common acceptance of his Gospel as the only saving truth.'[21]

I have spoken at some length of these books by Père Congar and Père Le Guillou,[22] not so much because of their influence on my thought as because they reflect a movement of theological reflection in the Catholic Church to which John XXIII's decision was to bring an unexpected answer. At the same time, I am not fogetting that on the eve of the Council there were other 'movements', linked with the first but still distinct from it and developing along other lines, and that these may well have

21. Op. cit., pp. 221, 222. Cf. É. Gilson, 'L'Esprit de chrétienté', in *La Vie intellectuelle*, 1945, Vol. I, pp. 34-5.
22. Other books, which I was unable to consult at the time of their publication, reflected the same ecumenical tone: for example, Père Dumont's *Les Voies de l'Unité chrétienne* and *L'Histoire doctrinale du Mouvement œcuménique* by Père Thils.

helped to pave the way in the Pope's mind and heart for an
enterprise that was so sharply contested by some and so warmly
welcomed by others.

The 'biblical revival' was developing with a vigour at which
Protestants should have been unanimous in rejoicing. The
liturgical movement, many of whose protagonists would never
have dared to go so far as the extremes popularized by the
Council's reforms, was winning over parishes in town and
country which had hitherto set their faces against the abandonment of venerable customs which had been exalted to the dignity
of infallible dogmas. The laity were beginning to refuse any longer
to be second-class Christians under the thumb of the hierarchy.
They were grieved, as were many priests and religious, to see
their Church resigning itself to being no more than a sort of
ghetto in a secularized world; and they were hoping, sometimes
with ill-concealed impatience, for the day to come when the
Catholic Church would remember that it does not exist for itself
but for the world, in which its Lord is waiting for it to serve him
in the persons of the most wretched of those to whom it has the
duty of proclaiming salvation and life.

The worker-priests were a symptom – and how prophetic a
symptom – of this thirst to go out and meet others, to seek them
out in the places where they live and toil and suffer and die. In
places where spoken languages can no longer be the vehicle for
witness to the most ardent faith, because it has become to millions
of men an alien language, all that remains is the incarnate Word:
the language the worker-priests sought to use was the language
of the love which makes a gift of self. Even though their attempt,
carried out with some lack of prudence maybe, was condemned,
it is none the less certain that it made it easier for many of the
Fathers of the Council to see more clearly what different roads
could enable the Church of Rome to make itself actively present
in the modern world.

Did John XXIII bring to light all the aspects of this presence
when, moved by the Holy Spirit, he came in the depths of his
mind to the decision which struck the Catholic Church like a
blow? He loved the poor and the humble too dearly not to
realize some of those aspects: and there can be no doubt but that

he foresaw that, if the announcement of the new Ecumenical Council was to create turmoil in the higher echelons of the Vatican, over large areas of Catholicism it would breathe a great wind of hope.

II

May I say that in our Churches of France, which I was still seeing close at hand as president of the Protestant Federation, particular attention was paid to the development of the Roman Church and to the influence of the movements I have just been appraising?

That an attitude of suspicion to Catholic institutions as a whole is congenital among a certain number of French Reformed, and that they regard all fraternizing, all dialogue and all interdenominational religious services, as abjuration and betrayal, is a fact so undeniable that one can do no more than note it. Its causes, historical, doctrinal, psychological and social, are many and varied. Contacts between priests and pastors, and between the laity of the two Churches – and even of the three, in places where Orthodox are to be found – can only be harmful and lead to a gradual falling away which ends in disastrous surrender. So at least we are assured.

It was in fact in connection with the Week of Prayer for Christian Unity and with the practical problems it raised for some of its pastors, that the Reformed Church of France was obliged to put before its regional synods, as a preliminary to its submission in 1955 to the National Synod in Strasbourg, the question of the 'external policy of the Reformed Church of France towards Catholicism': an odd formulation of a nice problem to which the National Synod gave its answer only after hearing two voluminous reports and the ramifications of a lengthy discussion in the course of which the opinions of several regional synods played their part. Pastor Albert Gaillard of Toulouse[23] concentrated on giving a picture of 'the lineaments and tendencies of French Catholicism'. Listening to his report I was struck by the fullness of his documentation, and his care not to overlook any of the aspects of the revival which could be witnessed in the Catholic Church in France since the end of the Second World War. At the same time,

23. Now general secretary of the Reformed Church of France.

in loyalty to his 'reformed' convictions and his evangelical faith, he felt obliged to point out that the biblical and liturgical revivals and the receptive attitude to the world called for in various quarters, take place within strict limits determined by the reactionary attitudes of the hierarchy, and still more by the fact that the dogmatic corpus of the Church includes elements that are foreign to (not to say contradictory to) the teaching of Christ and the testimony of the Apostles. His reservations, his doubts and fears, caused me some uneasiness, which was increased by his assumptions about the Roman Church's having closed the door in advance to the possibility of modifying any of its attitudes.

Re-reading his exposition today – and its value, let me repeat, is beyond dispute – I am surprised to note that the deliberations of Vatican 2 and a number of the constitutions and decrees it adopted and which were promulgated by Pope Paul VI, completely contradict what Albert Gaillard asserted, while at the same time on a number of points they exceed the pre-Council hopes of the 'reformists' who were frowned on by the Curia.

Professor Roger Mehl, of the Protestant faculty of theology in Strasbourg, one of the most vigorous thinkers of modern French Protestantism, gave a clear statement of the problem of the attitude the Reformed Church should determine towards *present-day* Catholicism, including, in all charity and with great lucidity, an estimate of the *present-day* development of French Catholicism. How admirable today is seen to be what Roger Mehl said in 1955: 'We must beware of in any way anticipating the future. We must, it is true, make a judgment if we are to define our attitude *today*, but this judgment holds good only here and now.'[24] With 'today' being 1966, Roger Mehl, I am sure, would reach conclusions very different from those he based on the 'today' of 1955.

He was right, however, in pointing out that 'all forms of biblical, exegetical and theological revival, and any boldness of initiative in the political and social sphere, are and remain at the mercy of a brake that may be applied by the hierarchy and the Roman Curia in particular. Such applications are quite unpredictable'.[25] What is still more unpredictable is the great wind of the Holy Spirit, breathing mightily over an assembly of 2,500 bishops and

24. *Forty-eighth National Synod*, p. 109.   25. Ibid.

inspiring them with words and decisions which cannot fail to produce a root and branch reform of the Curia, making it increasingly impossible to apply the brake in a way that even in the twentieth century has given rise to such grievous scandals.

The question Roger Mehl was asking was basically extremely simple: should we continue to regard the Church of Rome as a Church of Christ? Or must we recognize that with Catholic theology in its present stage of evolution, the structure and preaching of the Church of Rome no longer reflect the characteristics of a Christian theology and a Christian Church? To answer the second question in the affirmative is to assert that no ecumenical relationship between the two Churches is possible. To answer the first similarly, is to keep the door open to personal contacts, theological discussion, common prayer, and interdenominational biblical studies; it is to look on the Church of Rome 'as a sister Church, and to *try* to live with her the ecumenical venture to which we are manifestly summoned'.[26]

The discussion which followed the reading of these two reports turned not so much on their content as on the text of a message from the National Synod to the pastors and faithful of the Reformed Church of France, whose draft was before the members. As I was obliged to leave Strasbourg that same evening, I asked if I might speak first, and I briefly indicated my reservations. I must admit that I was once again disheartened by the 'buts' which in almost every paragraph introduced a clause which weakened or nullified the acknowledgment which the drafters felt themselves obliged to accord to a favourable element in the evolution of the Catholic Church. My intervention found no support.

It is unnecessary to reproduce here the text of this message: after the ecumenical events that have taken place since 1955, it seems out of date, much of it obsolete, full of hesitations which, accompanied by the counsels that a wise prudence demands, should have been replaced by a great act of faith and hope.

To balance this official attitude of the Reformed Church, which, as I shall soon be recording, was later reconsidered and more fully expressed, a number of personal studies should be noted.

In 1956, Hébert Roux, at that time pastor of the church of the

26. Op. cit., p. 117.

Holy Spirit in Paris, published a booklet on *Church and Mission* (*Église et Mission*).[27] His exposition, rich in biblical and ecclesiological substance, had been presented to a General Assembly of the Société des Mission évangéliques. I took the chair at this Assembly, and, in common with all the members, I had been struck by the vigour of thought and the breadth of outlook we had encountered. Père Le Guillou's book was not to appear until four years later. To French Protestants, whether their attachment was to the apostolic work of their Church or to the cause of Christian unity, Hébert Roux's reflections came with a new emphasis. From the outset he made his audience, and later his readers, face the serious problem raised for the Protestant Churches by the multiplicity of their missionary enterprises, working in ignorance of one another, and too often in competition. It was impossible, unless this missionary activity was to be impugned as somewhat dubious, not to ask oneself what were the causes of these divisions and by what means they could be cured. Any refusal to examine the question 'would tend to introduce a fatal divorce between faith as professed and faith as lived, between doctrine and life, between the institution, the internal order of the Church, and its work and practical effect in the world'.[28] The mission must be careful not to become a denominational 'good work', ceasing to exist integrally within the Church whose very being it is. The fragmenting of their apostolate inevitably raises for the Churches the problem of unity.

Oscar Cullmann, in a little book called *Catholics and Protestants, a Proposal for realizing Christian Solidarity* (*Catholiques et Protestants, un projet de solidarité chrétienne*),[29] looked at the problem from a different point of view. As Professor of New Testament Theology in the universities of Paris and Basle, he could count on an exceptionally favourable reception in Catholic circles for his *Peter, Disciple, Apostle and Martyr* (*Pierre, disciple, apôtre et martyr*), however contested some of his views might be. He is always welcome at the Vatican, where Paul VI treats him with marked confidence. His annual visits to Rome, long before the Council, have brought him into contact with the most diverse Roman

27. Société des Missions évangéliques de Paris.   28. Op. cit., p. 59.
29. London, Lutterworth, 1960.

circles. How, on the eve of the Council, did he see the problem of unity?

'The first condition for the bringing together of Catholics and Protestants', writes Cullmann, 'is absolute openness on both sides.'[30] Having made that clear, he starts from the Pauline definition of the Church as the 'Body of Christ', ruling out any possibility of schism as an infidelity and a contradiction. Since the Church is established by the Holy Spirit, a divided Church is unthinkable. By his own example the apostle Paul showed that the disciple of Christ must accept sacrifices on behalf of unity, but at the same time Paul says that there is a limit to these sacrifices: in Antioch he stands up to Peter because to yield to him would have been to sacrifice the very basis of his faith.[31] Is there not, between Catholics and Protestants, a limit beyond which the faith of each will not allow them to go? And what faith is it that intervenes? It is precisely 'faith in the Church and its unity'. It is a matter of fundamental concepts of our faith which we cannot sacrifice; and these concepts, unhappily, differ radically. The Catholic Church believes 'that according to the will of Christ himself the unity of the church is only guaranteed through the papacy; and that, as a consequence, unity can only be secured by the submission of all Christians, including the Protestants, to the Pope.'[32] The faith of Catholics in the Church founded upon Peter, of whom the Pope is the legitimate successor, prevents them from regarding our Churches as true Churches. 'The Roman Catholic and the Protestant ecumenical conceptions of unity are irreconcilable . . . The dividing line lies precisely at the point where the Roman Catholics would be forced to stop being Roman Catholics, and where the Protestants would be forced to stop being Protestants.'[33]

Thus, according to Cullmann, 'the unity of the *church* is no longer possible as far as Catholics and Protestants are concerned.'[34] Nevertheless discussion should continue. 'Perhaps we should see a hopeful sign in the fact that today this discussion is possible without any polemic.'[35]

In any case, friendship and co-operation can and must be sought

30. Op. cit., p. 7.   31. Galatians 2:13. Cf. pp. 17 ff.
32. Ibid., p. 19.   33. Ibid., p. 20.
34. Ibid., p. 23.   35. Ibid., p. 24.

in the effective practice of Christian solidarity. Thus, at the end of his book, Cullmann advocates the setting up of funds to which the faithful of each faith would subscribe in support of diaconal or social works of the other faith.

This book was written, or rather given as a lecture, more than a year before John XXIII announced his decision. I can still remember the feeling of pessimism I experienced as I listened to the lecturer. I wonder whether the Vatican Council, all of whose sessions Cullmann attended, modified his conviction: I shall have occasion to note his present position when I deal with the post-conciliar period.

The General Assembly of French Protestantism, meeting in Montbéliard from 29 October to 1 November 1960, was the last at which I presented a report in my capacity as president of the Protestant Federation of France. I had, in fact, decided not to accept this heavy responsibility for a further term – presuming my colleagues should wish me to – when the new Council of the Federation, which would follow the Assembly, elected its officials.

The question of unity was included in the considerations which I put before the many representatives of Churches, youth movements, societies, and communities assembled in Montbéliard. Wishing to communicate to them some of the causes for gloom and hope that I could then see in the situation as it was developing, I confessed that there was a shadow approaching which gave me a cold chill.

'I refer', I said, 'to the relations of the Protestant Federation with what is known as the ecumenical movement. A certain number of our fellow-Protestants seem to have succumbed to a curious obsession. As soon as they hear ecumenism mentioned, or the World Council of Churches, they see a Roman Catholic threat looming over the horizon; they completely forget that there is an ecumenism which, as a matter of extreme urgency, must be given a place within the Churches of the Reform; they are blind to everything that is being thought and done in the Protestantism of countries and continents outside our own, and even in the whole body of the non-Roman Churches. They shut themselves up, and allow themselves to be bogged down, in a negative attitude inspired by an anticatholicism which too often lacks authentic theological knowledge. Thus they subject our Churches, and the whole of Protestantism, to the danger of turning in on themselves, of an introversion that may well be fatal. They divert the attention of the Protestant Christians of France from the wide prospects which, during the last half-century, the ecumenical movement has opened up for the Churches of all denominations throughout the whole world. Let me, I beg you, tell you this: it is time for us once and for all to free ourselves, or rather to pray for the grace to free ourselves, from complexes which, if we are not careful, will imprison and isolate us in ghettos: there our eyes would finally and permanently be closed to the vision of the universal Church of Jesus Christ, whose Reformers, foremost among them Calvin and Theodore Beza, always wished her to be the light to guide evangelical communities along the road of faith.'

I make no apologies for this long quotation: it expressed a pain that had long been suppressed, the distress of having to recognize, just as I was parting from the Protestant Federation, that in the course of half a century devoted to the religious and moral unity of French Protestantism it had in effect confirmed, and perhaps hardened, the ecclesiastical distinctions or divisions of our Churches.

Visser 't Hooft delivered an address on the Church's mission, at the end of which, urging our Protestant Churches of France to collaborate even more closely, he gave us this warning:

'It must be said: in collaborating with one another, we are still not fulfilling the whole of the Church's mission. This full mission implies also the unity of the Church. This unity is not a pretty ornament, a superfluous luxury. It is necessary and essential. You have only to read the pages of the New Testament to be convinced of this.' His concluding words were a reminder that 'unity belongs to the essence of the Body of Christ'.

In January 1961 at the first meeting of the new Council of the Federation elected in accordance with the statutes then in force, I told my colleagues, after expressing my immense gratitude for their friendly and continual confidence, that they would now have to appoint my successor. That same day, to my extreme satisfaction, they elected Charles Westphal. I felt perfectly certain that with him as president there could only be a strengthening of the

link between the Protestant Federation of France and the World
Council of Churches.

It was during this decade of 1950 to 1960 that I began to give, in
numerous towns of France and abroad, lectures in which I
tended more and more to deal with the problem of Christian
unity. In the majority of cases, the greater part, sometimes even
the whole, of the audience was Catholic. On any number of
occasions I found that you can say everything you wish to
listeners whose convictions you do not share, provided you speak
with tact and charity and that there is no sign of denominational
self-interest.

   In November 1961, while preparatory work for the Council was
actively under way, I was invited by Mgr Elchinger, at that time
coadjutor-bishop of Strasbourg to lecture under the auspices of
Humanités chrétiennes on 'The World Council of Churches on the
Eve of the Vatican Council'.[36] Looking at the crowd of Catholics
and Protestants assembled in the Palais des Fêtes, and sitting
between Mgr Elchinger and Père Congar, I felt deeply moved. I
was conscious of an atmosphere of expectancy and hope, of something that was unexpressed but perfectly real: and I prayed God
to enable me to meet it.

   I was glad to have the opportunity of recommending my
audience to read two studies which I have not yet mentioned: the
first, by Pastor Bourguet, president of the National Council of
the Reformed Church, was one whose objectivity, loyalty and
fraternal understanding I had admired when I read it.[37] In the
other, by Professor Jean Bosc, on 'Protestantism and Roman
Catholicism',[38] I had met again one of my favourite convictions:
that, however small our Protestantism may be in numbers, it
can be a valuable partner in dialogue for the Catholic Church and
its theologians. This, wrote Jean Bosc, entailed a summons and
responsibility for French Protestantism. 'What has to be done is to
find out whether in its confrontation with Catholicism it can be
the vigorous and attentive collocutor, vigilant but without
prejudices, without whom dialogue would be fruitless.'

36. *L'Église en dialogue*, Éditions du Centurion, 1961.
37. *Protestantisme et Catholicisme*, Éditions *Je Sers*, 1949.
38. 'Protestantisme et catholicisme romain', in *Foi et Vie*, No. 3, 1960.

The Assembly of the World Council, called for New Delhi, was to meet some days after this Strasbourg Conference. I could not prejudge the decisions at which it would arrive, in particular, what it would think proper to say on the subject of unity. The Vatican Council would be opening the next year. I felt that I had the right to express the hopes and fears these two events were arousing among Protestants who were dedicated to the service of Christian unity. There were fears of a hardening in certain Catholic and Protestant circles, and of a tendency so to strengthen ecclesiastical institutions as completely to check the outpouring of the Spirit. And yet at the same time there were great hopes that New Delhi and Rome would make manifest a presence before whom we could all bow, a presence of love which brought with it the assurance, so often neglected, that 'what is impossible for men is possible for God'. It was only in such a climate that it would be possible to discuss such crucial questions as the Virgin Mary and St Peter in the dialogue between the various Christian denominations which would inevitably follow New Delhi and Vatican 2.

I would not like to give the impression of forgetting that even before the New Delhi Assembly (and still more after it) Orthodoxy took an increasing part in ecumenical deliberations. In a meeting such as the Rhodes Panorthodox Conference, as well as in ecumenical gatherings, Orthodox theologians and bishops were much concerned with getting ready for Vatican 2. Mgr Cassien, the saintly bishop who until his death was rector of the Paris Faculty of Orthodox Theology, kept in close and continual touch with the theological work of the committee for Faith and Order. He dreaded, it is true, the admission to the World Council of the Church of Russia, and did not spare us his warnings on that matter. When he spoke of the Vatican Council he made it quite clear that, even if the majority of the theological obstacles seemed to him surmountable, the Catholic doctrine of the Papacy, with the universal jurisdiction and infallibility of the Pope, would prove a serious stumbling-block.

Already extremely feeble, Mgr Cassien insisted on attending a number of sessions of the Council. It was in St Peter's, in the tribune where guests and observers sat, that I saw him for the last time. He left me with the memory of a man of God, of a generous heart, and of an Orthodox Christian whose filial devotion to his own Church never prevented him from loving all the Churches who confess Christ as their Lord.

III

As the Vatican Council drew closer, there was no end to the activities and talk that still call for mention. The visit paid by Dr Fisher, Archbishop of Canterbury, to Pope John X X I I I, strictly private though it was, produced conflicting reactions, but approval was more pronounced than criticism. This visit reminds me of a conversation I had in London, at the beginning of 1952, with my fellow-presidents of the World Council. Pope Pius X I I had expressed a wish to meet me. Since I did not want to do anything without my colleagues' agreement, I asked their opinion. With hardly an exception, they were against it. Among other arguments, it was urged that a visit to the Vatican would raise a scandal among the Protestants of Spain and Latin America. I bowed to their judgment; but when I learnt that after the Archbishop of Canterbury's visit, the Moderator of the Presbyterian Church of Scotland, one of the most Calvinist Churches in the world, and other Protestant Church leaders, had followed his example, I noted with satisfaction that in the course of a few years the ecumenical climate had fortunately grown more genial.

However, I must get back to the main point which, preceding the opening of the Vatican Council, was the Assembly of the World Council in New Delhi (19 November – 5 December 1961).

Since Evanston I was no longer either a president of the World Council or chairman of its Division of Ecumenical Action (in which position I had just been replaced by Mrs K. Bliss), and I accordingly decided not to go to New Delhi, to which I had been cordially invited. Later I was greatly to regret this, since there is no doubt that this third Assembly of the World Council marked a memorable date in the history of the movement towards unity.

There was already significance in the fact that the Assembly should be held in Asia, in Nehru's India: this sharply emphasized the universal character of Christianity: from five continents, there were gathered the 625 members (not counting the secretaries, advisers, observers, delegates of youth movements, and the Press), representing all the Christian Churches and communities, from the Salvation Army to the Orthodox Church, the only exception being the Church of Rome, whose fraternal attendance was nevertheless evidenced by the presence of five official observers. It was, indeed, a tremendous advance since Amsterdam, when all contact between Catholics and the Assembly had been forbidden.

The theme was 'Jesus Christ, the Light of the World'. For all the masterly skill with which it was developed, I shall leave it aside here in favour of two events which call for my attention. In the first place, the admission to the World Council of the Russian Orthodox Church and several other smaller Churches. Orthodoxy was henceforth to be represented in the Assembly by seventy-five members, which entailed considerable modifications in the running of the Council. A number of 'young' Churches were admitted at the same time, some of which, spiritual daughters of our Missionary Society, had only recently attained autonomy. The Afro-Asians (to use the now popular name) also witnessed an increase in the authority of their position. In New Delhi the 'catholicity' of the Church of Christ was manifest with incomparable brilliance.

The second event – prepared and awaited for many long years – was the final integration of the International Missionary Council and the World Council of Churches. This was much more than a simplification of administration. The final act of a long process inaugurated in the first years of the ecumenical movement is of cardinal theological importance. It finally puts an end to the distinction (too often the separation) between Church and mission. It proclaims that Church and mission are two aspects of one and the same reality. All that I have written in connection with Père Le Guillou's book can be seen in the fullness of the truth that the mission is the very being of the Church. The Christian Churches assembled in New Delhi solemnly declared this truth, and as a result the whole orientation of the World Council, and in the first place its structure, were inevitably modified.

Two other decisions made by the Assembly should be noted. The 'doctrinal basis' to be accepted by Churches seeking admission was formulated in a way that met the wishes expressed since 1939 by the Orthodox. Its trinitarian character was emphasized. I have already quoted the text adopted in Utrecht in 1938. The 1961 text was as follows:

'The World Council of Churches is a fellowship of Churches which confess the Lord Jesus Christ as God and Saviour according to the Scriptures and therefore seek to fulfil together their common calling to the glory of the one God, Father, Son and Holy Spirit.'

It is hardly necessary to note that a number of members of the Assembly were at pains to declare that the acceptance of this 'basis' did not imply adherence to any particular doctrine of the Trinity.

A new definition of unity, as conceived by the World Council, was similarly among the essential documents adopted in New Delhi. I mentioned in the appropriate context the 'Toronto declaration' (1950). Since that time, the Faith and Order Committee had reopened the study of the question. At the St Andrews Central Committee in 1960, it proposed the text which was adopted by the New Delhi Assembly in 1961. Its importance is such that I quote it in full:

'We believe that the unity which is both God's will and his gift to his Church is being made visible as all in each place who are baptized into Jesus Christ and confess him as Lord and Saviour are brought by the Holy Spirit into one fully committed fellowship, holding the one apostolic faith, preaching the one Gospel, breaking the one bread, joining in common prayer, and having a corporate life reaching out in witness and service to all and who at the same time are united with the whole Christian fellowship in all places and all ages in such wise that ministry and members are accepted by all, and that all can act and speak together as occasion requires for the tasks to which God calls his people. It is for such unity that we believe we must pray and work.'

Finally, I should add that the Assembly referred to this statement in the message it addressed to the member-Churches of the World Council and their faithful: '. . . in some things', it said, 'our convictions do not yet permit us to act together but we have made progress in giving content to the unity which we seek . . .'

Such, it seems to me, were the most decisive acts of the New

Delhi Assembly. Would I go so far as two dear friends of mine[39] and say that 'it marks the beginning of a new reform of the Christian world'? To appraise that judgment, we shall no doubt have to wait until the balance sheet of the Vatican Council can be examined: and that, too, of the vitally important 1966 Geneva Conference on 'Church and Society'.

39. Cécile and Jean Bodmer de Traz, *New Delhi*, p. 163.

CHAPTER 19

The Council
1962-1963

I. Opening of the first session. Death of John XXIII.
Paul VI and the 'separated brethren'. II. Faith and Order
Conference at Montreal 1963: Tradition and Catholicity.
Cardinal Bea in Geneva. III. Ecumenical work in France.

I

'THE Council which is now beginning is a day of light'; so spoke
Pope John XXIII, on 11 October 1962, in his opening address
at the Vatican Council. Since, on 25 January 1959, he had made
known his intention of calling an ecumenical council, a cloud of
uncertainty had to some degree overlaid his project, and the
highest hierarchical authorities had not always been at pains to
disperse it. The preparatory work had been carried out in a
mixture of order and confusion. There were ten thousand pages
of proposals submitted by bishops from all over the world, and
from these had to be selected the essential questions which the
Council would have to answer if it was not to be a failure. Ten
commissions were engaged in defining the features of the
aggiornamento sought by Pope John. The number of *schemas*
envisaged was awe-inspiring.

Nevertheless, at the solemn moment when he opened the
Council, Pope John had a perfectly clear picture of the twofold
aim he was proposing to it: the rejuvenation of the Church,
dangerously attacked by sclerosis, and the development of a
climate of respect, understanding and love between Rome and
the schismatic or heretical religious bodies separated from her.
The latter point was so constantly in his mind that as early as June
1960 he had set up a secretariat for the promotion of Christian
unity and, on Christmas Day 1961, in the bull *Humanae salutis* he
had announced his wish to welcome at the Council observers
appointed by the non-Roman Churches. A number of these were

already present on 11 October, and, even if they felt some discomfort at hearing the wording of the profession of faith to be accepted by the Fathers of the Council, their hopes were high when they heard the Pope assert that the substance of Catholic doctrine contained in the deposit of faith is one thing, the formulation it is given when it is determined, in its terms and emphasis, by the requirements of a magisterium and of a mode of expression that is primarily pastoral, is quite another.

I was not privileged to be present at the first two sessions of the Council (1962 and 1963). Nevertheless, having watched, in part at least, those of 1964 and 1965, I note here an impression that I felt from the opening of the assembly and which was confirmed when I was able to be present in St Peter's.

For the first time, the Catholic bishops from all parts of the world were gathered at the heart of Roman Catholicism, around and under the authority of the man whom they recognized as the successor of Peter and the Vicar of Christ. It was for them no ordinary event. They could see and watch one another, learn gradually to recognize one another, make contacts which in the course of the next four years would develop, pave the way to friendships and reinforce the consciousness of a solidarity that had until then remained theoretical. White, yellow, black and brown, these bishops received in the basilica of St Peter, the physical revelation – the revelation in the flesh – of their unity, and at the same time of the diversity, I might even say the opposition, of their views on the fundamental vocation of the Church in the second half of the twentieth century. The event, let me insist again, was tremendous both in itself and in the consequences, immediate or distant, with which it was pregnant.

It is not my intention to write the story of the Council. There is already a sufficiently imposing array of accounts and comments. Concentrating on the concern for ecumenism which is the inspiration of this book, I shall confine myself to drawing attention to what emerged from the life, and labours and decisions of the Council as assisting or hindering progress towards unity.

Some days after Pope John's intention had been made known, I had met a Catholic theologian engaged in the study of ecumenical problems. I asked him whether he thought the Council would include such matters in its deliberations. 'I pray God', he answered, 'that there may be nothing said at the Council about unity. That is the worst thing that could happen.'

Nevertheless, there was talk of unity. The presence of 'observers' in a gallery as near as possible to the papal throne and the table at which the presidents of the Council sat, was in itself a visible display of the grievous reality of the division of the Churches and of Pope John's hope that the Council would help to remove them. How many bishops, arriving in Rome, were ignorant of the ecumenical movement which for half a century had been forcing itself on the attention of what some still call the Christian West! And there, seated in the most favoured positions, facing the cardinals' tribune, side by side in fraternal companionship, they saw Orthodox priests, Anglican bishops, and theologians or pastors of many Protestant Churches. And they did not merely see them, they passed them in the aisles of St Peter's, they engaged them in conversation, exchanged impressions with them, and felt constrained to recognize that these schismatics and heretics gave evidence in their speech not only of sure theological knowledge but still more of an evangelical love that coloured their thoughts and their lives. Gradually, *the ecumenical challenge* asserted itself irresistibly in their minds and hearts; for four years it was to continue to become more imperative, penetrating, dominating some of the discussions and giving a completely new tone to the documents which derived from them.

As soon as I arrived in Rome, in September 1964, for the opening of the third session, I noted with joy and gratitude the respect, confidence and affection won by such observers as Hébert Roux, Professors Schlink and Skydsgaard, and Lukas Vischer, or guests such as Oscar Cullmann, Bishop Cassien, and Brothers Schutz and Thurian from Taizé.

These 'separated brethren' will never be able adequately to express their gratitude to Cardinal Bea, president of the secretariat for Christian Unity, to Mgr Willebrands, his principal assistant, and to Mgr Arrighi, whose solicitude and courtesy were constantly lavished on them. Every Tuesday there were meetings arranged by the secretariat, at which Catholic theologians could canvass the opinions, answer the questions and note the reservations of observers and give them their reply; and none will ever forget how enriching were these gatherings.

'A day of light', said Pope John, infusing his own faith and hope into the Council, at only the first session of which, unhappily, he was to preside. Many clouds were to dim the sunshine of that bright day.

Should one count among them the illness, the slow agony and death of 'Good Pope John', and the election to the supreme pontificate of Cardinal Montini, under the name of Paul VI? I think not. It is true that there was deep emotion not only in the Catholic Church but also in all the Christian Churches and even in the non-Christian world. Never had the illness and death of a pope created such a stir. Television, no doubt, accounted for much of this; but nevertheless John XXIII's humility and sincerity and the radiance of his loving kindness had won him in all quarters an unrivalled spiritual authority and devotion.

The election of Paul VI soon scattered the few clouds that gathered on the horizon on the eve of the Conclave. For all the difference between the new Pope and his predecessor, the intimacy of their relations was well known. No one, however ill-informed, doubted Paul VI's loyalty to Pope John's project; I was convinced of this at the first audience he granted me during the third session; let me record here and now the conviction I came to so quickly – John XXIII began what Paul VI would never have attempted, but Paul VI will finish what John XXIII would have been prevented from seeing through to the end. I shall have occasion later to return to this delicate point.

I could see the light of which John XXIII spoke shining through some of the papal addresses. In his opening of the second session, Paul VI, after saying that every human being is faced by three questions, exclaimed, 'Three questions, capital in their extreme simplicity, but with only one answer. And it is this answer which we have to proclaim here for ourselves and make heard by the world around us: the answer is Christ, the Christ who is our beginning, the Christ who is our way and our guide, the Christ who is our hope and our faith. May this Council keep fully in mind this relation between ourselves and Christ: may this assembly shine with no light but Christ, the light of the world: may no truth have weight with us, save the words of the Lord, our one Master!'

Pope Paul VI's address in Bethlehem, some passages of which

offended Protestant hearers, was also introduced by a presentation of the Church to Christ which radiated a pure evangelical fire. And I am convinced that, listening to Paul VI at the opening of the second session, very many of the Fathers felt themselves in living communion with him.

Whenever Paul VI received the observers he opened up for them a road of light. One of the spiritual peaks of the Council, all were agreed, was the service celebrated in St Paul's-without-the-Walls two days before the final closing of the assembly, when the papal allocution, addressed to the observers, introduced a prayer in common which will always be a treasured memory to those who took part, Catholic, Protestant and Orthodox.

I am well aware that in other circumstances, and sometimes in that same address, the Pope insisted more than once, and with an emphasis distressing to his 'separated' hearers, on the primacy of Peter and the oneness of the Roman Church. Shadows after the light! But in his own entourage, were there not, among the cardinals who had frequent access to him, a number always ready to urge on him that by supporting the collegiality of the episcopate he was jeopardizing the exercise of primacy? And what more natural than that he should seek to reassure them? Others, surprised and even scandalized by the presence of all these heretics a few paces from the papal throne, must have feared that Paul VI would allow himself to be drawn into compromises with the other Christian denominations. They, too, had to be appeased. This, I believe, is what accounts for repetitions that seemed excessive to us, and which, it would appear, were addressed more to certain Catholics than to us and our Churches.

Most of the documents adopted by the Council and promulgated by the Pope will have, and no doubt are already having, ecumenical consequences. I am thinking of the decree on the reform of the liturgy. It might be imagined that this concerns only the Catholic Church, and everyone knows the reactions it has produced, particularly among older people. Nevertheless in most places there can be no doubt about the welcome it has received from the youth of today.

From the ecumenical point of view its importance is fundamental: in the place given to the reading of Holy Scripture in the vernacular, accompanied by a homily that is in future obligatory, Catholic worship, which is almost exclusively a worship of the sacrament, is tending to become (or to revert to) worship of the sacrament *and of the Word*. At the same time, in many Protestant Churches, a renewal of the doctrine and practice of the Lord's Supper is giving our Sunday service the character of a liturgy of the Word *and of the sacrament*. The convergence is unmistakable.

One of my colleagues in the Académie française, speaking to me about a mass he had just attended, once said to me, 'But, Monsieur le Pasteur, they gave us a Protestant service!' It was an excellent opportunity to remind him that most of the Christian liturgies follow the same pattern from beginning to end, and I did not fail to do so. A remark of this sort, and others one heard in Rome ('The Church is turning Protestant') emphasize the ecumenical importance of the liturgical reform, which, violently criticized though it may be occasionally, will ultimately be universally applied.

The dogmatic constitution on the Church, *Lumen gentium*, has the same ecumenical repercussion. As most people know it continues and completes the work of the first Vatican Council, which was brusquely interrupted by the declaration of war between France and Prussia and the entry of Italian troops into Rome immediately after the adoption of the doctrine of the papacy. It is a *Roman Catholic* document, and inevitably, therefore, presents an ecclesiology with which we disagree on fundamental points. Nevertheless, it is a magnificent attempt to give the doctrine a scriptural basis whose solidity every Christian must recognize. The Council intended the Mystery of the Church, of which St Paul spoke in words which are too often misunderstood, to be offered to the contemplation of the people of God as something which takes precedence over every other consideration, and this people of God, as the New Testament constantly insists, includes the laity, however humble they may be in the eyes of the world, just as much as it does the priests, the bishops and the Pope. Any number of my Catholic friends often used to say to me, 'We are not the Church, we are in the Church': yet, even before the Council ended, a French layman, and one of some eminence, could entitle an article 'We are the People of God'.

On this point, the teaching of the Reformed Churches has always been quite definite. At the same time, they may well in practice, I fear, yield too often to the temptation of a clericalism which is all the more baneful in that it contradicts what we pastors teach from the pulpit, our consciences undisturbed by the absence in many of our parishes of any organization for the witness and service of the laity.

It is true that in spite of the assurance given to the Fathers of the Council, the Constitution on the Church could not be adopted during the second session, as was the case, too, with the decree on ecumenism, which again was discussed at length. This was perhaps one of the most distressing moments of the Council. With a desperation whose echoes could not always be contained within the walls of the papal library, cardinals and bishops of the Curia insisted that the vote on these two capital documents should be postponed to a third session – which they hoped would never be held. They had their way, but the future was to show once again that the great majority of the Fathers intended to remain true to its original approach.

II

While the examination of the schemas submitted to the Council was proceeding in the Aula of St Peter's, some notable events occurred for which the initiative of the World Council of Churches was responsible.

In the summer of 1963 there was a world conference in Montreal called by the Faith and Order Committee. It followed on the Lund Conference (1952), which itself continued from the Edinburgh Conference of 1937. After lengthy preparations in working committees, it included in its agenda the study of problems which the holding of the Council made strikingly actual: the Relation of Christ and the Church, Catholicity, Tradition and Traditions, and Worship.

Five official observers from the Catholic Church and journalist theologians of the same faith were present in Montreal, and the Orthodox Churches were largely represented. The second session of the Council was soon to open. What had already been said in Rome had an influence on the discussions in Montreal. It became abundantly clear that many Protestant members of the Conference were prepared to accord to Tradition an importance and a fruitfulness which had not been recognized before. 'It is the tradition of my Church to pay no attention to Tradition', said one delegate.[1] For the vast majority of the Conference, however, Tradition had an importance which the Catholic theologians confessed came as a pleasant surprise to them. In the same way the notion of catholicity, for the first time, it would appear, in an ecumenical assembly, gave rise to full expositions and exchanges of views which evidenced a new orientation of Lutheran and Reformed theology. Convergences of views could be distinguished in the offing, whose effects were not to be recognized until later.

Professor Albert C. Outler presented a study, 'From Disputation to Dialogue', which shed much-needed light on the conditions to be satisfied by participants in any ecumenical dialogue, if they really wish it to be not simply a matter of words but something lived in the communion of the Lord of the Church. I was greatly impressed by his insistence that 'the sovereign cure for ignorance and error in matters ecumenical is neither disputation nor mere toleration, but love' and that the apostolic rule 'speaking the truth in love' (Ephesians 4:15) is the 'scriptural charter of the entire ecumenical movement'. 'But', he added, *'neither truth nor love is served when we pretend to prefer either above the other. Dialogue must be intent upon the truth, or else be a deception; it must proceed in love, or else it will never come to the whole truth.'*[2]

Next year, the Central Committee of the World Council of Churches held its annual meeting in Enugu, in Africa. It drew up a statement, addressed to the Roman Catholic Church, proposing the setting up of a joint working group, made up of eight representatives of the World Council and six of the Catholic Church, to explore in common the possibility of dialogue and collaboration between the two.

It was this brief statement which was responsible for my meeting with Cardinal Bea in Geneva in February 1965, for our

1. I wonder whether the poor man had ever suspected that many Protestant Churches are embedded in sociological or paratheological traditions, inherited from the nineteenth century, which they mistake for the true tradition of the Reformers.

2. *Foi et Vie*, special number, May-August 1963, p. 197.

visit together to the new headquarters of the World Council and
for our dialogue in the Hall of the Reformation. I must say
something about this double event, which has been acclaimed as
'historic'.[3]

Paul VI lost no time in accepting the World Council's suggestion. Cardinal Bea himself would take the news to Geneva. It
had already been arranged, before the Enugu meeting, that the
two of us would have a public exchange of views on the ecumenical situation after the third session of the Council. There was
no difficulty in combining the two plans. On Thursday, 18 February 1965, I had, with Visser 't Hooft, the joy of welcoming the
Cardinal, accompanied by Mgr Willebrands, at the entrance to
the huge building which since 1965 has housed the numerous
departments of the World Council of Churches, and a number of
confessional organizations.

As, with our guests, we entered the hall prepared for the
solemn session about to open I felt an emotion that every reader
will appreciate. For sixty years it had been my ambition to see the
day when, in spite of all the obstacles, the Church of Rome
would agree to enter into brotherly dialogue with the other
Churches, the heretical Protestant no less than the schismatic
Orthodox. And at last that day had come.

'My very dear brothers in Christ', were Cardinal Bea's first
words. And he went on, 'the name "brothers in Christ" sums up,
in truth, all that is most profound in what we have in common by
virtue of baptism, that by which we are rooted and grounded in
love and therefore in Christ' (cf. Ephesians 3:17). No more was
needed for the great audience present – religious, civil and academic authorities, representatives of the diplomatic corps, officials
of the World Council – to be won over by the force of heart-felt
love emanating from the Cardinal, which drew from us a response
of love and made us all one in joy and gratitude. Visser 't Hooft,
in welcoming us both, had dwelt on the importance of the
Council's decree on ecumenism, and the part played in its drafting
by the secretariat for Christian Unity of which Cardinal Bea was
the life and soul. The latter emphasized the historical impact of
our meeting. 'Our brotherly love', he said before concluding, 'and
our love of unity will give us the courage required for frank

3. *Rencontre œcuménique à Genève*, Labor et Fides, p. 5.

dialogue, even on difficult questions.' In expressing our gratitude to the Cardinal, I had pleasure in pointing out that if this moment in our lives marked a completion, it was still more the starting-point of a new stage in the irreversible advance towards the unity which the eye of faith could already distinguish for us.

A book,[4] edited with great diligence by Pastor Bodmer, president of the Ecumenical Committee of the Churches in Geneva, brings back to life the excitement of those days. I shall not try, therefore, to describe the unforgettable evening of the next day. When I arrived in the Hall of the Reformation, hundreds of people, undeterred by the bad weather, were vainly trying to enter. It was a great pity that a loud-speaker had not been fitted up in the street. In the hall itself, I was overwhelmed by the sight of the vast gathering. All eyes were directed with a great air of expectation, to the dais on which the Cardinal and I were seated side by side. This was the most memorable of all those sessions, being, as it was, the official opening of a dialogue which had been carried on in private for many years and which, whatever diffi-culties and, perhaps, momentary checks it might meet, will never be abandoned.

I cannot forget the apprehensions of a certain number of Genevan Protestants, pastors and laity, as that evening approached. It was considered premature, and it was feared that I would agree to dangerous compromises. An official caution was sent to me as a fraternal warning. But, hardly was I back in Paris, when to my great satisfaction I received a letter signed by the highest Church authorities in Geneva, thanking me for my 'tact', my 'delicacy' and my 'courage'. My readers will, I am sure, forgive me for relating this incident.

III

During this period, punctuated by the successive meetings of the Council, I was constant in pursuing my ecumenical work in France. Since I was no longer president of the Protestant Federa-tion, I felt myself free to express my personal convictions; it was only myself I was committing, and so I could 'dialogue' with any-one who agreed to a public discussion with me on this or that ecumenical problem, or, more directly, on the progress of the

4. *Rencontre œcuménique à Genève*, Labor et Fides.

Council's work and the prospects opened up for us by Vatican 2. It was thus that on very many occasions I was to meet, before extremely large audiences, Père Daniélou, Père Le Guillou and others. With Mgr Delarue, at that time auxiliary bishop of Paris, a completely different subject was discussed. We held a meeting in the crypt of Saint-Honoré-d'Eylau, for members of the diocesan group of Women's Catholic Action and their husbands, at which there was a discussion in dialogue form of the Psalms, those living prayers, which was not without ecumenical overtones.

More than once I was invited by members of various orders to speak on the movement towards Christian unity or on the Council, and I accepted gladly. At the theological faculty in Lyons, directed by the Fathers of the Society of Jesus, I was received with heart-warming cordiality by the Rector, by Père de Lubac (my valued colleague in the Academy of Moral and Political Sciences) and by Père Étienne Girardon, spiritual prefect of the Jesuit Scholastics, and son of the admirable lady, who, as I mentioned earlier, showed me a friendship rooted in the love of the Lord.

In Chantilly, I was again received by the Jesuit Fathers, in the fine grounds which contain their school of philosophy and their library of half a million books. It was with great joy that I did my best, as in Lyons, to bear witness, in the presence of a large number of novices, to the fundamental convictions of a 'Reformed' Christian, but also to my vocation to serve the cause of unity, willed by the Lord of the Church, which the apostles Paul, Peter and John were the first to proclaim. It was the same with the Benedictines of Ligugé and the Cistercians of Tapié. Even in Madagascar, at the diocesan seminary of Tananarive, on that island where tragic conflicts had set Catholic missions against Protestant, the director asked me to tell the Malagash and European seminarists something about the origins and principal stages of development of the ecumenical movement.

The interest aroused by the Council brought me requests from many non-religious organizations, such as the Conférences des Ambassadeurs and the Cercle interallié.

And I must certainly not neglect to mention a new paper – which my colleagues of the Academy of Moral and Political

Sciences asked me to read on the subject of the 'Outlook for Ecumenism after the Third Session of the Vatican Council'.

What a mistake it would be to think that Protestants were still indifferent to what was maturing or being accomplished in Rome. If there were some whose chief concern was 'the defence of Protestantism' against encirclement by Rome, there were many who were anxious to receive clear and objective news, untainted by an optimism that is merely superficial or by a negative attitude that systematically refuses sympathy. I tried not to disappoint the latter, and in doing so I made valuable contacts. Local ecumenical committees would organize exhibitions of great educational value. The unreceptiveness of some was balanced by the keen interest of others. What I had always longed for, ecumenical education in the parish, was being intelligently and efficiently undertaken by pastors and laity.

Hébert Roux, on his side, was conducting a propaganda campaign addressed to the public in general, and in many pastoral meetings used to comment on the conciliar documents already published or in an advanced state of examination. Countless Protestant theologians, such as Jean Bosc and Roger Mehl, were busy in making known, in unimpaired fidelity to the faith of their Church, the spirit which animated the Fathers of the Council in their desire for reform, even while they emphasized their reservations on one or other of the subjects under discussion.

Our 'religious' Press, under fire from readers with contradictory views, was often hesitant and even suspicious. *Réforme*, which is read as much in lay and Catholic circles as in Protestant, in its desire to take a clear line, often displayed pessimism that in my eyes was unjustified.

It is time, however, to get back to the Council, much of the third and the fourth sessions of which, by Cardinal Bea's kind invitation, I was able to attend.

CHAPTER 20

Visits to Rome
1964-1965

I. The third session of the Council. First contacts in Rome.
II. Freedom of religious belief and Revelation. III. First
audience with Paul VI. IV. Lecture to the Cercle Saint-
Louis-de-France November 1964. Tumult in St Peter's.
Mixed marriages.

EVERY time I arrive in Rome I am overcome by the beauty and
charm of that unique city. The very first evening I cannot refrain
from walking up to the piazza of the Capitol and gazing at its
admirable harmony. The next morning I am impatient to see
again the places of which I am most fond: the Piazza Navona
with Bernini's fountain, the Spanish steps of the Trinita del
Monte, the Pincio, from which in one sweep I can survey the
whole city. And how I love meeting again, in front of the Albergo
Minerva, where at last I feel I am at home, the marble elephant,
standing solid under the weight of its Egyptian obelisk! What a
joy, too, to find my way again along those narrow pavementless
lanes, where so many of the *trattorie* are to be found! However,
on this occasion it was the Council that had brought me to Rome,
and I had to be content with occasional sightseeing in one of the
Roman horse-drawn cabs whose drivers guide them through the
medley of cars with such unfailing skill.

I

It was at the inaugural ceremony of the third session, on 14
September 1964, that I made my first physical contact with the
Council. The event was exceptional: for the first time Mass was
concelebrated by Paul VI and twenty-four of the Fathers of the
Council, representatives of the world-wide Church. Here the
liturgical reform was giving us one of the first of its fruits: 'The
celebration of the Eucharist by a number of priests at the same
altar, and their communion with the same bread and the same

chalice, are a clear manifestation of the unity of the priesthood and of the Church.'[1]

The spectacle – for one cannot but use the word – was impressive. Père Wenger, in a reference to my presence in his account of the third session,[2] notes that for me it was an unexpected but natural culmination of my long ecumenical career. He adds, 'The splendour of St Peter's, the pomp of the public session to which princes and ambassadors were invited . . . were such that he could only stand and wonder.'

On Low Sunday in 1951, before preaching in the Waldensian church of Quattro Novembre, I had been present at the Mass celebrated by Pope Pius XII. I had been moved by his ascetic face, but the sedia gestatoria, the costumes of the Roman princes, the helmets and halberds of the Noble Guard, and the acclamations of a vast crowd, had had a most depressing effect on me. In 1964 the sedia was less ostentatious, the tall fans had gone, and the Pope did not give the impression of playing up to, but rather deprecating, the cheering. Apart from the Fathers of the Council, there was a very large attendance of theologians, secretaries and other Council officials. There was not a single empty seat in the diplomatic tribune, where observers and guests were seated at the general assemblies. I recognized our Ambassador to the Holy See, and Mme Brouillet, whose warm welcome on each of my visits I remember with gratitude. My daughter Denyse Berthoud was with them as their guest, and it was a great joy to have her with me in Rome at this stage of my ecumenical life.

Mgr Arrighi, with unparalleled kindness, had given me a place in the middle of the observers and guests. There I met old friends from America, Germany, the Scandinavian countries, and above all Oscar Cullmann and Brothers Schutz and Max Thurian from Taizé. Being only a few steps from the *Confessio*, the pontifical throne and the altar, we were to miss no details of the liturgical actions or the words pronounced.

The concelebrated Mass dragged somewhat, and it was difficult to avoid having the impression that the liturgy was at a standstill; one felt impatient for it to end and for Paul VI to address us.

1. Introduction to the liturgy of the opening service for the third session, p. 10.
2. *Chronique de la troisième session*, Éditions du Centurion, p. 26.

Alas! We first had to listen to the profession of faith by the Fathers of the Council, a legacy from the Council of Trent which intended it to be uncompromisingly anti-Protestant: in the ecumenical climate produced by the two first sessions, how was it that it was not felt necessary to modify it?

At last, however, the Pope spoke. He dealt with collegiality, with the powers of bishops and their association with the Pope in the government of the Church. His voice and his tone were a disappointment to me; and then suddenly a new tone could be heard. His voice became stronger and warmer, betraying an emotion that communicated itself to all of us. When Paul VI addressed himself to the observers and spoke of the separated Churches, 'the objects of our hopes and tears', it was impossible not to be deeply moved. I mentioned this feeling in an interview I gave to *La Croix* and expressed the conviction that the Pope's appeal to the Churches had been directed to all the 'communities' not attached to Rome. 'This would accordingly be', I added, 'the first time that Paul VI has given our Churches born of the Reformation the name which they know they have the right to bear.'[3]

When, on 26 September, I was received by the Sovereign Pontiff, I asked him quite plainly whether my interpretation of his words was correct, and he was good enough to confirm it.

II

There was a full programme for the session which had just opened, for it included no less than thirteen schemas. I shall refer only to those which touched on my subject; the discussion of some of these was not to be completed until the fourth session.

Every morning I was driven to St Peter's by my friends from Taizé, whose kindness to me during my visits to Rome was a great blessing. As we turned into the Via della Conciliazione I used to see hundreds of bishops mounting the steps of the basilica, the purple of their soutanes often giving way to scarlet. Seen in the light of a bright autumn day, they formed a great wave of purple, gently fluttering in the light breeze. Every day the same sight was

3. *La Croix*, 18 September 1964.

to be seen, attracting a crowd of tourists. Entering by the Santa Maria door, I would make my way to the tribune reserved for observers and guests of the secretariat for unity, while the majority of the cardinals were still arriving. I would greet with pleasure the French cardinals, Feltin of Paris, Liénart of Lille, Richaud of Bordeaux, Gerlier of Lyons, Martin of Rouen, Lefèvre of Bourges. Cardinal Tisserant, who as Dean of the Sacred College was president of the board of presidents, was always one of the first and would already be there.

Entirely by chance rather than design, our little group of guests used to occupy the left-hand corner of our tribune: Cullmann, Mgr Cassien, the brothers from Taizé and I used to sit close to one another. Just below me, I could see the Sistine choir, or the choirs brought in to accompany the services of other rites. The corner of the tribune overlooked the table of the secretary-general, Mgr (now Cardinal) Felici, and his assistants: Mgr Villot,[4] coadjutor of Lyons, was one of them during the third session; when, on the death of Cardinal Gerlier, he became Cardinal Villot, he was replaced by another Frenchman, Mgr Le Cordier, Bishop of Saint-Denis.

A few yards away was the table of the moderators, Cardinals Agagnian, Lercaro, Suenens and Döpfner. Behind them, and a little raised, the long table of the presidents, with Cardinal Liénart sitting on the right of Cardinal Tisserant. The latter would vacate his chair when the Pope himself attended the general assembly.

This was opened by the conciliar Mass, preceded by the solemn 'enthroning' of the Gospel at one side of the conciliar altar. From my place I could follow every detail of the liturgical action; this began at 9 o'clock, and was followed, immediately after Cardinal Tisserant had read the prayer for the Council, by the opening of the general assembly under the presidency of one of the moderators.

It was by attending the conciliar Mass that I came day by day better to appreciate the importance of the reform of the liturgy. Saying Mass in the vernacular necessarily changed the rhythm of the readings and prayers. I regret to say that the speed at which

4. Cardinal Villot is now head of the Congregation of the Clergy. He played a leading part in the episcopal synod.

most of the celebrants recite or read the Latin makes it impossible for the faithful to *think* the words they are listening to, even when it is the *Pater Noster*. When the vernacular is used, it is quite different: the celebrant is forced to modify and slow down his rhythm, and the faithful *take in* the words, now that they are said more slowly; they no longer flow superficially over their minds but penetrate them. This is one of the reasons why, since the reform, the liturgy of the Word is acquiring an increasing influence.

There was a great deal said about the Virgin Mary during the early days of this session. The eighth and last chapter of the dogmatic Constitution *De Ecclesia* is devoted to her. I wonder whether I was mistaken in feeling, after listening to numerous lengthy expositions, that the majority of the Fathers did not wish to see any new developments in Mariology, and that an attitude of extreme reserve could be detected when the titles of co-redemptress or universal mediatrix were first used.

The discussion of the decree on freedom of religious belief opened on 23 September. I noted that on that day Paul VI attended the conciliar Mass, and displayed to the bishops the celebrated relic, the *head* of St Andrew, which he had decided to give back to the Orthodox Church of Greece.

The discussion was opened by a remarkable exposition from Mgr De Smedt, Bishop of Bruges. In all quarters it was expected that there would be an exchange of impassioned expressions of approval or dissent. Moreover, in all the Christian Churches, and in non-Christian religious bodies and lay circles, too, there was a readiness to judge the Council – and the Church of Rome – by the nature of the resolution it adopted.

Nine cardinals were the first to speak. Where on earth did their listeners, myself among them, think they were taking them? At some moments I could only wonder where I was: was I among theologians of the age when the Inquisition flourished? Or in a gathering of American Christians for whom Christianity means democracy and the rights of the human person? Or in a theological debate on thesis and hypothesis? Cardinals Cushing and Meyer of the United States, and Cardinals Ottaviani and Ruffini of Italy, contradicted one another violently. What a sight it was to see

Cardinal Cushing, who had come back specially for this debate, bellowing into the microphone, in almost inaudible Latin, his conviction that the Church, having always claimed freedom for herself, must finally recognize it for others!

From the other side, from Cardinals Ottaviani and Ruffini, and later from Cardinal Browne, very different language was heard. 'So!' exclaimed one of them. 'You proclaim the freedom of error! It is true, of course, that God has given man freedom, but he gives it in order that man may freely adhere to Catholic truth, outside which there can only be falsehood or heresy': which brought the reply: 'Error is always error, in our eyes as much as in yours; nevertheless we accord to the man who finds his truth in error the right openly to say so. And if we are to combat his truth, we may do so only with the weapons of light of which St Paul speaks.'

The one hundred and six expositions of this subject which I was to hear in the course of the third and fourth sessions did not, on the whole, lay much emphasis on what Holy Scripture teaches, implicitly or explicitly, on freedom of belief. Many observers noted this with great surprise. Later I shall have more to say about this great debate which the last session of the Council brought to a conclusion whose revolutionary nature had been unhesitatingly denounced by the opponents of the schema.

Here I shall simply note that the declaration on the Jews, originally attached to the Decree on freedom of religious belief, became later an integral part of the schema dealing with relations between the Church of Rome and non-Christian religions. At the beginning of the third session, in the debate I have just summarized, it raised violent conflicts which augured ill for its future.

III

All the Fathers of the Council, and with them the experts and still more the observers, were impatiently awaiting the discussion of the schema on Revelation, whose chequered history lies outside the scope of this book. The original text, amended and modified in its structure and substance, now bears the title 'On Divine Revelation', thus ruling out the assertion, implicit in the title of the first draft, that there are two distinct sources of Revelation, Scripture and Tradition.[5]

There is no need to emphasize the importance for ecumenism of the discussion which opened on 30 September 1964. Neither the Fathers nor the observers had forgotten the violent opposition aroused, during the Council's first session, by the text proposed by the preparatory doctrinal commission, which was profoundly influenced by the Holy Office and the Roman universities. John XXIII had decided to refer it back to a joint commission on which the secretariat for Christian unity would be strongly represented. It was on the result of this work that the Council now had to pronounce.

I was obliged to get back to France, where I was to preside at meetings of the Committee of the Société des Missions and of Cimade and lecture in several provincial towns; I was therefore able to attend only the general congregation, to which Mgr Florit, Archbishop of Florence, presented his report on the first two chapters of the schema. He emphasized the importance of Chapter II, 'On the Transmission of Divine Revelation'. Tradition is defined there as the living transmission of Revelation; it transmits everything that concerns the life, the faith and worship of the Church founded by the Apostles. 'Everything that the Church is, and everything it has, belongs to the domain of Tradition; and in the first place Scripture itself, as being indissolubly one with the Church and in consequence deriving life and strength from the witness of Tradition . . . Tradition is constantly regenerated from the sources of Scripture, and Scripture in turn is illuminated in the light of the developments of Tradition.'[6]

The spokesman for the minority, Mgr Franic, Bishop of Split, complained that the draft did not accord to Tradition its true place. It is Tradition alone that enables us to know truths which are not revealed by Scripture: an assertion which brought out into the open the profound divergence between the constant teaching of the Churches of the Reformation and that of the Church of Rome. It was most satisfactory to hear Cardinal Meyer, Archbishop of Chicago, having no hesitation in speaking of the

5. The schema presented at the first session was entitled, 'On the Sources of Revelation'.
6. Père Wenger, op. cit., p. 144.

shortcomings of Tradition, which can be made good only by the verdict of Scripture. This was bringing us uncommonly close to the *normative* authority of Scripture. In any case, the character of the schema was in no way anti-Protestant, at which Mgr Rougé, Bishop of Nîmes, expressed his satisfaction. I shall have occasion to refer again to this fundamental document when we come to the fourth session.

On the day after the opening ceremony I attended the regular Tuesday meeting between the observers and guests, and representatives of the secretariat for unity and Catholic theologians. They were generally presided over by Mgr Willebrands. Views were exchanged on the problems argued in the Council, Oscar Cullmann, Skydsgaard of Copenhagen, and Schlink of Heidelberg taking leading parts. I am grateful for having had the opportunity to benefit from such a rich store of spiritual and intellectual wealth shared so freely.

I used to meet the theologians again, and also the Fathers of the Council, in other places besides the Unitas centre, in the Piazza Navona, where the Tuesday meetings were held: and first of all in St Peter's itself. We did not always stay in our tribune to listen to the expositions succeeding one another every ten minutes, which were translated for us by the generosity of a young Jesuit to whom I still feel most grateful. There was a great deal of repetition, and it was tempting to make one's way closer to the *Confessio*, in the part behind Bernini's famous baldacchino, where private conversations could be carried on between Fathers of the Council, theologians, observers and guests, without in any way disturbing the discussion in the general congregation. I used to enjoy meeting Pères de Lubac, Congar, Villain, Chenu, Refoulé, and gather their impressions, sometimes pessimistic, sometimes hopeful and even jubilant. Bishops from France, Switzerland, England or Madagascar would recognize me and useful conversations would follow. At times these took place in the conciliar bars, of which there has been so much talk. These opened at 11 o'clock and were immediately well patronized. They offered a chance to relax and meet one's friends over a welcome *capucino* and brioche: most refreshing after two hours' solid listening, which was particularly tiring for the most recently consecrated bishops, who sat near the entrance to the conciliar Aula. The excellent amplification system enabled them to hear perfectly well, but they had only a distant view of what was going on near the *Confessio*.

By the kindness of the French Ambassador and Mme Brouillet I was able to meet French bishops at the Villa Bonaparte. I was invited to meals with the latter at the French Seminary or the Cercle Saint-Louis-des-Français. And it was there, towards the end of my first visit, that the four members of the Académie française who were in Rome met together – Cardinal Tisserant, Wladimir d'Ormesson, Jean Guitton and I.

The papal audience for observers and guests of the secretariat for unity was fixed for 26 September in the Sistine Chapel. Long before the time appointed we were all assembled, each in the place to which we had been directed by Mgr Arrighi. I thought of the times when I had been in this celebrated chapel: on the last occasion the crowd had been so packed and noisy that my wife and I had left almost immediately. Today, waiting in almost complete silence for the arrival of Pope Paul, we had time to examine Michael Angelo's work at leisure. It would be absurd presumption on my part to attempt to describe its beauty. I gazed, drinking in the wonders communicated to eye, mind and heart by that magnificent ceiling and those magnificent walls.

Cardinal Bea, accompanied by Mgr Willebrands, came in just before Pope Paul. The papal suite consisted of only a few persons; the Pope came to us, quite simply, as a brother to brothers. Cardinal Bea quietly emphasized the significance of the meeting. An Orthodox observer, on behalf of all of us (we were about seventy-five), expressed our gratitude to the Holy Father and the intense interest we found in sharing the life of the Council. Paul VI's reply was warm, brotherly and with a message of hope. At the same time this was not, as it was the year before, a sort of theological dialogue, an exchange of question and answer between the separated Churches and the Roman Catholic Church. The Pope went round our circle, saying a few words to each of us as we were introduced in turn by Cardinal Bea and giving us a copy of the recent Greek and Latin edition of the New Testament. He soon withdrew, walking with the quick step so noticeable to anyone who saw him attending the conciliar Masses or general congregations.

As Pope Paul stopped in front of me he reminded me of our recent conversation. He had, in fact, received me late on the morning of 26 September. It was not so much the Pope as the man I had met on that day. I had an overpowering feeling of solitude. A dozen or more rooms led to the library in which the Pope gave audience. On that day they were completely deserted except for a few of the Noble Guard. This emptiness made almost a physical impression on me. I seemed to be finding my way to a man who was completely *alone*. Finally I reached the room where I was received by the chamberlain on duty. A bell was rung, he opened the door, and I was in the presence of Paul VI.

There was a wonderful cordiality in his greeting, affection in his look, and strength in his handclasp. Immediately, seated side by side at a corner of his big table, we began to talk as though we were old acquaintances. The same devotion to the cause of unity was a close bond between us. I do not doubt that he recognized in the man he greeted so warmly one of the few survivors of the beginnings of the ecumenical movement. The Pope picked up, lying ready to his hand, a copy of the lecture I had given in Strasbourg the year before, and read out a passage which had struck him. We spoke about the Council. I raised the question of freedom of belief and mixed marriages. I told him how grateful I was for the first chapters of the Constitution on the Church: The Mystery of the Church, and the People of God.

I was in the presence of a man who suffered. It is impossible to have just a simple conversation with him without being aware of a heart, a Christian soul, that is tried by suffering. Whether or not it be hypersensitivity, of the suffering there can be no doubt. But what one sees is the suffering of the Sovereign Pontiff, who, there can be no question, is eager to carry through the great project of John XXIII, and day after day has to support the obstinate and skilfully applied pressure of its opponents. They are on the spot, right in the Vatican itself, with free access to his person and, as no one doubts, harassing the Pope with objections, doubts and prophecies of evil. Listening to Paul VI, I obtained some idea of the terrifying responsibility that lies heavy on him, the fear of splits in the unity of the Council, of mistakes into which the majority might allow itself to be drawn, of hidden wishes to have done with this Council which has already lasted too long. I could not refrain from telling him that we were praying to God to give him great courage.

At last I had reached this goal – nearly sixty years after my birth into ecumenical life, after experiencing so many disappointments, and so much pain, too, from the suspicions and refusals and condemnations of the Church of Rome. It had, indeed, been a long road for those who had, as I had, lived through this great adventure: and yet how many more stages lie ahead before our thirst for unity can truly be quenched!

After taking my leave, I thought of the loneliness which had struck me so forcibly. Had Paul VI friends with whom he could speak freely of the problems he had to face day after day? But is not a man always humanly alone on so exalted a peak? All his 'sons' and all his 'daughters', who cannot approach him without bending their knees – have they any idea of the crushing weight under which he can stand upright before God, or kneel before him, only by means of God's grace? Time and again, in recent years, when I have been speaking to many Catholic listeners, I have urged on them the duty of praying tirelessly for the man whom they call their Holy Father, that God may keep him, with the humility, the courage, the clear vision of the goal to be won – and with the love. We too, the 'separated brethren', have the duty of praying for this servant of Christ Jesus, who knows so well what a stumbling-block on the road to unity is the dogma of the papacy. His initiative, his decisions, his attitude towards non-Catholics, and what he rejects and what he accepts, can have great influence on the 'dialogues' Rome has opened, or will later open, with other Christian Churches. How, then, could we fail to include him in our prayers?

The Pope's journey to Fatima, regretted by many Catholics and almost unanimously criticized by Protestants, cannot excuse us from this ministry of prayer. Was it necessary for Paul VI, by going to Fatima to pray for peace, to risk an increased hardening of anti-ecumenism in non-Roman circles? The words he spoke about the devotion to Mary, with our Churches in mind, were designed to counter the uneasiness we were bound to feel: but whether in fact they did so, is something that I may be allowed to doubt.

On 1 October I was back in Paris, and plunged again into the life, full of bustle and overburdened with work and yet absorbingly interesting, which I had known for so many years.

IV

My return to Rome on 4 November had a more official character. M. Brouillet had asked me to give a public lecture to the Cercle Saint-Louis-de-France. The subject was 'Our Common Road to Unity'. The Ministry of Culture sponsored my visit, and on my arrival I was welcomed by Père Darcy, a Dominican and one of the theologians attached to the Embassy.[7]

I need hardly say more here than that the lecture took place on 11 November. Two patriarchs, some cardinals and many French or French-speaking bishops, Catholic and Protestant theologians, the Ambassador and his colleagues, were among my audience. I had occasion to quote some of Fallot's sayings, which I included in the early part of this book; several bishops were so struck by them that they asked if they might copy them out. The audience was attentive and warmly sympathetic.

The pastors of Rome and the professors of the faculty of theology had been good enough, during my first visit, to treat me with great friendliness. Several of them were old acquaintances. Every morning I used to meet in the Council Dean Subilia, observer on behalf of the World Alliance of Reformed Churches. On 24 October a dinner of Waldensians from Uruguay, whom I had known in their parishes in Rio de la Plata from my visit there in 1949, had already given me an opportunity of meeting some of the Roman pastors again. They asked me to preach in the big Protestant church in the Piazza Cavour. I accepted gladly and with gratitude, and so I took part in the worship on 15 November. Afterwards there was a most hospitable meal in the outskirts of Rome, where I was able to meet my colleagues of the Tavola

7. Père Darcy's sudden death in 1967 was a grievous blow to all who knew him.

Valdese[8] and their wives. I was to meet them again during the fourth session.

But to get back to the Council: the Pope attended on several occasions. However, on the first occasion, on 6 November, he was faced by a serious disagreement between the Fathers of the Council and himself. The subject under discussion was the schema on the Church's missionary work. Before withdrawing, Paul VI said that the document was sound and should be adopted. Of the sixteen or seventeen who spoke on the subject, all except one, if my memory is correct, were of the opinion that it should be rejected. Their view would have prevailed, had not the Commission asked, through Mgr Riobé, Bishop of Orleans, for the text to be sent back to them for complete redrafting.

On 13 November, in the presence of the Pope, Patriarch Maximos (the only conciliar Father who spoke in French at the general congregations), celebrated the Mass of the feast of St John Chrysostom. I was wondering whether the Pope would speak, but he preferred a practical gesture: Mgr Felici announced to the Fathers that, moved by the heart-rending references to poverty that punctuated the first discussions of schema 13, the Pope had decided to offer his tiara for the poor. Mgr Dante, the Pope's master of ceremonies, was then seen to hand the tiara to Paul VI, who silently placed it on the altar. He then withdrew, cheered by the crowds which had poured into St Peter's.

Although he was not seen in the Aula of the Council, the Pope was closely concerned in the events which marked the last days of the session. Mgr Felici delivered to the Fathers, 'by decision of higher authority', i.e. by decision of the Pope, a note explanatory of Chapter III of the Constitution *De Ecclesia*. This caused very considerable excitement among the majority, which was greatly heightened when on 19 November, even though it had been understood the day before that the Council would be invited on the 20th to vote in principle on the decree on freedom of religion, Cardinal Tisserant announced, somewhat brusquely it would appear, and certainly without any preparatory speech, that some bishops had asked for more time to study the completely redrafted text, and that their wishes would be met. No vote,

8. 'Tavola Valdese' is the name of the executive committee of the Reformed Waldensian Church of Italy.

therefore, was taken, and the whole matter was held over for the fourth session.

At this news great feeling was shown by all who were present. Hundreds of the Fathers left their tribunes and hurried across to the tables of the moderators, the presidential council and the general secretariat. There was a real hubbub and a chorus of violent protests. I have never witnessed such a scene in a synod of the Reformed Church.

Peace had hardly been restored when Mgr Felici produced another surprise by informing the Fathers of the Council of modifications which the Pope had asked Cardinal Bea to introduce into the decree on ecumenism. This decree, however, was none the less adopted almost unanimously and promulgated by Paul VI at the closing sitting on 21 November. On the same day he proclaimed Mary 'the Mother of the Church'.

I shall hasten over the schemas which, towards the end of the session, I heard the Fathers discuss, sometimes more fully, sometimes less, in the general congregations: the revival of the religious life, training for the priesthood, Christian education, and the sacrament of marriage, all produced contributions which were often noteworthy. I shall mention only the exposition given by Mgr Garrone, Archbishop of Toulouse, of the problem of the organization of seminaries and of the methods, 'calling for complete revision', of the Congregation for Seminaries. The authoritative position he thus won in that field brought, at the end of the Council, his nomination by Paul VI as sub-prefect of that important body. This was to be the first time a French archbishop had been given such a position.[9]

The problem of mixed marriages was to have been introduced before the end of the session. Observers and Protestant guests attached the utmost importance to this. The discussion, however, did not begin until the morning of the last day and, at Cardinal Döpfner's proposal, resulted in a motion addressed directly to the Pope. Later I shall describe the further developments of this ill-starred venture.

On the afternoon of the same day, Paul VI concelebrated the closing Mass with twenty-four bishops representing the principal

9. Mgr (now Cardinal) Garrone is today prefect of the Congregation of Catholic education.

Marian sanctuaries. The fatigue of over-many discussions and the emotions of the preceding days seemed to weaken the grandeur of the service. Nevertheless, when the Pope promulgated the dogmatic Constitution on the Church, and the decrees on the Eastern Churches and ecumenism, the breath of the Spirit seemed active in the basilica: the fourth session was approaching under the sign of hope.

CHAPTER 21

The Council Completes its Work
1965

I. Lectures in Morocco and France. II. Opening of the
fourth session of the Council. Freedom of religion.
Schema 13. III. Mixed marriages again. Paul VI's farewell
to the observers. The lifting of excommunications. Paul VI's
gesture in St Peter's Square.

THE months following my return from Rome were fully occupied, quite apart from the committees at which I still presided, by my own ministry of preaching and visiting, my share in the work of the Académie française and the Academy of Moral and Political Sciences and by almost constant ecumenical activities. In over fifty towns, in France, Switzerland, Belgium and Morocco, I was invited to give lectures, mostly on the Vatican Council, the problems it raised for the Reformed Churches, or some other aspect of the ecumenical movement.

I

I was hardly back in Paris before I left for Morocco, where the Evangelical Church always has an inspiring welcome for me. Whenever I am in Morocco I call on Mgr Lefèvre, Archbishop of Rabat. He was just back from Rome when he received me with his usual cordiality. He gave me his impressions of the Council, and I learnt a great deal from our conversation.[1]

I must not neglect this opportunity of expressing my gratitude to the fifteen cardinals, archbishops or bishops, whom I met or who received me in their residences during this last interval in the Council's meetings. I am indebted to them for the evidence of their trust in me, the information I received from them, and their answers to my numerous questions; and above all I am glad of the opportunity to pay tribute to their evangelical fervour, to their ecumenical spirit, stimulated by what they had seen and

1. Mgr Lefèvre died quite recently.

heard in Rome, and to their fraternal understanding. Many were the times when I wished that some of my Reformed brothers, incorrigible enemies of ecumenism, could have had the surprise and joy and benefit of an open-hearted conversation with some of these bishops, whose pastoral sense I found so perceptive.

The fact that during this period I was able to develop relations formed before the Council or at the meetings in St Peter's, I owed partly to the initiative of lay organizations; in the majority of cases, however, my debt was to pastors of town or country parishes or to ecumenical committees founded by them. A certain reserve or suspicion towards the ecumenical movement, and most of all to any approach to the Church of Rome, can be found in our Protestantism, it is true: but it is far from being general. Education in ecumenism has for a long time been organized by pastors, by no means all of whom belong to the younger generations. I feel great gratitude towards them, since it has very often been those men, by their personal relations with the Catholic clergy and their perseverance in making their parishioners face their ecumenical responsibility, who have made it possible for me to speak to audiences which were often very large and in which Catholics were in the great majority.

Some of those audiences showed a special interest in the ecumenical dialogues to which they were invited. At that time Père Daniélou and I had a number of public exchanges of views: in Paris, at the Catholic church of the Holy Spirit, at a Conférence des Ambassadeurs, in Le Mans, in Brussels (with Cardinal Suenens in the chair) and in various other places. Père Daniélou's lively intelligence, his readiness in giving a prompt reply, and his theological knowledge and skill make him an uncommonly fine partner in such a discussion.

In the early months of this period the ecumenical world was saddened by grievous blows, which struck me through some very old friendships.

I had known Professor Zander, of the St Sergius School of Orthodox Theology, since the inter-war period. He had been one of the initiators of the interdenominational meetings of which I wrote earlier, the presence at which of such men as Berdyaev, Laberthonnière or Maritain gave them enormous zest, characterized by violent oppositions. A disciple and friend of Bulgakov, the great Orthodox theologian of the last half-century, Professor Zander had an exhaustive knowledge of the thousands of pages written by his teacher and had translated a number of his works into French. He was an enthusiastic worker in the cause of Christian unity, which he served with passion but at the same time in strict loyalty to his conviction that Orthodoxy would have a leading part to play in the progress towards unity. I had the moving task of speaking in St Sergius over his bier.

A similar blow fell at the beginning of February 1965 when our beloved Bishop Cassien died, the rector of the same theological school. His failing health had not kept him from attending, as a guest, the first sessions of the Council. I have already mentioned that we were neighbours in the same tribune during the general congregations of the third session.

We all felt his death as a personal loss. He was above all a man of God, a man of prayer, who radiated an authentic love. He had been very familiar with the monastic life, and his personality as a Christian bore the stamp of Mount Athos.

Cardinal Gerlier, Archbishop of Lyons, was a great contrast to this monk-bishop. 'Prince of the Church' was the phrase almost invariably used to describe him: a name now happily consigned to oblivion. His great height, his piercing look, and his majestic air, gave him authority from the outset. It will be remembered that the Cardinal and I were very closely associated during the occupation years. At the Council, where I saw him often, everyone was struck by his increasing weakness. Back in Lyons, after the third session, he sank rapidly. Nevertheless he expressed a wish to attend the lecture I was to give on 19 January in the Burdeau hall . . . That same day I went to Fourvières to salute his mortal remains. Mgr Villot, coadjutor, and now Archbishop and primate of the Gauls, was just arriving from Rome. He joined me by the coffin of the man who had wished him to be his successor. To the astonishment of the faithful who had come to salute once more their pastor, Mgr Villot, his vicars-general who were present, my colleague Atger and I recited together the Lord's Prayer; such spontaneous ecumenical action was continued, at my lecture in the evening, by the words of Mgr Ancel, the 'worker-bishop'.

To the names of these builders of ecumenism, let me add that of one of my fellow-Academicians, Count Robert d'Harcourt, a fervent Catholic whose extreme strictness in 'practice' was combined with an ecumenical receptiveness that I constantly appreciated in our conversations.

I was director of the Académie française at the time when Robert d'Harcourt died, shortly after his wife. It fell to me, accordingly, to represent the Académie at his funeral, which took place on 22 June in Pargny-lès-Reims, where his home was. As we came out of the church into the village square, I paid our tribute to this noble and deeply Christian soul, in the presence of his large family and the whole population, all Catholics, of Pargny. It was a poignant opportunity to proclaim the gospel of the Resurrection, and to show that in the love with which God loves us in Jesus Christ, lies the source of the love with which we, who profess to be his disciples, should love one another in the 'unity of his body which is the Church' (cf. Ephesians 1:23).

In the months that followed I note a number of events which had ecumenical implications.

My young and well-loved colleague Jacques Maury – Pierre Maury's younger son – had asked me to lecture in Poitiers on 'French Protestantism and Some Major Problems of Today'. This gave me the chance of accepting an invitation from the Benedictine Fathers of Ligugé. Three talks in the course of a few hours, on the Council as seen by a 'separated brother', and a long conversation with Père Lefèvre, made this a most fruitful visit. I left them carrying a souvenir in the form of one of their beautiful enamels.

Some days later I was in Rouen, lecturing, at the request of Pastor Durand, in the former circus. Cardinal Martin was present. During the course of the day, I had been able to discuss with him at length the concern felt in Protestant circles all over the world about a number of problems still to be debated in the Council, and at the Pope's delay in replying to the petition concerning mixed marriages.

In May I was in the heart of the steel industry, at Villerupt, Longwy and Audun-le-Tiche. I was taking part in a discussion between local priests and pastors, at which we studied together the decree on ecumenism. In a number of priests I could detect an impatience for more far-reaching reforms than those promulgated at the first three sessions of the Council. These days were lived by us in a complete fraternal communion; and this was due to the ecumenical zeal of Pastor Jacques Diény, whose life is still devoted to Lorraine, the home for many years of such serious industrial and social problems.

I had continually to answer questions from Catholic laity and clergy about the divisions and separations of Protestantism in the widest sense of the words. Both before and after the last session of Vatican 2, I had endless opportunities of replying to the most diverse questions. At the theological faculty of Louvain, at the Foreign Missions Seminary of Bièvres, and at the friary of the Dominican travelling missionaries in Thil, I was glad to explain the position of our Churches in relation to the most controversial problems. It was the same, more recently still, in Flavigny, at the convent founded by Lacordaire when he restored the Order of Friars Preachers in France. There other Dominican sisters welcomed, with the most evangelical sisterliness, two teams of Protestant ladies, one Swiss and one French, who had met together for a study of the Lord's Prayer which they had asked me to direct. Those hours of illumination, alas, were only too brief.

On Radio Luxembourg, where my Sunday morning broadcast was still continuing week after week, I devoted a considerable part of my talks to ecumenical problems, to the preparations for the fourth session of the Council and to the many ecumenical gatherings taking place in France and abroad.

At the beginning of September, just before leaving for Rome, I paid another enjoyable visit to Taizé, where the Cimade workers had their camp. A long conversation with Brothers Schutz and Thurian was already a start of the big event we were in a few days to begin to live together: the last session of Vatican 2.

II

Rome, 14 September 1965. Nine o'clock in the morning; the tribunes of St Peter's beginning to fill up; the observers sitting this time below the ambassadors' tribune.

A little after 10 o'clock, the vast procession appeared at the entrance to the nave. The two thousand five hundred bishops, wearing the bright *cappa magna* and identical white mitres, made their way to their places. After them came the papal suite. The *sedia* was gone. Paul VI came in on foot, holding in his right hand not a crozier but a staff surmounted by a crucifix. He went up to the altar of the *Confessio* and concelebrated with the cardinals and bishops who had shared the responsibility of organizing the Council.

In his address, after extolling the love which the Council would radiate to the uttermost ends of the earth, he made an announcement which caused lively surprise: the creation, as soon as possible, of the Episcopal Synod envisaged in the schema on the pastoral duty of bishops. So quick a decision had not been anticipated. It was an indication of the Pope's desire to implement the Council's decisions without delay.

The next day Paul VI came in quite simply and seated himself in the presidential chair, in order to give more solemnity to the reading of the *Motu proprio* setting up the Synod announced the day before. While Mgr Felici was reading the document, he sat impassive, and withdrew immediately afterwards to an outburst of applause.

As Cardinal Tisserant had promised the Fathers at the end of the last session, the decree on freedom of religion was at the head of the agenda. Mgr De Smedt read his revised draft, in a calm atmosphere that betrayed no echo of 1964's violent arguments. Sixty-two Fathers spoke. I listened to them all, putting forward views that were often contradictory but expressed without passion. By 1,997 for, to 224 against, the Fathers entrusted the final drafting of the document to the secretariat of the Council.

This long succession of speeches, as did those I heard on other schemas, made me increasingly and more sharply aware of the conflict between two traditions, the supporters of each of which claimed to rely on the authentic tradition of the Church.

On one side there were those, generally older men, and following the guidance of the cardinals of the Curia (Italian or Spanish), who came out as guardians of the tradition born at the Council of Trent, and developed, consolidated and imposed during the following centuries. It was the tradition of a Church which, in its desire to defend itself against the Reformation and everything that was akin to its heresies, found it necessary to centralize its organization, exaggerate its juridical character, and strengthen the authority in all spheres of the Sovereign Pontiff and, in consequence, of the Curia which claims to speak in his name. Cardinal Ottaviani was the passionate interpreter in the Council of this tradition. He proclaimed it with his love of the Church, his determination to defend the primacy and universal jurisdiction of Peter, his keen consciousness of his pastoral duty and his convinced belief that those who contradicted him were leading the Church into the direst catastrophes.

On the other side there were bishops, of whom the most recently consecrated were the most ardent, who believed that the Counter-Reformation belongs to the past, and that if the Church is to satisfy the demands of the world, its suffering and its hope, it must decentralize itself and reduce as much as possible its juridical character. The true tradition of the Church is to be found again well on the other side of the Council of Trent and the Reformation. The best part of it, its ever-living dynamic force, comes from the theologians of the Middle Ages and, still further back in the past, from the Latin Fathers, of whom Augustine is the greatest, and from the Greek Fathers, so long unread or neglected, whose immense authority is now beginning again to be recognized. And, still further back, we have to return to the real source, the one source which is to be found in the Gospels and the witness of the Apostles.

It was a most interesting experience to meet this conflict and to follow it through the cross-currents of theological expositions. There can be no doubt at all that the vast majority of the Fathers of the Council believed that if the Church is faithfully to respond to the demands of the future, it is to that past, and not to yesterday, that it must look; for only there will it find again its true vocation.

On the same day as that on which the discussion on freedom of religion ended, schema 13 came up for consideration.

Gaudium et Spes: 'The joys and hopes, the sorrows and agonies of modern man, in particular those of the poor and suffering,

these are the joys and hopes, the sorrows and agonies, too, of
the disciples of Christ: there is nothing which is truly human but
finds an echo in their hearts.'

So runs the preamble to the fundamental document in which
the Catholic Church, through the voice of the Council, sets out
to tell the world how she looks upon it, seeks to serve it, and
loves it.

A whole book would hardly be long enough to summarize the
numerous expositions provoked by the discussion of a document
the final version of which was due to the work of the appropriate
committees, rewriting it, retouching and adding to it and expressing it more exactly. The French, it is known, had the biggest
hand in the definitive draft. Mgr Haubtmann, now Rector of the
Institut Catholique in Paris, 'was appointed to draw up the doctrinal part, to be responsible for the full text and to ensure so far
as possible the unity of the schema until its final adoption by the
Council'.[2]

It was, indeed, a frighteningly delicate and difficult task. I
would not go so far as to say that before the final version the
draft was made up of bits and pieces. Nevertheless, a large number
of bishops and theologians had collaborated in working it out,
men who differed in culture, language, theological and sociological views, and may well have differed even more in their view of
the world and the Church's mission. Moreover, there was such a
variety of subjects: atheism, marriage, culture, economics,
politics, war and peace. To give the document a real unity, to
place all its parts on the same level, to avoid excessive gaps, and
to use language intelligible to the 'average' man in the world,
was an impossible assignment. Even so, Canon Haubtmann and
his immediate colleagues faced it with an intelligence, an informed
skill, and a courage – combined with their love of the Church and
of the world – for which it would be difficult to find a parallel
in the history of the Christian Churches.

It is none the less true that side by side with powerful and striking pages there are some which give evidence of haste or lack of
thought, and an imperfect knowledge of the subject-matter. In
short, on important points, schema 13 is still provisional in
character.

2. Decision of the plenary joint sub-committee (November 1964).

In a book which collects some Protestant views on the Council,[3] some of our best thinkers, ardent ecumenists, closely examine, analyse and comment on the various sections of the schema. With great clarity, they bring out both its strength and its weakness. I quote a few lines from Georges Casalis's conclusion:

'I very much hope that the great new wind which blows through the document as a whole, in spite of its only too evident weaknesses or omissions, may come as a salutary challenge to us non-Catholics, and force us out of the rut of our routine and fears. Let us be satisfied to recognize with gratitude in this provisional text – which already, maybe, has been superseded – of *Gaudium et Spes* something of the Church's ever revolutionary dynamism.'[4]

There can be no doubt but that any number of omissions would have been made good and shortcomings avoided if the preparation and drafting of this great document had not been the work of almost exclusively clerical gatherings, and if the knowledge and competence of layfolk had been called on as well as their Christian faith and their filial devotion to the Church. In this respect, the World Conference on Church and Society, in July 1966, was soon to provide a salutary example.

III

Apart from the general congregations, there was the same pattern of theological conversations, meetings and receptions as the year before.

When I arrived in Rome on 13 September everyone was talking about the encyclical *Mysterium fidei*, which had been published the day before in the *Osservatore Romano*. Unexpected though it may have been, it was a serious appeal from the Supreme Magisterium to those who, for example in the Catholic Church in the Netherlands, were discussing the problem of eucharistic transubstantiation in terms that many Catholics found disturbing. It appeared to be designed as a reply to a letter by the Dutch hierarchy on the Eucharist, read from the pulpit on 9 May. We were soon to meet these *avant-garde* bishops again.

For my own part I was more concerned than ever by the

3. *Vatican II: Points de vue de théologiens protestants*, Paris, Éditions du Cerf.
4. Op. cit., p. 265.

question of mixed marriages. It was almost six months since the Pope had received the petition drawn up by the Council. What, everyone was wondering, was behind this great delay in replying to it? It was rumoured that the bishops of Great Britain and North America (often of Irish descent) were strongly opposed to it. It seemed to me that a note ought to be sent to Paul VI, stressing the urgency of a problem whose solution was anxiously awaited by many Catholic and Protestant families and most of all by engaged couples. I spoke about this to Hébert Roux, who was present this time as observer for the Protestant Federation of France, and left him a draft to discuss with Cullmann, Vischer, Skydsgaard, Schlink and others. The note being accepted in principle, a number of observers joined Roux in drawing up a text. After modification and final correction, this was signed by the majority of observers and guests and was delivered to the Pope the day before he left for the United States.

I took the occasion, too, to raise this thorny question with some of the Fathers of the Council. At the French seminary, to which I was invited by the bishops who were staying there, I urged them to intervene, if they could, in the hope of receiving an answer to their petition. At the Belgian Embassy, where Baron Poswick had the great kindness to invite me to meet the Fathers from his country, I saw Cardinal Suenens, Archbishop of Malines, and Cardinal Heenan, Archbishop of Westminster. This was an opportunity not to be missed. 'It would appear', I said to Cardinal Heenan, 'that you are opposed to the modifications of canon law proposed by the Council.' 'Not me', he answered, 'but the whole British hierarchy!' So the rumour-mongers were right.

Cardinal Bea, to whom the discussion on freedom of religion brought a heavy responsibility, nevertheless found the time to show his affection for the observers and the guests of his secretariat. He received us soon after our arrival, on 18 September. His address, compact of delicacy and kindness, sounded a note of confidence and hope for us.

I must mention an exposition by Canon Haubtmann of schema 13 which was exactly what we wanted and an absorbing lecture on the same subject by Père Chenu.

During this month of September, which drew to a close in days of wonderful luminosity, numerous visitors came, if I may use the phrase, to take the temperature of the Council. Meetings multiplied: at one there was a gathering of French-speaking Protestants. At the Waldensian Church's theological college we had the pleasure of meeting again the Lutheran and Reformed professors of our own faculties, and I listened with profit to several of their talks.

As I was obliged to spend October and November in Paris I missed a great deal of the discussion of schema 13. Before leaving Rome, I was able to go with my son Étienne to Naples and, on our way back, to stop at Monte Cassino, destroyed during the Allied advance on Rome, but now rebuilt by American generosity, brand new, with a profusion of marble and gold – but very few monks.

Back in France, various commitments to parishes or ecumenical committees gave me a chance of correcting some misunderstandings about the Council and providing objective news of it. At the beginning of November I had to preside at the General Assembly of the Paris Société des Missions évangéliques. All our 'young Churches' of black Africa, Madagascar and the Pacific were represented at it. The plan for a 'common apostolic work', inter-racial and inter-Church, was studied at length.

On the same day on which, a little later, I was lecturing in Pau on freedom of religion and could not, unhappily, be in Rome, Paul VI, back from his visit to the United Nations, presided at St Paul's-without-the-Walls at a *liturgy of the Word*, which was attended only by the observers, the guests of the secretariat and some cardinals and bishops. At the morning's general congregation the observers had arranged for Mgr Felici to read their message to the Fathers of the Council. 'The observers', it said, 'are firmly convinced that the communion which has so far been effected can become even more full and will undoubtedly do so.' During the first audience he gave to the observers Pope John said 'Praised be God, this day and every day'. His words may today be paraphrased, 'Praised be God for all that he has given us up till this day through the medium of his Holy Spirit and for what it is his will to give us in the future.'

It will always be a matter of great regret to me that I was unable to be present at the service in St Paul's-without-the-Walls, 'one of the finest and greatest hours in the life of the Council', as all who were admitted to it declared. The words of Pope Paul, speaking in French, went straight to the hearts of his listeners.

'Now', he said, 'we are about to part. Your going away is producing an emptiness around us such as we never knew before the days of the Council and which saddens us: we would like always to have you with us.

'Yet, friendship remains. And what still remains, too, as the first fruit of the Council's meetings, is the conviction that the great problem of re-incorporation in the unity of the Church, visible to all who have the happiness and responsibility of calling themselves Christians, must be the subject of the most profound study, and that the time for this is now ripe.'

I cannot quote the Pope's concluding words without deep emotion:

'You are about to leave us for your homes. Never forget the love with which the Roman Catholic Church will ever think of you and follow you. Do not believe that she is unfeeling and proud if she believes that it is her duty religiously to guard the "deposit" entrusted to her from the beginning [cf. I Timothy 6:20], and do not accuse her of having distorted or betrayed this deposit if, in the course of her centuries of reflection, scrupulous and instinct with love, she has found in it treasures of truth and life which she would be false to renounce. Consider that it is precisely from Paul, the apostle of ecumenicity, and you know with what inflexible firmness [cf. Gal. 1:6ff.], that she received her first training in the dogmatic magisterium. Remember, too, that truth is greater than us all, that it is truth that makes us free, and that truth is close, nay, very close, to love.'[5]

I was back in Rome on the evening of 5 December and the next morning I was present at the voting on the whole of schema 13. In the afternoon the observers and the guests of the secretariat gave a reception for Cardinal Bea, in the hall of the faculty of theology, in order once more to assure him of their gratitude and their confidence in the light of the work still to be done. All my friends were still feeling the impact of the liturgy of the preceding day; all were full of the words of Paul VI which I have just quoted. On all sides there was talk of nothing but the hour of illumination spent in St Paul's-without-the-Walls.

Tuesday, 7 December 1965: the Council met in public session under the presidency of the Pope. It was known that after the voting on the last four conciliar documents still to be promulgated, a decision, arrived at after long negotiation between Rome and Constantinople, was to be implemented and the sentence of excommunication passed nine centuries earlier on Patriarch Cerularius would be lifted. We did not know, however, what form this would take. When Mgr Felici began to speak with unusual solemnity we were all on tenterhooks. He announced that, since the Churches of Rome and Constantinople wished to follow the road of charity opened up by the Council by forgiving their offences against one another, the Pope and the Ecumenical Patriarch had decided to lift the ban of excommunication pronounced by each Church against the other.

Mgr Willebrands, whose voice was then heard by the Council for the first time, mounted the ambo and read out a joint statement by Paul VI and Athenagoras I. It was listened to in an impressive silence by the crowd which filled the basilica.[6] As Mgr Willebrands read the final words, a storm of applause broke out, which rose above the Sistine Choir's intonation of the motet, 'Ubi caritas et amor, Deus ibi est' – 'Where charity and love dwell, there dwells God'.

At the end of the Mass that followed these solemn moments we saw Metropolitan Meliton, delegated by Athenagoras I, go up to the altar and exchange, in reconciliation, the kiss of peace with Paul VI. It was a wonderful charism to be able to witness this gesture, expressing a revolutionary reality and perhaps heralding in the near or distant future the lifting of other excommunications.

At the same moment a no less moving ceremony was taking place in the modest church of the patriarchate in Phanar, the quarter of Istanbul in which the Greeks lived until their expulsion. There Athenagoras proclaimed the lifting of the sentences of excommunication, the Pope being represented by Cardinal Shehan.

In St Peter's the long ceremony was drawing to an end.

6. See the text in Wenger, op. cit., pp. 452 ff.

Paul VI, refusing to use the sedia, stepped down from his throne. The long procession formed up which was to escort him back to the entrance to the basilica, from which he would return to his own apartments. He came forward, holding the strange staff surmounted by a crucifix. I noticed that he was looking at me as I stood among the observers, beside Brothers Schutz and Thurian: suddenly he stopped and, coming towards me, put out his hand and said the single word, *'Merci!'*

'When I saw you', he told me some months later, 'I hesitated: but then I felt the Holy Spirit would guide me.'

Shall I ever be able to forget that moment of my ecumenical life, so impossible to foresee, so charged with hope?

Of the interminable ceremonial that took place the next day, celebrated in the piazza of St Peter's, all I remember is a series of messages addressed to various categories of persons by the Pope and the Council, read in French, but mostly without sufficient vigour to strike home to those for whom they were intended.

And so it was all over. Nevertheless, all of us were thinking of what was to follow. Was that really the end of the Council, we wondered. Will it not be continued, in countless different forms, in the Christian Churches to all of whom it meant so much, until one day, please God, a new and truly ecumenical Council will meet to set the seal upon unity?

CHAPTER 22

Crises in Catholicism
1965-1967

I. Difficulties arising from the problem of birth-control.
Reform of the Curia. II. The crisis of discipline. Celibacy
of the clergy. III. The crisis of faith. The Dutch Catechism.
Reforms or Reform. IV. Two great events: the Episcopal
Synod, the Congress of the apostleship of the laity.

SEVERAL months have already passed since I finished writing
the preceding pages. Some dear friends of mine have urged me,
in the course of long conversations, to let my memories lead out
into the prospects that now seem to me to await the Churches
and the ecumenical movement. I wonder, however, whether one
can speak of them without the risk of being contradicted by events
that are intervening as much in the Church of Rome as in the
Orthodox Church, the Reformation Churches and the World
Council itself.

The Vatican Council does not bear the sole responsibility for
the present crises. The influence, not only in Protestant circles,
of the theology and ethics of Bonhoeffer, and of the exegesis of
Bultmann and his disciples, is creating a ferment of opinion whose
further effects it is impossible to foresee. Things which only a few
years ago seemed incontestable are now challenged. Exegesis,
catechetical instruction, the 'new theology', and the 'new ethics',
are upsetting traditional ideas which the great majority of the
faithful of different Christian denominations used to regard as
impregnable. The age-old affirmations of faith are tottering on a
scriptural foundation which is itself shaken by 'demythologizing'
exegesis.

The institutions, again, which for centuries have been watching
over the 'deposit of faith' are in the eyes of the younger generation no more than antiquated rubbish, responsible to a great
degree for the cleavage between the Churches and the world;
and all that can be done today is to get rid of them.

At the root of today's chaos we should not overlook the importance of the economic and social problem which affects every nation. The destitution of the famine-stricken races, the poverty of millions which is increasing in direct ratio with the continual enrichment of the western world, the striking spread of atheism, all these have undoubted repercussions on the theological and ethical theorizing of Christian thinkers, no matter what their denomination. Nor can they fail to be shaken to the core by the staggering advances in the sciences, in particular the social sciences, and in technology, which are revolutionizing the lives of individuals and nations in the acceleration of history which Daniel Halévy foresees for us.

All the Churches are suffering from this crisis, or these crises, whose gravity cannot be denied. Is it even possible, then, to speak of prospects? Can one possibly look beyond the present chaos into the time when the new and the stable will have emerged and the Churches, like the nations, will have completed their 'mutation'? And, in this period of quest, of arguments and challenges, what will become of the ecumenical movement? It will soon be sixty years since that movement committed us to a road from which there is no turning back: but through what 'diversions' shall we have to travel before we approach the goal?

I do not know whether I shall succeed, in the concluding section of this book, in affording a glimpse of the end towards which the Holy Spirit seems to me to be guiding the Church of Christ through the crises of today; but I am anxious at least to make the attempt.

I

Eighteen months after the Fathers of the Council had finally returned to their dioceses, the Roman Catholic Church found itself confronted, in more places than one, by serious difficulties. They arose on different planes which it is important to distinguish, and this I can do only briefly.

There is not much to be said about the liturgical reform. The saying of Mass in the vernacular is, and for a long time will continue to be, a disappointment to many of the faithful who believe it to be impossible to give up what they have been accustomed to since childhood. Young people, on the whole, welcome it with real satisfaction, although they continue to find it puzzling that in some parishes the canon of the Mass is still said in Latin. There can be no doubt, all the same, but that the language used for the whole of Catholic services will ultimately be the vernacular, apart from such exceptions as will be allowed as a privilege to certain religious orders.

National conferences of the hierarchy have been organized and have got down to work without any disturbance or difficulty in the majority of countries in which the Catholic Church is represented. I have nothing but admiration for the wisdom, orderliness and efficiency with which the French hierarchy has solved the problems involved. The necessary steps, envisaged many years before, have been taken smoothly and without offending any susceptibilities. In future the conference of the hierarchy will be a normal organ of the Church. Its authority has been greatly increased in the eyes of the public by the answer it made, immediately after its Lourdes meeting in October 1965, to the questionnaire (surprising at least in its form) addressed by Cardinal Ottaviani on behalf of the Congregation *de fide* to all the national conferences.

Paul VI's obstinate silence on the question of birth-control is the cause of an uneasiness which affects Catholicism all over the world. On a number of occasions it was thought that, after studying the conclusions reached in lengthy deliberations by the new commission he had appointed, he was about to announce a decision which was awaited with impatience in millions of Catholic homes: and each time the Pope has thought that further delay was necessary.

During the last audience Paul VI was so kind as to grant me on 21 March 1967, he mentioned this delicate problem. It is a great disappointment to him that he is unable to satisfy as speedily as he could wish the expectations of so many of the faithful. Shortly before he received me, he believed that the time had come for a pronouncement; but once again the commission sounded the alarm: persistent disagreements were still making it impossible for them to submit a unanimous conclusion to him: and this made it impossible for the Pope to reach his own decision.[1]

1. On this question see the article by Père Perico, S.J., 'La super-pilule', in *La Documentation catholique*, 9 December 1967.

Meanwhile, conversations I had with priests from various countries made me realize the confusion produced by the birth-control question. For some considerable time, I was told, many Catholic homes had been solving the problem in the light of conscience, frankly balancing their Church's rules against the physical, social, and economic conditions in which married couples have to fulfil their fundamental vocation, which is unity in love and its full realization in the welcome given to children freely desired and greeted with joy. Nevertheless, other Catholics, who may well be even more numerous, refuse to disobey their Church's orders; their married life runs the risk of being embittered and thereby seriously damaged, and their faith is in danger of being shaken by the hesitancy and slowness of the supreme magisterium.

I have just mentioned the delays which Paul VI finds he has to accept in the examination of a particular problem. I should perhaps add that other instances of delay in coming to a decision or taking action have been held against him by priests or layfolk impatient to see the spirit of the Council permeate the Church more rapidly.

It is four years, for example, since the reform of the Curia was announced more than once by the Pope himself; and it was difficult to understand why it should take so long for words to be translated into actions. It was too easily forgotten, I believe, that there were a number of 'daring' acts, such as the nomination of Mgr Garrone as pro-prefect of the seminaries and universities congregation, and that of Canon Moehler to what used to be the Holy Office and is now the congregation *de fide*. The inadmissible methods used for centuries in the execution of 'justice' have been abandoned. Cardinals too infirm to manage a diocese have been asked to resign: though not all, it must be admitted, have complied.

And now suddenly, without any previous notification, the Pope has just, in a *Motu proprio* and an apostolic constitution, reformed the Curia in a way that can only be described as revolutionary.[2] There was considerable surprise and, in many Catholic circles, no small satisfaction. It had, it is true, been expected that the Curia would be given a more international character and that there would be changes in the names, the responsibilities and the

2. 6 and 12 August 1967.

constitution of some of the various departments. But greater changes were announced: there was the increase in the power of the Secretary of State, now becoming a real Prime Minister, the time limit for the holding of office in the Curia, apart from exceptions decided by the Pope, the inclusion of the 'secretariats' created by John XXIII and Paul VI, the reorganization of the Holy See's finances, and still further innovations. These are introducing changes into the government of the Church so profound that one can look for violent reactions in those circles (almost entirely Italian) in which a career in the Curia used to be the height of ambition.

There are some who regret that the reform strengthens the centralization of authority in the Church. Nevertheless it would appear that the new powers granted to the national conferences of the hierarchy meet the wish for decentralization expressed by many Fathers of the Council.

Both within the Catholic Church and to outsiders, Paul VI gives the impression of being a man who tries to hold the balance, or rather make concessions. I do not believe that that is so. It is true that during the Council he already seemed, after indicating his approval of the line followed by the 'majority', to agree to modifications designed to appease the 'minority'. In this connection it should be noted that some of his interventions (at times made at the last moment), which modified a text or postponed the voting on it, were justified as producing undeniable improvements in the wording. This was the case, for example, with the decree on freedom of religion, the postponing of which to the fourth session had greatly upset us all at the time.

No, I do not believe that the Pope is concerned to preserve a balance between conflicting tendencies. He dreads above all what might produce a crack and still more a split in the body which is responsible, under his supreme authority, for the government of the Church. He does not wish to break with either party: he wants agreement in charity, humility and love. What disturbs him most, in the post-conciliar period of the Church's life, are not problems of discipline, for these he will tell you are easily solved, but disputes that relate to faith. That no doubt was why he decided that 1967 should be the year of faith.

II

There are, in fact, formidable disputes of this sort, although they do not appear everywhere in the Church with the same vehemence. Nevertheless, there are few countries, at all events in what is still called the Christian West, that have not reverberated with the theological, moral and ecclesiological controversies that excite priests, religious and layfolk.

'During this post-conciliar year', Paul VI once said to the members of the Sacred College, 'the Church will find a new awareness of her reason for existence, will regain her original energy, will gather together in a well-ordered teaching the content and meaning of the life-giving word of Revelation, will offer herself to our brethren still separated from our communion with a humble and inspiring certainty, will lavish herself for the world as it is today, full of greatness and wealth and yet heartbreakingly in need of the faith's message of consolation.'[3]

All the Pope's words are weighed. Yet what exactly will be this 'gathering together in a well-ordered teaching' of the content and meaning of Revelation, at a time when, as we shall see, the foundations of doctrine are rocking?

A striking declaration by Mgr Ancel, auxiliary bishop of Lyons, may give some idea of the direction in which the thinking of the Roman Church is moving: 'If doctrinal deviations are being produced in the Church, they are a sign that we are providing only insufficient answers to real problems. That is why we must not regard these deviations as errors to be condemned, but as a summons to develop more fully the doctrine of faith and improve its expressions, so that our contemporaries may be able to find answers to the questions they are asking.'[4]

And what, then, are these questions? Père Congar does not hesitate to say that they are 'very difficult'. 'Questions are being asked on all sides today, and every day they are taking new and more acute forms. The Council was able to let them come out into the open, but it did not create them. It could loosen tongues – but the questions existed already and would imperatively have had to be faced . . .

3. *La Documentation catholique*, 16 July 1967, p. 1,307.
4. *Informations catholiques internationales*.

'Everything seems to be challenged, or to be going that way. The pull of modern currents in philosophy, contact with non-believers, the revival of questions in biblical hermeneutics, the problems raised by science, including the social sciences, all these are obliging us to reconsider positions which only yesterday could be held undisturbed.'[5]

For the faithful, and for many of the clergy too, this is producing an atmosphere of insecurity.

How could it be otherwise, when one realizes that, while the notion of the immutability of dogmas has penetrated deep into Catholic thought in the centuries since the Reformation, theologians, with an ever wider audience, are again asking – and asking as though it had never been officially settled – 'What is the nature and function of dogma in general, and what can they become in the light of the Gospel?'[6]

Indeed, they are under no illusion: they know that 'dogma appears to many to be a drag on the Church, self-applied, which checks her power to reform herself from within . . . They see in the Church an institution so tied to its past and its tradition as to have become, in Nietzsche's phrase, incapable of living'.[7]

Thus, while dogmas appear to many Catholics as being above Scripture and accordingly above the Gospel, today a new language is making itself heard. Men of my generation can remember how, after the condemnation of modernism, Laberthonnière, Maurice Blondel and Édouard Le Roy found that they had to face the problem of dogma. That was before the days of existentialism, but it is now this latter which is behind the new ways of thinking about this serious question and which is clearing a road for the answers put forward.

The Counter-Reformation, it is commonly held, made a great mistake in substituting a juridical and formal concept of dogma for the theological concept which prevailed in the first centuries of the Church, and it is against the former that modern theologians are directing their attack. They find support, with gratitude and hope, in the statement by John XXIII on the importance of which I remarked earlier: 'The deposit of faith, that is to say the

5. Ibid., 15 April 1967. Extracts from a lecture by Père Congar, 'Analyse critique des tendances actuelles', p. 26.
6. Walter Kasper, *Dogme et Évangile*, Paris, 1967, p. 11.   7. Ibid., p. 11.

truths contained in our venerable doctrine, is one thing; the way in which those truths are formulated, while retaining the same undoubted meaning and bearing, is another.'[8]

In this connection attention should be drawn to what Walker[9] has to say in his study, suggestive and full of substance, of the question of the nature of dogma and its function, its relation to Holy Scripture, in which the later Church saw 'the evidence of its normative apostolic origin',[10] of its eschatological significance, and its character of 'being not a terminal point but a starting-point'.[11] Dogma is confession, but it is also witness, given an external orientation 'in a missionary context of propagation'.[12] Nevertheless, its principal function is 'to make possible the "homologia", the profession of common faith in the Church, and thus to foster the love proper to the ecclesia'.[13]

This notion of open dogma, as opposed to the 'rigid barrier', underlies many books published since the end of Vatican 2. It clashes so violently with the ideas accepted by the vast majority of Catholics, clergy and layfolk, of yesterday and perhaps still of today, that its exposition by theologians of great merit cannot but produce the atmosphere of crisis in which the Catholic Church is now living.

In this respect there are some 'specially favoured nations'. The daily Press of the Netherlands, for example, is assiduous in keeping its readers in touch with theological opinion on the most controversial questions.

What those questions are, or what some of them are, may be learnt from a French publication issued by the 'Pastoral Institute of the Ecclesiastical Province of the Netherlands', a body set up by the Dutch hierarchy.

'Recent conversations', it tells us, 'among Dutch theologians might be interpreted as follows. Discussions on the way in which Christ is really present in the Eucharist, and on the Resurrection and the Virgin birth, should be regarded as attempts to examine these doctrines from the point of view of their value in relation

8. See above, p. 287.
9. A German theologian, professor in the University of Münster, in West-phalia.
10. Op. cit., p. 105.   11. p. 121.
12. p. 126.   13. Ibid.

to a life inspired by faith. The physical reality of these affirmations, which to a more traditional thinking are an assurance of the facts that concern salvation, seems more or less unimportant to modern thought. One can conceive the meaning of these truths, understand and accept them, without thereby seeking to make their physical or biological interpretation inevitable.'[14]

Thus the dogma of transubstantiation, defined at the Lateran Council of 1215, needs to be entirely reformulated. The words of John XXIII and Paul VI undoubtedly authorize such an attempt: but the real question is whether this could be done without impairing the substance of the dogma.[15]

An increasing number of young priests are questioning themselves, and their superiors, about the celibacy of the clergy. Some seminarists are challenging the obligation not to marry, and quote the example of the clergy of the Orthodox Churches and also that of pastors in the Protestant Churches. In the United States and the Netherlands the canonical regulation (which does not in any case have doctrinal character) is being openly condemned.

Controversy was legitimate so long as the supreme magisterium had not spoken. In October 1965 the Pope informed the Council of his 'plan to give more prestige and vigour to the celibacy of the priesthood, in the circumstances of the present day'. This he did in the encyclical *Sacerdotalis caelibatus* of 24 June 1967. Without disguising the extent and seriousness of the problems or the distressing desertions of priests, the responsibility for which some attribute to the Church's intransigence, Paul VI insisted on the necessity and the grandeur of the celibacy of the clergy, and maintained its incumbence upon all members of the priesthood.

There was a speedy reaction to the Pope's words. In the United States, the National Association for Pastoral Renewal 'hopes to continue to work for a reform of the law on the celibacy of the clergy, because we believe the new situation in which man is placed demands it'.

14. Cf. *Le Monde*, 19 July 1967, p. 7.
15. The Church has characterized the term 'transubstantiation' as 'most appropriate'. 'Nevertheless, this does not rule out the possibility of other formulations' (Walker, op. cit., pp. 126 ff.). It should not be forgotten that the studies of the Reformed theologian F. Leenhardt have helped to orientate the enquiries of Catholic theologians.

More weight should be given to the statement by the theologian Hans Küng, of Tübingen: 'Even if the encyclical has the merit of bringing the real difficulties out into the open, it is far from having solved them. Rather has it aggravated them. There will be no peace in the Catholic Church until the choice of celibacy has become, as it used to be, every individual's own business.'[16]

Nevertheless, in this field as in that of Marian teaching, Catholic opinion is so sensitive that a long time will be required, or some revolutionary step will have to be taken by the supreme authority, before the obligation of celibacy is abolished. Meanwhile, vocations to the priesthood are showing a regular decline.

The primacy of Peter, the personal infallibility of the Sovereign Pontiff and his universal jurisdiction are equally under attack. Could anyone today guarantee that continued and faithful use of episcopal collegiality will not sooner or later upset the dogma of the papacy as at present formulated? If Paul V I, as I have already emphasized, was at pains untiringly to reaffirm the rights, powers and responsibilities of the successor of Peter, was it not because a number of his immediate circle were expressing fears that collegial government of the Church would ultimately encroach upon the absolute power recognized since the first Vatican Council as belonging to the Bishop of Rome, *servus servorum Dei*?

If it was said before the Council, and if today it is still whispered in Rome or elsewhere that John X X I I I yielded to a wild impulse when he decided to summon Vatican 2, it is undoubtedly because some most genuine servants of the Church, cardinals and bishops of the Curia, considered that there was a threat, not to their own personal positions, but to the papacy and infallibility; any weakening of these, they maintain, would make the Pope into a sort of constitutional monarch and would involve the Catholic Church in the direst catastrophe.

Is the Pope right in throwing the weight of his authority into the world controversies aroused by the wars in Vietnam and the Middle East, by the destitution of the famine-stricken nations, by problems of capital and labour? There are some who fear that to do so does not strengthen but weakens his authority. Many Catholics, belonging to 'well-heeled' circles openly blame him for what they call his political and social orientation. They see

16. *Informations catholiques internationales*, 15 July 1967, p. 12.

this asserted in the encyclical *Populorum progressio*. Some go so far as to accuse him of condemning private property in it.

At the same time it cannot be denied that the encyclical is a great document, the necessary sequel to schema 13, new in style, and with a truly generous human tone. It is through the development of the whole man, to which the Church has a decisive contribution to make, that the life of the community will attain its full growth, 'in the quest for a new humanism which allows man to find himself again as he accepts the higher values of love, friendship, prayer and contemplation'.

The thought of the French Dominican, Père Lebret, whose recent death has been sadly felt in the Catholic world and by all, believers and non-believers alike, who have been helped by *Economie et Humanisme* of which he was the soul, had made a deep impression on Mgr Montini, at that time Archbishop of Milan. As Pope Paul V I he incorporated many of its fundamental theses in the encyclical: moreover, the original text was written in French.

III

Thus the Catholic Church is not untouched by the great currents of the 'new theology' which are sweeping through the Churches of the Reformation. At the Protestant bookshop in the Piazza Cavour in Rome young priests have no hesitation in asking for the works of Bultmann, Bonhoeffer, Tillich, Robinson, and of Cullmann, too, whose annual lectures at the faculty of Protestant theology are attended by many members of the Roman clergy as well as by religious of the great orders. The 'God is dead' movement, which has made great studies in the U.S.A., is carrying with it both Catholics and Protestants, united in the teaching of a 'religionless' Christianity and of 'Christian atheism'. In a number of countries, priests are coming up against the refusal by many of the faithful to continue to accept as certain truths the doctrines affirmed in the traditional catechisms. The questions they are being asked by the laity are obliging them to re-think their faith, and to call on the theologians of their Church to help them. The priests themselves are often shaken by doubt. Is there not a danger that the doctrine of God may be swept away by the mighty wave of atheism which is submerging a great many of the nations which are still described as Christian? What answer can be given to the challenge to the Church's traditional teaching thrown down by supporters of scientific materialism? The supreme magisterium multiplies its warnings and repeatedly sounds the alarm, but the principle of strict obedience to instructions coming from the Holy See is itself, there can be no doubt, now being questioned.

I shall have more to say about this doctrinal confusion when I come to consider the crisis in the Churches of the Reform. Meanwhile, it is important to note a recent essay from the Catholic Church in the Netherlands which has continued since its inception to have powerful repercussions.

A 'Catechism for Adults',[17] published in 1966 after long preparatory studies, completely upsets all the traditional catechetical methods. Cardinal Alfrink himself sees in it not so much a catalogue of truths to be believed as a source of inspiration: 'A starting-point and not an end', as it has been described by the Dutch bishops, in a pastoral letter.

The 'conservative' party in the Curia reacted violently against this publication. They gave a warm welcome to a protest from clergy and laity against 'the grave heresies' of the new catechism. The Pope did not overlook it.[18] However, it was of other theological disturbances, too, that he was thinking when in a public audience on 30 November 1966 he said that he was not merely 'concerned' but 'appalled' at the 'erroneous' opinions and 'arbitrary interpretations' of Catholic doctrine current 'even among believers'.

To return, however, to the Dutch Catechism: since 'reflection on the mysteries of faith' is never finished, and since 'the last word on any of them has not yet been said, nor will it be said tomorrow', this catechism is above all an invitation to reflection. It is founded upon tradition, it is true, but 'it does not regard tradition as a body of fixed definitions given once and for all'. It has no intention of making a break with the past; revelation still remains the same, but it 'is receiving a richer and more

17. *A New Catechism, Catholic Faith for Adults*, commissioned by the Hierarchy of the Netherlands, London, 1967.
18. In the summer of 1967 Paul VI appointed a commission of cardinals, international in membership, to examine the catechism in question.

fully developed content' from the evolution of human thought.

The dialogue to which the catechism invites the reader, involves a striking change in the point of view. It is not God but man who takes the stage first, with the search for God that can be seen asserting itself in him. God seeking for man appears only at the end: in the history of Israel which 'opens out . . . into the proclamation of Jesus who is the Christ'. Jesus Christ is the culmination of a long history. In him alone can man find the God he seeks and who seeks him.

The Church, starting from Jesus Christ, is gradually revealed in history and confronts the Christian with tasks that are continually being renewed. The Dutch Catechism endeavours to provide an 'interpretation of the Bible' by and for the man of today, whether it is treating of the sacraments, of morality, or of the kingdom of God already given and still to come, and it is impossible not to be impressed by its essential desire to give adults 'the emancipating dimension indispensable to the inspiration of love, without which a life cannot be Christian'. I am filled with delight whenever the poor mortal men we are, are introduced by one of our Churches to the adventure of love, to which 'the God of Abraham, of Isaac, and of Jacob, the God of Jesus Christ', has committed himself in order to prepare and accomplish our salvation. And what is our salvation if not, under the Cross which shines in the light of the Resurrection, our own birth, through death to ourselves and through forgiveness, into the love which gives itself to serve and save?

IV

There are not a few who believe that the most important of the documents published by the Council, either through their implementation or the discussions they have given rise to, are positive factors in the crisis I am describing.

Even if the decree on freedom of religion is meeting with general agreement in large sections of the Church, elsewhere it is coming up against resistance for which the hierarchy is not always responsible. Spain is an example. For a short time after the promulgation of Vatican 2's decree there was justification for the hope that the evangelical minorities would at last obtain freedom to practise their worship in churches again made available to them. The Spanish bishops seemed to be in favour of a loyal application of the Council's published decision. It was within the Government that opposition showed itself. Nevertheless, a plan that met the Council's wishes was presented to the Cortes; seriously amended, it became a law which is restoring the old unhappy situation of our Protestant brothers in Spain. May one hope that the Spanish bishops will feel it their duty to demand a radical modification of the law?

What a contrast this is with the breadth of mind shown by bishops and priests of other countries to their 'separated brethren'. Churches are placed at the disposition of pastors so that in those districts within their parishes that have no Protestant chapel they may fittingly celebrate their worship with their faithful, no matter how small their numbers. I know at least one Catholic district where a page in the parish magazine is reserved for the Reformed Church and its pastor. These are notable applications of the decree on ecumenism. In other places the decree has had a more doubtful reception. The various ways in which the bishops are encouraging its application are creating an impression of confusion. For my own part, I cannot but pay grateful tribute to the atmosphere of trust and brotherly love I am constantly meeting in those parts of France and abroad in which it falls to me to meet my Catholic brethren. My colleagues in the ecumenical movement are having the same experience. With some hesitancy, it is true, the same road is opening up in other countries: and it is not one of the least signs of the times that in Latin America priests and pastors can be found associated in action to remedy the distress of their peoples.

This brings us back to the vast field to which the 'Constitution on the Church and the Modern World'[19] applies. We saw earlier the concern the Council intended to satisfy when it undertook the examination of the draft produced by the preparatory commission. It accepted the impossibility of the Catholic Church's ignoring the great problems of modern civilization. On the threshold of the atomic age, whose formidable and magnificent potentialities we can only glimpse, the Council wished the Church to initiate a dialogue with the man she meets both inside her fold

19. The official title of schema 13 (see above, p. 319).

and outside, by showing him the vision that she, as a Christian Church, must have of him.

This capital document of Vatican 2 has been applied in a number of very different ways, some of which have caused surprise, and even protests and scandalized indignation. The approval of some meets the violent criticisms of others.

When bishops commit themselves to a position in conflicts between workers and employers, when they take part in public demonstrations, marching at the head of processions of strikers, they are expressing their desire to associate themselves with man in his problems, his distress and his demands against what he can only see as an injustice. It is hardly surprising that Catholic opinion should be divided when confronted by such action with which, moreover, Protestant pastors are at times associated. The divisions become more pronounced when, in Latin America for example, archbishops and bishops of undeniable spiritual authority consider it their duty to make their convictions publicly known in the social and political crises in which their countries are involved. Theology and ethics cannot but influence the motives that determine such attitudes. The vision of man that every Christian Church and every Christian receive from the Gospel, presents him in a dimension of eternity. And it is in order to reach man in his *heart*, in Augustine's sense and Pascal's, that so many bishops and priests and layfolk want to stand by his side when the pressure of economic and social realities produces such suffering.

A great risk is involved: for in going away to seek and share the life of the lost sheep – lost to itself and to its kind as much as to God – one might stray so far from the fold that one could never find the way back. There are obviously countless possibilities of danger in faithful application of the Constitution. It is introducing new aspects into the crisis of the Catholic Church which are emphasizing its gravity. We shall find the Protestant Churches confronted by the same dangers.

After the experience of so many different impressions, after so many exchanges of views and so much factual observation, and after pondering so many publications, can we at least glimpse what the Church of Rome will be when it emerges from this troubled period?

Vatican 2 intended finally to wind up the Counter-Reformation, of which the Council of Trent (1545-63) was the driving force.

Nevertheless, new attacks from circles within or closely associated with the present Curia are still possible.[20] It must not be thought that the resignation or death of a few very aged cardinals is sufficient to put an end to such attacks. 'Integrists' can be found in the next generation. The present Pope is undoubtedly anxious not to allow himself to be diverted from the road opened up by the Council. But what about his successor? Even so, it seems unlikely, particularly if the Episcopal Synod acquires a real authority, that the Catholic Church should have in the future a Sovereign Pontiff who would take her back to the time and outlook of Pius XII. And is there not a possibility that – no one could say when, but sometime – the Episcopal Synod may be entrusted with the election of the Pope?

The authority of the Episcopal Synod – that, too, is a problem. Can one say that in the first session, held in November 1967, it was asserted with a vigour that justified the great hopes its institution gave rise to? That was only partly true. Pope Paul's state of health at the actual moment of the Synod's meeting, the imminence of an operation which was preceded by pessimistic rumours, and the coming visit of the Ecumenical Patriarch, all, in various ways, overshadowed the meeting. Nevertheless, it had its grandeur, though very different from that of the Council. Its two hundred members, in the black soutanes which did not always proclaim the hierarchy's lofty responsibilities, were a far cry from the two thousand five hundred Fathers of the Council and their solemn processions. Nevertheless the great merits of a number of the expositions and the tone of the discussions gave the synod an undeniable greatness. Moreover, the recent nomination of Cardinal Seper, Archbishop of Zagreb, as sub-prefect of the Congregation *de Fide* (formerly the Holy Office) was proof that the Pope, now happily recovered, attached great importance to the indications reflected in the Synod's votes.

The problem of mixed marriages raised great difficulties. The discussion had an unfortunate introduction, in an atmosphere of constraint for which the secretariat for Christian unity was in no

20. This was written before 1 January 1968, the date when the reform of the Curia came into effect.

way responsible, and it brought out the impossibility, in the extreme diversity of local circumstances, of putting forward a uniform rule for the whole of the Church. The Synod asked the Pope, while maintaining a strict canonical framework, to authorize bishops in cases of which they would in future be the judges, to grant such dispensations from canonical form and written undertaking as seemed necessary to them. Should the Sovereign Pontiff grant their request, it is not difficult to see that great confusion may well be the result.

There can be no doubt at all but that such a step is one stage on a road that must inevitably end some day in the Church of Rome's recognition of mixed marriages which have been solemnized by a minister of a Reformed Church. Even so it will be necessary for the liturgy of that Church to express the doctrine that the bond of marriage can be dissolved only by death.

However, it was the 'crisis of faith' which called for most attention from the Synod. The ecumenical importance of the discussion it gave rise to is obvious, since all the Christian Churches are being required to live together this period of theological, ethical and ecclesiological controversies. Being in Rome during the meeting of the Synod, I was able to discuss the 'crisis' with a number of cardinals and bishops. The anxious pessimism of some was balanced by the confident optimism of others. A commission, appointed by the Synod and presided over by Cardinal Seper, in order to review a report on 'dangerous modern beliefs and atheism', frankly recognized that in a number of places 'arbitrary innovations, false opinions and even errors had been introduced into faith':[21] errors similar to those I have already mentioned.[22] These errors must be *denounced*, but always with charity; but this fundamental rejection must not rule out *approval* of the researches of theologians 'who have courageously and successfully worked to make the fruits of the Council available'.[23]

The remedies proposed by the commission are pastoral in character, and emphasis is laid on the necessity of integrating the witness of life and that of the Word.

21. Report of the commission, in *Informations catholiques internationales*, 15 November 1967, p. 10.
22. See above, p. 338.   22. Loc. cit., p. 9.

No Church could fail to endorse the prudent and loving counsel of the Episcopal Synod, which, moreover, stressed the responsibility of theologians, whose researches, based on the Word of God and in agreement with the magisterium, must be allowed legitimate freedom.[24]

At the very time when the Episcopal Synod was holding its first session, the international congress of the apostleship of the laity was meeting in Rome. About three thousand layfolk (priests, too) from all parts of the world had answered an appeal whose ecumenical significance was beyond doubt. Its deliberations, it is true, and its resolutions concerned the Catholic Church, but the vigour with which the layfolk present affirmed their wish to be treated as *adult* Christians, and their full consciousness of their responsibilities as members of a Church and their vocation to share in its priesthood, could not but have profound repercussions in the Churches separated from Rome; for, ever since the sixteenth century, these Churches have always endeavoured (often, unhappily, falling seriously short of their goal) not only to teach universal priesthood but to make it a living reality. I wonder, however, whether the laity gathered in Rome did not perhaps display an impatience calculated to jeopardize the effects of their resolutions.

At the congress of the laity, as in the episcopal Synod, the vast majority realized even more sharply than at the Council that there must be *reform* in the Catholic Church, in its government, discipline, canon law, preaching and instruction, and in its witness and service in the world.

At the same time, this reform will never be really fruitful unless it is also, as Luther's was, doctrinal. Whether such a reform will extend to the Church's body of dogmatic teaching is the question that really matters, both from the point of view of revealed truth in the first place and from that of ecumenism. Paul VI reacts vigorously to contentions which threaten the integrity of the faith. We should not, however, forget that, like John XXIII, he has recognized the possibility of modifying the formulation of dogmas without impairing their substance.

What is more, in a number of its constitutions, decrees and statements, the Council affirmed the fundamental priority which

24. Ibid., p. 10.

the Catholic Church attributes to the sovereign authority of the Word of God. It is quite certain that she intends it to become or to return to being, a Church of the Word in the same way as the Churches of the Reform; and this raises in consequence a central problem for the latter. In future Catholic exegetes will have the same scientific freedom as their Protestant colleagues, and they cannot fail, surely, to scrutinize very closely the solidity or fragility of the scriptural foundation attributed to certain dogmas. The years to come – to be marked, moreover, by the completion of the ecumenical translation of the Bible – will once again make it plain that the Word of God, heard in Holy Scripture, receives from the Holy Spirit, who warrants its truth, a power to reform which ultimately overcomes the most formidable obstacles.

Oscar Cullmann recently quoted to me this saying from an extremely well-known Catholic theologian: 'Everything is collapsing: we must start again from zero, in other words the Gospel.' That is perfectly true, but the Gospel contains explosive matter powerful enough to blow up, in the Church of Rome and in our own, everything that tends to shut them up in dogmatic or ecclesiastical constrictions from which our contemporaries are determined at all costs to escape. But the ruins must be allowed to fall in a place where the men of today can, as one, proceed with building up the Church of Christ on the sole foundation of the apostles and the prophets. Perhaps, when we come to look at the problems arising in the Churches of the Reform, we shall find a further warning to this effect.[25]

25. The resignations of Cardinals Ottaviani, Lercaro and others mark a new stage on the road to a real reform of the Curia.

CHAPTER 23

Problems in the Reformed Churches

I. Mixed marriages. II. The institutional crisis. The sense of
catholicity. III. Scripture and tradition. The *norm*. IV. The
specific vocation of the Reformed Churches in their confrontation with the Catholic Church, in the light of its
claim and desire to be the Church of the Word of God.
V. Did the Reformers intend to found a new Church?
VI. Was the Reformation the opening of a parenthesis?

I

A crisis of momentous import is shaking the Churches born of the
Reformation. Even if, seen from the outside, it sometimes seems
to be institutional, it is fundamentally theological. It does not
in any way originate from the ecumenical movement. It has been
to a large degree produced by the radically new interpretation of
the New Testament writings put forward by the German
theologian Bultmann and his followers. Their work in 'demythologizing', by destroying traditional exegesis, has brought to
light theological problems for which revolutionary solutions
are proposed. Nevertheless it is still more the amazing influence
exerted by a hero of the anti-Nazi resistance, the young Lutheran
theologian Dietrich Bonhoeffer, that is responsible for the
emergence of a 'new theology' which seems to have swept through
the Churches of the United States more rapidly than those of
Western Europe.

In the prison in which for many long months he awaited
execution, Bonhoeffer wrote letters, noted down his thoughts,
prayers and poems, which were published after his death. In
these we find him foretelling with astonishing prescience the era
in which we are now living. The era of the man, now master of the
universe, who has no need of religion. 'We are moving towards
a completely religionless time; people as they are now simply
cannot be religious any more... In human affairs generally, "God"
is being pushed more and more out of life, losing more and more

ground. . . . God would have us know that we must live as men who manage our lives without him. . . . Before God and with God we live without God. God lets himself be pushed out of the world and on to the cross. He is weak and powerless in the world, and that is precisely the way, the only way, in which he is with us and helps us.'[1]

Bonhoeffer himself does not proclaim 'the death of God', as did Hegel, Feuerbach, Karl Marx and Nietzsche; but the theologians who regard him as their teacher have adopted the words as the slogan of the 'new theology'. According to Bonhoeffer, however, the Church can henceforth proclaim the Gospel message only in the language of the world. Today Christianity has to be religionless. It is impossible to retain the traditional relationship between *faith* and *religion*. The Christian is doomed to live in permanent tension: he must joyfully welcome the secularized world which is the world of his life, and at the same time he must understand that this world is 'God's tomb'.[2]

In *The Joyful Wisdom*,[3] Nietzsche puts into the mouth of a madman the words, 'We have killed God'. For those who accept the 'new theology' the death of God has meanings that vary greatly. They proclaim it in terms that their readers or hearers find disconcerting and which scandalize many of them. Even so, before passing judgment on them it is essential to understand what the phrase means. What matters to us, however, at this moment is to see whether this great theological crisis can have repercussions on the ecumenical movement, and more particularly on the life of the World Council of Churches.

The Reformed Churches, as members of the World Council, have the duty of asking themselves that question. In 1961 at New Delhi, they emphasized the Trinitarian character of the Council's doctrinal basis. The Orthodox Churches see in this modification a necessary condition of their complete collaboration in the life and work of the World Council. And yet how can that basis not fail to be shaken, both by a hermeneutics which

1. *Letters and Papers from Prison*, 3rd ed., London, SCM Press, 1967, pp. 152, 178, 196.
2. See the lecture given by the Dutch theologian Hendrik Berkhof at the meeting of the World Alliance of Reformed Churches at Torre Pellice in the summer of 1967.
3. English trans., Edinburgh, J. N. Foulis, 1910, pp. 167 ff.

questions the historical reality of the 'facts of Christianity' which have been the foundation for twenty centuries of the dogmatic tradition of all the Churches, and by a theology which deprives God of all transcendence? This is a point to which I shall return in my last chapter. It is hardly surprising that the various currents which make up the present crisis are already strengthening the negative reactions of some Protestant circles to recent ecumenical happenings.

II

Some communities which are proud to describe themselves as evangelical, and have always shown themselves extremely chary of any contact with the Church of Rome, are hardening their anti-ecumenical attitude since Vatican 2. The disappointing reply to the Council's petition in connection with mixed marriages, Pope Paul VI's insistent exaltation of devotion to Mary, and his constant emphasizing of the primacy of Peter, are strengthening the opposition, not only of the fundamentalist Churches but of those, too, in which, all unconsciously, being 'Protestant' is more common than being 'Christian'.

The trouble can be seen in the fear that workers for unity may allow themselves to be drawn into concessions, compromises and sentimental gestures of friendship which leave doctrinal differences untouched. When some hear us speak with delight of the new atmosphere, redolent of respect and brotherly love, which accompanies our interdenominational meetings, they conclude that we are shutting our eyes to the dogmatic and ecclesiastical obstacles which still remain insurmountable.

Were these apprehensions justified, I would be the first to acquiesce in courteously expressed reservations. Nevertheless I am convinced that they are addressed to an imaginary ecumenism, and in any case bear no relation to the movement we have been serving for decades.

That ecumenism should be a fashion, as Bergsonism was and as we can see Teilhardism becoming, many of us deplore, and I never miss an opportunity of denouncing its mischievousness. It compromises our progress and forces us to multiply our precautions. It imposes on us, too, a strict discipline in what we say and write. Unfortunately, our words are so often distorted or quoted in a mutilated form that what is offered to us as 'Protestant defence' or 'confessional loyalty' cannot, any more than can sentimental ecumenism, divert us from the ecumenical line we have been following, not without disappointment and distress, for nearly sixty years.

The solution offered for the problem of mixed marriages, unhappy for all its necessarily provisional character, is one of those disappointments: and I am not proposing to say any more about it.[4]

III

However important that problem may be and however urgent the solution which so many Catholics and Protestants are waiting for, those are nevertheless minor matters in comparison with questions which the Reformed Churches are obliged to ask themselves at this juncture, or which the Church of Rome is raising for them in this post-conciliar period.

Winston Churchill's cruel remark is well known, when he was deciding to put forward to George VI the name of William Temple for the archbishopric of Canterbury, the primatial see of 'All England': 'In this penny bazaar I have chosen a shillings-worth.' This malicious quip brings out the gravity of the institutional crisis through which the great Churches of the Reformation are now passing, and it may be well to look at it a little more closely.

The Church of England, to deal with that Church first, is called upon to solve two problems: the problem of its 'establishment' and consequent links with the State, and that of its ecclesiastical organization and government.

To be 'established' brings the Church which is so privileged considerable moral advantages. After the sovereign, and before the Prime Minister, the Archbishop of Canterbury is the first person in the kingdom. He sits in the House of Lords, with the Archbishop of York, and other bishops, and does not fail to make known his views on matters of national concern or on bills to which the Churches of Great Britain cannot be indifferent. If, as has often been the case, he enjoys the confidence of the sovereign or the Prime Minister he can exert an influence that is by no means negligible. And the Church, through its episcopal body,

4. See above, p. 343.

can give warnings and express the demands of Christian morality, and call on the State not to close its eyes to social dangers. But a heavy price, undoubtedly too heavy, has to be paid for these privileges and rights: forfeiture of the right to elect its own archbishops, bishops and deans of cathedrals, and the risk that some day the Church's most legitimate undertakings may come up against the ill-will of a secularized State. People still remember the debates a good many years ago in the House of Commons on the revision of the Prayer Book: the prayers and eucharistic liturgy of the Church of England depended on the votes of members of parliament, Catholics, unbelievers, and Nonconformists just as much as Anglicans. In the new age into which we have been flung since the Second World War, can one imagine so astonishing a scene being repeated?

On the ecumenical plane, again, could there not be reason to fear that the connection between Church and State may have an unwholesome effect on the positions adopted by the Church in the examination of certain international problems? In the matter of its own government, the Church of England is going through a period of reflection and discussion. It would appear to be ready to adopt a synodal character, which would bring it closer to the Nonconformist Churches.

What I have just been saying about the Church of England may be applied without difficulty, subject to a few slight modifications, to the Churches of Scandinavia, where the nomination of the primate sometimes depends on considerations other than those which would have weighed with the Churches had they been free.

I know that in France certain theologians regret that Christendom no longer exists, by which they mean that there is no longer a Christianized mass which would enable the Churches to benefit from having an authentically Christian élite in the country.[5] At the very least, it is said, the State should adopt an attitude of benevolent neutrality to them. From the point of view of Christianity such a return, however modified, to the era of Constantine would have grave disadvantages.

The Lutheran and Reformed Churches of Alsace and Lorraine share the same character of State Churches. At the head of the

5. Cf. Père Daniélou, *L'Oraison politique. Prayer as a Political Problem*, London, Burns and Oates, 1967.

Church of the Augsburg Confession is a high official appointed by the Government. His freedom of initiative is limited by the Ministry of the Interior's control of religious bodies, which, though often liberal, might well become unsympathetic and even hostile if there were a change of policy. The Reformed Church of Alsace and Lorraine is governed by its Synod, but its association with the Reformed Church of France (of the interior, note) is becoming continually closer. Nevertheless its pastors will continue to be State-employed officials while the Organic Articles, retained after the 1914-18 war, remain in force.[6]

In our own country the institutional crisis makes itself felt in a different context. Young Reformed theologians resent the ecclesiastical institution on the ground that the whole organism is clericalized. Parishes, parochial ministry and the authority of the Synods, must be abolished because they do not correspond to the new conditions created for – or imposed on – the life of men, any more than they do to the demands of the Gospel. Young men, convinced of their vocation to serve Christ, believe in all honesty that their vocation to bear witness and to serve, and at the same time really to think out theological problems and to live the life of the community, cannot be fulfilled in forms of ministry, worship and ecclesial life which in their view are ineffective and impotent.

I have no hesitation in admitting that what I have been witnessing myself for more than sixty years of pastoral ministry provides ample justification for their contention. Parishes have been killed, some more rapidly than others, by a ministry which, confining itself to acts of worship which lacked any Christian substance, was no more than carrying out with the least possible effort a function accepted without a spark of love. At times, again, the ministry has been poisoned by bitterness and despair, and doomed to tragic suffering, by the spiritual mediocrity, the hostility, or, even more, the contemptuous indifference of 'Protestants' who are slaves to their parish-pump politics, and have no knowledge at all of the contribution the ministry of a true pastor could make to their lives, their homes and their towns.

6. The Concordat concluded between the Holy See and Bonaparte was followed by 'Organic Articles' which decided, among other questions, those relating to non-Catholic religious bodies.

Towards the end of the last century, Fallot, in an excellent little book on the Church,[7] was already speaking of dead churches. How, and by whom, were they killed? And how and by whom were pastors, who had entered the ministry with a vocation accepted in wonder and joy, gradually condemned to become gravediggers?

It is perhaps from asking themselves these questions, which have forced themselves on my own attention for so many years, that young theologians have believed themselves summoned to a work of demolition. The territorial parish seems to them a ghetto which the world no longer has any use for; and, shocking though it is to have to say so, the pastor's ministry is nothing to these younger men but a rotten cork which will have to be drawn as soon as possible. And what will pour out of the opening? Corruption? Or a flood of suffering bringing with it the thirst for renewal of souls – *souls*, mark you – who refuse to the very end to despair of Christ?

We should not condemn the younger generations who are moving away from the Churches, nor those who, within them, are trying to build up new communities on the ruins they have themselves helped to produce, to erect them not where so many human beings hardly do more than sleep and sometimes eat, but in places where men work, whether they are students or engineers, executives in private or public enterprises, or factory workers. We must listen to them, try to get inside them and understand them, and, above all, love them.

They see the world clothed in an atheism which is submerging many little islands which until this time have been Christian. They see that men – all men, and often Christians themselves – are living lives from which God is completely absent. And even if some still think that they enjoy his intermittent presence, what God is it who is present? Is it a blind, dumb idol, or is it the God of the prophets who demands our sanctity and whom alone Christ makes known to us as our Father?

There is a great deal I could easily say on this most important subject, but I must confine myself to only one point. It is indeed true that the Church must develop new structures for herself, must produce theologians, pastors and layfolk for all the

7. T. Fallot, *Qu'est-ce qu'une Église?*, Paris, Fischbacher, 3rd ed.

ministries which the family, economic, social and cultural situation of today is making indispensable. The Church must, indeed, abandon outworn liturgical formulas which are now meaningless and 'invent' assemblies of the faithful in which the necessary dialogue between all the participants may from time to time be inaugurated, and in which a rejuvenated reading of the Bible may be taught and practised. All this was strongly urged at the General Assembly of French Protestantism which met in Colmar in the autumn of 1966. Let me, however, express my conviction that, in many parts of France and all over the world, the territorial parish still can and must play a part which nothing can replace: that of being the place where the universal Church offers herself to the contemplation of all, without distinction of sex, age, occupation, culture, social position, or race; the place where the Body of Christ is, not only for the faithful assembled round the holy table, but in their daily lives, a magnificent reality by which they live and in which they live *together* in a community of true brotherhood.

I must add that to condemn ancient institutions is to expose oneself to a very grave danger. In the attempt to build anew there is a risk of cutting oneself off from the past and of pulling up roots through which the sap can still rise. I cannot help thinking once more of Fallot. He left the Church of Alsace when it became German because he refused to be a State-supported pastor in it; he was cruelly disappointed by the narrowness and absence of love in the free Churches in which he had hoped to find the purity and joy of the early Christian communities; but, knowing that, in spite of his wretched health, he was still called to be a messenger of Christ, he understood that all prophetic witness, if it is not to be fruitless, must be incarnate in an institution. Wretched though it was at that time, with its doctrinal and ecclesiastical quarrels, the Reformed Church of France offered itself to him as the institution to which he should attach himself. I witnessed that experience, punctuated at times by outbursts of righteous indignation, and it gave me a lesson I have never forgotten.[8]

In this connection the future of the ecumenical movement is also at stake. Problems of order, of authority, of particular

8. Cf. Marc Boegner, *La Vie et la pensée de T. Fallot*, Vol. 2, pp. 249 ff.

ministries within the ministry of the universal Church, are calling for study, not only in such bodies as Faith and Order, but also in the official dialogues to which theologians of all the Churches are invited. Local churches, too, have to understand this: their ecumenical education is the condition of progress towards unity.

IV

The biblical revival, so vigorous in the Catholic Church, and not in France alone, during the twenty or thirty years before the Vatican Council, was welcomed with joy, gratitude and hope by a great many of the faithful of the Reformed Churches. The Bible was becoming the best *ground* for ecumenical meeting in study, meditation and prayer.

The extensive discussions in the Council of the schema *De Revelatione*, and the final form of that document, brought out unmistakably the desire of the great majority of the Fathers that their Church should base its teaching, doctrine, liturgy and government on the Revelation given in the Holy Scriptures and proclaimed as the one source of Christian truth.

The problem remains, however, of what it is that emerges from this source. Is it a tradition, which, with no break in continuity from the Apostles to the Pope and Council of our own day, brings to maturity the seeds deposited in Revelation? Or did Revelation reach in the apostolic age a point of perfection, attested in the New Testament, which has been recognized as the *norm* of all the Church's later reflection? There we have the crucial question which governs all the differences between the Church of Rome and the Protestant Churches. Nevertheless, it remains true that we all find in the Bible the one source of what God bids us know about himself and about ourselves. It is in the Bible, and in the Bible alone, that we hear the Word of God.

It was this biblical revival, then, which was solemnly confirmed by the conciliar decree. Read and pondered in the vernacular at the Sunday services, Holy Scripture is taking its place beside the Eucharist as one of the two essential pillars of personal and community Christian life.

The Catholic Church, accordingly, is justified in claiming that she intends to be and now is just as much a Church of the Word of God as the other Christian bodies.

What problem does this raise for the Reformed Churches? For over four centuries they have been affirming, wherever they have taken root, that they, and they alone, are the Churches of the Word of God. In the face of *De Revelatione*, of the amazing circulation of Catholic vernacular versions of the Bible in many countries, and of the remarkable quantity and quality of Bible-study groups in Catholic parishes (often a source of jealousy for us) how can the Reformed Churches refuse the Church of Rome the right to put herself forward as a Church of the Word of God?

If that be so, what remains of the centuries-old vocation of our Churches? What is there to distinguish it from the vocation which the Church of Rome claims as hers? I wonder whether we have realized how serious is that question.

I can see only one answer. For all the Reformed Churches, whatever their differences in the various spheres of faith and Christian action, the Word of God, attested by the Holy Spirit in Scripture, is the *norm* to which all developments in dogmatic and moral teaching must be referred, in worship, too, and in the life of the Church with its ministries, apostolate, diaconate and service in the world. This is a principle to which our Churches must cling more firmly than ever.

Since the Council, I have read a statement by a Catholic theologian to the effect that *De Revelatione* makes it impossible henceforth to formulate any new dogmatic or moral teaching without express reference to the *normative* teaching of the New Testament. If only that had been so in 1854 and 1950, when the two Marian dogmas, completely without scriptural foundation, were defined, and so aggravated the doctrinal differences which separate our Churches from the Church of Rome!

However that may be, the one sovereign authority of the Word of God, heard in Holy Scripture, must remain, after *De Revelatione* as it was before, the basic principle on which the Reformed Churches found their inalienable vocation.

At the same time, it is essential accurately to define what we mean by the Word of God. This brings us back to Bultmann and the revolution he has produced in exegesis and theology. However plausible, and even indispensable, a certain 'demythologizing' may be, it cannot shatter the unity of Revelation. Beyond the myths there is a history for us to ponder: the history of God working throughout the centuries to realize the loving plan he has freely made for his creature, who resists him in his desire for autonomy which is the essential sin. A history of salvation is revealed to us in the old covenant which found its fulfilment in Christ, on the cross of Calvary shining forth in the light of the Resurrection. Oscar Cullmann is right[9] when he describes the stages in our history of mankind's salvation, our own salvation and that of other men, and shows that they are willed and, by roads that are often roundabout, accomplished by the eternal love whose plenitude is revealed to us by Christ. It is a history which comes from eternity, is made within time, and draws us towards eternity. The further I advance along the road of life, the more am I filled with wonder at the unity of the Revelation sealed on the Cross, the more I worship the God who is love and who in begetting his creature into the life of love and re-establishing him, through Christ, in his freedom, summons him freely to become, in the Church and in the world, a sign and an actualization of his love.

I realize, of course, that some modern readers of the Bible, who wish to live their Christian life in the spirit of the 'Church and Society' Conference,[10] attach great importance to the parable of the last judgment in the Gospel of St Matthew (25:31-46). They are eager to meet Christ, who has called them to serve him, in the poor, the strangers, the prisoners, the hungry, in whom he awaits them. But is not this Christ he whom the Father has *sent* in order to realize his loving plan for the world, the 'world he so loved'? Is it not through him and in him that the long history of salvation is fulfilled? And is he not today the Lord and Saviour who, 'a Lamb standing, as though it had been slain',[11] is to overcome the satanic powers before restoring the kingdom to God his Father? Christ awaits us not only in the unfortunate brothers of whom the parable speaks, but above all in his Church; there, in the cultal and ecclesial life of an authentically Christian community, and in pondering the Word of God, we have to learn how, through us and in the first place in us, Christ intends

9. Oscar Cullmann, *Salvation in History*, London, SCM Press, 1967.
10. See below, pp. 364-7.
11. Revelation 5:6.

to show his love to those to whom he will send us, as he himself was sent.

V

As I re-read what I have just written, I ask myself how there can be a presence of love in a Church of Christ which is torn by such divisions. What part has love played in the lamentable story of our secessions, major and minor?

It was from fidelity to the demands of faith, as imposed on their Christian souls and minds, that the Reformers, we are told, broke with Rome, before later dividing among themselves the bread of the Lord's Supper, the sign of love, of its demands and promises.

Countless Christians are convinced that they did in fact break with Rome, the Christian Church of the West, the Church of their baptism: but does history confirm their belief?

On this point the researches on which Jaques Courvoisier, professor of history in the faculty of Protestant theology in Geneva, has been engaged, seem to me to be conclusive.[12] Neither Luther nor Calvin had the intention, and still less were they anxious, to establish a new Church. They sought to reform the Church, their Church, whom evil shepherds had corrupted morally, led into vicious doctrinal betrayals, and involved in temporal enterprises with which the Gospel should have no concern. This Church condemned, excommunicated and exiled them. It was still none the less the Church in which they knew there was still smoke from the embers, and therein lay their hope. Daniel-Rops made a serious historical mistake when in his volume on the Reformation he denounced Calvin to Catholics as bearing the heaviest weight of responsibility for the tragic breach of the sixteenth century[13]—a mistake which I did not fail to point out to him.

The most violent of the criticisms and reproaches aimed at the Roman Church of that time never implied the desire to abandon her to the poisons that had eaten into all her organs. The Church was threatened by death but there was still life in her. And on the eve of the Reformation souls of light were still radiating the

12. Jaques Courvoisier, *La Dialectique dans l'ecclésiologie de Calvin*, Paris, 1964.
13. Daniel-Rops, *The Protestant Reformation*, London, Dent, 1961.

pure beauty of evangelical holiness. The vine must be pruned, not cast into the fire. That, I believe, was foremost in the minds of the Reformers.

A Catholic asked a Protestant, 'If the Catholic Church had presented the same picture in the sixteenth century as it did at the Council, would you have started the Reformation?' And the Protestant answered, 'But in that case, would you have thrown us out?'

Well, the Reformers were thrown out; and under the pressure of condemnation, of martyrdoms, of political and social upheavals, new communities had to be built up, they had to be given a discipline, they had to be brought to confess their faith, to formulate their teaching in catechisms and to set up the Church. The Church? The poison, alas, of division was inside her, and the last four centuries have been shocked and envenomed by the history of these separations, from which have been born denominations each of which claimed exclusive possession of the true faith. Would things have turned out in this way had love been preached, believed and lived as 'the fulfilling of the law'?[14]

VI

And here we meet the final question. Should we not hold that the Reformation opens a long parenthesis in the history of the Church, which can never be closed until, by the grace of God, the visible unity of the Body of Christ is restored, that 'the world may believe'? I know that the same may be said of the eleventh-century schism between the Greek and Latin Churches; the parenthesis opened at that time may well be easier to close.

The very word 'parenthesis' may shock many of my fellow-Protestants, I fear. But, in that case, what do they expect: that our Churches or denominations, often minute, lost in the vast and continually increasing mass of non-Christians and unbelievers, can retain a permanent significance? By what aberration can some 'children' of the Reformation shut themselves up in such an illusion?

The truth is that since the day when the unity of the Reformation broke on the conflicting interpretations of the words 'This is my body', there has been a sort of curse which blinds the majority

14. Romans 13:10.

to the scandal of our divisions and the suffering we inflict on Christ, 'in agony until the end of the world'.[15]

It is true that the cause of Church unity is continually becoming more familiar, closer to men's hearts and better served in the Reformed Churches of many countries, and sometimes in the humblest of their parishes. It is, however, only a minority that is so affected. The majority are still included among those who see in their Lutheranism, their Calvinism, Anglicanism, Methodism or Baptism, the faithful expression of revealed truth, and they believe that God will preserve it there, until the coming of his kingdom, from the contagion of the heresies that surround it.

Oberlin, Daniel Le Grand, Christophe Dieterlin, Tommy Fallot – these are men to whom I am ever thankful for having led me along the path, difficult but opening up horizons of inexpressible beauty, which becomes plainer as one advances along the royal road of love. It is to them I owe it that I can thrill with joy when I think that one day all Christ's disciples, sons and daughters of their heavenly Father, all his disciples, from St Paul to John XXIII, from St John to William Booth, from St Catherine of Siena to Blanche Peyron, will sing in unison the praises of the Lord in the communion of one and the same faith, hope and love.

This, however, is a personal feeling which I might do better, perhaps, to keep to myself. Our real concern is with the Reformed Churches not only in France but all over the world.

What matters is whether they will heed the summons addressed to them, through the ecumenical movement of these last years, by Christ, the Lord of the whole Church. In the lukewarmness of their faith, to which they are too often resigned, in their formalism, or, to go to the other extreme, in the lamentable excesses of the 'new' ethics and the spiritual void created in the Churches by negation heaped upon negation, will they recognize their duty to rediscover the secret of their prime vocation: to be, in the obedience of love, *living* communities, authentically Christian, in which Christ may in truth become the Lord of our life? If we are to go out to the world and there make felt a presence which is truly a Christian apostolate, witness and service, we must again become, we must *be*, *Christians*, radiating holiness and love in the image of him whose disciples we claim to be.

15. Pascal.

Will our Churches understand that, to approach this God, no problem of doctrine or Church allegiance, of diaconate or mission, can be expressed or solved except in the context of an ecumenism which is sought for and gradually consented to by all the Christian Churches? And will they understand, further, that this will be even more true in the decades to come?

Only a clear realization of this truth can enable the Reformed Churches to save themselves from the hazards of a muddle-headed or syncretic ecumenism which could only lead to a fatal weakening. The ecumenical context of which I am speaking will be produced only through an education which is based on a revitalized study of the apostolic doctrine of the Body of Christ, of the Church's mission and her unity. How right Père Villain is when he says that without this persevering education, undertaken and continued with love for the truth of God, who is love, the ecumenical movement can end only in stagnation and paralysis.

If we ask who is to provide ecumenical education for the parishes and believers whose allegiance is to the Reformation, the answer is that the task is too great for the theologians, the pastors and the layfolk whose ambition it is to help build up unity. Ecumenical institutes must be established in every country, whatever denominational differences they still contain, and these institutes must undertake the magnificent task of giving the Reformed Churches, still tragically attached to their divisions, the vision of the Church of Christ, restored to its unity, and alone capable of carrying out, in the world and for the world, its mission of witness and service.

It is by following this road that our descendants will, by the grace of God, see the closing of the parenthesis opened in the sixteenth century. But the Catholic Church, too, will have to have closed the parenthesis on her side: not simply the parenthesis opened by the Counter-Reformation which Vatican 2 aimed to close, but that which is opened by her claim to exercise a magisterium which asserts itself as the infallible organ of the truth revealed in Christ and, with a clear, and all unwitting, conscience, awaits the 'great homecoming' of all her separated brethren.

CHAPTER 24

Towards the Future

I. Orthodoxy and its approach to unity. II. The Church and Society Conference Geneva, 1966. III. Taizé and youth. IV. Cimade and its ecumenical significance. V. Problems of the World Council. VI. The Catholic Church and World Council Joint Working Group. Lukas Vischer's report and Mgr Willebrands's impressions. VII. Preparations for the Uppsala Assembly 1968.

As I come to the end of these memories, my mind turns to the possibility of focusing, not the crises that affect each particular Christian body, but the ecumenical movement as a whole, and of forming an idea both of the dangers that may lie in wait for it and the stages through which it will have to pass if it is to be true to its vocation. I have already commented on the difficulty of trying so to read the future; and the difficulty is increased by the fact that new events of ecumenical significance are continually occurring which I cannot afford to ignore; and before this book is in the reader's hand I have no doubt that this will be even more true.

I

The exchange of visits between Paul VI and Athenagoras I during the year 1967 gives me an opportunity of saying something more about the Orthodox Churches, to which I have not, I fear, given sufficiently close attention in the preceding chapters. Nevertheless, ever since the beginnings of the ecumenical movement I believe I have been one of those who have never ceased to hope that they may take the place to which they are entitled both in the Council and Assemblies, and also in the general secretariat.

When, on my way back from the Holy Land in the spring of 1964, I stopped in Istanbul, it was in order to meet the Ecumenical Patriarch.[1] The two first sessions of the Council were over. Paul

1. 25 May 1964.

VI and Athenagoras I had exchanged the kiss of peace in Jerusalem. All the Christian Churches felt a thrill of joy and hope: but we were all wondering what the sequel would be.

The ecclesiology of the Orthodox Churches, so different from that of the Catholic Church, is still unfamiliar to the Western world, even though during the last fifty years successive immigrations have brought a considerable increase in the numbers of Orthodox Christians in the West. Some of their bishops and theologians prefer us to refer to them not in the plural but as 'Orthodoxy', thereby emphasizing their doctrinal unity, which has so far spared them the crises from which, as we have just seen, the Catholic Church is no more immune today than are the Reformed Churches.

At the same time, each of these Orthodox Churches sets great store by its autocephalous character: each is self-governing, and recognizes no jurisdiction other than that of its patriarch or national metropolitan. It is the Church of a nation, intimately bound up with the life of that nation, in spite of political circumstances, spiritual and intellectual revolutions, and even persecutions.

While all the Orthodox Churches accord to the Ecumenical Patriarch, sometimes with reservations, a primacy of dignity (*primus inter pares*), they deny him the right to speak in their name without the consent of a synod in which they are all represented. That was why, when Athenagoras met Paul VI in Jerusalem, he did not have the support, or even the approval, of the whole of Orthodoxy.

Even so, the ecumenical significance of that event should not be minimized. When, some months later, I had the pleasure of an interview with Athenagoras, whom I had known of old, he told me that Jerusalem was a starting-point, and that he was determined to move on from there; and he informed me of his intention to make the most careful preparations for the return visit he had decided to make to Paul VI as soon as circumstances permitted.

There was first of all the political situation. The Turkish Government was not well disposed to certain members of the Patriarchate. Even though a Turkish citizen himself, Athenagoras was in a difficult position. Were he to undertake the journey to

Rome, and wish to precede or follow it by a visit to the Archbishop of Canterbury and the World Council of Churches, what would he find on his return?

Then there was the ecclesiastical situation. Archbishop Chrysostomos of Athens persisted in his rejection of any approach to the Roman Church, and was drawing the Church of Greece into an uncooperative attitude which would have prevented Athenagoras, even with the support of the other autocephalous Churches, from presenting himself to Paul VI as the spokesman of Orthodoxy.

Thus when I went to see the Ecumenical Patriarch in the Phanar he was confronted by some delicate problems. His serenity, his profound faith and his conviction that the visible unity of the Church of Christ must and will be restored, overcame any reasons he might have for anxiety. Over three years have passed by since that time; Athenagoras has at last been able to undertake the journeys he planned, with the somewhat grudging agreement of the Turkish Government; what is even more important, however, is that it is the result of an unforeseen improvement in the ecclesiastical situation.

Those who supported the separation of Church and State may find this rather startling. It was the *coup d'état* in Greece in 1967 and the violent action taken by the new régime against the Orthodox Church which brought about the change in the attitude of the latter towards Athenagoras and his attempts to establish dialogue between Rome and Orthodoxy. Archbishop Chrysostomos had been forced to retire; a new archbishop, Hieronymos, had been nominated at the instance of a purged synod, and one of the first things he did was to visit Patriarch Athenagoras.

Paul VI's lightning visit to Istanbul, where Roman protocol had been thrust aside by a great outburst of humility and charity, and the conversations in Rome, are a sign that on neither side is there any intention of allowing the cardinal question of restoring the unity shattered in the eleventh century to lie undisturbed. Both Pope and Patriarch are agreed that as soon as possible official dialogue between the two Churches must be inaugurated. The dogmatic and ecclesiological divergences are deeper than many of the faithful realize. Further, it will be necessary for Athenagoras I to secure the consent of the whole of Orthodoxy to this joint search for a road to unity. In some respects, the Orthodox Churches seem closer to coming to an understanding with the Reformed Churches, the Anglican Communion in particular, than with the Church of Rome.

While the Roman Church has always maintained the fundamental principle of the catholicity of the Church, founded on the authority of an episcopate whose continuity is guaranteed by apostolic succession, Orthodoxy has never ceased to affirm the unity of bishops, priests and laity, who together constitute the people of God, in the government of the Church. On this point, the Reformed Churches have found themselves much closer to Orthodoxy than to the Church of Rome.

II

Of all the ecumenical meetings during these last years, that which was held in Geneva in July 1966 will undoubtedly be found to have made the most impression. Organized by the Department on Church and Society of the World Council, the Church and Society Conference brought together hundreds of participants from all parts of the world, among whom, for the first time it would appear, the laity were in a majority. Catholics, Orthodox and Protestants debated together, not on subjects that had been discussed again and again on countless occasions, but on completely new themes, of which the most important was 'The Theology of Revolution'. 'A shattering event', noted a Swiss theologian, adding that 'this conference will have particular significance in the history of the Church, because the Church and theology are presented by the revolutionary world of today with a new task to which they have to adopt a positive attitude.'[2]

The number of delegates from the 'third world', and particularly from Latin America, was an eye-opener to many at the conference. Where these Christians live 'the question is no longer one of wanting or not wanting revolution, but of knowing who is going to make the revolution and how it is going to be made'.[3]

2. Professor Arthur Rich (of Zürich) in *Le Christianisme social*, January-February 1967, p. 11.
3. Ibid., p. 12.

'For all of us in Geneva', says André Dumas, 'Latin America was the really important continent, provocative and clamouring for attention . . . . Revolution was the watchword of its Christianity, a Christianity eager to fight, by violence if need be, the chaos of the existing order and to show the poor and suffering that God in Christ is identifying himself with their quest.'[4]

André Philip emphasized his conviction that revolution, in the traditional meaning of the word, has no longer any place in modern industrial society. In one of the preparatory publications, he had no hesitation in speaking of 'the end of revolution'. It is true, indeed, that profound changes in political, economic and social structures are indispensable. Nevertheless, in highly developed industrial societies, they can no longer be effected by classical revolutionary methods except at the cost of undermining the whole system of technical production, with a consequent general impoverishment of the masses. This position, imperfectly understood, was rejected by the majority of those taking part. On the other hand, all were agreed in recognizing that henceforth revolution and all it entails falls, for Christians, within their sphere of responsibility.

New differences of opinion were apparent when it became necessary to define 'the Christian's duty in a revolutionary situation'. While recognizing that no revolution can provide a final solution to the distress of mankind, and refraining from making an idol of revolution, the Christian must be perfectly clear in his mind about his duty. Is he to do this in accordance with a 'normative ethics' or a 'situation ethics'? It was the supporters of the latter who won the day after some vigorous exchanges.

Among many other questions, there still remains that of deciding whether the Christian may use violence in his revolutionary battle. The report of Section 2 faced this question squarely. The fight against unjust systems which oppress man 'raises the crucial issue of the methods of opposition which a Christian may validly use'. There can be no doubt but that the Christian must look for 'all possible peaceful and responsible non-violent means of action in society. . . . Even in the most adverse circum-

4. *La Conférence 'Église et Société'*, p. 5.

stances, the Christian should distinguish himself in his persistent challenge of evil through non-violent means'.

And yet violence, whether visible or invisible, is an obvious reality in our world. The bloodless violence which condemns millions of human beings to despair, such as the segregation of Negroes, is surely more murderous, ultimately, than the violence which seeks by brute force to overthrow a system which is founded on injustice and oppression. 'There are situations in which Christians are committed to violence. . . . Violence, however, should be regarded as the last resource, justified only in extreme cases.'[5]

The same problem was studied by the Theological Commission of the Christian Conference on Peace (at Prague). I think it may be opportune to quote some passages from its report.

Basing themselves on the authentically Calvinist recognition of the right and duty to resist an authority that is turning into a tyranny, and on the doctrine (today so disputed) of the 'just war', to which there should logically correspond a doctrine of the 'just revolution', the members of the commission held that thinking on theological lines they were unable to arrive at a formulation of principles. 'It is impossible to determine casuistically Christian principles which can guarantee the conditions in which it is permissible to have recourse to force. What we are being asked to do is to advise our fellow-Christians after a responsible and competent analysis of their specific situation. We can give them such advice only by praying that the Holy Spirit may grant us a prophetic boldness.'[6]

Will this 'prophetic boldness' authorize the use of violence by Christians? The German theologian Gollwitzer warns them against the danger of carrying advocacy of non-violence so far as to build it up into an ideology which takes the weapons out of the hands of those who feel obliged to have recourse to violent revolution. Every revolution implies violence, because the order to be replaced rests upon hidden violence, as, for example, on the immutable distribution of private property, which is the source of economic power. Nevertheless, the use of armed violence on behalf of a revolution can only be the ultimate argument, and the

5. *Christianisme social*, loc. cit., pp. 65-6.   6. Ibid., pp. 68-9.

Christian who makes up his mind to use it 'must always and in all circumstances give evidence of love, even love of his enemies, reconciliation and forgiveness'.[7]

I can readily imagine that on reading such declarations many of the faithful of the various Christian denominations will feel extremely puzzled. The commandment to love, it is true, is still operative and has lost none of its rigour. But if the Churches begin to recognize that in certain circumstances Christians may legitimately use revolutionary violence, many will wonder where this is going to lead us. That is precisely the question: or rather, where is it going to lead the Churches, whose younger clergy and layfolk are attending more and more conferences and round-table discussions on the problem of violence and insist on being heard by their elders, against whose 'gerontocracy', moreover, they are in rebellion? These young people must be listened to, and efforts must be made – not paternalistic but with a perceptiveness that is rooted in the Gospel and is shot through with love – to understand them from within and 'get inside their skin'; and we must try, too, not to reject their theology and their ethics and their sociology out of hand. I cannot help wondering, though, whether youth is yet prepared for dialogue with age.

III

This was not the case, it would appear, with the 1,500 young people assembled at Taizé at the beginning of September 1966, some weeks after the Geneva Conference. Prominent ecclesiastical and theological figures of various denominations had come to Taizé at the invitation of the Prior, Brother Roger, in order to listen to the young people and have discussions with them. As I was not there myself, I can only say what I learnt from the account given to me a month later by Brother Roger and from the text of the discussion he himself had with the young people. The latter listened politely to a lecture by Cardinal Bea; they then preferred to remain on their own in their fifty discussion groups, leaving the Church and theological 'authorities' to exchange their views on the ecumenism of today and tomorrow in another part of Taizé.

One of the essential features of this gathering was the force,

7. Ibid., pp. 69-72.

one might even say the vehemence, with which it brought out the *ecumenical impatience* of Christian youth.[8]

'We are disturbed and disappointed', say the inspirers of the discussion groups, 'at the prospect of an ecumenism which is becoming too institutional and losing its dynamic character of pressing on towards the unity which we are ready to believe is not far distant.

'... We are waiting for the authorities (of our Churches) to give real support to the efforts of youth to achieve visible unity.

'... Bound together by a true communion and living a common prayer, we are distressed that we cannot share the bread of the Eucharist. We believe that the impossibility of this sharing is robbing us of a specially effective means of rebuilding visible unity: and we are waiting for the authorities of our Churches and their theologians to think again and give us a definite answer.'

One cannot but be struck by the tone of this appeal. It expresses a distress (of which I was poignantly aware as early as 1932),[9] but also the conviction that youth must exert its authority in the ecumenical movement in order to prevent it from declining into a fatal institutionalism.

Brother Roger had a discussion with the young people on his own. He gave full answers to the carefully thought out questions they had prepared. They were the questions of Christians who were on fire with eagerness to communicate Christ to men, knowing that what they were involved in was not merely a life of personal salvation but a living of Christianity for the world, and anxious at all costs to find communication with man. What, then, does ecumenism count for, what can it achieve, in the face of the immense difficulty of realizing such a plan? What has it done so far? Is it not in danger of becoming no more than an institution if it loses sight of the urgency of restoring the visible unity of all who are baptized? And how can we envisage a solution, for which we cannot afford to wait?

The Prior's answers showed his anxiety to maintain contact with youth, in the conviction that the Church would be heading for

8. This impatience made itself felt on countless occasions: on Fanö (1934), in Amsterdam (1939), Lausanne (1960), and New Delhi (1961).
9. See above, p. 91.

At a lecture given by Dr. Martin Luther King, Paris, 1965

In his study

youngest brothers and novices, of which I retain
memory, tinged only with gratitude. Between
ning and Monday morning I attended their services
nited with the brothers in the community's beautiful
was I alone, for with me there were many of the
m France, Switzerland, Germany and the Netherlands.
e tourist's curiosity that brought them? or an interest in
m? or was it the desire for closer contact with a living
yearning to find a place, were it but for a moment, in a
ouse of love and unity whose driving force bears the
f Jesus Christ? I am inclined to think that the last of these
es is closest to the truth.

eed hardly repeat here all that Taizé represents for me,[10]
may be well to add this: a Catholic writer recently described
é as the capital of ecumenism. I can hardly accept that descrip-
. Whether one likes it or not, the capital of the ecumenical
vement, after Vatican 2 as before, is in Geneva: it is there, at
e present moment, that you will find not an institution but a
hole organization of departments in which are incarnate the
vision and the challenge from which it was born, and through
which it fulfils its vocation. Taizé is something else: a stronghold
of French and international Protestantism, in spite of anything its
critics and detractors may say, and above all a symbol of the
hunger for unity which gnaws at an increasing number of
Christians who want in the first place to be *Christian*. Taizé, at
least in some degree, is a prophecy of restored unity. Side by side
with the liturgical life, the life of the community, and economic
and social work, there are the writings of Brothers Schutz and
Thurian to give more than ample evidence of this. Nevertheless,
this unity of the Church is not desired as an end in itself: it is
to serve the unity of the great community of man. 'If we are to
hasten the coming of unity', said the Prior to the young people
meeting at Taizé in 1966, 'we must make the Christian community,
even if only provisionally, a reality.' Indeed, in this corner of the
earth where I constantly gaze in wonder at the expanse of the
horizon, I can fill my lungs with the life-giving air of the 'Christian
community' and I can only say, and say again, 'Praise be to God'.

10. See above, p. 248.

At the Convent of St Anne,
Jerusalem

Looking at the Dead Sea Scrolls

In the Holy Land, 1964

Visiting the ruins of Qumran

By the Jordan

disaster if it were to lo[...]
he said (as John XX[...]
in putting history on t[...]
was wrong: but I wonde[...]
he went on to say, 'We ca[...]
which postpone for some c[...]
unity. We are no longer w[...]
imprisoned in a history and[...]
themselves and their own petty[...]
Roger felt that one cannot ans[...]
oneself with its rejection of 'individ[...]
histories'. He had no intention – and[...]
of questioning the history of salvation[...]
Within that history the ecumenical n[...]
'act of God'. Ecumenism is not one mo[...]
and disseminated by an institution over w[...]
threat of sclerosis; it is a vocation, calling[...]
answer of faith – it is a life.

Space forbids further quotation, but I may[...]
inclined I may be to make reservations about on[...]
of the Prior of Taizé's conception of ecumenism[...]
agreement with him on the fundamentals upon wh[...]
build 'the unanimity of the baptized', so that the c[...]
the baptized may once again find the 'joy, the peace,[...]
charity, in other words the dynamism of the Gospe[...]
alone will enable him to 'communicate the life of C[...]
secularized man'.

A further meeting of young people took place at Taizé i[...]
summer of 1967. Although there was a bigger attendance tha[...]
the earlier meeting, the impatience does not seem to have be[...]
so unrestrained. I am one of those who believe that the Holy
Spirit, the 'activator', of whom you will hear much talk at
Taizé, clears a road for himself through the discussions, arguments,
claims and declarations of *Christian* youth with a passion for
Christ, and that he will make this youth into a force which will
help the World Council of Churches to remain faithful to the
prophetic event from which it was born.

In October 1966 I went once again to Taizé. My long conversations with the Prior did not prevent me from spending a little

370

time with the[...]
an uncloude[...]
Saturday eve[...]
four times,[...]
liturgy; no[...]
faithful fr[...]
Was it th[...]
ecumenis[...]
reality,[...]
power-[...]
name[...]
motiv[...]
I n[...]
but i[...]
Taiz[...]
tion[...]
m[...]
th[...]
w[...]

IV

From that citadel of unity, Taizé, it is a natural step to Cimade, where again fidelity to the summons of ecumenism is the fundamental characteristic. Cimade has already appeared on many pages of this book. Ever since the time, in the sad summer of 1939, when it emerged as the answer to a great distress, it has never ceased to note the most urgent demands of mankind's suffering and destitution, and to do its utmost to meet them in renewed acts of faith and love.

I am too closely involved in the life of Cimade to be able to express myself as freely as I could wish on the subject of its rationale and work. When in January 1962 I finally gave up my work with the Protestant Federation of France, I asked most earnestly to be still allowed to work for the Société des Missions évangéliques and Cimade.[11] My association with both these meant that the demands of ecumenism were never relegated to the background of my mind. I have written about the Mission in an earlier chapter; but in spite of my intimate personal connection with Cimade I cannot refrain from saying something about it here.

When, as early as 1940, Cimade heard the call to devote itself to the care of the non-Aryan refugees who were flocking into our country, its answer was given in close co-operation with the World Council of Churches. I need not repeat what I have already said about its work in camps for refugees – or internees – of which Gurs remained the most hateful example, or about the labour of love and the lavish display of courage aroused by the persecutions of non-Aryans. The name of its first general secretary, Madeleine Barot, will always be remembered in connection with those years, during which Cimade won the respect and gratitude of the whole Christian world.

After the end of the war, while setting up its teams in numbers of towns and suburban areas, Cimade planned to meet the urgent needs it recognized in occupied Germany. Thus it founded a centre in the University of Mainz, and later another one, for clandestine refugees from the East, in one of the districts of Berlin. As I write these lines I can see in my mind's eye the face

11. See above, p. 136.

of Otto Dibelius, the intrepid Bishop of Brandenburg, by whose side I was present on the day when the new enterprise was inaugurated. This developed later into the homes for Orthodox refugees, for whom Cimade, as representing the World Council, has made itself responsible, in common with the Tolstoy Foundation and the Massy international and ecumenical students' centre. Then came Dakar and its Bopp dispensary, which was the prelude to increasingly close contacts with the Moslems of the Arab quarter.

Jacques Beaumont, who succeeded Madeleine Barot as general secretary, was able to organize a favourable reception for Cimade's work in Algeria at the height of that country's political and military troubles. It was his wise counsel that was behind the representations that Cardinal Feltin, Archbishop of Paris, Chief Rabbi Kaplan and I made to the French Government, and that inspired our attempts to influence public opinion. The establishment of Cimade teams in the Kasbah of Algiers and in the Medea area, raised many problems, whose solution at times involved an element of danger. The young men and women who made up the teams, working in the middle of the most dreadful destitution and suffering, particularly affecting the women and children (for the men were fighting), were a living witness to the presence and power of a dynamic love: a love that sprang up in answer to the ecumenical challenge which Cimade can never dissociate from the witness it strives, wherever it goes, to render to Christ. Today our Algerian teams are attached to the C.C.S.A. (Christian Committee for Service in Algeria), whose work has the backing of the World Council of Churches. These teams are teaching people to read, replanting devastated forests, working to produce citizens who are conscious of their duties and responsibilities, and caring for sick children. Without the help of the World Council very little of this great work would have been possible.

It is true that Cimade has gradually won an increasingly wide hearing in our French Churches; but I wonder whether people realize all that it has accomplished at home in France, where the number of refugees from so many nations is still increasing under the pressure of political events. Harkis from Algeria, Vietnamese, Hungarians who fled from their country after the suppression of the 1956 rising, illiterate North Africans, Albanians, Angolese, Portuguese, Negroes from French-speaking Africa, numbers of ex-prisoners – and this does not complete the list – receive from our teams of both sexes the assurance that there is someone at hand, fraternal, considerate, selfless, and ready to do anything that can possibly be done. Moreover, the Cimade teams do not work independently of one another. *As one whole*, they all constitute a true community, its unity in thought and work reinforced by two annual retreats. Communion in prayer, too, is one of the characteristics of Cimade.

Towards what near or distant lands will Cimade direct our faith, weak though it still is? Today it cannot be deaf to the appeal of the Middle East. Wherever refugees are suffering Cimade knows that it is needed. Jacques Beaumont, who has done so much to increase its reputation among the great international organizations for help and assistance in development, insists that Cimade must be prepared to deal with every urgent situation. The keen sense he has always had of Cimade's vocation has often helped us not to shrink from what at first appeared a rash undertaking to our puny faith.

v

There have been many references in this chapter to the World Council of Churches, but they have mostly been indirect. This is an appropriate moment at which to bring it into focus and to ask into what sort of future it is moving.

Great changes have been introduced into its organization and control and cannot fail to be introduced during this year. The complete incorporation of the International Missionary Council, effected at New Delhi in 1961, and the welcome extended at the same Assembly to the great Churches of Orthodoxy, have called for important modifications in the administrative services of the World Council. An evangelism and missions division, directed until 1965 by Bishop Newbigin, is practical evidence of the reality of the incorporation. The Bossey Ecumenical Institute now has an Orthodox director, Dr Nissiotis. The Department of Information, the Translation Office and the Publications Office have become the Department of Communications.

Changes in personnel have an importance of another nature.

The retirement of Visser 't Hooft, who was asked to continue as an 'adviser', could not but have profound repercussions in its effect on the staff. Eugene Carson Blake, his successor, displays rare qualities of intelligence, energy, and ability to diagnose the dangers of the present day; his age, however, makes it impossible for him to draw up a long-term programme of work, and some distressing losses make his task even more difficult. Leslie Cooke, the admirable director of the Division of Inter-Church Aid and the Refugee and World Service, died in 1966 after a long illness, and Philippe Maury, director of the Department of Information, was taken from us, still a very young man, in 1967. Such men are not easily replaced, particularly when national and denominational questions are concerned. Fortunately Philip Potter has been appointed as director of the Division of World Mission and Evangelism: but will he win the attention of the young 'ecumenists'?

For after all the young, and the not so young too, are asking the World Council questions of ever more insistent urgency. We have already met these at the Taizé and Geneva conferences; and the whole of the religious Press reverberated their echoes after the Central Committee's meeting in Heraclion. These arguments cannot be dismissed without a few more words about them.

I can quite well understand that the institution, the indispensable instrument of witness and service, can raise problems for some minds and inspire some apprehension. Looking at things from the outside, one cannot but be impressed by the great expansion of the Council, both in personnel and in buildings. Nevertheless, the prime reason for this, outweighing all others, is surely the rapid increase in the appeals made by Churches which are anxious to deal with human sufferings, in particular those of refugees, the underfed, and the victims of wars, of segregation and hatred. They can do this only if the Council helps them with the funds it collects or which are made available to it. That is one of its vocations and, since the Council 'in formation' was born in 1938, the directors or the secretary general have never allowed their fundamental concern with being faithful to that vocation to be relegated to the background. It would be an endless task to enumerate all the proofs of that assertion.

There is a risk involved, it is true, and I think I have mentioned this more than once. It is an anxiety that I have shared myself. And this, I believe, gives me all the more right to express the great gratitude of many to those who, in always difficult and sometimes critical circumstances, have kept the ecumenical movement to the prophetic road of its origins.

Nevertheless, the World Council is blamed for its institutionalism. I have just explained what I think is the answer to such a reproach. But may I not add that it comes from a generation which, almost throughout the whole Church world, considers that all ecclesiastical institutions, great and small, denominational, interdenominational and ecumenical, are suffering from sclerosis, and that the clericalism of the 'authorities' is reducing them to impotence? I believe that while in many cases the accusation is well-founded, it does not hold good as regards the World Council of Churches. That some re-direction, some new infusion of youth, is necessary, is true enough, and we are justified in thinking that the coming Uppsala Assembly will see to this: the members of the Central Committee are the first to be convinced of that necessity.

At the same time it remains true that the World Council raises a number of debatable questions.

There can be no effective increase in the number of member-Churches, which now stands at 223.[12] It should even decrease if the plans for organic reunion, now being examined in many Churches, should mature in the near future. It is already difficult, if not quite impossible, for the Secretariat General to remain effectively in contact with all the member-Churches. The most serious problem seems to me to be that of bringing the Churches up to an *ecumenical scale of thinking*, of making them conscious of their responsibility in the quest for unity, as defined at the New Delhi Assembly. No one can deny that, particularly since the Evanston Assembly in 1954, ecumenical education has been a matter of permanent and fundamental concern; but it is doubtful whether that education has stressed with sufficient force the central significance of the New Delhi definition of 'the unity we seek'.[13]

12. Unless the Pentecostal communities apply for and obtain membership of the Council.
13. See above, p. 284.

I do not believe that the Council needs any urging towards a more accurate appreciation of its great educational task. This is something in which all its divisions play their part. It would be impossible ever to estimate the educative value of the work done by a Madeleine Barot, a Hans-Rudi Weber, a Philip Potter, and many more whom I could mention. In carrying out their mission, such people bring to light everything that has to be undertaken, to be studied more fully, to be brought home to the mind and conscience of the Churches; they are the first to be painfully aware of the shortcomings that still persist, and all the time they are coming up against the problem of men and money. Nevertheless, how could one possibly cope with such an accumulation and diversity of needs and appeals, if there were not an institution at hand to find the indispensable men and resources, to decide an order of priority in urgency, to co-ordinate efforts and always and everywhere to allow the authority of the Holy Spirit to prevail?

So many Churches, again, are not yet ecumenically of age. This is a weakness which the Bossey Ecumenical Institute is helping to rectify; and this it is doing through its numerous annual sessions, and above all through the teaching given year after year to dozens of clergy, theologians and Christian layfolk who are studying for the degree in ecumenism awarded by the University of Geneva. The benefit of this is passed on in the form of ecumenical education in churches and parishes: nor is it the fault of Bossey if the large Churches appear to neglect the wealth of knowledge and experience that some of their young theologians might well derive from this course.

'There is a lack of dynamism in the World Council' is the complaint in more than one quarter. It must be admitted that according to some of those who took part in or attended the meetings of the Central Committee in Heraclion, it left them with a general impression of lifelessness. It is said that the committees did a great deal of work and that sometimes there were lively discussions. But at the public meetings, except when political problems came up, it would seem that a somewhat dismal silence prevailed.

And yet the secretary general's report, the first to be given by Eugene Carson Blake, should have stimulated a brisk exchange of views. He made a stand against the 'new theology', declaring, and with justification moreover, that the World Council is in some way founded on faith in the transcendence of God. One has only to re-read the New Delhi 'basis' to endorse that statement. Dr Blake's remarks, it is true, were noted, appraised, criticized, and occasionally severely condemned. But no storm burst at Heraclion.

Moreover, Heraclion was a mistake. It is true that when the decision was made and the necessary preparations had been put in hand no one could foresee the military *coup* of June 1967. To cancel a meeting prepared with such care, a matter of weeks before the appointed date, seemed impossible. Even so it would have been better to postpone the Central Committee's meeting to a later date and a different place. Whether one likes it or not, there was an almost universal impression that, quite unwittingly it is true, but at the same time with the sanction of its spiritual authority, the Council's failure to speak out evidenced an ill-advised acceptance of a régime which it could not but condemn. What a contrast, indeed, to the haste with which, at the time of the Suez affair, the Churches' Commission on International Affairs made authoritative representations to the member-Churches of the countries engaged in the war.

VI

And now we come to what today appears to many Christians to be the thing that really matters. The slowness or progress towards unity is deplored and, in a number of different quarters, it is attributed to an alleged passivity on the part of the World Council of Churches in comparison with the ecumenical activity displayed by the Catholic Church. This is a question that needs to be cleared up.

The reader will remember that in February 1965 Cardinal Bea came to Geneva on an official visit to the World Council, and to inform Visser 't Hooft of Paul VI's decision to accept the Council's suggestion of forming a joint working group of the Church of Rome and the World Council, instructed to 'work out the principles which should be observed in further collaboration and the methods which should be used'.[14] Since that time suc-

14. Instructions to the Joint Working Group, in the *Ecumenical Review*, 1965, 2, pp. 171 ff.

cessive meetings of the group have produced two reports. In August 1967 Lukas Vischer, director of Faith and Order and joint secretary of the group with Fr Jérôme Hammer, read to the Central Committee in Heraclion the second report, which had already been approved by Cardinal Bea and to which the Pope, after studying it, had raised no objection. I note this tribute to Lukas Vischer's complete objectivity; as the World Council's observer at the Vatican Council, on several occasions he reported the proceedings with a no less remarkable objectivity.

What mutual relationship should there be between the World Council of Churches and the Church of Rome; and what form should it take 'in order to bear witness to Christ and better serve the unity desired for his Church'? It has been asked whether the answer to this fundamental question is not that the Catholic Church should belong to the World Council. Nevertheless the working group held that such a solution 'would not allow the common cause of Christian unity to be better served'. That decision seems to me eminently reasonable. It seems to me quite unrealistic to believe that in the present state of theology the entry of the Roman Church into the 'family' of 223 member-Churches of the Council can be envisaged for a single moment; and I am quite certain that in the World Council there is an exact appreciation of the immensity of the problems that must be studied in common and which neither party can dream of leaving open. Has not a certain Catholic 'ecumenist' reproached the Council for supporting an ideology according to which all that is needed to *realize* unity is to gloss over anything that hinders its appearance?

Pace those of both persuasions who are still impatient, 'problems must be solved, not shelved'. By precipitating the theological enquiries of Catholic ecumenists, the World Council, presuming it had such an intention, would succeed only in jeopardizing the collaboration effected in an atmosphere of complete frankness and in doing a disservice to the ecumenical movement which it is its vocation to promote.

The Joint Working Party has a notable programme of theological reflection and work in common. A number of points of prime importance should be noted. A theological commission has been set up for the study of 'Catholicity and Apostolicity'.

The problem of the authority of the Bible and its interpretation, in view of the present orientation of theology and exegesis, will be the object of a searching examination. The same is true of the question of the common witness which the Churches *should* be able to render in 'mission situations'. Mission, Church, Unity: these are three words which for some years now have given rise to fruitful discussions. At the same time it is important not to confine oneself to the theological study of their relationship. There are practical problems which are urgently in need of solution. They require, however, the establishment of an ecumenical agreement on the distinction, often extremely nice, between evangelism and proselytism.

Conversations on the role of the laity, following on from the Rome Congress, closer co-operation between women's organizations, and joint action in the service of mankind in everything that concerns international peace and social justice are similarly envisaged and have even been started. Difficulties of every order will, no doubt, have to be overcome; but, only ten years ago, few would have entertained the hope that, in the ecumenical atmosphere developed in the last half-century, such a programme of fraternal co-operation between the Catholic Church and the World Council would be drawn up, in a common determination actively to seek for its realization. This beginning of a joint advance into the future gives added strength to my hopes.

We should not forget that, in this same year of 1967, there appeared the first part of the directive implementing the decree on ecumenism adopted by the Council and promulgated by Paul VI at the end of the third session. More striking still are the adoption, in a number of countries, of an ecumenical text of the Lord's Prayer and the putting in hand of ecumenical translations of the Bible. The French version, in which over a hundred biblical scholars are co-operating, is well under way. No doubt I shall never see its completion; but the moving gathering in the Sorbonne to greet the publication of the Epistle to the Romans gave me a foretaste of the joyfulness of this great event.

It is, indeed, an event of the first importance, saluted as such during the fourth session of the Council at a meeting at which I had the honour of presiding with Cardinal Martin. Many of the Fathers of the Council attended and listened with great attention while details of the plan adopted were given them by the two key men in the enterprise, Père Refoulé and Professor Georges Casalis.

VII

The fourth Assembly of the World Council of Churches was fixed for Uppsala in July 1968. Uppsala is the primatial see of the Lutheran Church of Sweden. Archbishop Soederblom's body lies in the cathedral in which so many years ago the voice of that great author of the ecumenical movement could be heard. But Uppsala has also a university renowned for centuries. Church and university will join the Swedish Ecumenical Council in welcoming some two thousand persons who in various capacities will share in or be present at the Assembly's work. Already, apart from the criticisms and arguments I have just mentioned, many people are asking whether this fourth Assembly is going to give them what they hope to find.

The general theme is expressed in the words of Revelation (21:5): 'Behold, I make all things new.' There are some who see in this an allusion to the 'new theology' – will it be possible, they wonder, to clear up the perplexing confusions of modern theology and (as some hope) create a living unity, now more necessary than ever, between the World Council's heritage from Life and Work (Stockholm, 1925) and what is learnt from Faith and Order (Lausanne, 1927).

Two hundred and twenty-three Churches will be represented in Uppsala, as compared with one hundred and ninety-one in New Delhi, an increase which is partly accounted for by the joining of large Orthodox Churches and of 'young Churches' enrolled in New Delhi. It will no longer be possible to say that the World Council is 'a western set-up with a few eastern trimmings'. The preponderance of English-speaking Churches, so pronounced for many years, is disappearing more and more.

Roger Mehl foresees that the Uppsala Assembly will come down on the side of a new mode of life for the Churches, deliberately rejecting the idea that 'they should continue to be administrators of the sacred'. A change I would indeed welcome, provided that, in their desire to assume their proper responsibility both in social and economic development and in international affairs, the

Churches do not lose sight of their prime vocation: which is always, and even more than ever before in our secularized age, to be heralds and witnesses, through the life of their communities and of their faithful, of the saving power of the Gospel and the Holy Spirit who makes it possible to *live* that life.

The Assembly will most certainly listen to some extremely valuable expositions and the discussion on particularly controversial questions is sure to be heated. New presidents will have to be nominated, and a new Central Committee elected. The choice of a chairman for the latter will be of great importance. There are men and women, young (as compared with those who will make way for them) but at the same time thoroughly acquainted with the history of the ecumenical movement, its sorrows and joys, its reverses and successes, who guard the vision of the *Una Sancta*, who have heard the summons of ecumenism which they will now have to pass on to others; and it is these, I ardently hope, who will be the inevitable choice of the hundreds of representatives of the Churches of the whole world.

Official observers from the Catholic Church will be present. I hope they will come to Uppsala realizing how true it is that all the members of the Assembly are very much alive to the importance of the stage in ecumenism through which the Roman Catholic Church and the World Council of Churches are now passing side by side. It is hardly possible for a man of my generation, who has met with so many disappointments in the relations between Catholicism and Protestantism, to believe that Rome is now willing to discuss with the separated religious bodies, the Reformed Churches in particular, as one equal with another, questions which she used to propose to solve by her own authority alone. And yet it is precisely this that we are now witnessing.

It should be noted, however, that the Catholic Church, through Mgr Willebrands, has made it quite plain to us that she cannot accept that the World Council should yield to the temptation of monopolizing the ecumenical movement. Rome may perhaps agree that the Council is a specially useful instrument of ecumenism; but the Catholic Church regards herself as closely participating, in her own way and in accordance with her own principles, in the *World Movement for Ecumenism* in the development of which she asserts her readiness to co-operate with the *World Council*.

Further, Mgr Willebrands rightly distinguishes between the *Movement* and the *Council*. The latter is an institution, exposed to many dangers and always patient of improvement, which Rome today looks on as an indispensable partner in dialogue. The Movement belongs to another order of realities. As a fruit of the action of the Holy Spirit, it leads all those associated with it, Churches and faithful, towards a fulfilment which infinitely transcends any institutional action: the visible restoration of the unity of the Body of Christ. And this movement grows in width and depth in an ever purer atmosphere of mutual respect in humility, of a common quest for truth in brotherly love, and in constant prayer one for another.

Some ardent ecumenists, I know, are annoyed when they hear talk of 'dialogues'. The time for these, they believe, has gone by. How mistaken they are – the beauty and joy of brotherly love lived in Christ cannot and must not make us forget that, in the quest for unity, truth is inseparable from love. To by-pass the problems of truth would be a betrayal of love.

We must attach as much importance to the necessity for dialogue as do Cardinal Bea and his colleagues, who contribute to its preparation a vast body of biblical, theological and ecclesiological knowledge, combined with an ardent love of unity. At the same time it is essential that the Uppsala Assembly find a way of introducing order and method into dialogue. It may well find that the Council is somewhat embarrassed by the eagerness of certain Churches or denominational alliances which sometimes give the impression, in their haste, of wanting to take over all its responsibilities.

The visit of Patriarch Athenagoras to Geneva and London will undoubtedly have profound repercussions at Uppsala. The Orthodox members will rightly emphasize the ecumenical importance of this double move. One remembers all the prophecies that the three meetings between Paul VI and Athenagoras gave rise to. 'Catholics and Orthodox are going to come to terms at the expense of the "separated brethren"—what will be left of Orthodox-Protestant collaboration?' Once again the Patriarch showed his complete loyalty and his desire to serve the cause of a total ecumenism. Moreover, in the name of whom or of what could one take it ill that Orthodox and Catholics should study together the problems raised by the breach in the eleventh century, while seeing nothing to complain about in an official dialogue between Catholics and Lutherans? Are we not only too glad to see the place that Luther's theology is regaining in the thought of Catholic theologians?

The lesson we have to learn is to be more obedient to the guidance of the Holy Spirit.

This awareness of the difficulties and problems of today, this vision of the future of the ecumenical movement, this picture in my mind's eye of restored unity – these are things that are continually with me while in the evening of my days I still press on along the road I entered upon over sixty years ago.

The reader will remember from what I have already written that in its original impulse the ecumenical movement aimed primarily at bringing together the Churches born of the Reformation, at the breaking down of their 'denominational' partitioning, and at the elimination of the proliferance of 'communions' alien to and often anathematizing one another. How has this affected French Protestantism?

Now that I no longer have any official responsibility in our French Churches, I welcome with hope and gratitude the news of what is being done to build up, as soon as possible, the Evangelical Church of France for which I made a plea in 1961 at the Montbéliard General Assembly.[15]

A small committee, made up of the directors of the Lutheran and Reformed Churches of France, Alsace and Lorraine, is organizing and co-ordinating the theological and ecclesiological studies which the search for unity calls for. This echoes the wishes of the great majority of the laity. It cannot fail one day to reach the goal that has been defined on countless occasions since Montbéliard, for the unity we seek is spiritually logical and, even more, in harmony with the truth of the Gospel and of apostolic teaching.

Once again, at the beginning of 1967, I had the pleasure of an ecumenical dialogue with Père Congar. A large audience seemed to take a lively interest in our discussion, which was published

15. See above, p. 277.

shortly afterwards.[16] It took place during the Week of Prayer for Christian Unity. Even more than in preceding years, the numerous services and meetings associated with the week drew crowds of people in whom one could see evidence of confident hope. In Saint-François-de-Sales, Père Le Guillou and I conducted a vigil of prayer.

Let no one think that all this is illuminism, romanticism, or sterile sentimentality. As builders of Christian unity, we keep a cool head for the dialogues whose importance is still fundamental, but 'our hearts burn within us'[17] because in this movement which is leading Christ's Church towards the visible realization of his unity, we recognize the will of Christ himself, the head of the Church.

I speak of the 'ecumenical movement'. The reader will have noticed how often I use those two words. I greatly prefer them to the word 'ecumenism'. This latter suggests the idea of an intellectual system, of an ordered body of teaching, like Thomism or Calvinism. It contains no demand for a way of life. When, after 'my birth into ecumenical life',[18] I felt my first thrill of excitement at contact with John Mott, Oldham, and others too, it was by a movement that I was swept up and carried along; and it is this same movement that still does so today. In the end it will certainly triumph over our denominational pride and self-centredness, because the love which produced it and gives it its enduring vigour carries within it the almighty power of God, revealed on Calvary. It is this love which will unite us at the appointed hour through the divine mercy. Gathering us all under the sovereign authority of the eternal Word, it will make us bow down before the splendour of truth, contemplated, believed, and lived in the freedom of love and the unity of faith.

Could I offer my readers any finer conclusion? We are pressing on towards the Kingdom. Even if its perfect realization is of the order of the eternal, yet is it already present in the midst of us, and the ecumenical movement is one of the signs that announce and pre-figure its coming. More than half a century has gone by since the movement first sprang into life. It has known great disappointments and great sufferings, but it has had its share of

16. *Conférences des Ambassadeurs*, Paris, 1967.   17. Luke 24:32.
18. See above, Chapter 1.

exhilarating joy. It has witnessed miracles that attest with compulsive force the design of God. The ecumenical challenge has shown how rich is the fruit it bears. And so it is with an ever stronger faith that I await the fulfilment of the Lord's priestly prayer, 'that they may be one even as we are one . . . so that the world may believe'.[19]

Vulaines-sur-Seine, July 1966 – Paris, December 1967

19. John 17:21-22.

Appendices

1. Extracts from the encyclical *Mortalium animos* (1928) (see p. 68).
2. Note drawing attention to a secret circular sent to police headquarters (see p. 167).
3. Letter to the Minister of Justice, 14 February 1941 (see p. 168).
4. Letter to Admiral Darlan, 26 March 1941 (see p. 171).
5. Letter from Pastor A.-N. Bertrand to Marshal Pétain, June 1942 (see p. 175).
6. Letter to Marshal Pétain, 20 August 1942 (see p. 176).
7. Letter to M. Pierre Laval, 27 August 1942 (see p. 176).
8. Resolution of the Council of the Protestant Federation of France, 5 May 1944 (see p. 194).
9. Text of telegrams exchanged between the German Ambassador in Paris and the Foreign Ministry in Berlin, June 1943 (see p. 194).

Appendix I

Extracts from the encyclical *Mortalium animos*, on the means of achieving religious unity.

After denouncing efforts made by non-Catholics to bring about unity, the Pope condemns all collaboration between the faithful of the Church of Rome and those whom he calls *pan-Christians*.

'So far from being a few isolated individuals, [they] have formed an entire class and grouped themselves into societies of extensive membership, usually under the direction of non-Catholics, who also disagree in matters of faith. . . . In reality, however, these fair and alluring words cloak a most grave error, subversive of the foundations of the Catholic faith.'

After referring to the congresses organized by 'pan-Christians' and detailing some of their opinions, the Pope continues:

'This being so, it is clear that the Apostolic See can by no means take part in these assemblies, nor is it in any way lawful for Catholics to give to such enterprises their encouragement or support. If they did so, they would be giving countenance to a false Christianity quite alien to the one Church of Christ. Shall we commit the iniquity of suffering the truth, the truth revealed by God, to be made a subject for compromise? . . .

'Thus, Venerable Brethren, it is clear why this Apostolic See has never allowed its subjects to take part in the assemblies of non-Catholics. There is but one way in which the unity of Christians may be fostered, and that is by furthering the return to the one true Church of Christ of those who are separated from it; for from that one true Church they have in the past fallen away. . .

'Let our separated children, therefore, draw nigh to the Apostolic See . . . and let them come, not with any intention or hope that "the Church of the living God, the pillar and ground of truth", will cast aside the integrity of the faith and tolerate their errors, but to submit themselves to its teaching and government.'[1]

Less than forty years later the Second Vatican Council adopted, and Paul VI promulgated, the decree *De Oecumenismo*!

Appendix 2

Protestant Federation of France.

Pastor Marc Boegner, President of the Protestant Federation of France, has been informed that a *secret* circular, ordering a special police supervision of pastors, was received in the early days of December by police headquarters in departments of the unoccupied zone. This circular, which has all the appearance of originating from the Ministry of War, bears only the date of its forwarding to police headquarters in the chief town of the department, and its number in the forwarding register. It refers to an organization described by the name of 'Liberté'. It alleges that the first three numbers of a publication bearing this name were composed by some pastors of the Gard department. All pastors, it adds, are to be objects of special police supervision, and this is to include their correspondence and movements. Enquiries concerning pastors are to be made from heads of the Légions des Combattants,[2] employers, and *ministers of the Catholic religion*. In suspicious cases, search warrants will be authorized.

There can be no doubt that the circular has in fact been received by police headquarters and that enquiries have followed. The document is either genuine or a forgery. If it is the work of a

---

1. Eng. trans., 'True Religious Unity', in *Selected Papal Encyclicals and Letters 1928-1931*, London, Catholic Truth Society, 1932, pp. 11, 16, 20, 22.
2. A Vichy organization of ex-servicemen, originally patriotic and civic, but later infected by totalitarianism and anti-Semitism. See Robert Aron, *The Vichy Régime*, London, Putnam, 1958, pp. 176-7, 306.

forger or if it originates from an organization which wishes to disturb public opinion, it should be immediately and publicly disowned.

If it is genuine, Pastor Boegner cannot but protest vigorously against a suspicion that has been gratuitously thrown upon all the pastors of France. He solemnly affirms that pastors, exclusively engaged in their spiritual ministry, have no connection whatsoever with any secret organization of any sort or kind. He insists on being given the names of the alleged pastors of the Gard who are said to have been responsible for the issues of *Liberté*. It is, moreover, unthinkable that any authority whatsoever should have dreamt of having enquiries about pastors made from ministers of the Catholic religion. It would be the surest way of reawakening in many parts of France religious differences which would be a serious threat to public order.

Appendix 3

Nîmes, 14 February 1941.
10, Rue Claude-Brousson.

Monsieur le Garde des Sceaux,

The cordial welcome you were good enough to extend to me a few days ago justifies me, I believe, in raising with you a matter of some delicacy which has had wide repercussions in the whole Protestant world.

Pastor Dürrleman, Director of the well-known evangelizing organization known as *La Cause* was arrested in Carrières-sous-Poissy where he lives, on Wednesday 22 January, by officers of the German political police. M. Dürrleman would appear to have been denounced following a religious service he had conducted in the cemetery of Carrières-sous-Poissy, at the funeral of an Englishman who had died in a concentration camp. The search conducted in the *La Cause* building led to the seizure in M. Dürrleman's office, of a leaflet which, it would seem, he had agreed to duplicate. I am perfectly certain that he is not the author, but I am quite sure, too, that he would never reveal the author's name. The fact remains that it is this leaflet, probably anti-German, which led to the immediate arrest of Pastor Dürrleman and his internment in the Cherche-Midi prison, where he has now been held in solitary confinement for some time.

From what I have just learnt, M. Dürrleman would appear to have been handed over to the French judicial authorities and is to appear before them. I shall be most grateful if you will be so good as to look into this matter, and I allow myself to hope that in your kindness you will draw the attention of the French judges to Pastor Dürrleman's character. For many years now, he has used his great oratorical powers in conducting a tireless campaign against Communism and in denouncing the evil effects of its anti-religious activities. His arrest has aroused great feeling in our churches. He has, no doubt, been guilty of an imprudent act; but I am certain that this has been due solely to the generosity of his heart and the ardour of his patriotism.

MARC BOEGNER.

Monsieur Joseph Barthélemy,
Garde des Sceaux,
Ministère de la Justice,
Vichy.

Appendix 4

The National Council of the Reformed Church of France
To Admiral of the Fleet Darlan,
Vice-President of the Council of Ministers.
26 March 1941.

Amiral,

We have just held a meeting in Nîmes, for the first time since the coming into force of the law of 3 October 1940 on the status of Jews. On the day before our meeting we learnt, from a note in the Press, of your intention to appoint a High Commissioner for Jewish Questions. We believe it to be our duty to inform you, on behalf of the Reformed Church of France, which includes the vast majority of French Protestants, of our feelings about this unhappy question.

We are in no way unmindful of the gravity of the problem presented to the State by the recent mass immigration of a great number of foreigners, many Jewish in origin, and by the hasty and unjustified naturalizing of some aliens. We are convinced that this problem should and can be solved while preserving respect for the human person, and with due care for the justice whose ready champion France has always been.

We know, too, that in the present circumstances it was inevitable that strong pressure should be applied to the Government of France with a view to persuading it to promulgate an anti-Jewish law.

We are none the less deeply disturbed, both as Frenchmen and as Christians, by a law which introduces the principle of racialism into our legislation, and one whose rigorous application entails cruel ordeals and poignant injustices for Jewish Frenchmen and Frenchwomen. In particular, we abhor the principle in virtue of which the State has broken formal undertakings entered into with men and women the vast majority of whom have served it loyally and selflessly.

We are assured that the law of 3 October 1940 is not a law of religious persecution. If, then, there is still complete freedom of worship for Jews, as much as for Catholics and Protestants, why is it already in actual fact denied or threatened in certain areas? It is a fact that a religious minority has been dealt a severe blow. Our Church, which has experienced all the sufferings of persecution would be failing in its fundamental mission if it did not raise its voice in support of that minority.

We know, Sir, that it is your earnest desire, by the very appointment of a High Commissioner for Jewish Questions, to do all that is in your power to save French Jews from even more severe trials. We believe that we are justified in assuring you that the Christian religious bodies will support you unreservedly in your attempt, whose difficulty they fully appreciate. At the same time we beg you with the utmost urgency to go further, and here and now to consider a revision of the status imposed on French Jews which will be such as on the one hand to prevent or rectify great injustices, and on the other to dissipate the disastrous impression made on a great part of the civilized world by the law of 3 October last. The defeat whose grievous consequences we are now experiencing is one reason more for France to hold fast to what, in the moral order, has won her the respect and affection of the Christian nations.

> Believe me, etc.
> On behalf of the National Council
> of the Reformed Church of France,
> Marc Boegner, President.

Appendix 5

> The Vice-President of the Council
> of the Protestant Federation of France
> (occupied zone)
> To the Marshal of France,
> Head of the French State.
> June 1942.

Monsieur le Maréchal,

The Council of the Protestant Federation of France, meeting in Paris, takes the liberty of addressing itself to the Head of the French State, with respect and confidence, in order to express to him the extreme distress of the Churches within the Council's jurisdiction at the new measures with regard to Jews taken by the occupation authorities.

The order of 29 May obliging our fellow-countrymen of Jewish race to wear a distinctive symbol has without any doubt aroused profound feeling in Protestant circles in the occupied zone.

Our President, Pastor Marc Boegner, had the honour of

informing you, at the appropriate time, as also Admiral of the Fleet Darlan, then Vice-President of the Council of Ministers, of the unanimous wish of the Protestants of France to see an attempt made to find a solution, in a spirit of justice and understanding, for the Jewish problem, whose importance we all recognize.

We now find ourselves presented with a measure which, far from contributing to a reasonable solution of the problem, seems to us to rule it out. With no social or economic validity, this measure seeks to impose upon Frenchmen, a number of whom have shed their blood under our flag, a gratuitous humiliation, affecting to set them apart from the rest of the nation; it exposes children six years of age to forms of bullying which are always possible in the disturbed atmosphere in which our population is living; finally, it forces baptized persons, Catholic or Protestant, to display openly before men the name of Jew, whereas they count it an honour to bear before God the name of Christian.

The Churches of Christ cannot, therefore, be silent in the face of an unmerited suffering which strikes at Frenchmen, sometimes Christian, in their dignity as men and believers. The Council of the Protestant Federation has accordingly instructed me, Sir, to express to you on its behalf the deep distress it feels. The Council hopes that you will have the goodness to take into consideration, as evidence of its trust and respect, the fact that it confides this sorrow and emotion to the heart of the great soldier, the Head of the French State.

> Believe me, etc.
> For the Council of the Protestant Federation
> (occupied zone),
> André-N. Bertrand,
> Vice-President.

Appendix 6

Monsieur le Maréchal,

When you did me the honour of receiving me on 27 June last, I handed to you the letter in which the Council of the Protestant Federation of France confided to your heart, as Christian and soldier, the sorrow and emotion felt by the Protestant Churches at the new measures taken in the occupied zone with regard to Jews and to Christians classed as Jews by the law. I now, unhappily, find myself obliged to write to you today, on behalf of the same Council, to express to you the unspeakable distress of our Churches at the news of the steps decided on by the French Government against foreign Jews (whether converted to Christianity or not), and of the way in which they have been carried out.

No Frenchman can remain unmoved by what has been happening since 2 August in the refugee and internment camps. It will be urged in reply, we know, that France is doing no more than sending back to Germany Jews whom the latter sent here in 1940. The truth is that there have just been handed over to Germany men and women who sought sanctuary in France for political or religious reasons, numbers of whom know in advance the terrible fate which awaits them.

Hitherto Christianity had instilled into the nations, France in particular, respect for the right of asylum.

The Christian Churches, whatever the differences in their professions of faith, would be false to their essential vocation if, in face of the abandonment of their principles, they did not raise their sorrowful protest.

I must add, Sir, that the 'handing over' of these unfortunate aliens was affected in many places under conditions so inhumane as to revolt the most hardened consciences and to draw tears from those who witnessed these proceedings. Packed into goods-wagons without any care for hygiene, the aliens selected for despatch were treated like cattle. The Quakers, who do so much for those who suffer in our country, found that they were refused permission to distribute food to them in Lyons. The Jewish Consistory would also appear to have been forbidden to provide them with any supplies. Respect for the human person, which you have been at pains to write into the Constitution you wish to present to France, has on countless occasions been trampled under foot. Here again the Churches are constrained to protest against so grave a neglect on the part of the State of its undeniable responsibilities.

The Council of the Protestant Federation appeals to your high authority in the hope that entirely different methods may be introduced into the treatment of aliens of Jewish race, Christians by religion or not, whose handing over has been agreed. No defeat, as you yourself have reminded us, can oblige France to allow her honour to be stained.

The persistent loyalty of France, even, and particularly, during the tragic time she has been living for the last two years, to her traditions of human generosity and of spiritual nobility, is still one of the essential reasons for the respect which certain nations continue to accord to her.

As Vice-President of the World Council of Churches, which associates all the great Churches, I cannot but inform you of the deep emotion felt by the Churches of Switzerland, Sweden and the United States, at the news, already known all over the world, of what is being done in France at this very moment.

I beg you, Sir, to enforce measures which are indispensable if France is not to inflict upon herself a moral defeat whose grievous consequences would be incalculable.

Believe me, etc.
Marc Boegner.

Appendix 7

Nîmes, 27 August 1942.
10, Rue Claude-Brousson.
To Monsieur Pierre Laval

Monsieur le Président,

Being entitled to speak on behalf of the Protestant Churches of the whole world, numbers of whom have already requested my intervention, and knowing the facts that have occurred during these recent days, I have the honour to ask you, with the utmost urgency, to be good enough to give me your assurance that in no case will foreign nationals be sent into the occupied zone who have been sentenced in their own country for a political reason, or who have asked for asylum in France for such reason.

Believe me, etc.
Marc Boegner,
President of the Protestant Federation of France,
Vice-President of the World Council of Churches.

Appendix 8

Council of the Protestant Federation of France
Meeting on Wednesday 5 May 1944

Resolution

Informed by the National Council of the Reformed Church of France of the suggestion which Dr Reichl had officially forwarded to the Council through Pastor Marc Boegner, the Council of the Protestant Federation of France wishes to express its surprise at the question put to it.

It is true that it has already had occasion, and no doubt will have so in the future, to make clear to the faithful the position on essential problems which seems to the Council to be demanded from them by fidelity to the Christian faith. But our Churches of France, separated from the State for much the greater part of their history, have always taken the initiative themselves in such pronouncements. It would be contrary to the Churches' most firmly established principles, and would create a serious precedent, to allow themselves to be guided in this matter by the intervention of a temporal power. The Church of Jesus Christ can raise its voice only at the bidding of its Head.

Moreover, the Council deduces from a very recent example the certainty that, were it to be led publicly to express its opinion on all the atrocious consequences of total war, its statement would not be published in its entirety and French Protestants would obtain only a fragmentary version of it.

In these circumstances, whose importance cannot be overlooked, the Council of the Protestant Federation of France finds itself obliged to abstain.

It authorizes its President to forward the text of this resolution to Dr Reichl.

Appendix 9

225/150877·86   7 June 1943.
Schleier to AA
Tel. 3701

Persons against whom the Embassy proposes that preventive security measures should be taken:

1. Persons important for constitutional reasons: Lebrun, Jeanneney.

2. Persons against whom immediate preventive measures should be taken: Frossard, Champetier de Ribes, François-Poncet, Hutin, Delbos, Vermeil, d'Ormesson.

3. Persons to be arrested in the event of a landing: Boncour.

Baudouin, Caziot, Lamirand, Lehideux, Noël, Peyerimhof de
Fontenelle, Spinasse, Tirard, Maurras, Boegner, Sarraut (Albert),
Sarraut (Maurice), Marin.

4. La Porte du Theil.

242/158145-51   23 June 1943.
Schleier to AA
Tel. 4131

Do not advise deportation of Caziot, Lehideux, Maurras,
Boegner, Ménétrel, Bonnet. Embassy reasons.

242/158169-70   25 June 1943.
Sonnleither (Minister's Private Office) to Paris
Tel. 3940

Ribbentrop agrees to the non-deportation of Caziot, Lehideux,
Maurras, Boegner, Bonnet and requests further information on
Ménétrel. Herriot to be sent to Germany.

Acknowledgments

The translator and publisher gratefully acknowledge their indebtedness for permission to reproduce copyright material as follows: from *Letters and Papers from Prison* by Dietrich Bonhoeffer, 3rd edition, published by SCM Press, London, 1967; from *Catholics and Protestants, a Proposal for realizing Christian Solidarity* by Oscar Cullmann, published by Lutterworth Press, London, 1960; from *Selected Papal Encyclicals and Letters 1928-1931*, published by the Catholic Truth Society, London, 1932; and from documents published by the World Council of Churches, Geneva.

Index